SQL SERVER 2005
FOR DEVELOPERS

SQL Server 2005
for Developers

Robert Ericsson

Jason Cline

CHARLES RIVER MEDIA
Boston, Massachusetts

Cover Design: The Printed Image

CHARLES RIVER MEDIA
25 Thomson Place
Boston, Massachusetts 02210
617-757-7900
617-757-7969 (FAX)
crminfo@thomson.com
www.charlesriver.com

This book is printed on acid-free paper.

Robert Ericsson and Jason Cline. *SQL Server 2005 for Developers.*
ISBN: 1-58450-388-2

All brand names and product names mentioned in this book are trademarks or service marks of their respective companies. Any omission or misuse (of any kind) of service marks or trademarks should not be regarded as intent to infringe on the property of others. The publisher recognizes and respects all marks used by companies, manufacturers, and developers as a means to distinguish their products.

Library of Congress Cataloging-in-Publication Data
Ericsson, Robert.
  SQL Server 2005 for developers / Robert Ericsson and Jason Cline. -- 1st ed.
     p. cm.
  Includes index.
  ISBN 1-58450-388-2 (pbk. with cd : alk. paper)
  1. SQL server. 2. Client/server computing. 3. Relational databases. I. Cline, Jason. II. Title.
  QA76.9.C55E75 2006
  005.2'768--dc22
                            2006016156

Printed in the United States of America
06 7 6 5 4 3 2 First Edition

CHARLES RIVER MEDIA titles are available for site license or bulk purchase by institutions, user groups, corporations, etc. For additional information, please contact the Special Sales Department at 800-347-7707.

Requests for replacement of a defective CD-ROM must be accompanied by the original disc, your mailing address, telephone number, date of purchase and purchase price. Please state the nature of the problem, and send the information to CHARLES RIVER MEDIA, 25 Thomson Place, Boston, Massachusetts 02210. CRM's sole obligation to the purchaser is to replace the disc, based on defective materials or faulty workmanship, but not on the operation or functionality of the product.

From Jason:
To Shey and Jake, whose love, laughs, and support helped
make this book a reality.

From Rob:
Many thanks go out to Kate, Sophie, Jack and Ellie for your
understanding and encouragement during the writing of this book - I
couldn't have done it without you!

Contents

1 Introduction

In this Chapter

- What is SQL Server?
- SQL Server History
- What is in this Book?

Microsoft SQL Server 2005 is a complete data management package that goes beyond simply providing the data management we expect from a database to providing an entire platform for developing data-centric applications. This book is intended for developers who have some knowledge of relational database concepts and want to use SQL Server 2005 in their applications.

WHAT IS SQL SERVER?

SQL Server is designed to provide enterprise-class data management and *business intelligence* (BI) tools as a part of the Microsoft Windows Server system. At the heart of SQL Server is the data engine that provides relational database services. In addition, SQL Server provides a full complement of management, reporting, analysis, integration, notification, and replication services.

These services are used by other pieces of the entire application infrastructure. As an example, SharePoint might be used to display reports from Reporting Services. Microsoft Office Excel might be used to analyze data from Analysis Services. Visual Studio might be used to create a custom application that accesses the relational database through ADO.NET. Figure 1.1 shows how the services provided by SQL Server integrate with other elements of an enterprise infrastructure.

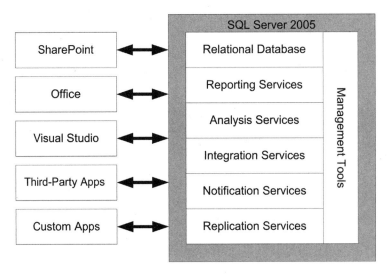

FIGURE 1.1   The services provided by SQL Server are part of an overall enterprise architecture.

SQL SERVER HISTORY

The first version of SQL Server was released in 1988, jointly developed by Sybase® and Microsoft® for the OS/2 operating system. In the early 1990s, Microsoft began to develop its own version of SQL Server specifically for Windows NT. This version was released in 1993 and became very popular because of its combination of low cost, solid performance, and easy operation. In 1995, Microsoft released SQL Server 6.0 with improved performance and administration features. SQL Server 6.5 was released a year later and was followed by the 6.5 Enterprise Edition in 1997. In 1998, SQL Server 7.0 was released. This version was a complete rewrite of the original Sybase product and added online analytic processing (OLAP) support for analytics and an extraction, transformation, and loading (ETL) tool for data integration. SQL Server 2000 was released two years later, continued to build on the 7.0 application, and added many important features and improvements, including data mining. Subsequent to the release of SQL Server, XML support for SQL Server and Reporting Services were shipped as add-ons.

SQL Server 2005 is a major new release and has many improvements and new features. This book describes many of the new features and enhancements in some detail.

WHAT IS IN THIS BOOK?

This book is organized into 16 chapters (including this one), each of which focuses on a specific SQL Server 2005 topic. The following subsections detail what you will find in each.

Chapter 2: "Database Design"

Chapter 2 establishes the basics of database design and has a roadmap to produce solid foundations for building relational databases in SQL Server 2005. It covers topics like entities, relationships, and tables that are fundamental to database design, and offers some advice on how to structure your design for the best results.

Chapter 3: "Database Security for Developers"

Chapter 3 covers the topic of database security in SQL Server 2005. Because of the importance of the data stored in databases, security is a major concern. This chapter describes important security concepts in SQL Server 2005 and offers advice on how to secure your database applications.

Chapter 4: "Transact-SQL for Developers"

Chapter 4 describes the relational language used in SQL Server 2005—Transact SQL. Knowing Transact SQL is an important element in being able to effectively define structures and retrieve and manipulate data. This chapter describes the important syntax elements and keywords used in Transact SQL.

Chapter 5: "Programmability"

Chapter 5 covers the programmability options in SQL Server 2005. It starts with a description of creating custom assemblies and types in .NET, and then describes how to use stored procedures, functions, and triggers to create custom business logic in SQL Server 2005.

Chapter 6: "ADO.NET 2.0"

Chapter 6 explains ADO.NET, which is used to integrate SQL Server (and other) databases into .NET code. First, the main components of ADO.NET are described, and then some of the more interesting new features are explored, including asynchronous operations, multiple result sets, user-defined types, and others.

Chapter 7: "Notification Services"

Chapter 7 covers Notification Services, which deliver information from SQL Server 2005 to interested subscribers as events occur. Notifications are an excellent way to integrate applications with SQL Server asynchronously.

Chapter 8: "XML in SQL Server 2005"

Chapter 8 explores the use of XML in SQL Server 2005. XML is integrated to the very core of SQL Server. The XML data type establishes XML as a first-class citizen in SQL Server. XML Query allows XML to be flexibly retrieved from the database through the standard XQuery language. Schema management allows definition and management of XML schemas in the database. In addition, XML is the core of the native Web services offered by SQL Server 2005.

Chapter 9: "Service Broker"

Chapter 9 describes the Service Broker in SQL Server 2005. The Service Broker provides support for asynchronous queuing, which enables many new application paradigms for integrating with SQL Server.

Chapter 10: "Performance Analysis and Tuning"

Chapter 10 covers the important topic of performance tuning and analysis in SQL Server 2005. Performance is an important aspect of application acceptance for users, and this chapter describes some of the important determinants of performance and basic tools and techniques used to maximize performance in your SQL Server applications.

Chapter 11: "Business Intelligence"

Chapter 11 introduces the topic of business intelligence, an important emphasis in SQL Server 2005. It describes the challenges in establishing a credible business intelligence program, how you can add value with a business intelligence solution, and outlines the features in SQL Server that support business intelligence goals.

Chapter 12: "Data Warehouse"

Chapter 12 is about data warehousing, a consolidated and organized repository of data used for analysis. It describes the important differences between transactional applications and analytic applications, and describes the process of designing and building a data warehouse in SQL Server.

Chapter 13: "SQL Server Integration Services"

Chapter 13 covers SQL Server Integration Services. Integration Services is the replacement for Data Transformation Services (DTS) and provides enterprise-class extraction, transformation, and loading (ETL) services for SQL Server. This chapter describes the fundamental pieces of Integration Services and illustrates how to build Integration Services solutions.

Chapter 14: "SQL Server Reporting Services"

Chapter 14 introduces SQL Server Reporting Services, a Web-based reporting environment for SQL Server and other data sources. It describes the basics of good report design and covers the architecture and extensibility of Reporting Services.

Chapter 15: "OLAP"

Chapter 15 describes online analytical processing (OLAP) for SQL Server. OLAP allows "slice and dice" dimensional analysis and is part of the services provided by SQL Server Analysis Services. This chapter describes the basics of the multidimensional data model, the architecture of Analysis Service, the Multidimensional Expressions (MDX) query language, and includes an example of building a cube.

Chapter 16: "Introduction to Data Mining in SSAS 2005"

Chapter 16 introduces the Data Mining features in SQL Server. Data mining is a part of Analysis Services and provides the capability to search for hidden patterns in data. This chapter describes some data-mining fundamentals, a process for data mining, and how to construct and interpret a data-mining project.

2 Database Design

Good design is the cornerstone of all successful database development projects. Developers, however, sometimes see the process and techniques of database design as purely theoretical, obscure, and even in some cases, unnecessary. Developers often view the database design as a byproduct of application development and thus employ no particular design techniques. This chaotic approach to database design can lead to designs that have severe repercussions in terms of performance, scalability, and maintainability. To help minimize these risks and show you how proper database design can have a positive impact on your projects, this chapter explains some important database design principles that provide tangible benefits and can be applied to any relational database design project. For readers experienced in the practice of database design, this chapter will be a review. For others who may be less experienced, this chapter provides a crash course in the basics of database design.

The goal of relational database design is to organize data into an efficient and practical structure. Real-world data is often unstructured, so breaking down this unorganized data into a tabular, structured format is one of the most important, and difficult, aspects of database design. Database design approaches may take many forms, some very informal and others quite structured. Keep in mind that no single design approach will work for all projects, so scale your design formality to match your project.

We would be remiss if we proceeded to cover database design practices and principles without emphasizing the importance of establishing and understanding the database requirements before doing so. A good understanding of the requirements (or purpose) of the database is essential to creating a good design—even a great design cannot make up for bad or misunderstood requirements. Just as there is no one-size-fits-all solution for database design, the same is true for requirements. The process for gathering and documenting requirements can be as informal or as formal as needed depending on the project. At a minimum, you need to know what data the database needs to store, what users want to know about the data, and what they want to do with the data before beginning the design process.

Before we begin covering guidelines for database design, let's examine a few key terms and concepts that will help you understand the material in this chapter and other literature on the topic of database design.

Entities, Relationships, and Tables

Entities are the foundation of relational database design. An *entity* is a person, place, or thing of interest in the system being designed. An example of an entity for a chain of bookstores would be a customer, book, or bookstore. Entities generally map to the tables of a database.

Associations between entities are called *relationships*. These associations or mappings between entities are typically classified as:

- One-to-one
- One-to-many
- Many-to-many

These classifications are known as the cardinality of a relationship and define the way entities are associated. Let's look at each of the cardinality types.

A one-to-one relationship defines that entities of one class may be associated with entities of another class, through a given relationship, at most one time. To illustrate this example, let's say we have an entity called Book and it has a relationship with another entity called TableOfContents. The relationship between Book and TableOfContents would be considered one-to-one since books have one and only one table of contents. Figure 2.1 illustrates the one-to-one relationship between Book and TableOfContents.

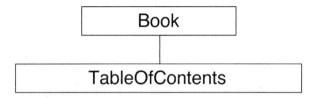

FIGURE 2.1   The one-to-one relationship between Book and TableOfContents.

A one-to-many relationship defines a mapping where one entity may be associated with one or more other entities through a relationship. Continuing the Book example, the relationship between a Book entity and a Chapter entity is a one-to-many relationship, because books generally contain several chapters (Figure 2.2).

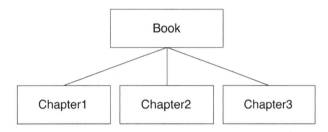

FIGURE 2.2   A one-to-many relationship.

Many-to-many relationships are defined as relationships in which many entities of one class may be associated with many entities of another class. This type of cardinality is demonstrated by the relationship between retail bookstores and the books that are sold by each store. For example, Store1 may sell Book1 and Book2, while Store2 sells Book1 and Book3. Figure 2.3 illustrates this many-to-many mapping.

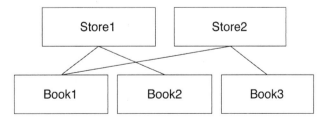

FIGURE 2.3   A many-to-many mapping.

Attributes and Columns

In database design terms, an attribute is a property of an entity. Attributes describe the qualities or characteristics of an entity that are of interest to the application. For example, the attributes for a Book entity might include:

- ISBN
- Title
- Author

Attributes of an entity are typically mapped to the columns of a table.

Values and Cells

Values represent the data for an attribute of an entity instance. In terms of a physical database, the intersection of a row and a column—a cell—stores a value. Some sample values for the Book entity attributes might include:

- Title = "SQL Server 2005 for Developers"
- ISBN = 1-58450-388-2
- Author = Ericsson/Cline

Logical Design versus Physical Design

Database design occurs in two phases: the logical design and the physical design. Logical design is concerned with mapping business requirements to a model that represents the business data elements. Physical database design translates the logical database design into a technology-specific design.

During the logical design process, a database designer reviews data requirements with stakeholders and constructs entity relationship diagrams (ERDs). An ERD is a technology-independent model of the data elements and relations that are needed to support the business requirements. Entity relationship diagrams use simple shapes to capture and communicate entities, relationships, and attributes to stakeholders. A typical ERD uses rectangles to represent entities, diamonds to represent relationships, and ellipses to represent attributes. Figure 2.4 illustrates an example entity relationship diagram.

Physical database design takes the logical database design and maps it to a specific database technology. When completing a physical design, logical elements are transformed into physical database objects; for example, entities are transformed into tables, attributes are transformed into columns of a table, and relationships are transformed into referential constraints. In addition to the translation of the logical ERD into physical objects, this design process makes any necessary technology-specific decisions, including:

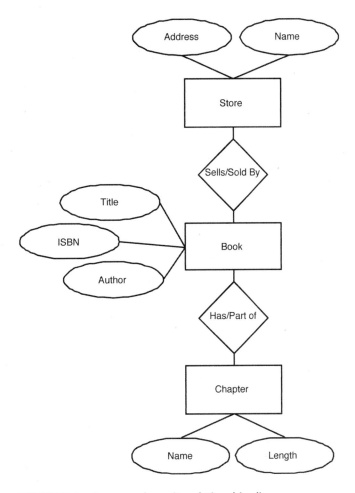

FIGURE 2.4 An example entity relationship diagram.

- Data types for attributes
- Index selection
- Constraint identification

Physical database design typically results in the construction of a data model diagram (Figure 2.5).

Now that we have covered some basic database design terminology, let's look at some simple guidelines to help you create good database designs.

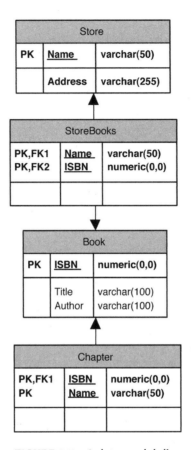

FIGURE 2.5 A data model diagram.

INFORMAL RULES OF DATABASE DESIGN

The basic rule of database design is to organize data in the most efficient way possible and prevent data integrity problems. Here are some rules to help you do this.

Design Meaningful Tables

When designing a database, it's important that the tables created as part of your design are significant and meaningful. This concept, simply put, means that for every table in your database, it should be clear and evident what data is contained in each table. To help you create designs that contain meaningful tables, a few simple guidelines can be applied to your design process.

The first guideline is that tables should be organized so they contain only one type of entity. For example, let's take an e-commerce database that needs to capture the following customer order information:

- Customer ID
- Customer Name
- Email
- Phone Number
- Address
- Credit Card
- Order Number
- Order Date
- Order Description

As the database designer, we have several options for organizing this data. The first option is to capture all the data in a single table called Orders. Storing this data in a single table, however, would not be very efficient because a customer who made multiple orders would have duplicated information in the database. What if a customer made a single order and then cancelled it? In this design, we would delete the row containing the order information, but a side effect of that deletion would be that all record of the customer who made the order would be removed. A better option would be to segment the data to be stored in two tables—a Customer table and an Order table. The resulting Customer table would capture the following data elements:

- Customer ID
- Customer Name
- Phone Number
- Email
- Address
- Credit Card

and the Order table would capture:

- Customer ID
- Order Id
- Order Date
- Order Description

In this design, customer information is not duplicated for each order, and it avoids the delete anomaly we encountered in the single table approach.

The second guideline for designing meaningful tables is that an individual row in a table should represent a single instance of an entity. Continuing the customer orders example, this guideline implies that every row in the Order table contains information about a single order.

After creating a database design, you can test if your design includes meaningful tables by writing a very brief description of the contents of the table. If the description becomes lengthy or is difficult to describe, you may need to revisit your design.

Design Separate Columns for Independently Accessed Data

Data that may be referenced or validated independently should be separated into another column. To illustrate the application of this simple principal, let's take, as an example, storing a customer shipping address. A standard customer shipping address would be similar to the following:

Apt. 1A
100 Main St.
Roanoke, VA 24011

In our database design, we have several options for storing customer address data. One is to store the entire address as a single string value. This design approach would make it possible to accept any address format; however, the process of querying the data to, for example, retrieve all customers in Virginia would be very difficult.

Another option would be to separate the address into individual lines and store each line independently:

- AddressLine1 = "Apt. 1A"
- AddressLine2 = "100 Main St."
- AddressLine3 = "Roanoke, VA 24011"

This approach would also be very flexible in capturing different address formats, but again is cumbersome to query and difficult to validate. Querying for all customers in Virginia or all customers in a particular zip code in this scenario would be quite awkward.

Both design approaches have maximized data flexibility, but minimized retrieval and query capabilities. Too little structure in a database design can lead to real business problems. Databases provide structured data storage so it is possible to apply business rules that validate the data, and it's possible to efficiently retrieve or operate on that data at a later time. The design possibilities outlined thus far have been *too* flexible. It would be extremely difficult in the previous two design options to ensure valid address data. For example, these designs make it difficult to ensure that data entry personnel always enter a five-digit zip code and a valid two-digit state abbreviation. Invalid addresses allowed by the database design have real implications and could result in delayed or lost shipments and decreased customer satisfaction.

Avoiding these pitfalls is quite simple if you follow the pattern of separating independently referenced or independently validated data into separate columns. A better design for storing customer shipping addresses would be to define separate columns for city, state, and zip while keeping the street address format flexible by creating columns to capture the first line and second line of the address as illustrated here:

- AddressLine1 = "Apt. 1A"
- AddressLine2 = "100 Main St."
- City = "Roanoke"
- State = "VA"
- Zip = "24011"

Each Cell Holds Only One Piece of Data

Cells should store single values. Storing sets or arrays in a relational database cell results in a database design that makes data queries unnecessarily difficult. To illustrate this principle, let us continue the "Customer" example and say that our business requirements dictate the need to capture customer phone numbers. Customers may have any combination of home, work, and mobile phone numbers. As the database designer, it's up to you to create a design that is flexible enough to handle this requirement. One option is to define a column that would capture any and all phone numbers in a single cell; for example, PhoneNumber="(540) 555-1212, (540) 555-5555." This design approach would allow capturing multiple phone numbers for a customer; however, which phone number is the work number and which is the home number? The database design does not make any distinction as to the "type" of the phone numbers, which makes queries for data such as the work phone numbers for all customers impossible.

A better design choice that follows the principle that cells should contain single values would be to create separate columns to store data for home phone number and work phone number. In this case, each cell would contain a single phone number and be much easier to query. For example, the previous phone numbers would be stored as:

- HomePhoneNumber = "(540) 555-1212"
- WorkPhoneNumber = "(540) 555-5555"

Every Table Needs a Primary Key

One of the foundations of relational database theory is that an instance of an entity can be uniquely identified, and the way entities are identified is through the use of keys. Every row in a table needs a key, which is comprised of one or more columns that uniquely identify the remainder of data in the row. A key comprised of two or more columns is referred to as a *composite key*, because it is the composite of the multiple values that uniquely identify the entity. Every column (or composite of columns) in a table that could uniquely identify a row is called a *candidate key*. From the collection of all candidate keys for a table, the database designer chooses one and only one candidate key to be the primary key.

In addition to being unique, a primary key should not change over the life of the entity. It's very important to understand this at design time and choose a primary key that will remain constant, since the key may be used by other entities as a reference. For example, Phone Number, Email, or Customer ID may uniquely identify a customer. Of these three options, Phone Number and Email have the potential of being changed over time, since customers may change locations or email providers. The best choice in this case would be Customer ID, which would be uniquely assigned to a customer at the time his account was created and would likely not change over the life of the customer.

Tables Related with Foreign Keys

Foreign keys allow for linking two tables together using the columns the tables have in common. To demonstrate the concept of foreign keys let's look at our Customer table and an Order table. The Customer table captures individual customer data such as name, addresses, and phone numbers, while the Order table stores a record of each order for a customer. We have already identified the Customer ID column as the primary key of the Customer table. Now we will define the Order ID column as the primary key of the Order table, and the Customer ID column of the Order table as a foreign key to the Customer table. This foreign key rule ensures that every order record is associated with a valid customer. Properly constrained foreign keys would prevent a scenario in which a user tries to create an order record with a missing or invalid customer, thus guaranteeing referential integrity.

Avoid Redundant Data

Another informal rule of relational database design is to minimize the amount of duplicate data. Redundant data is an inefficient use of available storage space and may also lead to problems updating data when copies of the data exist in multiple places. To prevent these problems, we can use primary keys and foreign keys to separate data into other tables, and then refer to the single copy of the data when needed.

Minimize Empty Cells

Database tables should be designed to minimize the number of empty cells. A table that contains numerous empty cells should be modified so that the columns containing the empty cells plus the foreign key columns are moved to a new table. To illustrate the application of this rule, let's assume that customers may subscribe to three weekly newsletters.

Designing the Customer table to capture newsletter subscriptions, we add the following three columns: NewsletterSubscription1, NewsletterSubscription2, and NewsletterSubscription3. A non-null value in these columns would mean the user has subscribed to the newsletter. The resulting Customer table would contain the following columns:

- Customer ID
- CustomerName
- PhoneNumber
- Email
- Address
- CreditCard
- NewsletterSubscription1
- NewsletterSubscription2
- NewsletterSubscription3

Customer newsletter selections are likely to widely vary. Some customers may elect to receive all newsletters, some only one or two newsletters, and others may elect not to receive any newsletters in Figure 2.6.

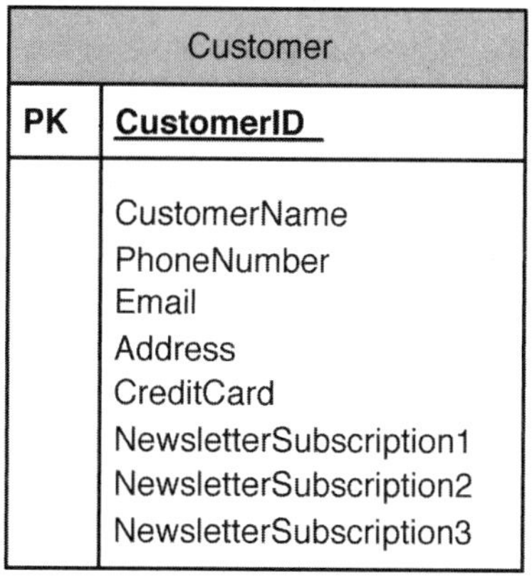

FIGURE 2.6 The Customer table.

This wide variability means that many of the cells for the newsletter subscription columns are likely to be empty and should be moved to another table. Therefore, following the informal design rules outlined in this chapter, we create two new tables: CustomerNewsletters and Newsletters. The Newsletters table stores the Newsletter ID and description, while the CustomerNewsletters table would contain a foreign key to the Customers table and a foreign key to the Newsletters table. Additionally, the combination of the Customers table foreign key and the Newsletters table foreign key will serve as the primary key for the table. The modified customer table now contains the following columns:

- Customer ID
- Customer Name
- Phone Number
- Email
- Address
- Credit Card

Additionally, the newly created Newsletters table contains:

- Newsletter ID
- Description

To capture which customers subscribe to particular newsletters, the CustomerNewsletters table contains:

- Customer ID
- Newsletter ID

A graphical representation of the resulting data model is shown in Figure 2.7.

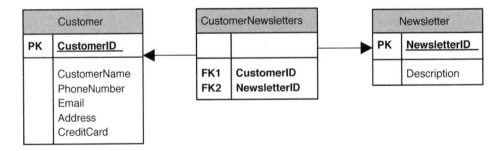

FIGURE 2.7   The Customer, CustomerNewsletter, and Newsletter tables.

In this section, we covered some informal database design guidelines that can help you create better database designs for your projects. Although we call these guidelines "informal," they each have a foundation in more formal database design approaches and set theory—we simply explained the guidelines in informal, non-mathematical terms. Next, we will look at the specific formalized technique of Normalization for optimizing database design.

NORMALIZATION

Normalization is the application of a set of formal design rules to organize data efficiently. Normalization reduces the necessary database storage space and helps ensure data integrity. Databases may be normalized to various levels called *normal forms*. The most common normal forms, and those we cover here, are called first normal form (1NF), second normal (2NF) form, and third normal form (3NF). Other normal forms exist, but are primarily academic in nature and not applicable to most business situations.

Normal forms are cumulative; that is, a database that meets the criteria of second normal form must also meet the criteria of first normal form, and a database that meets the criteria of third normal form must also meet the criteria of both second normal form and first normal form.

First Normal Form

In practical terms, a table is in first normal form if the table does not duplicate data for a given row. More specifically, first normal form eliminates duplicate columns from tables and creates separate tables for groups of information, with each row in the tables uniquely identified by a primary key. Let's look at an example that transforms a table into first normal form.

An example table, MovieRentals, needs to capture persons who rent movies and the movies they have rented. For the purpose of this example, let's assume there is a business rule in place that says a person may rent up to five movies at a time. If you were using a standard spreadsheet to capture this information, you might use one column to enter the customer name, and five other columns to capture the movie rentals. A table created to match the spreadsheet is defined in Figure 2.8.

Looking at Figure 2.8 we see that the first row lists "Bob Smith" renting *Top Gun*, *What About Bob?*, and *Rocky IV*. This table clearly does not meet the criteria for first normal form because the movie information is duplicated multiple times per row. Therefore, we will need to make some changes to the table before we can consider it being in first normal form.

Name	Rental1	Rental2	Rental3	Rental4	Rental5
Bob Smith	Top Gun	What About Bob	Rocky IV		
Jane Seasharp	Goonies	Top Gun			
Joe Codealot	Office Space	The Matrix	Star Wars	Tomb Raider	

FIGURE 2.8   The initial structure and sample data for the MovieRentals table.

One approach that is often tried during the normalization process is to combine columns into a single column as demonstrated in Figure 2.9.

Name	Rentals
Bob Smith	Top Gun, What About Bob, Rocky IV
Jane Seasharp	Goonies, Top Gun
Joe Codealot	Office Space, The Matrix, Star Wars, Tomb Raider

FIGURE 2.9   A modified MovieRentals table.

This approach, however, does not meet the criteria for first normal form. Instead of having duplicate data in multiple columns, this approach has simply combined the columns into one column whose cells contain multiple values. To transform this table into one that meets the requirements of first normal form, we need to move the duplicate column data into separate rows. The resulting structure is shown in Figure 2.10.

Now we can see that "Bob Smith" has a separate row for each movie he has rented and all the duplicate information per column has been removed. The table, however, is still not in first normal form. Remember that to be in first normal form, a table must not have duplicate data per row and must uniquely identify each row. There must be several Bob Smiths in the world, so our MovieRentals table does not meet the uniquely identified row criteria. We can easily satisfy this requirement by substituting Bob Smith's name with his unique customer identifier as shown in Figure 2.11.

Second Normal Form

Second normal form includes all the criteria of first normal form and requires additional reduction of duplicate data from rows. Second normal form simply takes data that is duplicated in multiple rows of a table, extracts a single copy of that data into a new table, and then uses foreign keys to link to the new table. Continuing with the example we used in transforming a table into first normal form, we see that the table

Name	Rental
Bob Smith	Top Gun
Bob Smith	What About Bob
Bob Smith	Rocky IV
Jane Seasharp	Goonies
Jane Seasharp	Top Gun
Joe Codealot	Office Space
Joe Codealot	The Matrix
Joe Codealot	Star Wars
Joe Codealot	Tomb Raider

FIGURE 2.10 A transformed MovieRentals table that eliminates multiple values per cell.

CustomerID	Rental
100	Top Gun
100	What About Bob
100	Rocky IV
200	Goonies
200	Top Gun
300	Office Space
300	The Matrix
300	Star Wars
300	Tomb Raider

FIGURE 2.11 The MovieRentals table using unique customer identifiers in place of customer names. This table is now in first normal form.

has duplicate data in multiple rows. Specifically, customer 100 and customer 200 have both rented copies of *Top Gun* and the data is duplicated. Because of this duplication, the table does not meet the criteria for second normal form.

Applying the rules of second normal form to the table design, we see that we can extract the movie name column into a separate table and use the movie key as a foreign key to link the two tables. The resulting table structures adhering to second normal form are shown in Figure 2.12.

CustomerID	CustomerName
100	Bob Smith
200	Jane Seasharp
300	Joe Codealot

CustomerID	MovieID
100	1000
100	2000
100	3000
200	4000
200	1000
300	5000
300	6000
300	7000
300	8000

MovieID	MovieName
1000	Top Gun
2000	What About Bob
3000	Rocky IV
4000	Goonies
5000	Office Space
6000	The Matrix
7000	Star Wars
8000	Tomb Raider

FIGURE 2.12 The tables in second normal form.

Third Normal Form

As previously mentioned, normal forms are cumulative, so third normal form includes all the criteria from both first and second normal forms. Additionally, third normal form removes the columns that are not directly dependent on the primary key. Columns identified as having a primary dependency on column(s) other than the primary key are moved to a new table and linked through a foreign key. Tables in third normal form do not allow these transitive dependencies on the primary key. Let's look at an example to help illustrate the application of this rule.

We have a Customers table that contains a customer number, customer name, street, city, state, and zip code as shown in Figure 2.13.

CustomerID	CustomerName	Street	City	State	ZipCode
100	Bob Smith	100 Main St.	Anytown	VA	12345
200	Jane Seasharp	200 Elm Ave.	Anyothertown	VA	12346
300	Joe Codealot	300 Broad St.	Anytown	VA	12345

FIGURE 2.13 The Customers table.

The customer number is the primary key, and it's easy to see that customer name and street are only dependent on the customer number. However, one may derive the city and state from a zip code. To transition this table into third normal form, we must remove this transitive dependency by creating a new table called zip codes, and move the city and state attributes into that table. Figure 2.14 shows the new tables that are in third normal form.

CustomerID	CustomerName	Street	ZipCode
100	Bob Smith	100 Main St.	12345
200	Jane Seasharp	200 Elm Ave.	12346
300	Joe Codealot	300 Broad St.	12345

ZipCode	City	State
12345	Anytown	VA
12346	Anyothertown	VA

FIGURE 2.14 A transformed customer table in third normal form.

As you can see, there are many similarities between the normalization process and the informal database design guidelines we introduced earlier in the chapter. The correct design approach for your project depends on the formality of the project itself. Generally speaking, moderate- or large-sized IT projects will require producing designs in 3NF, while for smaller IT projects, it could be sufficient to follow the informal design guidelines. Next, we will review the overall database design process and the application of the concepts covered in this chapter in a real-world scenario.

DESIGN PROCESS

The database design process may take many forms and, as with most design processes, no one approach works best in all cases. Some design approaches, however, give you a better chance at a good design than others. We'll cover a simple design process that is easily applied to nearly any project.

The basic approach is to iteratively follow a process that identifies and analyzes requirements, identifies data needs, and then refines those needs using good design rules. A graphical representation of this approach is illustrated in Figure 2.15.

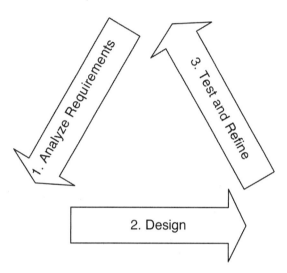

FIGURE 2.15   An iterative design process.

DESIGN OF EXAMPLE APPLICATION

The remainder of this chapter contains a sample design of a database for an online movie rental application that will be used throughout the book. This sample will demonstrate application of the principles we identified earlier in the chapter.

Identify Database Requirements

The requirements for the movie rental application database take the form of use cases. Use cases and user stories are two of the most common formats for capturing and presenting user requirements because of their focus on the system's interaction with the end user. These use cases outline an online movie rental subscription service application where a user creates a list of requested movies, and as the movies become available, the customer is sent three movies at a time. In addition to capturing the user movie requests, the system must also allow the distribution manager to generate a fulfillment schedule and warehouse employees to process movie fulfillments and rental returns. The example use cases include:

- Sign up for an account
- Sign in to account
- Find a movie
- View movie details
- Play movie trailer
- Update movie request list
- Update account information
- Generate movie fulfillment list
- Process movie rental
- Process movie return

Identify Entities

Next, we need to identify key entities from our analysis of the requirements. An entity is analogous to a noun in a sentence. One common approach to identifying the initial set of entities for a database design is to define entities for each unique noun in the system requirements definition. To identify relationships between entities, look for verbs that infer a role between the entities; for example, a requirement such as "A customer shall be able to optionally subscribe to newsletters." Dissecting this sentence, we see the nouns *customer* and *newsletter*, which we note as entities. Additionally, the verb *subscribe* links customers and newsletters, so we will note a relationship of "subscribe to" between the customer and newsletter entities. Key nouns in the use case names help us easily identify several entities. This first-pass set of entities includes:

- Customer
- Movie
- MovieRental
- RentalRequest

Assign Attributes to Entities

Following our design process we now need to assign attributes to the entities we have identified. To identify the attributes of these entities, we must review the details of the use case looking for entity-specific properties. Taking the Customer entity as an example we can identify the following attributes from the requirements:

- Name
- EmailAddress
- PhoneNumber
- Address
- Password
- CreditCard

Refine

With the attributes identified, we now need to refine the example Customer entity so it meets the criteria of first normal form. First, we need to identify or create a primary key uniquely identifying the customer. We could potentially leverage an email address for a primary key because of its uniqueness, but sometimes people change email addresses, so it's better to add a customer number column to the table as the primary key. Next, to further our quest for first normal form, let's remove all multivalued attributes; in this case, Name, PhoneNumber, CreditCard, and Address must be further decomposed. Name is decomposed into FirstName, MiddleName, and LastName. We can also divide PhoneNumber into Daytime-PhoneNumber and EveningPhoneNumber. Additionally, we will break CreditCard into CreditCardType, CreditCardNumber, and CreditCardExpirationDate. Lastly, Address may be divided into ShippingAddress and BillingAddress. The attributes for the Customer entity now include:

- CustomerId
- First Name
- Middle Name
- Last Name
- DaytimePhoneNumber
- EveningPhoneNumber
- ShippingAddress
- BillingAddress
- EmailAddress
- Password
- CreditCardType
- CreditCardNumber
- CreditCardExpirationDate

Testing our entity for compliance with first normal form, we quickly see that there exists duplicate data for a given row—duplicate phone numbers and addresses. The table mixes entity types as well because credit cards and customers are two distinct things and therefore should be stored in separate tables. Additionally, we notice that we really haven't removed all of the multivalue attributes, because ShippingAddress is really made up of a street, city, state, and zip code.

First, we will remove the duplicate columns of data and then further refine the multivalue attributes. To remove the duplicate columns of data we need to create a new entity called Address that has a primary key of AddressId and uses the CustomerId as a foreign key to the Customer table. The full list of attributes we have identified for the Address table includes:

- AddressId
- CustomerId
- AddressType
- StreetNumber
- StreetName
- City
- State
- ZipCode

Now we must apply a similar procedure to the phone number attributes of the customer entity. In this case, we will create a PhoneNumber entity that has a primary key of PhoneNumberId and uses the CustomerId as a foreign key to the Customer table. Attributes of the Phone entity include:

- PhoneNumberId
- CustomerId
- PhoneNumberType
- PhoneNumber

Finally, the credit card information is extracted to a new entity named CreditCard. The CreditCard entity has a primary key called CreditCardId and uses the CustomerId as a foreign key to the Customer table. Attributes of the CreditCard entity are:

- CreditCardId
- CustomerId
- CreditCardType
- CreditCardNumber
- CreditCardExpiration

After making these changes, the number of attributes on the Customer entity has been greatly reduced. The Customer entity attributes now include:

- CustomerId
- FirstName
- MiddleName
- LastName
- EmailAddress
- Password

Let us again test the tables for compliance with first normal form. This time, all tables contain only one type of entity, every row is uniquely identified, and duplicate data per row has been eliminated so the tables are now in first normal form.

With the tables in first normal, we can move on to check for compliance with second normal form. As you may recall, for a table to be in second normal form it must meet the criteria of first normal form. Additionally if a key consists of two or more fields, then nonkey attributes must be dependent on all key fields. Entities that are in first normal form and have a key consisting of a single field are automatically compliant with second normal form. In this situation, all of the entities we have defined have a single field key and we have the conversion to first normal form; therefore, the tables are automatically in second normal form.

Finally, we test the tables for adherence to third normal form. Tables in third normal form must be in second normal form, and all nonkey attributes must be dependent directly on the primary key and may not be dependent on other nonkey attributes. The Customer, PhoneNumber, and CreditCard entities meet these criteria, but the Address entity does not, so the table fails the test for third normal form.

Transformation of the Address entity into third normal form is quite simple. First, we extract the duplicate attributes into a new entity called Zip. This new entity has the attributes:

- ZipCode
- City
- State

The ZipCode attribute serves as the primary key of the new entity. Next, we add a ZipCode attribute to the Address entity to serve as a foreign key to the Zip table, leaving the Address entity to consist of the attributes:

- AddressId
- CustomerId
- StreetAddress
- ZipCode

Now with our database design in third normal form we are ready to create physical database structures in SQL Server 2005. To review the physical tables created for this design, install the example database included on the companion CD-ROM.

ON THE CD

CONCLUSION

In this chapter, we provided you with the terminology, guidelines, and processes needed to create good database designs for your projects. The next chapters in the book cover the features of the SQL Server 2005 platform. However, keep in mind that all successful projects begin with a quality design.

3 Database Security

Database applications are evident in almost all aspects of our lives—almost every purchase, payment, or interaction we have with a corporation or government is recorded in a database application. Much of this data is privileged information regarding our lives and livelihoods. In addition, the decentralization of IT systems and the spread of the Internet changed the way we access information. We no longer telephone Federal Express and speak with a service agent to see where our package is; we go online and access their systems directly. Similarly, to place a mail order for clothing or other goods, we use the Internet to choose what we want and complete our purchase without necessarily talking to another human being.

Unfortunately, this more pervasive and convenient access is not limited to legitimate uses. The Internet allows some of the most dangerous thieves, criminals, and hackers potential access to your applications and data. A quick look at the exponentially increasing number of reported security incidents shows how quickly things have changed in the past decade (Figure 3.1). We must adapt to the less trusted, more hostile environment in which we find ourselves today.

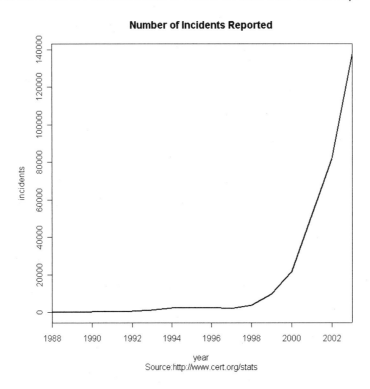

FIGURE 3.1 The number of computer security incidents has increased rapidly.

In this increasingly insecure environment, solid security can become a competitive advantage. If you can adapt to security risks faster than your competition, you will maximize your chances of being available when opportunities present themselves and minimize the potential cost of security breaches.

Unfortunately, security is often seen as an additional cost and bother. If your system has valuable data, attackers will find you. The real question is, will they be able to successfully penetrate your security measures? In too many cases, security doesn't become important until it has been broken, by which time it is too late and the damage has been done. You don't want to read about your company on the front pages and see it profiled on the evening news after a significant security incident. There is no sure way to avoid the embarrassment or worse of a security exploit on your application, but you can maximize your chances of avoiding a problem by taking security concerns seriously from the beginning of your application project.

At its core, security is a risk management issue. You need to fully understand the risks inherent in your design and implementation to make the right decisions about how much risk you can tolerate. There is no such thing as a 100% secure application in the real world—every moderately complex application has some available avenue of attack. The key to proper security is understanding what measures are worth the cost in terms of the other attributes of the application: cost, complexity, performance, and usability. Overall application security is only as good as the weakest link.

The overall topic of application security is much too broad and complex to be covered in one chapter, so we will focus on overall best practice and the aspects of security that directly touch the database and will ignore the policy and legal implications of security. Since security is systemic in nature, we will mention other specific aspects of application security but only in passing.

In this chapter, we will show how analysis, design, and understanding of the security features in SQL Server 2005 can be used to make your application as secure as possible, while minimizing cost, complexity, performance, and usability impacts. Some of the SQL Server 2005 features discussed are likely to be in the realm of activities performed by a database administrator (DBA) than an application developer. However, a database developer having a solid grasp of the security features available in SQL Server 2005 will be able to create more secure application designs that take advantage of the relevant features. Applications that are designed to be secure from the beginning are more likely to be secure throughout their lifecycles.

ACCESS CONTROL

Broadly speaking, application security can be thought of as controlling access to resources. In the case of most database applications, the most valuable resource is the data the application uses. Viewed in this light, security is based on six principals that apply whether the data is in transit on a communications channel or at rest inside a database. Later in this chapter, we discuss how SQL Server 2005 enforces each of these principals through specific security features. The six principles are:

- Authentication
- Authorization
- Confidentiality
- Integrity
- Nonreputability
- Accountablity

Authentication positively identifies the user of a system. Authentication is necessary for the other elements of security, but is not sufficient by itself to secure an application. To authenticate, users present some type of credentials that uniquely identify them to the system. These credentials can be something they know (e.g., a username and password combination), something they have (e.g., a key card) or something they are (e.g., a fingerprint), or, ideally, some combination of these. This is a familiar process to all of us. On almost every current computer operating system, you authenticate yourself by username and password every time you want to use it.

Authorization verifies that an authenticated party has permission to use a specified resource. Authorization happens after authentication, since it is impossible to determine permission if the system doesn't know who is requesting access. Simply being authenticated does not mean the user is authorized to access specific information. The details of who is authorized to do what are kept in access control lists (ACLs). For example, presenting your username and password does not allow you to shut down a Windows 2003 Server unless you have specific authorization to do so represented by your name in the ACL that determines who can shut down the server.

Confidentiality is the prevention of unauthorized information disclosure, and ensures that only those entities (both users and computer resources such as printers) authorized to access data may do so. If confidentiality fails, the data is said to be compromised. Confidentiality is not the same thing as privacy, even though they are easily confused. Roger Clarke's definition (*www.anu.edu.au/people/Roger.Clarke/DV/Intro.html#InfoPriv*) of information privacy is that it "is the interest an individual has in controlling, or at least significantly influencing, the handling of data about themselves." Confidentiality and privacy are related in that confidentiality can imply privacy in that information access is controlled and the protected information is kept secret, but the achievement of privacy in practice is more of a right implied by policy and law. For example, it would not be a breach of confidentiality for an authorized transaction to share confidential information, but it may be a breach of privacy. In most instances, confidentiality is enhanced by encryption. This is true whether the data is being sent over a communications channel or is sitting in a database.

Integrity assures that data has not been modified in an unauthorized or unknown way. If integrity fails, the data is said to be corrupted. It is important that integrity be combined with confidentiality so that sensitive data is not read without being altered (an audit trail) or altered without being read (corrupted). Providing a "fingerprint" for data that can be checked later to make sure the data has not changed is the most typical technique. A hashing algorithm or a digital signature can create the fingerprint. A hashing algorithm is a one-way operation that calculates a value from a given set of data. This value can later be calculated and will match the original value if the data has not changed. A digital signature carries this one step further by encrypting the hash value using a key that is only known to the sender. The hashed value is then decrypted using a public key and can be verified against the original.

Digital signatures are also used to ensure nonrepudiation, which assures the origin, contents, and creation time of the data. The goal is to prevent false denial of involvement in a transaction. For example, a signature on receipt insures that the recipient of a package cannot claim the package was not delivered. Nonrepudiation is an indispensable ingredient for e-commerce applications.

Accountability is a crucial element of a secure system and requires that activities on a system can be traced to specific entities, who may then be held responsible for their actions. Accountability requires authentication and auditing. Auditing is the process of compiling a list, called an audit trail, of all security-relevant events, including the user initiating the event. Accountability supports many other aspects of security, including nonrepudiation, deterrence, and intrusion detection, and provides a basis for postevent recovery and legal action.

C2 is a security standard on accountability that is specified in TCSEC (Trusted Computer System Evaluation Criteria), commonly known as The Orange Book. The Orange Book defines security in classes ranging from D (minimum) to A1 (highly secure) that define security capabilities required to meet a specified level of trust. Most commercial products are evaluated at level C2, and levels higher than that are generally only required by government agencies with very strict security policies. The main criterion for a C2 system is that it enforces DAC (Discretionary Access Control), assigning individual accountability for actions through login procedures, auditing of security-relevant events, and resource isolation.

SQL Server 2000 was awarded the C2 rating in August 2000 (*www.radium.ncsc. mil/tpep/epl/entries/TTAP-CSC-EPL-00-001.html*) by the NSA (National Security Agency). The security evaluation cited SQL Server's on-demand disk space management, dynamic memory management, full row-level locking, centralized administration, and tight integration with the Windows NT identification and authentication as strengths. Since SQL Server 2005 has improvements on these and other security areas, we can probably expect C2 or better certification for SQL Server 2005.

Although a C2 certification is indicative of the overall security capabilities of a product, these evaluations on done on very specific hardware and software configurations and only apply to the application being tested. Inadequate security practices or insecure application designs will undermine the most secure platforms. Be sure to develop with security in mind and adhere to security policies that match the requirements in your application environment.

SECURITY ANALYSIS

Solid security begins with understanding the nature of the application and data that needs to be protected. Design documents are useful during this phase of the analysis because they show how the application should be constructed. Beware that sometimes the as-designed and as-built condition of a system can vary, sometimes considerably. If you suspect that the as-built system deviates significantly from the design documents, you may want to do a full audit of the application to understand the data flows. Some documentation-light application development approaches (such as eXtreme Programming) generally do not produce sufficiently detailed documentation to really understand what data is going where. This does not mean that lightweight techniques are necessarily insecure; just that there may be more documentation work required to make sure all the relevant data flows are considered. A properly designed XP application project that follows security principles from the outset is likely to be more secure than an application that is fully designed upfront using elaborate documentation that doesn't take security considerations into proper account. The amount of documentation and analysis required depends on the security requirements for the application and sensitivity of the information therein.

If security is a consideration from the beginning of the design process, the resulting application will be much easier to secure no matter what project management style is pursued. Security testing and auditing should be done early and often. It isn't enough to have test cases that merely ensure the application functionality works. Test cases should be constructed that evaluate boundary conditions and known threats.

In addition to testing for security during development, it is essential to perform security code reviews during development. It is all too easy to introduce security holes into an application during implementation, no matter how watertight the design is. The more eyes that see the implementation code, the more likely you are to catch potential holes before they go into production. In addition, the act of going through code in a public setting with security tops on the agenda helps to raise awareness in the development team that security is important and helps to propagate knowledge and best practice throughout the organization.

To perform code reviews, you need to have a set of code standards against which to review. Depending on the nature of your development project, these standards may be extremely specific or a set of guidelines regarding best practice.

The first step for a threat analysis is to understand the functions, interfaces, and interactions for your application. This threat analysis consists of three parts:

1. Collecting application information.
2. Modeling the system.
3. Determining threats.

Figure 3.2 provides a high-level schematic of this process.

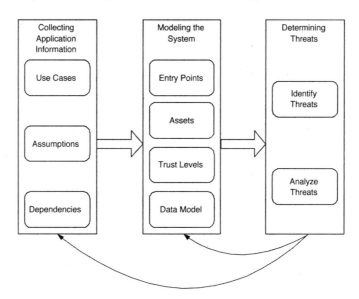

FIGURE 3.2 Threat analysis is a three-part process: collect information, model the system, and determine threats.

Creating a data flow diagram is an important step in understanding the boundaries of the system and potential threat areas. A data flow diagram uses the symbols shown in Figure 3.3.

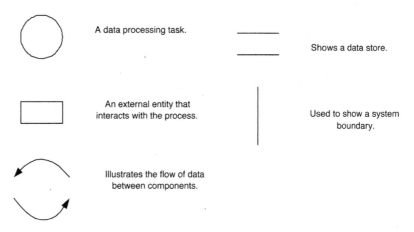

FIGURE 3.3 The symbols used in a data flow diagram define the flows and boundaries of a system.

Armed with specific application knowledge, the threats can be examined to identify the vulnerabilities of the application and possible countermeasures. Understanding the threats allows you to implement an application with those threats in mind. To do a good job, you must be methodical and complete at constructing the threat profile. Approaching the possible threats in a structured fashion is a good way to make sure all the relevant categories of threats are considered and can be included in your design and implementation. One such useful model for threat analysis is STRIDE, which is an acronym for six general threats to application security:

Spoofing. Spoofing involves impersonating a user or a system to gain unauthorized access to an application or data. A spoofing attack can be countered by a strong authentication and authorization facility.

Tampering. Tampering is changing data without authorization. Tampering is best prevented by strong authentication and minimizing the potential access paths to the data (minimizing the profile of the application).

Repudiation. Repudiation is concealing the evidence of an attack. Proper authentication and control of credentials is a solid countermeasure against the threat of repudiation.

Information disclosure. Information disclosure is simply the exposure of confidential information. A solid defense against information disclosure is to minimize the amount of confidential information that is stored. For example, retaining customer credit card numbers or account routing information should be approached very carefully.

Denial of service. Denial of service (DoS) is any action that makes an application less available than it otherwise would be. An effective defense for DoS attacks is to throttle requests so that a particular stream of service requests can't overwhelm the application and cause software or hardware faults.

Elevation of privilege. Elevation of privilege is not typically harmful in itself, but the improper acquisition of credentials can lead to manifestations of other types of threats. All other security measures are seriously compromised when an unauthorized user gains trusted access to a system.

The next step after categorizing the possible vectors of attack using the STRIDE framework is ranking the severity of the potential issues. A popular method for doing this follows the acronym DREAD, which ranks issues on a scale of 1 through 10 on each of the following:

Damage potential. Damage potential is an assessment of the damage that would result if a specific threat were realized. Damage can include data loss, application downtime, and the like.

Reproducibility. Reproducibility measures how easily the attack can be replicated in a variety of circumstances. The more easily reproducible an attack is, the more dangerous it is. For example, a threat that is present in the default installation of the system is most dangerous.

Exploitability. Exploitability measures the amount of time and expertise needed to succeed in the attack. An attack that requires a great degree of expertise is less threatening than one that can be easily exploited with a low degree of sophistication.

Affected users. This is a metric to capture the number of potential affected users. The more people affected by a security issue, the worse the potential effects of the issue.

Discoverability. Discoverability measures the likelihood of the issue being found and exploited. This can be very difficult to estimate, so it is usually safest to assume the issue will be found and exploited.

DREAD does not apply any weight to the difficulty of fixing an issue. It may turn out that a risk/reward justification of a particular security fix is not worth it, but this is not a factor in assessing the threat itself.

SQL SERVER SECURITY DESIGN PRINCIPLES

To help you secure your database applications, you must build them on a securable platform. SQL Server 2005 was designed with security in mind and makes some significant improvements in this area. Microsoft spent a three-month period in the development cycle devoted to making SQL Server as secure as possible. This included extensive training for all the SQL Server team members, code reviews, documentation scrubbing for security correctness, and a detailed threat analysis of the product. Because of this work, SQL Server 2005 is much more secure than its predecessors were.

Four of the principles followed in the SQL Server 2005 product are:

Secure defaults. SQL Server is secure as installed out of the box. It is intentionally difficult to change settings to make the server less secure.

Principle of least privilege. Minimal permissions are granted to objects and roles. Service accounts have very low levels of security privilege.

Granular permissions. Minimal escalation of privilege necessary to accomplish tasks.

Reduction of surface area. Only the necessary components are installed by default. Installing additional components must be done explicitly.

SQL SERVER 2005 SECURITY MODEL

SQL Server security is based on the Windows and Active Directory security model. A basic understanding of the relevant features of the overall Active Directory security model is essential to making the most of the security features in SQL Server. These concepts include domains, global groups, local groups, and user accounts.

There are two basic ways to maintain security in SQL Server. The first is to assign the Windows users to a global group. These global groups are in turn mapped to a Windows local group that has permissions assigned to access SQL Server and the appropriate catalogs. This mapping is shown in Figure 3.4.

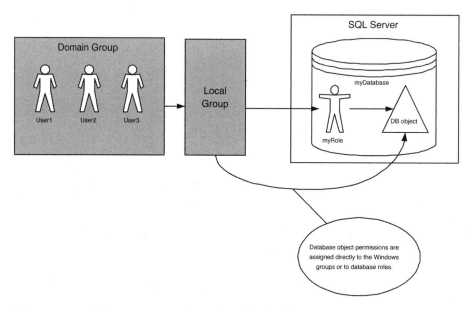

FIGURE 3.4 Windows users can be assigned to local groups that are mapped to SQL Server permissions.

The second method is to use database roles primarily. User accounts are mapped to roles. Object permissions are assigned to the roles. This mapping is shown in Figure 3.5. The basic difference is that the latter approach maintains security within SQL Server, while the former focuses on using Windows accounts directly.

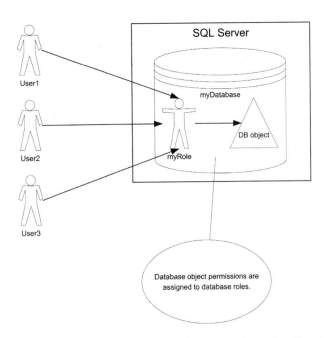

FIGURE 3.5 User accounts can be mapped to roles directly.

SQL SERVER 2005 SECURITY FEATURES AUTHENTICATION MODES

Access to SQL Server can be controlled by two distinct authentication modes: Windows Authentication Mode and Mixed Mode.

Windows Authentication is the default on SQL Server. In Windows Authentication Mode, SQL Server employs the Windows authentication credentials of the user as the sole source of authentication on the server. In this mode, Windows users and groups are granted permissions to access the server thorough *trusted connections*.

In Mixed Mode, users are authenticated either by Windows credentials or by SQL Server authentication. SQL Server authentication manages the username and password pairs in SQL Server. In Mixed Mode, a client capable of authenticating with Windows using NTLM or Kerberos can be authenticated that way. If Windows cannot authenticate the client, the username and password stored in SQL Server are used for authentication. Connections made using SQL Server authentication are called *nontrusted connections*.

In SQL Server 2000, Windows authentication is inherently more secure than SQL Server authentication because the authentication happens without sending the password. This has been improved in SQL Server 2005 with digest authentication that does not require the password to be sent over the wire. Digest authentication is the new default for SQL logins and is designed to be seamless to applications.

The old SQL authentication, which sends the username and password pair, unencrypted except by an obfuscation algorithm, is still supported, but not recommended. The obfuscation algorithm is well known, so if any traffic between the client and server is intercepted, the username and password pair could become known. If you are using Mixed Mode, be sure to use an encrypted communications channel to minimize the risk of interception of sensitive data.

ENCRYPTION

SQL Server encryption relies on a hierarchy where each layer encrypts the layer below it, providing security all the way down the tree as shown in Figure 3.6. At the top, the SMK (Service Master Key) is encrypted with the Windows DPAPI (Data Protection Application Programming Interface). The DPAPI provides simple yet powerful data encryption for any application (for more details on DPAPI, see the MSDN article at *http://msdn.microsoft. com/library/default.asp?url=/library/en-us/dnsecure/html/win-dataprotection-dpapi.asp*). The SMK is a 128-bit 3DES key used to encrypt all database master keys and server-level secrets such as credential secrets or linked server login passwords. There is just one SMK per database server, which is created the first time the server is used using the credentials of the SQL Server service account, and it can never be dropped (it can be changed with an ALTER statement, as we discuss later).

Each database can then have its own unique 128-bit 3DES key, the Database Master Key (DMK). Each DMK is encrypted by a password and the SMK. Each DMK is used to protect database secrets such as the private keys of certificates or asymmetric keys. The reason the DMK is encrypted by the SMK is to allow the server to decrypt each DMK without requiring a password. This means that every sysadmin has access to each DMK. If this is not acceptable, the SMK encryption can be removed, but then a password is required to use the DMK.

The DMK can then be used to create certificates and keys that are used to sign and encrypt data in the database. A certificate is a digitally signed document that binds a public key to the holder of a private key. Certificates are issued by a certification authority (CA) and contain a public key, an identifier for the subject, the validity period, and a digital signature of the CA that binds the subject public key to the identifier. Every certificate is valid for a limited period of time, and a new certificate is generated after the old one expires. A certificate can be revoked by the issuer and is then placed on the revocation list used to verify certificate validity. The benefit of certificates is that they relieve the need to authenticate by password—presentation of the certificate is the means of authentication. SQL Server creates standard x.509 certificates.

There are two types of keys used in SQL Server. The first is an asymmetric key, which consists of matched private and public keys. The private key can decrypt data encrypted by the public key and vice versa. Asymmetric encryption is a resource-intensive process, so it is typically used to encrypt a symmetric key used for bulk data encryption. A symmetric key is simply a single key that is used for both encryption and decryption. To maintain security, it is essential that a symmetric key remain secret.

Since the SMK is one of the most important pieces of information in the server, it is an excellent idea to back up the SMK on a regular basis. This can be done using the BACKUP SERVICE MASTER KEY statement. BACKUP SERVICE MASTER KEY takes two parameters: a file path specifying where the key should be stored in the filesystem, and a password used to encrypt the SMK in the backup file. This password must match the password policy on any Windows platform that enforces the platform policy API. For example:

```
BACKUP SERVICE MASTER KEY TO FILE = 'c:\temp\sql_smk' ENCRYPTION BY
PASSWORD = 'chOub@uprlet ';
```

RESTORE SERVICE MASTER KEY is similar. It has two required parameters and an optional FORCE parameter that will force the replacement of the SMK, risking potential data loss. The basic RESTORE operation reads the SMK from the specified file, decrypts it, and then migrates the data encrypted with the current SMK to the restored key. If there are errors, the whole action is rolled back and no data is changed. The FORCE parameter will allow the operation to proceed even if there are errors, which can be useful in recovering from a corrupted SMK. Data that cannot be decrypted using the current SMK will be left in place when the FORCE option is used. Restoring from the previous example would be:

```
RESTORE SERVICE MASTER KEY FROM FILE = 'c:\temp\sql_smk' DECRYPTION BY
PASSWORD = 'chOub@uprlet ';
```

If you have a need to regenerate the SMK either because it has been compromised in some way or as a part of general security policy, you use the following statement:

```
ALTER SERVICE MASTER KEY REGENERATE
```

This will regenerate a new random SMK and migrate all of the data encrypted with the current SMK to be encrypted with the new one. If it fails, no data will be changed.

Managing the DMKs is similar to managing the SMK, and you can find more information on that in the SQL Server Books Online.

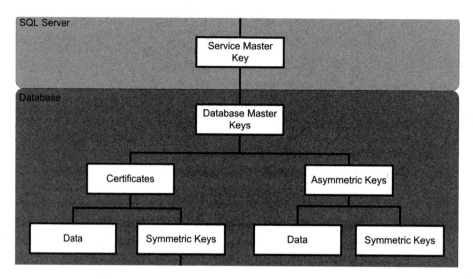

FIGURE 3.6   SQL Server encryption is based on a hierarchy of keys.

USER AND SCHEMA SEPARATION

In earlier versions of SQL Server, server logins were directly mapped to users in the database. The concept of schema in SQL Server 2000 is very weak. In database terms, *schema* is a collection of objects that are owned by a user and form a namespace. Essentially, every user owns a schema that has the same name as the user. Therefore, in SQL Server 2000, database users were also assigned ownership of objects in the database. This tight binding between users and schemas creates a few problems. For example, direct ownership of objects complicates dropping or changing a user. Since the user defines a schema, all the objects that user owned would have to be dropped or reassigned to a different schema before dropping or changing the user.

To solve this problem, SQL Server 2005 separates the users from object ownership. Users are now associated with a default schema that owns all the objects the user creates. These schemas can be owned by database roles so users can manage the database objects without having permissions on all objects in the database. In addition, this solves the problem outlined previously by allowing users to be dropped or changed without changing ownership of database objects.

In SQL Server 2005, a *securable object* or *securable* is a resource that has access control maintained by the SQL Server authorization system. Some securables are contained within a hierarchy of securable items called a *scope*. The three scopes are server, database, and schema. Items in the server scope include Logins, Certificates, Connections, and Databases. Items in the database scope include Users, Roles, Assemblies, and Schemas. Items in the schema scope include Tables, Views, Functions, Procedures, Types, and Defaults. In general, securables have the following four permissions:

CONTROL. Ownership-type privileges.

ALTER. Can change the properties of the securable. Typically grants the ability to change (CREATE/DROP/ALTER) contained items. For example, ALTER permission on a schema allows CREATE/DROP/ALTER on tables, views, etc. in that schema.

ALTER ANY. Can change the properties of any securable of a specific type. ALTER ANY ASSEMBLIES allows ALTER privilege on all assemblies in the database.

Take Ownership. Can take ownership of any object.

In SQL Server 2005, the term *principal* means an entity that can access securable objects. A primary principal represents a single SQL Server or Windows login. A secondary principal is a role or Windows group. Principals have a scope that depends on where they are defined. The Windows-level principals are Windows Domain Login, a Windows Local Login, and Windows Group. The SQL Server level principals are SQL Server Login and Server Role. The individual database level principals are Database User, Database Group, Database Role, and Application Role. An overview of principals and securables in SQL Server 2005 is shown in Figure 3.7.

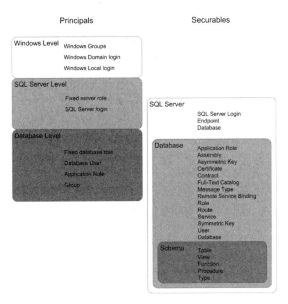

FIGURE 3.7 Principals and securables work together to give SQL Server 2005 a granular and flexible security model.

There are some default schemas created in each new database in SQL Server 2005. The first, sys, contains all the system tables and views. The sys schema is always checked first when trying to access an object, so you must not name your objects the same as any of the objects in sys. The next schema is the default schema, dbo. A user can be assigned a default schema that is used for name resolution. If no schema is specified, the default schema dbo is used.

The DDL for creating, altering, and dropping schemas is presented here:

```
CREATE SCHEMA schema_name_element [schema_element […n]]
schema_name_element ::=
{
schema_name [AUTHORIZATION <owner_name>]
}
<schema_element> ::=
{ table_definition | view_definition | grant_statement}
```

If no explicit AUTHORIZATION is specified, the user running the statement will be the schema owner. The <owner_name> must be either a database user or role. This role will be granted permissions to CREATE/ALTER/DROP objects in the schema. CREATE permissions need to be assigned explicitly. While the CREATE SCHEMA statement is running, the new schema is treated as the default schema for that user. Therefore, objects created during CREATE SCHEMA will be created in the new schema by default. It is possible to specify an explicit schema to create objects in another schema if required.

```
ALTER SCHEMA schema_name
AUTHORIZATION owner_name>
```

ALTER SCHEMA can only be run by a member of the db_owner role and is used to set ownership of a schema.

```
DROP SCHEMA schema_name
```

DROP SCHEMA can only be run by a member of the db_owner role and will fail if the schema contains objects. You must drop any objects in the schema before dropping the schema itself.

Database permissions can be associated with users. The DDL for creating, altering, and dropping users is presented here:

```
CREATE USER <user_name>
[FOR LOGIN <login_name>]
[WITH DEFAULT_SCHEMA <schema_name>]
```

If no explicit login_name is specified in CREATE USER, the user is associated with a login name that matches the username. If no matching login name exists, the statement will fail.

```
ALTER USER <user_name>
WITH <set_item> [ ,…]
set_item ::=
NAME = <user_name>
| LOGIN = <login_name>
| DEFAULT_SCHEMA = <schema_name>

DROP USER <user_name>
```

A user cannot be dropped if it owns any schemas or roles. The schemas or roles must be dropped or assigned to a different ownership to drop the user.

EXECUTION CONTEXT

SQL Server 2005 offers a great deal of flexibility in defining the execution context of modules allowing a user to perform actions as if he were authenticated as a different user. By *module*, we mean any code that is executed on SQL Server. This includes stored procedures, functions, and triggers.

A simple example of this is provided by the case where the application developer wishes to allow a user to truncate a specific table. Since there is no specific permission for truncation, a possible solution is to allow the user alter table permissions. However, alter table allows many more privileges than just truncation—the user could then change the DDL of the table. A better solution would be to write a stored procedure to truncate the table and then allow the user to execute the procedure as an account with truncate permissions. In this way, the specific permission to truncate a table can be granted to a user.

Like the previous version of SQL Server, SQL Server 2005 also supports ownership chaining to allow permissions to be inherited down the chain of ownership. This allows access to underlying elements in a database without explicitly granting access to those objects. Many types of database objects depend on other types of objects. Views depend on tables and other views. Stored procedures can depend on tables, views, functions, or other stored procedures. These dependencies imply a chain of ownership from one item to another. If one user owns a sequence of objects (e.g., a view that depends on a table), the ownership chain is considered unbroken. If different users own the table and view, the ownership chain is broken.

SQL Server uses the ownership chain when evaluating permissions to SELECT, INSERT, DELETE, UPDATE, and EXECUTE. If the ownership chain is unbroken, SQL Server checks each branch of the ownership chain to determine permissions. If the user has been granted permissions to those objects, the statement is executed. If not, the operation is not allowed.

An unbroken ownership chain makes things simpler. In the case of an unbroken ownership chain, SQL Server just checks permissions on the source object. This allows a user to grant permissions directly on the views or stored procedures instead of on every object that is used by the operation.

The more flexible execution context can be used to augment ownership chaining to make it easier to grant permissions to objects without having to grant permissions to every object that is used, minimizing the impact of broken ownership chains. In addition, ownership chaining is available for dynamic SQL so that a dynamically generated SQL statement can be run in the context of a different user with permissions checked against the execution context, not necessarily the current user.

There are some different options for EXECUTE AS:

CALLER. This option means that the statements are run in the context of the caller of the routine. This is the default.

SELF. This option runs the statements as the user specifying the module code. This is equivalent to specifying your own username in EXECUTE AS USER.

USER = user_name. This runs the statements in the user specified. You must have permissions to impersonate the user specified.

OWNER. Statements are run as the current owner of the module. When set, you must have permissions to impersonate the owner. If ownership changes, the context is also changed.

When a statement is run, permissions are first checked that the current user has permissions to run the statement. Then, permissions for any statements in the routine are run in the context of the EXECUTE AS user.

SIGNED MODULES

As described in the previous section, a common problem that arises in database applications is the need for users to access resources they should not otherwise have permissions to use. One solution, already described, is to use EXECUTE AS. However, EXECUTE AS breaks the audit trail since the user actually making the call is not in the execution context. Instead, the user configured to be the AS user is in the logs. Although EXECUTE AS will do the job in many cases, there is another option.

SQL Server 2005 cryptography offers a way to archive the same thing—module signing. Signed modules can be used to allow access to sensitive resources without granting permissions to users. To do this, we sign the module with a certificate with permissions to access the resource. Then, we give the users permissions to access the module. At runtime, the module will temporarily be granted a token granting access to the resource, but the calling context of the execution remains with the calling user. We can even grant both server- and database-level permissions to a certificate, allowing the certificated module to do server-wide and database-specific tasks.

To illustrate, let's create a procedure that allows the creation of a new login by a user who would not normally have the permissions to do so. Creating a new principal requires the ALTER ANY LOGIN permission at the server level and ALTER ANY DATABASE permission at the database level. We will do this by granting these permissions to a certificate and then using the certificate in the code module.

Log in to the database as a user with permissions to create databases, create a database, and create a master key and certificate in the database:

```
CREATE DATABASE [Foo];
USE [Foo];
CREATE MASTER KEY ENCRYPTION BY PASSWORD = 'BIE*P&A9';
CREATE CERTIFICATE MyCert WITH SUBJECT = 'Test cert';
```

Next, we create the code to create a login and user in a database:

```
CREATE PROCEDURE CreateLogin
 @name VARCHAR(256),
 @password VARCHAR(128)
AS
      DECLARE @cmd VARCHAR(400);

      BEGIN TRAN;

      SET @cmd = 'CREATE LOGIN [' + @name + '] WITH PASSWORD = ' +
      QUOTENAME (@password, '''')+ ', DEFAULT_DATABASE = [Foo]';
      EXEC (@cmd);
      IF @@ERROR <> 0
      BEGIN
       ROLLBACK TRAN;
       PRINT 'LOGIN CREATION FAILED'
       RETURN;
      END

      SET @SQLCMD = 'CREATE USER ' + QUOTENAME(@NAME);
      EXEC (@SQLCMD);
      IF @@ERROR <> 0
      BEGIN
            ROLLBACK TRAN;
            PRINT 'CANNOT CREATE USER'
            RETURN;
      END

      COMMIT TRAN;
   GO
```

If you try to run the CreateLogin procedure using a user account without ALTER ANY LOGIN privileges at server level and ALTER ANY USER privileges at database level, it will fail. To sign the code so the user can execute the procedure, we sign the first code with the certificate:

```
ADD SIGNATURE TO CreateLogin BY CERTIFICATE MyCert;
```

Next, we grant the appropriate privileges to the certificate by creating a user with ALTER ANY USER privileges:

```
CREATE USER MyCertUser FROM CERTIFICATE MyCert;
GRANT ALTER ANY USER TO MyCertUser;
```

Next, back the certificate up to a file and import it into the master database so we can create a user with the server-level ALTER ANY LOGIN privileges:

```
ALTER CERTIFICATE MyCert REMOVE PRIVATE KEY;
BACKUP CERTIFICATE MyCert TO FILE = 'MyCert.cer';

USE MASTER;
CREATE CERTIFICATE MyCert FROM FILE = 'MyCert.cer';
CREATE LOGIN MyCertLogin FROM CERTIFICATE MyCert;
GRANT ALTER ANY LOGIN TO MyCertLogin;
```

Now, any user with permissions to run the CreateLogin procedure will be able to create a login and user in a given database.

PASSWORD POLICY ENFORCEMENT

Passwords are essential to authentication in SQL Server. Older versions of SQL Server did not enforce password policies, which is a significant security weakness. SQL Server 2005 can either enforce these in the database or apply password policies from Windows 2003.

In SQL Server 2005, the CREATE LOGIN and ALTER LOGIN DDL statements have been created to accommodate for the improvements in login management. These statements replace the system-stored procedures formerly used to manage logins (sp_addlogin, sp_droplogin, etc.). These system-stored procedures have been deprecated and, although they will still work on SQL Server 2005, you should begin using the updated syntax to ensure forward compatibility.

Only members of the sysadmin and securityadmin roles and those logins with ALTER ANY LOGIN permissions can create or alter logins. Other logins can only alter the DEFAULT_DATABASE, DEFAULT_LANGUAGE, and PASSWORD for the own logins. The syntax for the CREATE LOGIN statement is:

```
CREATE LOGIN login_name
{WITH option_list | FROM WINDOWS [WITH option_list2[,…]]}
option_list ::=
    PASSWORD password [HASHED] [MUST CHANGE] [, option_list3[,…]]
option_list2 ::=
    DEFAULT_DATABASE = database | DEFAULT_LANGUAGE = language
Option_list3 ::=
    | SID = sid
    | DEFAULT_DATABASE = database
    | DEFAULT_LANGUAGE = language
    | CHECK_EXPIRATION = { ON | OFF }
    | CHECK_POLICY = { ON | OFF }
```

Each of the arguments means the following:

login_name. Specifies the name of the SQL Server or Windows login that is to be created.

PASSWORD password. Specifies the password for the login being created, which might be subject to password policies depending on other arguments.

HASHED. Specifies that the given password is already hashed. If not specified, a hash will be applied. Valid only for SQL Server logins.

MUST_CHANGE. Specifies that the password must be changed when the user first logs in. Valid only for SQL Server logins. If specified, CHECK_POLICY must be ON.

SID = sid. Specifies the GUID of the SQL Server login. If not specified, a new GUID will be created. Valid only for SQL Server logins.

DEFAULT_DATABASE = database. Specifies the default database assigned to this login. If not specified, the default database will be set to MASTER.

DEFAULT_LANGUAGE = language. Specifies the default language assigned to the login. If not specified, will be set to the default language of the server. The default language is not updated automatically if the default language of the server is changed.

CHECK_EXPIRATION. Specifies that the password expiration policy will be enforced on this login. The default value is ON. Valid only for SQL Server logins. If CHECK_POLICY is OFF, CHECK_EXPIRATION cannot be ON.

CHECK_POLICY. Specifies that the password policies will be enforced on this login. The default value is ON. Valid only for SQL Server logins. If specified as OFF, CHECK_EXPIRATION will be set OFF as well.

The syntax for the ALTER LOGIN statement is:

```
ALTER LOGIN login_name WITH set_option [,…]
```

```
set_option ::=
    PASSWORD = password [OLD PASSWORD = oldpassword
    | secadmin_pwd_option [secadmin_pwd_option]]
    | SID = sid
    | DEFAULT_DATABASE = database
    | DEFAULT_LANGUAGE = language
    | NAME = login_name
    | CHECK_EXPIRATION = { ON | OFF }
    | CHECK_POLICY = { ON | OFF }
secadmin_pwd_opt ::= MUST CHANGE | UNLOCK
```

The arguments are identical to those specified in CREATE LOGIN with the exception of:

UNLOCK. Specifies that a locked login should be unlocked.

NAME. Specifies a new name for the login. The SID associated with the login does not change. Usernames in each of the associated databases are also unchanged.

OLD PASSWORD = *oldpassword*. Specified by a login to change the password to *password*.

To get password policy information about SQL logins, the new LoginProperty function has been added. LoginProperty takes a login name and the property to be examined as arguments and returns an integer indicating whether the property is set (−1) or not (0). The syntax for the LoginProperty function is:

```
LoginProperty('login_name', 'property')
where login_name is the name of the SQL login we are interested in and
the property is one of the following:
IsLocked
IsExpired
IsMustChange
```

Some examples of the CREATE LOGIN and ALTER LOGIN follow:

```
CREATE LOGIN Fred
WITH PASSWORD = '%foo77Cash', DEFAULT_DATABASE = pubs

ALTER LOGIN Fred
WITH NAME = Charlie
```

ROW-LEVEL SECURITY

Previous versions of SQL Server only supported table- and column-level permissions. Row-level security was established at the application level or through the use of explicit SQL filters. SQL Server 2005 builds on the table- and column-level permissions and has a built-in mechanism to provide fine-grained access control at the row level that leverages its query processing capability.

The general approach to provide row-level security is to create expressions at the table level that restrict SELECT, BEFORE/AFTER UPDATE, DELETE, and INSERT rights to those requests that match the expression criteria.

As a simple example, consider the requirement that employees can select from records in the same department, but can only update their own. This would require creating an expression to filter the records by department:

```
CREATE EXPRESSION 'Filter' ON EmpRecords AS (DeptID = GetDept())
```

and an expression that filters their own record:

```
CREATE EXPRESSION 'updateself' ON EmpRecords AS (EmpName =
CURRENT_USER)
```

Then the proper permissions can be granted:

```
GRANT SELECT, UPDATE to Employees
GRANT SELECT,UPDATE (Address, Phno) ON EmpRecords TO Employees
GRANT SELECT WHERE (filter) ON EmpRecords TO Employees
GRANT BEFORE UPDATE WHERE (updateself) ON EmpRecords
TO Employees
```

A permission can be revoked by name:

```
REVOKE SELECT WHERE (Filter) ON EmpRecords FROM Employees
```

GRANULAR PERMISSIONS

In addition to the GRANT statements that were available in previous versions, SQL Server 2005 adds a number of new permission verbs. GRANT CONTROL allows the grantor to give another principal the rights of ownership, including dropping the object. GRANT ALTER allows the grantor to give another principal permission to do almost everything to an object except change ownership or drop the object. These allow the granting of permissions without having to include a particular principal in a role membership and more fully support the principal of least privilege—assign only those rights that are required.

Both GRANT CONTROL and GRANT ALTER apply to contained objects. For example:

```
USE DATABASE Foo
GRANT CONTROL TO Jim
```

allows Jim to control all the objects in the database Foo.

In addition to specifying the specific object, GRANT ALTER and GRANT CONTROL support a more general control over all the elements of that type. The syntax is:

```
GRANT ALTER ANY <securable_object>
```

where securable object is any securable that allows the principal to alter any element of that type. Therefore, GRANT ALTER ANY LOGIN allows the principal to alter any login, and GRANT ALTER ANY SCHEMA allows the principal to alter any schema in the database.

Note that these new permissions do not supersede the older permissions for creation of objects. For example, to create a table in a database, you still need to have CREATE TABLE permissions in that database. DENY permission at any level takes precedence.

CATALOG SECURITY

In previous versions of SQL Server, any user could see the metadata in the database. In SQL Server 2005, this has been changed and only users with permissions to use an object can see the metadata. This is implemented by the system catalog views using row-level security by default. If a user selects data from the sys views, he will see only those objects he has permissions to use. If he has no permissions, an empty row set will be returned. The SA role can view all the metadata in the server, and a database owner can see all the metadata in a database. The objects that are protected by permissions are anything that has GRANT, DENY, or REVOKE permissions available to it. This includes tables, views, assemblies, schemas, and databases.

In addition to securing the visibility of metadata, the module definitions are also secured. Simply having permissions to execute a module does not automatically grant permission to view the module source. There is a VIEW DEFINITION permission to allow the viewing of the source of a module. It can be applied at various levels of scope—database, schema, and instance.

SQL SERVER 2005 SECURITY BEST PRACTICES

Understanding security vulnerabilities requires a great deal of study and knowledge. Creating a secure application is much more than following a checklist, but having a good list of best practices is a good way to start. Applying each of these will not make your application bulletproof, but it will at least give you a head start down the path toward a secure application.

- Use strong passwords. A strong password is at least seven characters long and contains a combination of letters, numbers, and symbols. Configure SQL Server to enforce password complexity.
- Use the most granular permissions possible. Never grant more permissions than necessary to a particular user.
- Use integrated security. Network-wide authorization makes it simpler to efficiently control access to resources.
- Run Microsoft Baseline Security Analyzer on a regular basis to ensure that no insecure changes have been made to the configuration.
- Audit authentication successes and failures and check the logs on a regular basis. Additional application-level logging is also useful in spotting patterns of abuse.
- Keep current with operating system and application patches. Using an automated tool like Windows Update or Software Update Service is a big help with this.
- Establish an incident response plan. A complete and well-rehearsed incident response plan will allow you to minimize disruption in case of a security incident and potentially capture and prosecute the attacker.
- Establish a disaster recovery plan. This should include at a minimum frequent backups with off-site media storage and practice on the procedure to restore the system to operation. The benefits of this go well beyond security, but intrusions can require a recovery operation.
- Use a small administrative group with experienced people.
- Establish a corporate security policy. Such a policy might include things like minimum specification of password length and expiration period, logon and audit policies, intruder prevention policies, and ownership of user accounts.
- Use encrypted channels for transmitting sensitive information.
- Use encryption to store sensitive information.
- Isolate applications as much as possible. Don't install applications on a domain controller. Run services with the minimum privileges necessary. Do not run your application within the context of an administrator. Disable or remove unneeded services. Separate different tiers of applications with firewalls.
- Do not allow direct access to the data tier. Use a layered approach to security.
- Don't hide passwords in the client tier.
- Validate all user input to an application. Unvalidated user input enables many different kinds of attacks, including SQL script injection and buffer overruns. When working with XML documents, validate all data against its schema as it is entered. Never build Transact-SQL statements directly from user input. Never concatenate user input that is not validated. String concatenation is the primary point of entry for script injection.

- Use strong authentication methods in your applications, such as Kerberos authentication and client authentication certificates, to prevent spoofing.
- To defend against DoS attacks, use a packet-filtering firewall to separate legitimate and malicious packets. In addition, bandwidth throttling and resource throttling can be used to prevent malicious overloading from bringing down an entire server.
- Contract an independent security audit firm to evaluate your application and environment.
- Establish a perimeter network to protect your application servers. Run multiple firewalls.
- Create safe error messages. Do not allow an attacker to learn about the internal structure of your application through returned error messages. Do not return information that might be useful to attackers, such as a username.
- Subscribe to the Microsoft Security Notification Service. This will allow you to keep current on new security threats and issues.

CONCLUSION

Database security needs to be taken seriously and designed in from the beginning. In this chapter, we introduced some techniques useful in designing secure application and features of SQL Server 2005 that can be used to enforce a secure design. The design of SQL Server itself is intended to promote database security with a robust security model, strong encryption, user and schema separation, a definable execution context, enforceable password policy, and granular permissions. We closed the chapter with a set of best practices to enhance security that can be applied to many different situations.

4 Transact-SQL for Developers

In this Chapter

- Syntax Elements
- Basic Statements
- Additional Transact-SQL Language Enhancements
- Conclusion

Contemporary developers need to be competent in two, three, or sometimes four or more programming languages to accomplish their daily tasks. Take, for example, a Web application developer working on a simple data-driven Web site. The developer would need to have skills in VB.NET or C# for building the pages, ECMAScript or JavaScript for some browser-based scripting, and SQL for interacting with the data. That's a very large set of skills to hone for today's busy professional. In this environment, developers focus their learning efforts on the more traditional programming/scripting languages and often neglect to gain a solid understanding of SQL and its variations. Now, it's okay in certain situations not to have a deep knowledge of SQL (e.g., if you are building a mathematical calculation engine), but developers constructing data-driven Web applications and, generally speaking, any business application will be able to construct more performant, scalable, and robust solutions with these skills. Throughout this chapter, we provide you with a foundation for learning the Transact-SQL language, starting from the basic elements of the language and continuing through coverage of the new features added to Transact-SQL with Microsoft SQL Server 2005.

Transact-SQL is Microsoft's language for interacting with SQL Server 2005. Transact-SQL, often referred to as T-SQL, is an extension to the SQL standard that provides support for defining database structures and retrieving and manipulating data. The Transact-SQL language, like any contemporary, mainstream language, consists of identifiers, data types, functions, expressions, operators, comments, and reserved keywords. Transact-SQL has all of the components to make it a full-fledged programming language. Even with the advanced features of SQL Server 2005 such as tightly integrating the Common Language Runtime, Transact-SQL continues to be the primary language for retrieving and manipulating data in SQL Server 2005.

With the release of Microsoft SQL Server 2005, there has been some confusion about the use of Transact-SQL versus the integrated Common Language Runtime (CLR) and whether the CLR integration would make Transact-SQL obsolete. We will cover the CLR integration in the next chapter, but in the meantime, let us say that the CLR integration is not a replacement for Transact-SQL, and the clear direction coming from Redmond is that Transact-SQL is the way to retrieve and manipulate data while the CLR integration is the way to build very complex mathematical calculations. Figure 4.1 graphically illustrates the selection criteria.

FIGURE 4.1 Guidelines for choosing Transact-SQL or CLR integration.

SYNTAX ELEMENTS

The Transact-SQL language is comprised of a relatively small set of language elements, including identifiers, data types, functions, expressions, and reserved keywords. The language elements are arranged in a multitude of combinations, or statements, that give the Transact-SQL language its flexibility and power. The next sections cover these basic syntax elements and provide a foundation for constructing basic Transact-SQL statements.

Identifiers

Identifiers are the names of database objects. Nearly all database objects—including tables, views, variables, parameters, and columns—have identifiers, which makes identifiers one of the most commonly used Transact-SQL syntax elements. Transact-SQL identifiers are specified when the object is created and then the identifier is used to reference the object later. For example, the following statement creates a new database table named MyFirstTable containing a single column named MyFirstColumn:

```
CREATE TABLE MyTable (MyColumn INT IDENTITY)
```

There are two identifiers used in this statement: `MyTable` and `MyColumn`. The previous statement shows how identifiers are specified when database objects are created. Now let's look at the following example statement that uses the identifiers to reference the objects:

```
SELECT MyColumn FROM MyTable
```

Here we use the identifiers `MyColumn` and `MyTable` to define the table and column on which the statement should operate.

As we have seen, identifiers in Transact-SQL are names used to define and reference database objects. Many database objects, including columns and variables, are defined by using an identifier and a data type. Next, we will take a brief survey of the Transact-SQL data types available in Microsoft SQL Server 2005.

Data Types

Transact-SQL data types specify the type of data that will be stored in database objects. For example, columns, variables, and parameters must be defined to contain a particular type of data. At a conceptual level, data types in Microsoft SQL Server 2005 are categorized as numeric, character, date and time, binary, or user-defined. Each data type category has specific data types that define the types, ranges, and properties of values that may be stored in an instance of that type.

Developers who have worked with SQL Server 2000 data types will find SQL Server 2005 data types nearly identical. One significant enhancement to SQL Server 2005 data types is the introduction of several new data types that simplify working with large character and binary data. The new data types include `varchar(max)`, `nvarchar(max)`, and `varbinary(max)`, and are replacements for the `text`, `ntext`, and `image` types that are being deprecated in SQL Server 2005. Now let's look at common data types available in Transact-SQL, starting with the numeric data types.

Numerics

Numeric data types supported by SQL Server 2005 include exact numerics such as `integer` and `decimal` and approximate numerics such as `float`. As the name implies, exact numeric types store an exact representation of a value, while approximate numerics store a very close approximation of the value based on the IEEE 754 floating-point standard. For example, the value 19.999 can be stored as an exact decimal value, whereas 1/3 (e.g., 0.33333…) is represented as an approximate float value. Floating-point numbers are called approximations because the actual number is not what is stored; rather, floating points are represented by a sign, an exponent, and a mantissa. So, for example, we could represent 1/3 as $333333333333333 \times 10^{-15}$ as an approximate representation. Because of its very flexible representation of numeric values, floating-point numbers can be very large or very small.

The various numeric data types available support different ranges of values. Table 4.1 summarizes the range of values supported by some common numeric data types.

TABLE 4.1 Commonly Used Numeric Data Types

Data Type	Description
INT	Stores exact numeric values ranging from -2^{31} to $2^{31}-1$.
DECIMAL/NUMERIC	Stores exact numeric values ranging from $-10^{38}+1$ to $10^{38}-1$. The Decimal and Numeric data types are equivalent.
MONEY	Stores exact monetary values raging from -2^{63} to $2^{63}-1$. Values stored using this data type are accurate to one ten-thousandth of a unit.
FLOAT	Stores floating-point approximated values ranging from $-1.79E + 38$ to $1.79E + 38$

When defining columns, variables, and parameters as a `decimal` or `numeric` data type, SQL Server 2005 supports variable precision and scale of the numeric data. The precision of a number is the number of digits in the number, while the scale of a number is the number of digits to the right of the decimal point. For example, the decimal value 123456.789 has a precision of 9 and a scale of 3. Other exact numeric data types have predefined precision and scale values. For example, the INT data type supports values ranging from −2147483648 to 2147483647, making the precision of the data type equal to 10 and, because the INT data type does not support fractional values, a scale of 0. The FLOAT data type, following the IEEE 754 floating-point specification, does not support specification of a scale for values. The FLOAT data type uses a floating scale but imposes a maximum value of 15 for the precision float data. That means that no matter how large or small a number is, the number of digits that represent the number is limited to 15, and SQL Server 2005 will round up any values that exceed this precision.

The data types available in Transact-SQL offer flexible options for working with numeric data. These options allow designers and developers working with numeric data to tune their particular designs and implementations to capture the necessary data in the minimal amount of space. Next, we'll look at character data types in Microsoft SQL Server 2005.

Character Strings

Just as we saw the flexible options in Transact-SQL for storing numeric data, a corresponding set of flexible data types exists for storing character data. In SQL Server 2005, there are two major subcategories of character data types: traditional character data types and Unicode character data types. Traditional character data types store a character as a single byte. These traditional character data types work well for storing ASCII characters, which have 128 characters in the standard (nonextended) character set, but cannot support other character sets such as traditional Chinese, which has thousands of characters. To support these large character sets, SQL Server 2005 provides support for Unicode character data. The Unicode standard provides a unique representation for every character and every language in the world. The traditional character data types represent each character using a single-byte encoding, while the Unicode data types in Microsoft SQL Server 2005 represent characters using a double-byte encoding known as UCS-2. In SQL Server lingo, the Unicode data types are called National Data Types and are easily identified because their names are the same as the traditional character data types but are prefixed with an "N." For example, a traditional character fixed-length string data type is named CHAR; the corresponding Unicode data type is called NCHAR. Table 4.2 lists the more commonly used character data types supported by Microsoft SQL Server 2005 and the maximum number of characters each type may store.

TABLE 4.2 Commonly Used Textual Data Types

Data Type	Description
CHAR	Stores up to 8000 single-byte characters.
VARCHAR	Stores up to 8000 single-byte characters.
VARCHAR(MAX)	Stores up to 2 GB of single-byte character data.
NCHAR	Stores up to 4000 Unicode characters.
NVARCHAR	Stores up to 4000 Unicode characters.
NVARCHAR(MAX)	Stores up to 2 GB of variable-length Unicode data.

Defining an object to use a character data type requires specifying the maximum length of character data that can be stored in the object. For example, the following statement creates a table with a single varchar column that holds a maximum of 8000 characters:

```
CREATE TABLE MyTable ( MyColumn varchar(8000) )
```

The max keyword in SQL Server 2005 provides a new option for specifying the maximum length of variable-length character columns. The varchar(max) and nvarchar(max) data types are provided for objects that may exceed the 8000 character maximum length for varchar or the 4000 character limit for nvarchar data types. When varchar(max) or nvarchar(max) data types are specified, the object may hold up to 2 GB of data. Varchar(max) and nvarchar(max) are replacements for the deprecated SQL Server 2000 data types text and ntext, respectively. The text and ntext data types were notoriously difficult to work with because many of the string functions did not support these data types. These legacy data types are being phased out in favor of varchar(max) and nvarchar(max), which provide better overall programmability. To illustrate the new data type, the following statements create a table with a single varchar(max) column that stores up to 2 GB of data, inserts two records into the table, and runs a query using a standard string function on the column:

```
CREATE TABLE MyTable (MyColumn varchar(max))
INSERT INTO MyTable(MyColumn) VALUES('This is a test')
INSERT INTO MyTable(MyColumn) VALUES('This is another test')
SELECT LEN(MyColumn) FROM MyTable
```

Running this example script in a SQL Server 2005 database will return 14 and 20 representing the character length of the data stored in MyColumn of MyTable.

When choosing character data types, it is important to understand the typical length of character data stored in the object, because certain data types offer more efficient storage of variable-length character data. Both the varchar and nvarchar data types are more efficient than their char and nchar counterparts are when storing variable-length character data. The efficiency is achieved for varchar and nvarchar data types because the database will allocate just enough storage for the specific value being saved, not the maximum amount of data the column could store as in the case of char and nchar data types. Figure 4.2 shows the applicable data types for Unicode/Non-Unicode and fixed/variable-length character data.

To illustrate the difference between fixed- and variable-length character data types, let's say that we have a table with a column named BillingName. The BillingName column is required to store names up to 25 characters in length. The following is a list of sample names stored in the column:

```
JIM ROSS
PATRICIA HENDERSON
JOHN COLEMAN
LINDA JENKINS
MICHAEL PERRY
MARY POWELL
```

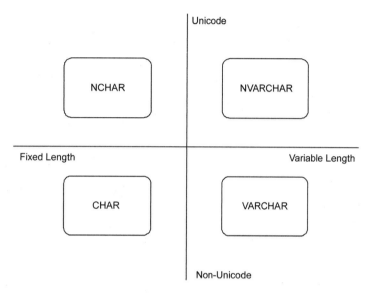

FIGURE 4.2   The character data type options in Transact-SQL.

Defining the `BillingName` column as a char data type of length 25 (e.g., `char(25)`) would result in a total storage size of 150 bytes (25 bytes for each value.) Electing to use a variable-length character data type such as `varchar` would reduce the storage requirement to 75 bytes. In this small example, we saved 75 bytes, or 50%, of the maximum space required.

Date and Time

Microsoft SQL Server 2005 provides two data types to store both date and time information. Table 4.3 describes the SQL Server 2005 date and time data types.

While SQL Server 2005 does not have a separate data type for storing only time or only date data, the date and time data types do support a user specifying only time or only date portions of a `datetime` or `smalldatetime` value. When only the time portion of a date and time data type is specified, SQL Server 2005 will default the date portion of the value to January 1, 1900. Additionally, if only the date portion of a date and time data type is specified, the time portion will default to 12:00 A.M.

TABLE 4.3   Common Date and Time Transact-SQL Data Types

Date Type	Description
DATETIME	Stores dates and times between January 1, 1753, and December 31, 9999.
SMALLDATETIME	Stores dates and times between January 1, 1900, and June 6, 2079.

Binary Strings

Binary data types store binary data such as images, audio, and video files. Binary data types, much like character data types, support both fixed-length and variable-length definitions. Again, much like the character data types, the variable-length binary data type also provides a new max length keyword that supports storing up to 2 GB of data and deprecates the image data type. Table 4.4 lists the SQL Server 2005 binary data types.

TABLE 4.4   Common Binary Transact-SQL Data Types

Data Type	Description
BINARY	Stores up to 8000 bytes of fixed-length binary data.
VARBINARY	Stores up to 8000 bytes of variable-length binary data.
VARBINARY(MAX)	Stores up to 2 GB of variable-length binary data.

Other Data Types

Other commonly used data types offered by SQL Server 2005 include bit and uniqueidentifier. Table 4.5 contains a brief description of each data type.

TABLE 4.5   Other Common Transact-SQL Data Types

Data Type	Description
BIT	Stores the value 0 or 1.
UNIQUEIDENTIFIER	Stores a 16-byte globally unique identifier (GUID).

The bit data type is often used as a replacement for the boolean data type. When the bit data type is used as a boolean substitute, the bit value of 0 is the boolean equivalent of false, and a bit value of 1 equates to true.

The uniqueidentifier data type is a globally unique identifier that consists of 32 hexadecimal digits (or 16 bytes) and is considered universally unique. Because of this universal uniqueness, the uniqueidentifier data type can be used to uniquely identify an object across multiple databases. Uniqueidentifier columns are commonly used to uniquely identify data in systems that require database replication or systems that aggregate data from multiple source databases.

As we have seen in this section, Transact-SQL offers a variety of data types to meet the requirements of nearly any situation. This section covered many of the most common data types; however, it did not provide comprehensive coverage of all the available data types. To learn more about other data types supported by Transact-SQL, we encourage you to see the Transact-SQL documentation that ships with Microsoft SQL Server 2005.

Variables

Microsoft's Transact-SQL supports defining and operating on variables, which are local objects that hold temporary values. Variables are an extremely import part of any language because they support computation of partial results, which allows program logic to proceed by computing results in smaller portions and then combining them for a final result. A Transact-SQL variable is comprised of the two language elements we just covered, identifier and data type. The identifier is used when defining variables is prefixed with the @ symbol. To define a variable, use the DECLARE statement. The basic syntax of the DECLARE statement is:

```
DECLARE @local_variable [AS] data_type
```

To assign a value to a variable, use the SET statement. The SET statement is defined as:

```
SET @local_variable = expression
```

Now let's look at a simple example that pulls together both the DECLARE and SET statements to perform some useful work. This example calculates the total for a given tax rate and subtotal:

```
DECLARE @SubTotal AS MONEY
DECLARE @TaxRate AS MONEY
DECLARE @Total AS MONEY
SET @SubTotal = 100.00
SET @TaxRate = 1.05
SET @Total = @TaxRate * @SubTotal
SELECT @Total
```

Executing this example returns the value 105.00. Also note how the example uses the partial results of subtotal and tax rate to determine the result. As we have seen, variables are a powerful aspect of the Transact-SQL language, and using them effectively can make your Transact-SQL programs more efficient and easier to maintain.

Functions

A function is a Transact-SQL language element that packages multiple statements or operations into a single referencable unit. Transact-SQL functions are very much like functions or methods in any modern programming language such as Transact-SQL. Functions accept parameter values and return results. The results returned by functions may be either scalar values or tables of values. Microsoft SQL Server 2005 provides many built-in functions and supports user-defined functions. The remainder of this section covers the commonly used built-in functions, while the discussion of user-defined functions is covered in Chapter 5, "Programmability."

Date and Time Functions

SQL Server 2005 provides several built-in functions for working with date and time data types. Table 4.6 lists some of the available date and time functions.

TABLE 4.6 Common Date and Time Transact-SQL Functions

`DATEADD(datepart, number, date)`	Adds the specified number of days, months, years, etc., to a given date and returns the resulting date.
`DATEDIFF(datepart, startdate, enddate)`	Returns an integer value representing the number of days, months, years, etc., between the start date and end date.
`DATEPART(datepart, date)`	Returns an integer value representing the portion of the date identified in the datepart parameter.
`DAY(date)`	Returns an integer value between 1 and 31 representing the date portion of the specified date and time.
`GETDATE()`	Returns the current date and time.
`MONTH(date)`	Returns an integer value between 1 and 12 representing the month portion of the specified date and time. →

`YEAR(date)`	Returns an integer value between 1753 and 9999 representing the year portion of the specified date and time.

Transact-SQL Date and Time functions make common programming tasks very simple. The following example uses the date and time functions to extract the year portion of two different date values and compare the values.

```
/* Define two date variables */
DECLARE @date_1 AS DATETIME
DECLARE @date_2 AS DATETIME
SET @date_1 = '1-JAN-2004'
SET @date_2 = '1-APR-2004'

/*
Call the DATEPART and YEAR functions
to get the year portion of the dates
*/
DECLARE @year_1 AS INT
DECLARE @year_2 AS INT
SET @year_1 = DATEPART(yyyy, @date_1)
SET @year_2 = YEAR(@date_2)
/*
Compare the year parts and
return the result
*/
IF(@year_1 = @year_2)
    SELECT 'YEAR PART IS EQUAL'
ELSE
    SELECT 'YEAR PART IS NOT EQUAL'
```

Mathematical Functions

SQL Server 2005 provides many powerful, built-in mathematical functions. The mathematical functions generally accept a numeric value and return the same data type as the data type of the input value. Table 4.7 contains a partial listing of available mathematical functions.

TABLE 4.7 Common Transact-SQL Mathematical Functions

Function	Description
`ABS(numeric_expression)`	Returns the absolute value of the specified numeric expression. →

Function	Description
CEILING(numeric_expression)	Returns the smallest integer that is greater than or equal to the numeric expression.
FLOOR(numeric_expression)	Returns the largest integer value that is larger than or equal to the specified numeric expression.
RAND(seed)	Returns a random float value between 0 and 1.
ROUND(numeric_expression, precision)	Returns the specified numeric expression rounded to the precision.
SQRT(float_expression)	Returns the square root of the expression.

System Functions

SQL Server 2005 system functions perform a wide variety of tasks. Table 4.8 is limited to the description of a few common system functions used in typical development scenarios.

TABLE 4.8 Common Transact-SQL System Functions

Function	Description
CAST(expression AS data_type)	Returns the expression value converted to the specified data type.
@@IDENTITY	Returns the last value inserted into an identity column.
NEWID()	Returns a new globally unique identifier.
@@ROWCOUNT	Returns the number of rows affected by the last Transact-SQL statement.

Aggregates and Grouping Functions

Aggregate functions operate on multiple values and return a single result. Table 4.9 describes the most common aggregate functions.

String Functions

String functions operate on char, varchar, varchar(max), nchar, nvarchar, and nvarchar(max) data types. Table 4.10 lists a subset of the available string functions.

TABLE 4.9 Common Transact-SQL Aggregate Functions

Function	Description
AVG(expression)	Returns the average of all non-null values in the expression.
COUNT(expression)	Returns the number of values, null and non-null, in the expression.
MAX(expression)	Returns the maximum non-null value in the expression.
MIN(expression)	Returns the minimum non-null value in the expression.
SUM(expression)	Returns the total of the non-null values in the expression.

TABLE 4.10 Common Transact-SQL String Functions

Function	Description
LEN(expression)	Returns an integer indicating the number of characters in the expression.
LOWER(expression)	Returns the specified character expression with all characters converted to lowercase.
UPPER(expression)	Returns the specified character expression with all characters converted to uppercase.
LEFT(expression, integer)	Returns the leftmost characters from the character expression. The number of characters returned is specified by the integer parameter.
RIGHT(expression, integer)	Returns the rightmost characters from the character expression. The number of characters returned is specified by the integer parameter.
REPLACE(string1, string2, string3)	Searches string1 for string2 and replaces each occurrence of string2 with string3 and returns the resulting string.
SUBSTRING(expression, start, length)	Returns a portion of the string expression beginning at the location specified by the start parameter and continuing for the number of bytes specified in the length parameter.

Operators

Operators are the glue that combines multiple expressions. In essence, they specify the actions to be performed on two expressions. The Transact-SQL language in SQL Server 2005 includes arithmetic, comparison, logical, and string concatenation operators. In this section, we briefly discuss the most common operators and provide a brief description of each.

Arithmetic Operators

Arithmetic operators are used to perform a mathematical calculation using two expressions. Table 4.11 lists the Transact-SQL numeric operators.

TABLE 4.11   Transact-SQL Arithmetic Operators

Operator	Description
+	Addition. For example: 2 + 2 = 4
-	Subtraction. For example: 2 - 2 = 0
*	Multiplication. For example: 2 * 2 = 4
/	Division. For example: 2 / 2 = 1
%	Modulo. For example: 2 % 2 = 0

Comparison Operators

Comparison operators evaluate two expressions and return a boolean value, which is the result of the comparison. Table 4.12 lists the Transact-SQL comparison operators.

TABLE 4.12   Transact-SQL Comparison Operators

Operator	Description
>	Greater Than. For example: 1 > 2 = FALSE
<	Less Than. For example: 1 < 2 = TRUE
=	Equals. For example: 1 = 2 = FALSE
<=	Less Than or Equal To. For example: 1 <= 2 = TRUE
>=	Greater Than or Equal To. For example: 1 > = 2 = FALSE
!=	Not Equal To. For example: 1 != 2 = TRUE
<>	Not Equal To. For example: 1 <> 2 = TRUE
!<	Not Less Than. For example: 1 !< 2= FALSE
!>	Not Greater Than. For example: 1 !> 2 = TRUE

Functions and robust function libraries are staples of all popular languages, and Transact-SQL is no exception. The built-in functions available in Microsoft SQL Server 2005 can perform functions such as string replacement, square root calculation, and summation of a set of values. For a comprehensive list of functions available in Microsoft SQL Server 2005, we encourage you to review the Transact-SQL documentation.

Expressions

Expressions are combinations of identifiers, operators, and values that evaluate to a single value. In Transact-SQL, an expression may include constants, variables, column names, or functions combined using various operators. For example, a valid expression would be:

```
1 + 1
```

This expression includes two constants joined together by an operator and the evaluation of the expression resulting in a single value. The syntax definition of a Transact-SQL expression is:

```
expression ::=
{
constant | scalar_function | column_name | variable |
( expression ) | expression { operator } expression
}
```

The order of operations for an expression occurs from left to right with the operator precedence and parentheses controlling the expression evaluation. For example, the following Transact-SQL statements show two expressions whose results differ because of the order of operations.

```
DECLARE @calculated_value_1 DECIMAL
DECLARE @calculated_value_2 DECIMAL
/* standard operator precedence rules apply */
SET @calculated_value_1 = 1 + 5 * 2
/* operator precedence overriden by parenthesis */
SET @calculated_value_2 = (1 + 5) * 2
/* returns: 11, 12 */
SELECT @calculated_value_1, @calculated_value_2
```

Transact-SQL expressions are very similar in function to expressions in programming languages such as C#, VB.NET, and C++. Expressions are a powerful language feature that helps you build robust solutions in Transact-SQL.

Logical Operators

Logical operators combine and test multiple expressions that result in a boolean value. Table 4.13 lists the Transact-SQL logical operators.

TABLE 4.13 Transact-SQL Logical Operators

Operator	Description
ALL	TRUE if all of a set of comparisons are TRUE. For example: `ALL(1 > 2, 2 > 1) = FALSE`
AND	TRUE if both boolean expressions are TRUE. For example: `(1 > 2) AND (2 > 1) = FALSE`
ANY	TRUE if any one of a set of comparisons is TRUE. For example: `ANY( 1 > 2, 2 > 1) = TRUE`.
BETWEEN	TRUE if the operand is within a range. For example: `(15 BETWEEN 10 AND 20) = TRUE`
EXISTS	TRUE if a subquery contains any rows.
IN	TRUE if the operand is equal to one of a list of expressions.
LIKE	TRUE if the operand matches a pattern.
NOT	Reverses the value of any boolean operator. For example: `NOT (1 > 2) = TRUE`
OR	TRUE if either boolean expression is true. For example: `(1 > 2) OR (2 > 1) = TRUE`
SOME	TRUE if some of a set of comparisons is true. For example: `SOME(1>2, 2>1, 2>3) = TRUE`

String Concatenation Operator

The plus sign (+) is the Transact-SQL string concatenation operator. Using the plus (+) sign between string expressions results in the combination of the string expressions. For example:

```
'Hello' + 'World'
```

results in the string:

```
'HelloWorld'
```

Comments

If a programming language doesn't support comments, is it really a programming language? Of course not! Luckily, Transact-SQL provides support for this indispensable documentation technique. To put it in very strict terms, a comment is text that is not evaluated by the database engine. The primary use of comment text is to describe the purpose of Transact-SQL statements. The Transact-SQL language supports single-line and multiline comments. Single-line comments are denoted by -- at the beginning of a line; for example:

```
-- This is my comment
```

Multiline comments start with /* and continue until a */ is found, as in the C, C++, and C# programming languages. For example:

```
/* My comment begins here
          and includes this line
          and this line
          but it finally ends here */
```

Providing good comments in your Transact-SQL programs is essential to their maintainability. The quality of comments is also very important. It's not necessary to provide a comment on every line in a Transact-SQL program, but as a best practice you should provide a comment describing the function of the unit (e.g., the function, procedure, etc.) and comments describing any complex logic.

Control Flow

Transact-SQL statements typically execute in sequential order, from left to right and top to bottom; however, using the control-of-flow elements of the Transact-SQL language statements can be conditionally executed. Table 4.14 lists the Transact-SQL control of flow statements.

TABLE 4.14 Transact-SQL Control of Flow Statements

Statement	Description
BEGIN…END	Specifies a set of Transact-SQL statements.
BREAK	Exits a while loop.
CONTINUE	Returns to the start of a while loop.
GOTO label	Moves the execution to the statement following the specified label.
IF…ELSE	Specifies a set of statements to execute if a boolean condition is met or not met. →

Statement	Description
RETURN	Exit.
WAITFOR	Specifies a set of statements to execute after a specified period of time or at a specific time.
WHILE	Specifies a block of statement to execute while a particular condition is met.

The following example illustrates the IF...ELSE and BEGIN...END statements.

```
DECLARE @MyVariable int
DECLARE @EvaluationResult varchar(30)
SET @MyVariable = Day(GetDate())
IF @MyVariable = 1
BEGIN
    SET @EvaluationResult = 'First of the month'
    SELECT @EvaluationResult
END
ELSE
    BEGIN
        SET @EvaluationResult = 'Not the first of the month'
        SELECT @EvaluationResult
    END
```

Error Handling

Transact-SQL in SQL Server 2005 provides a new, robust method of error handling using TRY...CATCH blocks. Previous versions of SQL Server required additional checking of the error status and using control-flow elements (GOTO and RETURN) to handle and process errors. With the introduction of the TRY...CATCH statement, the error checking happens automatically and all processing can occur in the CATCH block of the statement. The basic definition of the TRY...CATCH statement is:

```
BEGIN TRY
    sql_statements
END TRY
BEGIN CATCH
    sql_statements
END CATCH
```

The TRY...CATCH statement ensures that anytime an exception occurs in one of the Transact-SQL statements within the TRY block, the CATCH block is immediately executed. If the TRY block executes all statements without an exception, the statements in the CATCH block are not executed.

Transactions

A transaction is a set of changes, and either all changes are completed successfully or no changes are made. A transaction must exhibit the properties listed in Table 4.15.

TABLE 4.15 Properties of a Database Transaction

Property	Description
Atomicity	All work completes or no work completes.
Consistency	When work is completed, all data must be consistent.
Isolation	Transactions are isolated from changes made by other concurrent transactions.
Durability	After a transaction has completed, the changes are permanent (e.g., committed to disk).

These properties are termed the ACID properties of a transaction and ensure consistency and data integrity in databases. One significant enhancement to SQL Server 2005 is the SNAPSHOT isolation model. As defined in the previous table, isolation is the separation of operations performed by a transaction so that the results of the transaction are not visible to other users until the transaction has committed. Previous versions of SQL Server provided different levels of isolation, including READ UNCOMMITED, REPEATABLE READ, READ COMMITED, and SERIALIZABLE. Each isolation level offered different degrees of adherence to the ACID properties of a transaction, with SERIALIZABLE being the most stringent and ensuring that transaction changes are fully isolated. SERIALIZABLE transactions are perfect from a purist, transaction isolation, and consistency perspective, but real-world applications can suffer severe, often needless, performance penalties when using SERIALIZABLE transactions.

To combat the performance problems of SERIALIZABLE transactions, which take a pessimistic approach to read and write locking, SQL Server 2005 introduces a new isolation level called SNAPSHOT isolation that provides optimistic read and write locks. Basically, SNAPSHOT isolation allows a SERIALIZABLE transaction to execute as if it were running under a READ COMMITTED isolation level, and then at a point just before the transaction is committed, the transaction is checked to see if it meets the requirements of a SERIALIZABLE transaction, and if so, the transaction is committed; if the requirements are not met, the transaction is rolled back. SNAPSHOT isolation is, in a sense, the best of both worlds providing the performance characteristics of a READ COMMITTED transaction with the strict isolation and consistency of a SERIALIZABLE transaction.

Transact-SQL has both implicit and explicit transactions. Implicit transactions happen automatically and the scope of the transaction is a single statement. For example, a single DELETE statement is an implicit transaction. With explicit transactions, however, it is up to the developer to specify the beginning and end of transactions and when the partial work of a transaction should be rolled back to its original state. This means that an explicit transaction can include multiple Transact-SQL statements functioning as a single unit of work. The basic statements controlling explicit transactions are listed in Table 4.16.

TABLE 4.16 Transact-SQL Transaction Control Statements

Statement	Description
BEGIN TRANSACTION	Specifies the starting point of an explicit transaction.
COMMIT TRANSACTION	Specifies the transaction completed successfully.
ROLLBACK TRANSACTION	Specifies that all work done by the transaction should be undone and the database returned to the state just prior to BEGIN TRANSACTIONS.

BASIC STATEMENTS

Now that we have covered the basic syntax elements of the Transact-SQL language, we will learn how to use the language to perform tasks ranging from defining the structure of data to retrieving and operating on data. The Transact-SQL language contains two distinct language subsets: Data Definition Language (DDL) and Data Manipulation Language (DML). The DDL statements define database structures, including tables, columns, indexes, and security rights, while DML statements support the retrieval and modification of data contained in the structures defined using DDL. For example, we can use the DDL statement CREATE TABLE to define a table named Movies, but to retrieve data from the Movies table we would use the DML SELECT statement. The next few sections introduce common DDL and DML statements that are important for developers using the SQL Server 2005 platform.

Data Definition Language

The first part of our overview of the basic Transact-SQL statements is devoted to coverage of DDL. DDL statements are used to manage all database objects. Now we will cover some of the most common Transact-SQL DDL statements.

Database DDL Statements

The CREATE DATABASE DDL statement creates a new SQL Server 2005 database. When creating a new database you can specify the name of the database, the storage location of the database files, constraints on the size of the database, plus several other configuration options. Creating a new database does not create an empty database; instead, it creates a copy of the "model" system database. The Transact-SQL CREATE DATABASE statement is defined as:

```
CREATE DATABASE database_name
[ ON <filespec> [ ,...n ] ]
[
    [ LOG ON { <filespec> [ ,...n ] } ]
    [ COLLATE collation_name ]
]
<filespec> ::=
[ PRIMARY ]
(
    [ NAME = logical_file_name , ]
    FILENAME = 'os_file_name'
        [ , SIZE = size [ KB|MB|GB|TB ] ]
        [ , MAXSIZE = { max_size [ KB|MB|GB|TB ] | UNLIMITED } ]
        [ , FILEGROWTH = growth_increment [ KB|MB | % ] ]
) [ ,...n ]
```

The arguments are:

database_name. Specifies the name of the database to create.

NAME=logical_file_name. Specifies the name that will be used to reference the file in Transact-SQL statements. NAME=logical_file_name is required when FILENAME is specified.

FILENAME='os_file_name'. Specifies the path and filename used by the operating system when creating the file. The path must already exist and must be a path on the local SQL Server machine.

SIZE=size. Specifies the initial size of the file. The default size of data files will be equal to the "model" data file size, and the log file size will be 25% of the data file size. When specifying size, you must include a whole number and optionally one of the following units of measure: KB, MB, GB, and TB. The default unit of measure is MB.

MAXSIZE=maxsize. Specifies the maximum size of the file. The maxsize parameter has the same parameter definition as the size parameter with the exception that you may use the keyword UNLIMITED in place of the number and unit of measure to grow a file until the disk is full.

FILEGROWTH=filegrowth. Specifies the autogrowth increment of the file when space is needed. Much like the size parameter, you may specify a whole number and unit of measure and a whole number and % to increment the files size by a percentage of the current file size. The default growth increment for data files is 1 MB and for log files is 10%. Using a value of 0 for the filegrowth parameter will turn off the autogrowth feature, preventing the data file or log file size from increasing automatically.

COLLATE collation_name. Specifies the collation name for the database. The default collation_name will be the server's collation setting.

The only required element of the CREATE DATABASE statement is the database name, so an example of the simplest form of the statement to create a database called CavalierMovies, using all default configuration options, would be:

```
CREATE DATABASE CavalierMovies
```

Executing this DDL statement will create a database with a default data file size equal to the "model" database that will grow incrementally in 1 MB chunks and a log file size equal to 25% of the model data file size that will grow incrementally by 10%. Such a small database size is typically not sufficient for most applications. Although, by default, the database will automatically grow in size, there is a significant performance penalty incurred while the database resizes itself. For this reason, it is important to estimate the size of the database and plan maintenance intervals and windows to minimize the impact of data and log file resizing. When you have estimated the initial size of your database, you can specify the file size for both data and log files using one of the optional forms of the CREATE TABLE statement. The following Transact-SQL statement creates the CavalierMovies database with an initial data file size of 100 MB and a log file size of 25 MB:

```
CREATE DATABASE CavalierMovies
ON PRIMARY
(
NAME = N'CavalierMovies',
FILENAME = N'D:\DATA\CavalierMovies.mdf',
SIZE = 100MB,
MAXSIZE = 500MB,
FILEGROWTH = 10%
)
LOG ON
(
NAME = N'CavalierMovies_log',
FILENAME = N'D:\DATA\CavalierMovies_log.ldf' ,
SIZE = 25MB,
MAXSIZE = 500MB,
```

```
FILEGROWTH = 10%
)
```

Properties of existing databases are modified using the ALTER DATABASE command. The ALTER DATABASE command supports changing database properties such as the database name and file properties. The Transact-SQL ALTER DATABASE statement is defined as:

```
ALTER DATABASE database_name
{
    | MODIFY FILE <filespec>
    | MODIFY NAME = new_dbname
}
<filespec> ::=
(
    NAME = logical_file_name
    [ , OFFLINE ]
    [ , NEWNAME = new_logical_name ]
    [ , FILENAME = os_file_name' ]
    [ , SIZE = size [ KB | MB | GB | TB ] ]
    [ , MAXSIZE = { max_size [ KB | MB | GB | TB ]| UNLIMITED}]
    [ , FILEGROWTH = growth_increment [ KB | MB | % ] ]
)
```

To illustrate the usage of the ALTER DATABASE statement, we will change the maximum size of the CavalierMovies database. The following statement updates the CavalierMovies database, allowing the data file to grow until all available disk space is consumed:

```
ALTER DATABASE CavalierMovies
MODIFY FILE
(
NAME = N'CavalierMovies',
MAXSIZE = UNLIMITED
)
```

Databases can be deleted using the DROP DATABASE Transact-SQL statement. The syntax for the DROP DATABASE statement is:

```
DROP DATABASE { database_name } [ ,...n ]
```

Dropping an existing database will delete the database and all objects contained in the database.

Snapshot DDL Statements

OnLine Transaction Processing (OLTP) systems typically have requirements to maximize the system availability. A classic example of a highly available database system would be that of a bank. Banks try to keep their systems processing transactions 24 hours a day, 7 days a week so that we as consumers can use our debit cards to purchase a much needed cup of coffee at 2 A.M. from the local 24-hour gas station. These systems cannot be taken offline for things such as monthly reporting—if the system were offline, how would you purchase your coffee? Using the snapshot feature of SQL Server 2005 it is possible to handle a situation such as this and make a read-only copy of the data so as not to interfere with the production system.

The SQL Server 2005 snapshot feature is also a very useful safeguard for applying changes to production systems. Simply create a snapshot before making any changes to the production system and if something goes wrong while making your changes, you can restore the snapshot to the original database. Creating a snapshot does not require any special administrative rights and any SQL login that can create a database may also create a database snapshot. To create a snapshot, use the following variation of the CREATE DATABASE command:

```
CREATE DATABASE database_snapshot_name
    ON
    (
        NAME = logical_file_name,
        FILENAME = 'os_file_name'
    ) [ ,...n ]
    AS SNAPSHOT OF source_database_name
```

The arguments are:

database_snapshot_name. Specifies the name of the snapshot database to create.

NAME=logical_file_name. Specifies the name that will be used to reference the file in Transact-SQL statements.

FILENAME='os_file_name'. Specifies the path and filename used by the operating system when creating the file. The path must already exist and must be a path on the local SQL Server machine.

source_database_name. Specifies the name of the source database used for creating the snapshot. The source database and the snapshot database must be on the same instance.

To create a snapshot of the CavalierMovies database we created earlier in the chapter, execute the following command:

```
CREATE DATABASE CavalierMovies_YearEndSnapshot
```

```
(
    NAME = N'CavalierMovies_YearEndSnapshot',
    FILENAME = N'D:\DATA\CavalierMovies_YearEndSnapshot.mdf',
)
AS SNAPSHOT OF CavalierMovies
```

Table DDL Statements

Database tables are at the heart of any relational database system because they are the primary database objects used to aggregate and operate on data. A database can contain many tables. Conceptually we think of database tables as a collection of rows and columns where the individual columns define the type of data that will be stored at each row-column (e.g., cell) intersection. Transact-SQL DDL statements support creating, modifying, and deleting individual database tables.

Creating a new database table involves specifying table information plus the individual column definitions. In Transact-SQL, database tables are defined using the CREATE TABLE DDL statement. The Transact-SQL CREATE TABLE statement is defined as:

```
CREATE TABLE table_name(<column_definition>)
< column_definition > ::=
column_name <data_type> [NULL|NOT NULL]
    {
[DEFAULT constant_expression]
| [IDENTITY [(seed ,increment)] ]
}
    [ ROWGUIDCOL ] [ <column_constraint> [ ...n ] ]
<data type> ::=
type_name [ ( precision [ , scale ] | MAX ) ]
    sql_server_native_type | type_name

<column_constraint> ::=
[ CONSTRAINT constraint_name ]
{
{ PRIMARY KEY | UNIQUE }
 [ FOREIGN KEY ]
          REFERENCES
referenced_table_name [(ref_column)]
          [
ON DELETE
{ NO ACTION | CASCADE | SET NULL | SET DEFAULT }
]
          [
ON UPDATE
{ NO ACTION | CASCADE | SET NULL | SET DEFAULT }
]
}
```

The arguments are:

table_name. Specifies the name of the new table.

column_name. Specifies the name of a column in the new table.

type_name. Specifies the data type of the column. The data type can be a native SQL type, an alias type based on a native SQL type, or a CLR user-defined type.

Precision. For numeric data types, precision specifies the total number of digits that may be stored in a column.

Scale. For numeric data types, scale specifies the number of digits allowed to the right of the decimal.

MAX. This new option available in SQL Server 2005 allows varchar, nvarchar, and varbinary types to store up to 2 GB of data.

DEFAULT constant_expression. Specifies the value that will be used when a value is not explicitly provided in an insert statement. DEFAULT can be used for all columns except IDENTITY and timestamp columns.

IDENTITY [(seed, increment)]. Specifies that the column is an identity column. Identity columns automatically provide a unique, incremental value when new rows are inserted. The seed parameter specifies the first value, while the increment parameter specifies the incremental value added to the identity after each insertion.

ROWGUIDCOL. Specifies that the column is a global unique identifier. ROWGUIDCOL, unlike IDENTITY, does not enforce uniqueness of the value stored in the column or automatically generate values for new rows.

CONSTRAINT. Indicates the beginning of a PRIMARY KEY, NOT NULL, UNIQUE, FOREIGN KEY, or CHECK constraint. Constraints are used to enforce data integrity.

NULL | NOT NULL. Specifies whether null values are valid values for the column.

PRIMARY KEY. Specifies a constraint that the column values must be unique.

UNIQUE. Specifies a constraint that the column values may not be repeated.

FOREIGN KEY...REFERENCES. Specifies a constraint that provides referential data integrity.

referenced_table_name. Specifies the name of the table referenced by the FOREIGN KEY constraint.

(ref_column[,... n]). Is a column, or list of columns, from the table referenced by the FOREIGN KEY constraint.

ON DELETE { NO ACTION | CASCADE | SET NULL | SET DEFAULT }. Specifies what action takes place to rows in the table created, if those rows have a referential relationship and the referenced row is deleted from the parent table.

ON UPDATE { NO ACTION | CASCADE | SET NULL | SET DEFAULT }. Specifies what action takes place to rows in the table created, if those rows have a referential relationship and the referenced row is updated in the parent table.

CHECK. Specifies a constraint that enforces data integrity by limiting the values that may be entered into a column.

[ASC | DESC]. Specifies the order in which the column or columns participating in table constraints are sorted.

Now let's look at an example using the CREATE TABLE statement. The following statement creates a new table named "Genre" having two columns and a primary key:

```
CREATE TABLE Genre
(
    GenreId uniqueidentifier ROWGUIDCOL NOT NULL
    CONSTRAINT DF_Genre_GenreId DEFAULT (newid()),
    [Name] varchar(50) NOT NULL,
    CONSTRAINT PK_Genre PRIMARY KEY CLUSTERED (GenreId ASC)
)
```

Even with the best possible requirements gathering and design there will be occasions where changing business needs dictate alterations to table structures. Adding columns, changing columns, and deleting columns are just a few of the changes supported by the Transact-SQL ALTER TABLE statement. A summarized definition of the ALTER TABLE statement is as follows:

```
ALTER TABLE table_name
{
ALTER COLUMN column_name
    {<data_type>[({{precision,scale}|max})][NULL|NOT NULL]}
}
| {
ADD column_name
    {<data_type>[({{precision,scale}|max})][NULL|NOT NULL]}
}
| {
DROP
{[CONSTRAINT] constraint_name|COLUMN column_name}[ ,...n ]
}
```

The ALTER TABLE statement definition presented here is a subset of the full definition. The options documented here are the most commonly used variations of the ALTER TABLE statement, but for reference, the full definition of the ALTER TABLE statement can be found in SQL Server Books Online.

Let's look at an example of using the ALTER TABLE statement. Using the "Genre" table we created earlier, the following example adds a new column named "Summary" to the table:

```
ALTER TABLE Genre ADD Summary varchar(255) NULL
```

Now let's change the Summary column data type to varchar(MAX). The varchar(MAX) data type is new to SQL Server 2005 and allows a varchar column to contain variable-size text data up to 2 GB in size. To modify the Summary column:

```
ALTER TABLE Genre ALTER COLUMN Summary varchar(MAX)
```

Finally, we will remove the Summary column from the Genre table to restore the table to its original state. To remove the Summary column:

```
ALTER TABLE Genre DROP COLUMN Summary
```

Tables are removed from a database using the DROP TABLE statement. Dropping a table removes the table and all data stored in the table. The definition of the DROP TABLE statement is:

```
DROP TABLE table_name
```

As an example, the DROP TABLE statement to delete the previously created Genre table would be:

```
DROP TABLE Genre
```

Index DDL Statements

An index is a structure that stores key values of a table in an efficient tree structure to speed the retrieval of rows from a table. Indexes generally speed the retrieval of data but slow the execution of updates and inserts so it is necessary to be selective in the tables and columns chosen for indexing. When identifying candidate columns/tables for indexing, ask the following questions:

- Are the values stored in the column seldom modified?
- Is the column often included as a condition in SELECT queries?
- When the table is queried is it generally true that a small subset of the rows is returned?

If the answer is yes to all three questions, the column is a good candidate for indexing.

To create new indexes, use the Transact-SQL CREATE INDEX DDL statement. The statement is defined as:

```
CREATE [ UNIQUE ] [ CLUSTERED | NONCLUSTERED ] INDEX index_name
    ON table_name ( column [ ASC | DESC ] [ ,...n ] )
```

The parameters for this statement are:

UNIQUE. Creates a unique index (one in which no two rows are permitted to have the same index key value) on a table. A clustered index on a view must be unique.

CLUSTERED | NONCLUSTERED. Creates an index in which the logical order of the key values determines the physical order of the corresponding rows in a table. The bottom (leaf) level of the clustered index contains the actual data rows of the table. A table is allowed one clustered index at a time. With a nonclustered index, the physical order of the data rows is independent of their indexed order.

INDEX index_name. Specifies the name of the new index.

ON table_name (column [ASC | DESC] [,...n]). Specifies the table and columns in that table index. The ASC | DESC options specify the sort order of the index. Specifying two or more columns in a table creates a composite index on the combined values of the columns. Columns that have .NET CLR data types may be indexed provided the data type supports binary ordering. The specifics of implementing a .NET CLR data type supporting indexes is covered in Chapter 5, "Programmability."

Continuing with the Genre table we created earlier in the chapter, we note that the Name column is a candidate for indexing because the column would often be included as a condition in SELECT queries, the genres are not often updated or changed, and queries would likely be for a subset of the rows in the table. To create an index on the Name column:

```
CREATE INDEX Genre_Name_Ind ON Genre([Name] ASC)
```

Although Transact-SQL provides an ALTER INDEX statement, the column definition or structure of an index may not be altered. Execution of the ALTER INDEX statement rebuilds indexes and eliminates tree fragmentation caused by inserts, updates, and deletes in the table. The definition of the ALTER INDEX statement is:

```
ALTER INDEX { index_name | ALL } ON  table_name REBUILD
```

The ALTER INDEX statement can rebuild an individual index or all indexes for a specified table by using the ALL keyword in place of the index name. To change the column definition of an index it's necessary to delete the index and then create a new index with the new structure.

To delete an existing index, use the Transact-SQL DROP INDEX statement. It is often a good idea to delete indexes before executing a large number of INSERT or UPDATE statements such as would occur during an initial data load. With the indexes removed, the operations can execute much faster and then the indexes can be recreated to speed the execution of SELECT queries. The DROP INDEX statement is defined as:

```
DROP INDEX  index_name ON table_name
```

To illustrate an example of dropping an index, the following statement drops the Genre_Name_Ind index we created earlier in the chapter:

```
DROP INDEX Genre_Name_Ind ON Genre
```

View DDL Statements

Database views are virtual tables having columns and rows of data. Views can simplify queries of highly normalized databases by combining and filtering data from multiple tables into a single virtual table. Views are defined using a SELECT query and the CREATE VIEW statement. The CREATE VIEW statement is defined as:

```
CREATE VIEW view_name [ (column [ ,...n ] ) ]
AS select_statement
```

The parameters for this statement are:

view_name. Specifies the name of the view.

column. Specifies the name to be used for a column in a view. Specifying column names is optional unless the column is an expression, function call, or a constant. When the column name is not specified, the column names from the SELECT statement will be used.

select_statement. Specifies the SELECT statement that defines the view.

Let's look at an example of the CREATE VIEW statement. Continuing with the Genre table created earlier in the chapter, we add a new table named Movie that has a foreign key to the Genre table as illustrated in Figure 4.3.

Let's say that we need to get the count of movies available in a particular genre. One way to meet this requirement is to create a view that combines the genre information with the count of the movies available in that genre. The following statement creates a new view called GenreMovieCount that combines the genre information with the movie count for the particular genre:

```
CREATE VIEW GenreMovieCount AS
SELECT g.[Name] GenreName,
(SELECT COUNT(*) FROM Movie m WHERE m.GenreId = g.GenreId) MovieCount
```

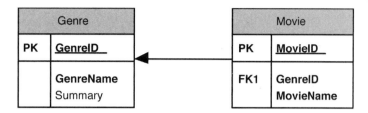

FIGURE 4.3 Entity-relationship diagram for the Genre and Movie tables.

```
FROM Genre g
```

Views are modified using the ALTER VIEW statement. Similar to the CREATE VIEW statement, ALTER VIEW requires the view name and the SELECT statement defining the view. The definition of the ALTER VIEW statement is:

```
ALTER VIEW view_name [ (column [ ,...n ] ) ]
AS select_statement
```

To illustrate the ALTER VIEW statement, let's modify the GenreMovieCount view to include the GenreId:

```
ALTER VIEW GenreMovieCount AS
SELECT g.GenreId,
g.[Name] GenreName,
(SELECT COUNT(*) FROM Movie m WHERE m.GenreId = g.GenreId) MovieCount
FROM Genre g
```

Views are deleted using the DROP VIEW statement, defined as:

```
DROP VIEW view_name
```

To delete the GenreMovieCount view we created earlier in this section, execute:

```
DROP VIEW GenreMovieCount
```

Synonym DDL Statements

Synonyms provide alternate names for database objects, including stored procedures, tables, views, aggregates, and functions. Synonyms are useful for database developers because they abstract the physical location of database objects allowing the developer to reference remote objects as if they were local. The definition of the CREATE SYNONYM statement is:

```
CREATE SYNONYM synonym_name FOR
{[server_name.[database_name]|database_name.] object_name}
```

The arguments are:

`Synonym_name`. Specifies the alternate name to use for the specified database object.

`server_name`. Specifies the name of the SQL Server where the object exists.

`database_name`. Specifies the name of the database where the object exists.

`object_name`. Specifies the name of the database object for which the synonym is being created. The database object must be a stored procedure, function, aggregate, table, or view.

To illustrate synonyms, let's look at an example. We will create a new synonym for the Genre table called Classification. The CREATE SYNONYM statement for making this change would be:

```
CREATE SYNONYM Classification FOR Genre
```

After creating the new synonym, the data held in the Genre table can be referenced using the name Genre or Classification. For example, the following two SE-LECT statements would return the same set of data:

```
SELECT [Name] FROM Genre ORDER BY [Name]
SELECT [Name] FROM Classification ORDER BY [Name]
```

Synonyms cannot be modified once they have been created. To change a synonym, you must first delete the existing synonym and recreate the synonym with the updated parameters. To delete a synonym, use the DROP SYNONYM statement. The definition of the DROP SYNONYM statement is:

```
DROP SYNONYM synonym_name
```

The following example deletes the Classification synonym created earlier in this section:

```
DROP SYNONYM Classification
```

Data Manipulation Language

The Transact-SQL data manipulation language (DML) statements provide the ability to retrieve, update, insert, and delete rows from tables. Transact-SQL DML statements have numerous alternative structures and options that are beyond the scope of this text. The following section presents the most common Transact-SQL DML statements.

Select Statement

The Transact-SQL select statement is an extremely powerful and expressive statement for retrieving data. SELECT statements can retrieve data from one or more tables or views, include rows conditionally, evaluate and return results from expressions, and group and sort data. The SELECT statement can be divided into six clauses: SELECT, FROM, WHERE, GROUP BY, HAVING, and ORDER BY. Because of the complexity of the SELECT statement, we will first present the basic form of the SELECT statement and then cover each of the clauses of the SELECT statement. The basic definition of SELECT is:

```
SELECT select_list
[INTO new_table_name]
FROM table_list
[WHERE search_conditions]
[GROUP BY group_by_list]
[HAVING search_conditions]
[ORDER BY order_list [ASC | DESC]]
```

The parameters are:

select_list. Specifies the columns and expressions that will be returned by the query; if multiple columns or expressions are included, they are separated by commas.

[INTO new_table_name]. Specifies the results from the query will be inserted into a new table.

table_list. Specifies one or more tables or views that will be included in the query. If the query contains more than one table or view, they must be separated by commas.

[WHERE search_conditions]. Specifies a filter, which will be evaluated as a boolean expression, to determine the rows that will be included in the search results.

[GROUP BY group_by_list]. Specifies the columns that are used as a basis for grouping the results.

[HAVING search_conditions]. Specifies an intermediate filter that will be applied to the results.

[ORDER BY order_list [ASC | DESC]]. Specifies the columns that determine the sort order of the results and whether the sort will be in ascending or descending order.

The SELECT statement is the most common SQL statement used by developers. The following example illustrates a SELECT query returning data from the Genre table created earlier in the chapter:

```
SELECT GenreId, [Name] FROM Genre WHERE [Name] = 'Comedy'
```

Update Statement

To update data in tables, use the Transact-SQL UPDATE Statement, which provides the ability to update data in a single table. When updating data, it's necessary to specify the name of the table being updated, the new values of particular columns, and optionally an expression that determines which rows will be updated. The definition of the UPDATE statement is:

```
UPDATE table_name
    SET
    { column_name = { expression | DEFAULT | NULL } } [ ,...n ]
    [ WHERE < search_condition > ]
```

The parameters are:

table_name. Specifies the name of the table being updated.

column_name = { expression | DEFAULT | NULL }. Specifies the columns being updated and the new value for each column. When multiple columns are updated, a comma separates each column/value pair.

[WHERE < search_condition >]. The search condition specifies a logical expression that determines which rows will be updated.

To illustrate usage of the UPDATE statement, let's say we have a requirement to modify the genre name to include parentheses around the name. The following UPDATE statement modifies the genre names to append parentheses:

```
UPDATE Genre SET [Name] = '(' + [Name] + ')'
```

Delete Statement

Deleting data from tables is accomplished using the Transact-SQL DELETE statement. The DELETE statement removes rows of data from a single table where the rows match a logical expression in the WHERE clause. If no WHERE clause is specified, all data will be removed from the table. The DELETE statement is defined as:

```
DELETE
    [ FROM ] table_name
    [ WHERE < search_condition > ]
```

The parameters are:

`table_name`. Specifies the name of the table from which data will be deleted.

`[ WHERE < search_condition > ]`. Specifies a logical expression that determines which rows will be removed from the table.

ADDITIONAL TRANSACT-SQL LANGUAGE ENHANCEMENTS

We have now covered many of the elements of the Transact-SQL language and many of its new features introduced in SQL Server 2005. This section describes some of the notable Transact-SQL language enhancements in SQL Server 2005 that didn't fit neatly into the more general language coverage in the preceding sections.

Common Table Expressions

One of the new features of the Transact-SQL language is Common Table Expressions (CTEs). CTEs enhance the expressiveness of the Transact-SQL language by providing a clean way of creating temporary tables that can be used for a variety of purposes, including traversing a hierarchy. CTEs are actually part of SQL Server 2005's compliance with the SQL-99 standard and provide a huge step forward for SQL Server's capability to retrieve hierarchical data. Previous versions of Transact-SQL could retrieve hierarchical data; however, it required very complex queries that generally relied on either creating temporary tables programmatically or using derived tables, which essentially involves using a SELECT statement as a table. Both of these approaches left much to be desired and neither provided an elegant mechanism to recursively traverse hierarchical data. CTEs are not limited to just SELECT statements; in fact, they may be used in INSERT, UPDATE, or DELETE statements. The basic format of a CTE is:

```
WITH <cte_name> (<columns>) AS
(<cte_statement(s)>)
```

If you think of CTEs as temporary tables, then the WITH clause of CTEs is essentially the definition of the structure of a temporary table that defines the name of the table and the columns in the table. The statements portion of CTEs specifies the content for the structures defined in the WITH portion of the CTE. Let's look at an example to demonstrate the use of CTEs in SQL Server 2005. Our example involves a Genre table that contains hierarchical genre information, such as Action as a subgenre War, Comedy as a subgenre Slapstick, and so forth. We create the Genre table and populate it with data as follows:

```
CREATE TABLE Genre ([Name] VARCHAR(50), Parent VARCHAR(50))
INSERT INTO Genre VALUES('Action', NULL)
INSERT INTO Genre VALUES('Sci-Fi', 'Action')
INSERT INTO Genre VALUES('War', 'Action')
INSERT INTO Genre VALUES('Comedy', NULL)
INSERT INTO Genre VALUES('Slapstick', 'Comedy')
INSERT INTO Genre VALUES('Satire', 'Comedy')
INSERT INTO Genre VALUES('Martial Arts', 'War')
```

Now, we define the CTE that will be used to retrieve the entire hierarchical sub-tree of the 'Action' genre. Based on the data we entered with the previous statements, the results of the CTE should include the two direct children of the Action genre—Sci-Fi and War—along with the single direct child of the War genre called Martial Arts. We define our CTE as follows:

```
WITH GenreCTE ([Name], Parent)
AS
(
    SELECT Genre.[Name], Genre.Parent
FROM Genre WHERE Genre.Parent = 'Action'

    UNION ALL

    SELECT g.[Name], g.Parent
FROM Genre g JOIN GenreCTE cte ON g.[Parent] = cte.[Name]
)
select * from GenreCTE
```

Executing the previous statements will begin by retrieving the first level of genres whose parent is the Action genre, and then proceed to execute recursively for each of those genres retrieving their children and their children's children, and so forth until there is no more data to recurse. As you can see, this is a very powerful and expressive feature of SQL Server 2005.

Set Default, Set Null

There are many very good reasons to store data in a normalized database as opposed to other formats such as spreadsheets or XML files. One very good reason to prefer storing data in a relational database is that it can provide referential integrity. That is, you can define relationships among tables, and changes to one table can cause changes to occur in other related tables. These actions may be specified when creating or altering tables. SQL Server has always provided these constraints, but with the release of SQL Server 2005 there are two new options for cascading changes to tables: SET DEFAULT and SET NULL. These constraints may be specified for DELETE and/or UPDATE actions and have the format:

```
ON {DELETE|UPDATE} {NO ACTION|CASCADE|SET NULL|SET DEFAULT}
```

When specifying the SET NULL option, deleting a row in a parent table will result in the foreign key columns value being set to NULL. Alternatively, when specifying the SET DEFAULT option the foreign key column will be set to its default value. This provides developers some flexible alternative behaviors for cascading referential integrity constraints.

Pivot and Unpivot

Database applications are generally constructed to help businesses capture information and then use that information to answer questions and spot trends that may not be readily apparent. Pivot and Unpivot are two new features of Microsoft SQL Server 2005 that provide a way of grouping and arranging data such that it can be easier to spot some trends. This feature is not to be confused with the business intelligence features of SQL Server 2005. Pivot and Unpivot are a "poor man's" method of data analysis, but they do provide very useful views of data for reporting. Pivot works by taking unique values from a column and turning those values into the columns of the returned data.

Ranking Functions

It is a fairly common development task to retrieve a set of data from a database and rank each row based on certain criteria. A concrete example of this would be a movie rating Web site that allows movie viewers to assign "star" ratings to movies they have watched; the results of all the ratings may be compiled, and a list of the top-rated movies displayed. In previous versions of the Microsoft SQL Server product it was certainly possible to achieve the result we described, but the approach was inelegant and often error prone. With the release of Microsoft SQL Server 2005, the Transact-SQL language has a set of built-in functions that make this task quite simple. The functions are called ranking functions and provide a built-in mechanism for assigning a numeric position to rows of data based on ordering criteria. There are four new ranking functions: ROW_NUMBER, RANK, DENSE_RANK, and NTILE. All these functions have a similar syntax, which is defined as:

```
<ranking_function> OVER( [<partition_by_clause>] <order_by_clause>)
```

The partitioning clause portion of ranking functions divides the ranking into different groups and takes the form PARTITION BY <column>. To continue with the movie-rating example, the PARTITION BY clause could be used to rank movie ratings by state so you could see the most popular movies for each state.

Ranking functions use the ORDER BY clause to specify the criteria that determines the rank and takes the form of the typical ORDER BY clause we covered earlier in this chapter. We will be continuing the movie ratings example in our coverage of each of the ranking functions. If you wish to run the ranking examples, run the following commands to create the necessary tables and load them with example data:

```
CREATE TABLE Ratings(Rating DECIMAL(3,2), Title VARCHAR(50))
INSERT INTO Ratings(Rating, Title) VALUES(4, 'Movie 1')
INSERT INTO Ratings(Rating, Title) VALUES(4, 'Movie 2')
INSERT INTO Ratings(Rating, Title) VALUES(3, 'Movie 3')
```

The ROW_NUMBER function is the simplest of the ranking functions, as it returns an increasing value for each row returned based on the ORDER BY clause specified for the function. You can think of the ROW_NUMBER function as returning a value that represents the position of the row if the ORDER BY clause were applied to the whole query. For example, the following select statement:

```
SELECT ROW_NUMBER() OVER(ORDER BY Rating DESC),
Title FROM Ratings
```

returns the following data:

1 Movie 1
2 Movie 2
3 Movie 3

As you can see, the row number assigned to each row is the same as the visible row index if the ORDER BY were applied to the select statement.

Next are the RANK and DENSE_RANK functions, which are very similar in the results they return. RANK and DENSE_RANK, unlike the ROW_NUMBER function, are not guaranteed to return unique values for each partition; that is, the functions may return the same value for multiple rows if the order by results in a "tie." To put this in terms of a concrete example, if there are three movies and two of them received ratings of four stars while the third received a rating of three stars, then the two top-rated movies would both receive a rank of 1. The difference in the RANK and DENSE_RANK functions lies in how the functions rank the third movie in our example. RANK assigns the row following a tie with the value of the ROW_NUMBER; in the case of our example, that means the third movie would be assigned a RANK of three. DENSE_RANK, however, assigns the row following a tie with the next integer value after the tied rank; in our example, the third movie would have a DENSE_RANK of two because the first two movies tied for a rank of one. Now, let's look at the statements we have described and the specific data returned by each. First, the statement, which includes the RANK function:

```
SELECT RANK() OVER(ORDER BY Rating DESC),
Title FROM Ratings
```

returns:

1 Movie 1
1 Movie 2
3 Movie 3

As described earlier in the section, the RANK function can return tie values, and the row following a tie rank is assigned a RANK equivalent to the ROW_NUMBER. The following example DENSE_RANK function:

```
SELECT DENSE_RANK()OVER(ORDER BY Rating DESC),
Title FROM Ratings
```

returns:

1 Movie 1
1 Movie 2
2 Movie 3

This demonstrates the difference between RANK and DENSE_RANK, with the DENSE_RANK following a tie rank being assigned the next integer value after the tie.

The last of the new ranking functions is NTILE, which is a mechanism to assign rows to different "buckets." The function accepts an integer parameter that specifies the total number of buckets, and then the function will divide the rows evenly, if possible, into each of the buckets. For cases where the number of rows can't be divided evenly into the number of buckets, the number of rows assigned to some of the buckets will be larger than the number of rows assigned to the remaining buckets. To continue our example of movie ratings, we can use the NTILE function to rank the movies into a good movie bucket and a bad movie bucket based on the viewer ratings. The following statement includes the NTILE function we described:

```
SELECT NTILE(2) OVER(ORDER BY Rating DESC),
Title FROM Ratings
```

and returns the following values:

1 Movie 1
1 Movie 2
2 Movie 3

In this case, we defined two buckets, with the first two movies being assigned to the first buck and the third movie being assigned to the second bucket.

The ranking functions introduced with SQL Server 2005 are powerful tools you can use to address some common development scenarios. These functions allow you to eliminate portions of code that you would write to calculate these ranking values, and provide better performance than you could achieve calculating rankings outside of the database.

TOP **Clause**

Many applications present users with lists of data retrieved from a database. Often, users of these applications are interested in only a portion of the total set of data that could be retrieved. The TOP clause in Transact-SQL provides the ability to limit a query to the top few rows by specifying either a number of rows that should be included or a percentage of the total rows that should be included. The TOP clause received some major enhancements in Microsoft SQL Server 2005. Prior to SQL Server 2005, the TOP clause was limited to a constant number or constant percentage value representing the number or percent of results that should be returned from a SELECT statement. The number had to be a constant and could not be a variable value, which limited the overall usefulness of the feature in building applications. With the latest version of Transact-SQL, this constraint has been removed and the TOP clause may now be a variable value. Another feature added to the TOP clause is that it may now be used in UPDATE, DELETE, and INSERT statements in addition to SELECT statements.

The basic format of the TOP clause is defined as:

```
TOP (<numeric_expression>) [PERCENT]
```

The same TOP clause syntax is used in SELECT, INSERT, UPDATE, and DELETE statements. Now let's look at some examples of using the TOP clause in SQL Server 2005.

First, let's look at an example using the traditional format of the TOP clause. The following example shows the TOP clause used in a SELECT statement with a constant number of rows specified:

```
SELECT TOP(1) Rating, Title FROM Ratings ORDER BY Rating DESC, Title ASC
```

Executing the previous statement returns the first row from the Ratings table. Next, let's look at an example of using the TOP clause with a variable number of rows.

The new option for using a variable number of rows in the TOP clause may seem trivial, but it is actually a significant enhancement that makes it easier to build certain dynamic applications. For example, we can now add a feature to our movie rating example that allows an individual viewer to define how many of the available top movies he wishes to see in his list. First, we need to create a Viewer Profile table to hold the viewer name and the number of movies he wants in his list:

```
CREATE TABLE ViewerProfile
([Name] VARCHAR(50), TopMovieCount INT)
INSERT INTO ViewerProfile([Name], TopMovieCount)
Values('Jason', 1)
INSERT INTO ViewerProfile([Name], TopMovieCount)
Values('Rob', 2)
```

Next, we declare an integer variable, which holds the top number of rows from the user's profile:

```
DECLARE @MovieCount INT
```

Finally, we can retrieve the defined number of rows from the user's profile and then select that variable number of rows from the ratings list:

```
SELECT @MovieCount = TopMovieCount
FROM ViewerProfile WHERE [Name] = 'Jason'
SELECT TOP(@MovieCount) Rating, Title
FROM Ratings ORDER BY Rating DESC, Title ASC
SELECT @MovieCount = TopMovieCount
FROM ViewerProfile WHERE [Name] = 'Rob'
SELECT TOP(@MovieCount) Rating, Title
FROM Ratings ORDER BY Rating DESC, Title ASC
```

Finally, let's look at the usage of the TOP clause in INSERT, UPDATE, and DELETE statements. It's important to note that specifying a TOP clause in INSERT, UPDATE, and DELETE statements can produce unexpected results. The reason for this unpredictability is that these statements do not guarantee the order of the rows involved; therefore, we recommend using extreme caution with this option. Let's say, for example, if we wanted to update the top-two rated movies, appending "Top Rated" to their title, we may consider using:

```
UPDATE TOP(2) Ratings SET Title = Title + ' - Top Rated'
```

This statement is not guaranteed to produce the desired results because the order of the rows in the Ratings table are not guaranteed. In fact, the preceding statement will update two random rows. If you find yourself using the TOP clause in INSERT, UPDATE, or DELETE statements, make sure your intention is to operate on random rows.

OUTPUT **Clause**

Some applications require maintaining an audit trail of changes made to data. This requirement is often imposed for purposes of regulatory compliance such as Sarbanes-Oxley. Traditionally, database developers have used triggers to capture modifications to data. Both the advantage and disadvantage of triggers is that they are invoked with every action on the table. For example, a BEFORE DELETE trigger will be invoked before every delete operation on the table. For occasions when you want to conditionally snapshot the data, SQL Server 2005 has the OUTPUT clause, which allows you to capture data modified by INSERT, UPDATE, or DELETE statements. Prior to SQL Server 2005 when you executed INSERT, DELETE, or UPDATE statements, the records that were modified were not returned. With SQL Server 2005's OUTPUT clause it is possible to capture the modified data in the same INSERT, UPDATE, or DELETE statement. In addition to being useful in capturing a trail of modifications, the clause is also handy for retrieving calculated values that have been changed due to an INSERT, UPDATE, or DELETE STATEMENT—including identity values. The basic syntax of the OUTPUT clause is:

```
OUTPUT {DELETED|INSERTED|from_table_name}.{*|column_name}[,…n]
    INTO output_table(column_list)
```

To see an example of the OUTPUT clause, let's say we want to capture modifications to the movie ratings table. To do this, we first create a new table to hold the modified values:

```
CREATE TABLE ModifiedRatings
(Action VARCHAR(50), Rating NUMERIC(3,2), Title VARCHAR(50))
```

Next, we modify the INSERT, UPDATE, and DELETE statements, adding the OUTPUT clause to insert the modified data into the ModifiedRatings table. The following is an example of an altered INSERT statement:

```
INSERT INTO Ratings(Rating, Title)
    OUTPUT 'INSERTED DATA', INSERTED.Rating, INSERTED.Title
INTO ModifiedRatings(Action, Rating, Title)
    VALUES (1, 'Movie 5')
```

Executing the statement results in a new row being added to both the Ratings table and the ModifiedRatings table. The corresponding UPDATE and DELETE statements are very similar, so we will leave that as an exercise for the reader.

CONCLUSION

As demonstrated in this chapter, Transact-SQL is a very powerful and robust language. We covered all the language elements and the most common statements and built-in functions. Additionally, we saw that the language is evolving, with powerful new features being released with Microsoft SQL Server 2005. That being said, this chapter only scratched the surface of all of the capabilities of the Transact-SQL language. For those inclined to learn more about Transact-SQL, we encourage you to review the documentation provided with SQL Server 2005, and there are also entire books devoted to the subject. In our next chapter, we will expand on the language foundation laid in this chapter and cover the programmability features of Microsoft SQL Server 2005 and Transact-SQL.

5 Programmability

In this Chapter

- Assemblies
- User-Defined Types
- Stored Procedures
- User-Defined Functions
- Triggers
- Aggregates
- Conclusion

In addition to being a world-class relational database, Microsoft SQL Server 2005 provides robust programming capabilities, which include support for user-built stored procedures, triggers, functions, aggregates, and data types. Additionally, SQL Server 2005 provides some powerful new language choices, in addition to the standard Transact-SQL support, for implementing programmability features.

Transact-SQL has long been the only viable option for programming stored procedures, functions, triggers, and types inside Microsoft SQL Server. Transact-SQL is a powerful language for data access but lacks robust support for implementing complex programming and computation logic. With the release of SQL Server 2005, the Common Language Runtime (CLR) and the Microsoft .NET Framework are integrated into the database, allowing developers to use any .NET language to write stored procedures, functions, triggers, and types. Microsoft .NET integration means that developers can now use the robust features of the .NET Framework to perform complex operations that would be impossible using Transact-SQL.

Microsoft SQL Server 2005's multiple language options means that developers must choose either Transact-SQL or a .NET language for writing stored procedures, triggers, and functions. Each language option provides a distinct set of benefits. There is no strict guide for when to use a .NET language or Transact-SQL, but in general, Transact-SQL is optimized for data access with minimal programming logic while .NET languages and the .NET Framework are optimized for implementing complex logic and computations. Figure 5.1 illustrates the driving factors for choosing Transact-SQL versus CLR integration.

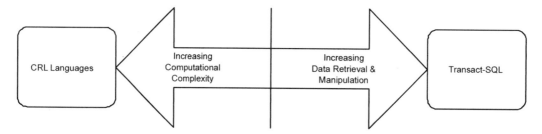

FIGURE 5.1   Guidelines for choosing Transact-SQL or CLR integration.

In addition to the technical reasons to choose Transact-SQL or a .NET language, one must also consider training and code reuse. All stored procedures, triggers, and functions written using .NET languages are constructed using either the .NET Framework 2.0 SDK or Microsoft Visual Studio 2005. Using .NET languages also allows developers to reuse the extensive .NET Framework Base Class Library or write their own custom libraries to share inside or outside your organization.

This chapter covers the programmability features of Microsoft SQL Server 2005. Each feature is presented using both the Transact-SQL and .NET language options.

ASSEMBLIES

All programmability features implemented using a .NET language are packaged into an assembly. Assemblies are created when .NET code is compiled; for example, using Microsoft Visual Studio 2005 or the .NET Framework SDK. An assembly can be either a DLL or an EXE and can contain multiple code modules plus a manifest. The manifest is like the table of contents for a book, listing the information the book contains and where each piece of information can be found.

Because SQL Server 2005 uses standard .NET assemblies, all of the standard .NET development tools may be leveraged. To illustrate the simplicity of creating SQL Server 2005 compliant assemblies, let's walk through an example using that time-tested Windows developer tool—Notepad. First, create a new file, named My-FirstClass.cs, having the C# content listed here:

```
using System;
public class MyFirstClass
{
    public static void MyFirstMethod()
{/* add your custom logic here */}
}
```

Next, create a key file. A key file is a cryptographic key that .NET uses to verify that code has not been tampered with after being compiled, a process known as giving an assembly a "Strong Name." The first step in this process is to use the SN.exe application and generate a key file the compiler can use to sign the compiled code. To generate a key file, open a command prompt, change to the directory where My-FirstClass.cs was saved, and type the command:

```
SN.exe -k keypair.snk
```

This will generate a new file named keypair.snk, which we will use to sign the compiled code.

The last step of the process is to use a compiler to convert the source code into an assembly. For compiling our C# source file we will use the C# Compiler (CSC) that ships with the .NET Framework V2 SDK. To invoke the compiler, open a command prompt, change to the folder containing MyFirstClass.cs and keypair.snk, and type the command:

```
CSC.exe /target:library /out:MyFirstAssembly.dll /keyfile:keypari.snk
/recurse:*.cs
```

Executing this command will generate a new file named MyFirstAssembly.dll.

After creating an assembly, it's necessary to load the assembly into SQL Server. The process of loading an assembly will assign the assembly a name and a security configuration that controls the external resources an assembly may access. Additionally, during the loading process SQL Server will evaluate the assembly's dependencies and begin loading dependent assemblies. All assemblies implementing programmability features must be registered with and loaded into Microsoft SQL Server 2005 to become accessible from inside the database. The registration and loading process of Microsoft SQL Server 2005 is invoked through the CREATE AS-SEMBLY statement, defined as:

```
CREATE ASSEMBLY assembly_name
FROM { '[path\]assembly_file_name' [,...n] }
[WITH PERMISSION_SET = {SAFE | EXTERNAL_ACCESS | UNSAFE}]
```

The parameters are:

assembly_name. Specifies the name of the assembly. The name must be unique within the database and a valid SQL Server identifier.

FROM { '[path\]assembly_file_name' [,...n] }. Specifies the location where the assembly being uploaded is located and the manifest filename that corresponds to the assembly. The path may be either a local path or a remote path using the UNC name of the network resource. `assembly_file_name` specifies the filename of the assembly. Any dependent assemblies of the assembly specified are automatically loaded.

WITH PERMISSION_SET = { SAFE| EXTERNAL_ACCESS | UNSAFE }. Specifies the permissions granted to the assembly. If not specified, the default permission set is SAFE. Code executed with SAFE permissions cannot access any external system resources, including external files or network resources. EXTERNAL_ACCESS allows assemblies to access certain external system resources, including files, network resources, and the Windows registry. UNSAFE allows assemblies unrestricted access to resources.

For example, to register the assembly we created earlier in this section, execute:

```
CREATE ASSEMBLY MyFirstAssembly
FROM 'C:\AssemblyTest\MyFirstAssembly.dll'
WITH PERMISSION_SET = SAFE
```

After registering an assembly, it is sometimes necessary to update the assembly; for example, to a new version that may include bug fixes or functional enhancements. To update an assembly that is registered with Microsoft SQL Server 2005, use the ALTER ASSEMBLY statement. The ALTER ASSEMBLY statement can update the permission set and refresh the assembly file loaded into the database. However, the assembly may not change the signature of any methods implemented nor can it change the set of dependant assemblies. The ALTER ASSEMBLY statement is defined as:

```
ALTER ASSEMBLY assembly_name
[FROM { '[path\]assembly_file_name' [,...n] }]
[WITH PERMISSION_SET = {SAFE | EXTERNAL_ACCESS | UNSAFE}]
```

For example, to update the assembly registered earlier in this section and change its permission set to allow access to external resources, execute:

```
ALTER ASSEMBLY MyFirstAssembly
FROM 'C:\AssemblyTest\MyFirstAssembly.dll'
WITH PERMISSION_SET = UNSAFE
```

To remove and unregister an assembly from the database, use the DROP ASSEMBLY statement, defined as:

```
DROP ASSEMBLY assembly_name
```

For example, to remove the MyFirstAssembly assembly, execute:

```
DROP ASSEMBLY MyFirstAssembly
```

Before deleting the assembly, the system will first check if any programmability features are referencing the assembly, and if references are found, the assembly may not be deleted until the objects referencing it are removed.

We have now covered the basics of managing assemblies in Microsoft SQL Server 2005. The remaining sections cover programmability features that may be implemented using Transact-SQL or .NET languages. All features implemented using .NET languages and external assemblies use the same registration features covered in this section.

USER-DEFINED TYPES

As you saw in Chapter 4, "Transact-SQL for Developers," Microsoft SQL Server 2005 supports a wide variety of data types; however, there are occasions when it is necessary to have a data type not available in the default set of SQL Server data types. Take, for example, an international shipping company that transports packages between Europe and the United States. The company needs to track package weight in a single system, but the European offices use kilograms (KG) and the United States offices use pounds (LBS). We can imagine a table design in a traditional relational database that would capture the weight in two separate columns: a value column and a unit column. However, it would be more convenient and logical to store the package weight and unit together as a single value. Microsoft SQL Server 2005 has an extensible type system called user-defined types that allows the creation of custom types that can, for example, store weights as a value and unit of measure.

User-defined types are implemented using a .NET class. User-defined type classes have special attributes that mark the class for use in SQL Server 2005. An attribute is a programming construct available in .NET that allows developers to associate metadata with assemblies, types, methods, and properties. User-defined types rely heavily on metadata defined in attributes to integrate the .NET class with

SQL Server. There are several requirements, including several attributes, for a user-defined type class:

- The class must be marked with the `Serializable` attribute.
- The class must be marked with the `SqlUserDefinedType` attribute.
- The class must have a public constructor that accepts no parameters.
- The class must implement the `INullable` interface and provide a public static `Null` property.
- The class must override the `ToString` method.
- The class must implement a public `Parse` method.

The `Serializable` attribute marks a class as persistable; that is, an instance of the class can be saved and reconstructed in a different environment. One way to conceptualize serialization is to think of an object instance as being similar to a traveling circus. A traveling circus is set up in one town and then deconstructed and shipped to the next town on trucks where it is reassembled. This is conceptually equivalent to a serializable object, which is deconstructed, or serialized, and transferred to a different environment where it is reconstructed, or deserialized.

The next requirement of a user-defined type class is that the class must be marked with the `SqlUserDefinedType` attribute. This attribute defines the storage format for the user-defined type. The attribute provides properties to specify the following properties of a user-defined type:

- `Format`
- `IsByteOrdered`
- `IsFixedLength`
- `MaxByteSize`

The `format` property controls the persisted format for the user-defined type. Options for the persisted format are Native or UserDefined. Choosing the proper format depends on the properties of the user-defined type being implemented.

Native format uses the SQL Server serialization format. It is the fastest serialization format, but all properties of the user-defined type must be fixed-length, which means you couldn't use string properties in your user-defined type.

The most flexible, but slower performing, format option is UserDefined. When a user-defined type is marked as having a UserDefined persistence format, the user-defined type implements the code necessary for the type to persist itself and, of course, to recreate itself. Using the UserDefined format brings additional implementation requirements; for example, implementing the IBinarySerialize interface, which provides the methods SQL Server will call on the class to serialize and deserialze the user-defined type.

Microsoft SQL Server 2005 uses the `IsByteOrdered` property to determine how the database will compare values of the user-defined type. When a user-defined type sets the `IsByteOrdered` property to true, the database will use the serialized type's binary representation (e.g., the bytes that are stored on the disk) for all comparison purposes. Comparison of values for a byte-ordered user-defined type is much faster than non-byte-ordered types because, in effect, SQL Server compares two byte-ordered user-defined type values as two binary numbers, which allows it to be blazingly fast. Additionally, only user-defined types that are byte ordered may be indexed. Implementing a byte-ordered user-defined type is quite simple for Native format, but more complex for UserDefined format.

The `IsFixedLength` property specifies whether all the user-defined type values are the same size when serialized, which allows SQL Server to optimize the storage of user-defined types. Native format user-defined types will be fixed-length, but types whose format is UserDefined may not be fixed-length.

The last property available in the `SqlUserDefinedType` attribute is the `MaxByteSize` property, which simply controls the amount of space SQL Server allocates to store a serialized user-defined type value. `MaxByteSize` must be specified when using the UserDefined format, but is not required for Native format user-defined types.

The next requirement for a user-defined type class is that it have a public, parameterless constructor. The reason for this requirement is straightforward: the database has to be able to create an instance of type, and to create an instance of a class the constructor must be public.

Columns storing values for user-defined types, just as other standard SQL Server data types, can store NULL values. SQL Server 2005 allows user-defined types to control when the database should interpret user-defined type values as NULL. User-defined types are able to inform the database that a value of the user-defined type should be interpreted as NULL by implementing the `INullable` interface. The `INullable` interface is a standard .NET interface that specifies a single boolean property named `IsNull`. When implementing the `IsNull` property, the user-defined type should implement logic that returns a `True` value from the property if the value should be interpreted as NULL, and a `False` value from the property if the value is non-NULL.

As mentioned previously, user-defined types are implemented using standard .NET classes, and all .NET classes implicitly derive from the Object class. The Object class provides some common overridable methods, including, for example, `Equals`, `GetHashCode`, and `ToString`. SQL Server 2005 user-defined types rely on this implicit derivation and the `ToString` method to provide a common way for user-defined types to present a textual representation of user-defined type values.

User-defined types must be able to provide a textual representation of user-defined type values, and convert a textual value into an instance of the user-defined type. This conversion is needed, for example, in INSERT SQL statements that can only work with strings and numbers as value inputs (e.g., when you insert a value of type UNIQUEIDENTIFIER into SQL Server using an INSERT statement, the value specified in the INSERT statement is the string representation of the UNIQUEIDENTI-FIER value, not the actual binary format). The Parse method must be a public method that accepts a single string value as a parameter and returns an instance of the user-defined type.

Now let's look at an example user-defined type that implements the requirements we just covered. The following class implementation represents a SQL Server 2005 user-defined type that provides the ability to store weight values along with the unit of measure in which the weight was measured:

```csharp
using System;
using System.Data.Sql;
using System.Data.SqlTypes;
using System.Data.SqlServer;
using System.Runtime.Serialization;

[Serializable()]
[SqlUserDefinedType(Format.UserDefined,IsByteOrdered = true,
MaxByteSize = 8000)]
public class Weight : INullable, IBinarySerialize
{
    private const string POUND = "LBS";
    private const string KILOGRAM = "KG";

    private decimal _value = Decimal.MinValue;
    private string _unit = null;

    public Weight()  {}

    bool System.Data.SqlTypes.INullable.IsNull
    {
        get
        {
            return (_value == Decimal.MinValue || _unit == null);
        }
    }

    private static void ParseValueAndUnit(SqlString s, out decimal val,
out string unit)
    {
        string[] parts = s.Value.Split(' ');
        string valuePart = parts[0];
        string unitPart = parts[1];

        valuePart = valuePart.Trim();
        unitPart = unitPart.Trim().ToUpper();
```

```
        try  { val = Decimal.Parse(valuePart); }
        catch { val = Decimal.MinValue; }

        unit = unitPart;
        return;
    }

    public static Weight Parse(SqlString s)
    {
        Weight weight = new Weight();

        if (s == null || s.IsNull || s.Value.Trim() == string.Empty)
            return Weight.Null;

        decimal value;
        string unit;
        ParseValueAndUnit(s, out value, out unit);
        if (value == Decimal.MinValue && unit == null)
            return Weight.Null;

        weight.Value = value;
        weight.Unit = unit;
        return weight;
    }

    public static Weight Null
    {
        // null by default
        get { return new Weight(); }
    }

    public override string ToString()
    {
        if (_value == Decimal.MinValue && _unit == null)
            return "NULL";

        return _value.ToString() + " " + _unit;
    }

    public decimal Value
    {
        get { return _value; }
        set { _value = value; }
    }

    public string Unit
    {
```

```
        get { return _unit; }
        set { _unit = value; }
    }

    void IBinarySerialize.Read(System.IO.BinaryReader reader)
    {
        string s = reader.ReadString();
        SqlString sqlString = new SqlString(s);
        ParseValueAndUnit(sqlString, out _value, out _unit);
    }

    void IBinarySerialize.Write(System.IO.BinaryWriter writer)
    {
        writer.Write(this.ToString());
    }
}
```

Type DDL Statements

After compiling your user-defined type into an assembly and loading the assembly into the database, you must inform the database of the new type's information by using the CREATE TYPE statement. CREATE TYPE specifies the name of the new type and where the implementation of the user-defined type may be found. More formally, CREATE TYPE is defined as:

```
CREATE TYPE  type_name
EXTERNAL NAME assembly_name.class_name
```

type_name. Specifies the name of the alias or user-defined type. Type names must conform to the rules for identifiers.

assembly_name. Specifies the assembly that contains the user-defined type class implementation. The assembly_name is the same name used in the CREATE AS-SEMBLY statement used to load the assembly into the database.

[.class_name]. Specifies the class within the assembly that implements the user-defined type.

Assuming the assembly name is WeightDataType, the following command creates the Weight user-defined type:

```
CREATE TYPE Weight
EXTERNAL NAME WeightDataType.Weight
```

At this point, you can use the data type just as you would any other native SQL Server data type. The following commands illustrate using the data type:

```
/*
```

```
Create a table using the Weight user-defined type as one of the column
data types
*/
CREATE TABLE Packages (PackageID UNIQUEIDENTIFIER, PackageWeight
Weight)
GO
/*
Insert some new rows into the table.  Notice the type is parsing the
string value into an instance of the type to be stored in the database
*/
INSERT INTO Packages VALUES (newid(), '5 KG')
INSERT INTO Packages VALUES(newid(), '10 LBS')
GO
/*
Retrieve the values we just inserted and prove that it worked ☺
*/
SELECT * FROM Packages
GO
/*
Now let's show that we can invoke methods on the class!
*/
DECLARE @MyWeightValue Weight
SET @MyWeightValue = Weight::Parse('100 LBS')
INSERT INTO Packages VALUES(newid(), @MyWeightValue)
```

As you can see, user-defined types provide a very powerful construct in SQL Server 2005, opening the door to designs leveraging aspects of relational and object-oriented databases design. Technology choices aren't typically clear-cut; most times, there are benefits and trade-offs that must be weighed in the context of a larger system. This is certainly true of user-defined types. If you find yourself forcing the technology to fit your problem, or if squeezing that last ounce of performance out of the database is important, then user-defined types may not be the best choice. Effective use of user-defined types will fit naturally into a design.

STORED PROCEDURES

SQL Server developers have, for many years, packaged functionality into database procedures. A procedure is a group of statements that can be executed as a single unit. Stored procedures provide a layer of abstraction that helps insulate your application from changes in the underlying physical structures of the database.

Traditionally, stored procedures have been developed using the Transact-SQL language. Previous versions of SQL Server supported developing procedures using other languages such as C++ for writing procedures, called extended stored procedures. The overall integration of extended stored procedures was quite clunky and did not provide first-class support for interacting with SQL Server. With the release of SQL Server 2005 and its integration of the Common Language Runtime (CLR), you can extend the functionality of SQL Server using any .NET language without many of the complexities and drawbacks previously associated with Extended Stored Procedures.

Before we dive into the implementation of stored procedures let's look at how stored procedures are managed in SQL Server 2005. The CREATE PROCEDURE DDL statement creates a new stored procedure in an existing SQL Server 2005 database. To create a new procedure you must specify the name of the procedure, the procedure arguments, and the body of the procedure. The Transact-SQL CREATE PROCEDURE statement is defined as:

```
CREATE PROCEDURE procedure_name
    [{@parameter data_type}[OUTPUT ][ ,...n ]
    [WITH  EXECUTE AS { CALLER | SELF | OWNER | 'user_name' }]
AS
{
        {
    BEGIN
            sql_statements
    END
      }
        |  {EXTERNAL NAME assembly_name.class_name[.method_name]}

}
```

The parameters to the CREATE PROCEDURE statement are:

procedure_name. Specifies the name of the new stored procedure.

@parameter data_type [OUTPUT]. Specifies a parameter name and data type. The optional OUTPUT keyword indicates that the parameter is an output of the execution of the procedure.

[WITH [EXECUTE AS { CALLER | SELF | OWNER | 'user_name' }]]. Specifies the security context under which the stored procedure will execute.

{EXTERNAL NAME assembly_name.class_name.method_name}. Specifies the procedure will execute a method of a .NET Framework assembly. The method must be a public static method of the class.

Syntactically speaking, creating a standard Transact-SQL stored procedure in Microsoft SQL Server 2005 is very much like creating procedures in previous versions. The procedure definition is comprised of three basic parts:

- The procedure name
- A list of input/output parameters and parameter data types

■ A group of Transact-SQL statements that will be executed when the procedure is called

The following example Transact-SQL stored procedure calculates the monthly payment for a loan with a specified rate and payment schedule, and keeps a running average of the rate used for all submitted payment calculations:

```
CREATE PROCEDURE CalculateMonthlyPayment
    @rate FLOAT,
        @nper INT,
@pv MONEY,
@pmnt MONEY OUTPUT
  AS
  BEGIN
      DECLARE @monRate FLOAT
      DECLARE @denom FLOAT
      SET @monRate = @rate/12
      SET @denom = POWER((1+@monRate),@nper)-1
      SET @pmnt = ROUND((@monRate+(@monRate/@denom))*@pv,2)
      UPDATE AverageRate SET Rate = ((TotalRate +
@rate)/(NumPaymentCalculations+1)), TotalRate = TotalRate + @rate,
NumPaymentCalculations = NumPaymentCalculations + 1
  END
```

After creating the procedure, we now need to execute it and test the results. To execute procedures in Microsoft SQL Server 2005, use the EXEC command and specify the name of the procedure and a list of parameters. The syntax of the statement is:

```
EXEC procedure_name [parameter_list]
```

For example, to calculate a monthly payment using the CalculateMonthlyPayment procedure and return the payment value, use:

```
DECLARE @payment MONEY
EXEC CalculateMonthlyPayment
    0.05,
    180,
    150000,
    @payment OUTPUT
/* returns a payment of 1186.19 */
SELECT @payment
```

Now that we have covered traditional Transact-SQL stored procedures, we will look at the new Managed Stored Procedure feature in SQL Server 2005.

Managed Stored Procedures

Writing managed stored procedures is amazingly simple in SQL Server 2005. You can turn nearly any public static method into a stored procedure. For example, instead of using Transact-SQL to implement our payment calculation, we could use a managed stored procedure and C# to implement the same logic as shown here:

```
using System;
using System.Data;
using System.Data.Sql;
using System.Data.SqlServer;
using System.Data.SqlTypes;

public class MonthlyPaymentCalculator
{
    [SqlProcedure]
    public static void CalculatePayment(double rate, int nper, int pv,
out double payment)
    {
        double monthlyRate = rate / 12;
        payment = Math.Round(Convert.ToDouble((monthlyRate +
((monthlyRate)/((Math.Pow((1 + monthlyRate),nper))-1)))*pv),2);
        SqlCommand cmd = SqlContext.GetCommand();
        cmd.CommandText = String.Format("UPDATE AverageRate SET Rate =
((TotalRate + {0})/(NumPaymentCalculations+1)), TotalRate = TotalRate +
{0}, NumPaymentCalculations = NumPaymentCalculations + 1", rate);
        cmd.ExecuteNonQuery();
    }
};
```

Once we have compiled the class, we must load the resulting DLL from the file system into the database. This is accomplished in Transact-SQL by using the CRE-ATE ASSEMBLY command, illustrated here:

```
CREATE ASSEMBLY MonthlyPaymentCalculator
FROM 'C:\MonthlyPaymentCalculator.dll'
WITH PERMISSION_SET = SAFE
```

At this point, you may now create the procedure, referencing the managed code implementation we just created. For example, to create a stored procedure that invokes the CalculatePayment method, execute:

```
CREATE PROCEDURE CalculateMonthlyPaymentUsingManagedCode
    @rate float, @nper int, @pv int, @pmnt float output
AS
    EXTERNAL NAME
MonthlyPaymentCalculator.MonthlyPaymentCalculator.CalculatePayment
```

Managed stored procedures are executed using the same commands as Transact-SQL stored procedures. For example, we can execute this managed procedure using:

```
DECLARE @payment MONEY
EXEC CalculateMonthlyPaymentUsingManagedCode
    0.05,
    180,
    150000,
    @payment OUTPUT
/* returns a payment of 1186.19 */
SELECT @payment
```

Those with a very keen eye may have noticed some differences between the data types specified in the CREATE PROCEDURE parameter list and the data types of the corresponding parameter in the managed code implementation. For example, the CREATE PROCEDURE command lists @rate as the first parameter and it's of type FLOAT, while the managed method lists rate as the first parameter but it's of type double. Microsoft SQL Server 2005 will automatically provide this conversion between intrinsic database types and their corresponding CLR types. Table 5.1 lists the Transact-SQL data types and their CLR equivalents.

Stored Procedures, whether implemented using traditional Transact-SQL or using managed code, provide the ability to package logic and/or data access into functional groupings. In most cases, this segmentation is a very effective layer providing insulation from changes to underlying data structures. In general, using stored procedures when building data-driven applications is an accepted practice

TABLE 5.1 Mapping of Transact-SQL Data Types to Their Equivalent CLR Data Type

Transact-SQL Data Type	CLR Type
char, varchar, text, nvarchar, ntext	String
decimal, numeric	Decimal
bit	Boolean
binary, varbinary, image	Byte[]
int	Int32
smallint	Int16
tinyint	Byte
float	Double
real	Float
Money, smallmoney	Decimal
datetime, smalldatetime	Datetime

and a very good idea. The choice between using managed procedures or Transact-SQL procedures will ultimately be driven by your project's requirements, but the general approach is that managed procedures are much better suited for implementing computationally intensive logic, while Transact-SQL stored procedures are better suited for implementing data manipulation logic.

USER-DEFINED FUNCTIONS

User-defined functions are very similar to stored procedures in that both package logic into groupings that can be executed as a whole. Functions, like procedures, also accept a list of parameters, but that's where the differences between functions and procedures begin to appear. Parameters to functions may only be passed by value; that is, a function parameter cannot be marked as an OUTPUT parameter. Another key difference between functions and procedures is that functions return a single value, while procedures return a code indicating the success or failure of the procedure, and any data returned from the execution of the procedure must be returned through output parameters. The final notable difference between user-defined functions and stored procedures is that because functions return a value, they can be embedded directly in queries, whereas stored procedures may not be embedded in other commands.

User-defined functions are created in SQL Server 2005 using the CREATE FUNCTION command. The Transact-SQL CREATE FUNCTION statement is defined as:

```
CREATE FUNCTION function_name
    ( [ { @parameter_name [ AS ] data_type } [ ,...n ]] )
RETURNS data_type
AS
{BEGIN
    function_body
    RETURN scalar_expression
END} | {EXTERNAL NAME assembly_name.class_name.method_name}
```

function_name. Specifies the name of the user-defined function.

@parameter_name. Specifies a parameter in the user-defined function.

data_type. Specifies the data types for parameters and the return value of a scalar user-defined function.

scalar_expression. Specifies the scalar value that the scalar function returns.

function_body. Specifies a series of Transact-SQL statements that define the value of the function.

EXTERNAL NAME assembly_name.class_name.method_name. Specifies the static method of a class, in the specified assembly that will be executed.

Now, let's look at an example user-defined function. Using the Weight user-defined type we created previously in this chapter, we'll create a function that can convert between pounds and kilograms:

```
CREATE FUNCTION ConvertWeightTSQL
        (
        @weightToConvert Weight,
        @convertTo VARCHAR(3)
        ) RETURNS Weight
AS
BEGIN
    if (@weightToConvert.Unit = @convertTo)
            return @weightToConvert
    DECLARE @conversionResults FLOAT
    if (@weightToConvert.Unit='KG' AND @convertTo='LBS')
            SET @conversionResults=@weightToConvert.Value*2.2
    else
            SET @conversionResults=@weightToConvert.Value/2.2
    Return Weight::Parse
(cast(@conversionResults as VARCHAR) + ' ' + @convertTo)
END
```

Using the Packages table we created previously, we can see the results of the function by including a call to the function in the SELECT list of a query against that table. For example, to convert all weight values returned in the query to kilograms, we would execute:

```
SELECT PackageID, dbo.ConvertWeightTSQL( PackageWeight, 'KG') FROM
Packages
```

The second column returned by the query will contain values that have been converted to kilograms.

With the CLR integration in SQL Server 2005 the same conversion can be implemented in managed code. In fact, the conversion function can easily be added directly to the class implementing the user-defined type, which provides a very clean packaging of functionality. The requirements for implementing a user-defined function in managed code include:

- The method must be a public static method of a public class.
- The method must return a value of the same type as the user-defined function.
- Parameters to the method may not be reference parameters or out parameters.
- The method must be marked with the SqlFunction attribute.

The reasons for the first three requirements are self-explanatory. For the class and the method to be invoked from SQL Server, it needs to be public and static, the method certainly has to return a value that's of the same type as the user-defined function definition, and functions don't support OUTPUT parameters so neither can managed functions. The SqlFunction attribute, which identifies the method as a valid user-defined function for SQL Server 2005, requires more discussion.

The SqlFunction attribute provides the ability to specify the following four properties of the user-defined function:

- IsDeterministic
- DataAccess
- SystemDataAccess
- IsPrecise

The IsDeterministic property accepts a boolean value that identifies whether the function will always generate the same output value for a given set of input values (e.g., a deterministic function), or if the function may generate a different return value for the same set of input values (e.g., a nondeterministic function). Why is this important? For two reasons: only deterministic functions can be indexed, and performance. SQL Server 2005 can cache the results of deterministic functions so that the next time the function is executed using the same set of input values, the database can simply return the cached result without having to re-execute the function. If a function is nondeterministic, then SQL Server can't guarantee that a set of inputs will generate any particular output, and therefore the database is unable to reuse cached results.

The DataAccess and SystemDataAccess properties mark whether the function involves reading data from the local database or system catalogs, respectively. These two properties help SQL Server 2005 understand what, if any, data the function may access, allowing the database to optimize execution of the function. The value for the DataAccess property is specified using the DataAccessKind enumeration, specifying DataAccessKind. None indicates that the function does not read local database data, while specifying DataAccessKind.Read indicates that the function will read data from the local database. The SystemDataAccess property behaves in the same way as the DataAccess property, except the valid enumeration values are SystemDataAccessKind.None and SystemDataAccessKind.Read. If unspecified, the SqlFunction attribute will assume the user-defined function does not access local data or system catalog data.

The last property of the SqlFunction attribute marks whether a method involves any floating-point arithmetic. Floating-point computations, by their nature, are approximations and are not precise calculations. The IsPrecise property of the SqlFunction attribute specifies this using a boolean value to indicate whether the function is precise. Nonprecise function cannot be indexed.

Now, let's look at an example of a user-defined function that implements these attributes. This example adds a new `ConvertWeight` method to the `Weight` user-defined type class. For brevity, only the `ConvertWeight` method is listed—the remainder of the class is listed in the user-defined type section in this chapter.

```
[SqlFunction(IsDeterministic = true, IsPrecise = true)]
public static Weight ConvertWeight(Weight weight, string to)
{
    decimal toValue = 0.0M;
    // 1 KG == 2.2 LBS
    decimal conversionFactor = 2.2M;

    if (to == POUND && weight.Unit == KILOGRAM)
        toValue = weight.Value * conversionFactor;
    else if (to == KILOGRAM && weight.Unit == POUND)
        toValue = weight.Value / conversionFactor;
    else
        return weight;

    return Weight.Parse(toValue.ToString() + " " + to);
}
```

After compiling the class and updating the `WeightDataType` assembly using the `ALTER ASSEMBLY` command, execute the following statement to create the user-defined function for converting weight values to different data types:

```
CREATE FUNCTION ConvertWeight
        (
    @weightToConvert Weight,
    @convertTo NVARCHAR(3)
        ) RETURNS Weight
EXTERNAL NAME WeightDataType.[Weight].ConvertWeight
```

Executing the managed user-defined function is accomplished in the same manner as a Transact-SQL user-defined function. Running the following query returns all package weights displayed in pounds:

```
SELECT PackageID, dbo.ConvertWeight( PackageWeight, 'LBS') FROM
Packages
```

SQL Server 2005 user-defined functions provide yet another tightly integrated and powerful CLR feature. The guidelines for choosing whether to use managed functions or Transact-SQL functions are very much like the guidelines for choosing the appropriate method of implementing stored procedures; namely, if calculations are involved, managed code will perform better.

TRIGGERS

Most developers using today's modern programming languages have been exposed to the concept of events, which is simply an asynchronous notification that something you're interested in has happened. In the realm of databases, a trigger is the conceptual equivalent of an event. Triggers are blocks of code that are executed when a subscribed event occurs. Microsoft SQL Server 2005 supports triggers for DML and DDL events. The possible DML events include execution of INSERT/UPDATE/DELETE commands on tables or views, while the possible DDL events include CREATE/ALTER/DROP and GRANT/DENY/REVOKE on database objects and security privileges, respectively.

DML triggers have two variations for each of the event types (INSERT/UPDATE/DELETE): INSTEAD OF and AFTER. An INSTEAD OF trigger executes the trigger code instead of the event (the trigger is responsible for performing whatever data changes are required), while an AFTER trigger executes the trigger code after the event has occurred. A viable scenario for using an INSTEAD OF trigger is a situation in which the trigger needs to modify the data before the table is changed, while AFTER triggers may be used for logging actions, updating values, and so forth.

DDL triggers can be created to respond to events from a specific database or for every database on a server. DDL triggers can be invoked for all types of DDL operations.

Like all of the programmability features we have covered, triggers, both DDL and DML, allow for using either Transact-SQL or managed code for their implementations. Before diving into the implementation of triggers, let's look at the DDL for creating triggers. The syntax for creating a DML trigger is defined as:

```
CREATE TRIGGER trigger_name ON { table | view }
{ AFTER | INSTEAD OF }
{ [ INSERT ] [ , ] [ UPDATE ] [ , ] [ DELETE ] }
AS
{
sql_statement [ ...n ] |
EXTERNAL NAME assembly_name.class_name[.method_name]
}
```

trigger_name. Specifies the name of the trigger.

table| view. Specifies the table or view on which the trigger is executed.

AFTER. Specifies that the trigger is fired only when all operations have executed successfully.

INSTEAD OF. Specifies that the DML trigger is executed instead of the SQL statement, causing the trigger to fire. INSTEAD OF cannot be specified for DDL triggers.

{ [DELETE] [,] [INSERT] [,] [UPDATE] }. Specifies the type of operation the trigger should fire in response to.

sql_statement. Specifies the SQL commands to be executed in response to the triggering event.

EXTERNAL NAME assembly_name.class_name[.method_name]. Specifies the trigger is a managed trigger and can be found at the provided method name in the specified assembly and class.

The syntax for creating a DDL trigger is defined as:

```
CREATE TRIGGER trigger_name ON { ALL SERVER | DATABASE }
AFTER { event_type | event_group } [ ,...n ]
AS
{
sql_statement [ ...n ] |
EXTERNAL NAME assembly_name.class_name[.method_name]
}
```

trigger_name. Specifies the name of the trigger.

ALL SERVER | DATABASE. Specifies that the DDL trigger is either limited to the current database or is for all databases on the current server.

AFTER. Specifies that the trigger is fired only when all operations have executed successfully.

event_type. Specifies the DDL event type the trigger should respond to.

event_group. Specifies a grouping of DDL events the trigger should respond to.

sql_statement. Specifies the SQL commands to be executed in response to the triggering event.

EXTERNAL NAME assembly_name.class_name[.method_name]. Specifies the trigger is a managed trigger and can be found at the provided method name in the specified assembly and class.

Now let's look at an AFTER INSERT DML trigger. The following trigger responds to an insert event on the Rentals table and updates the data on another table:

```
CREATE TRIGGER RemoveRentalFromRequestList ON Rentals AFTER INSERT
AS
    DECLARE @customerId UNIQUEIDENTIFIER
    DECLARE @movieInventoryId UNIQUEIDENTIFIER
    DECLARE @movieId UNIQUEIDENTIFIER
```

```
DECLARE @priority INT

SELECT @customerId = CustomerId, @movieInventoryId =
MovieInventoryId
    FROM inserted

SELECT @movieId = I.MovieId, @priority = R.Priority
    FROM MovieInventory I JOIN RentalRequestList R
    ON R.MovieId = I.MovieId
    WHERE I.MovieInventoryId = @movieInventoryId

UPDATE RentalRequestList SET Priority = Priority - 1
    WHERE CustomerId = @customerId AND Priority > @priority

DELETE FROM RentalRequestList
    WHERE CustomerId = @customerId AND MovieId = @movieId
```

With the power of CLR integration, triggers can now be easily extended to do things that have traditionally been relegated to applications or application servers. For example, the following code listing illustrates a trigger that sends an email to a customer informing him that his product has shipped:

```
using System;
using System.Data;
using System.Data.Sql;
using System.Data.SqlServer;
using System.Data.SqlTypes;
using System.Web.Mail;

public class EmailTriggers
{
    [SqlTrigger(Name = "NotifyCustomerOfShipment", Target = "Rentals",
Event = "FOR INSERT")]
    public static void NotifyCustomerOfShipment()
    {
        SqlTriggerContext triggerContext =
SqlContext.GetTriggerContext();
        SqlPipe pipe = SqlContext.GetPipe();

        if (triggerContext.TriggerAction == TriggerAction.Insert)
        {
            SqlCommand command = SqlContext.GetCommand();
            command.CommandText = "SELECT C.EmailAddress, M.Title FROM
INSERTED I JOIN Customer C ON C.CustomerId = I.CustomerId JOIN
MovieInventory MI ON MI.MovieInventoryId = I.MovieInventoryId JOIN
Movie M on MI.MovieId = M.MovieId";
            SqlDataReader reader = command.ExecuteReader();
```

```
        if (!reader.Read())
            throw new Exception("Unable to retrieve customer
information.");

        string emailAddress = reader.GetString(0);
        string movieTitle = reader.GetString(1);

        MailMessage message = new MailMessage();
        message.To = emailAddress;
        message.From = "donotreply@cavaliermovies.com";
        message.Subject = movieTitle + " has shipped";
        message.Body = "We have shipped " + movieTitle + " on " +
DateTime.Now.ToShortDateString() + ".";
        SmtpMail.Send(message);


    }
  }
}
```

Now let's switch gears and review a sample DDL trigger that logs DDL events
to a table. First, execute the following command to create the log table that will
store the DDL events:

```
CREATE TABLE DDLLog
(
LogId UNIQUEIDENTIFIER,
LogDate DATETIME,
Action VARCHAR(20),
Data XML
)
```

Next, create the DDL trigger using the DDL_DATABASE_LEVEL_EVENTS group,
which will be fired for all DDL events in the current database:

```
CREATE TRIGGER DDLTrigger
ON DATABASE FOR DDL_DATABASE_LEVEL_EVENTS
AS
    DECLARE @xmlEventData XML
    SET @xmlEventData = EVENTDATA()

    INSERT INTO DDLLog
            VALUES
            (
                    NEWID(),
                    GETDATE(),
                    Convert(varchar(20),
@xmlEventData.query('data(//EventType)')),
                    eventdata()
```

```
                    )
```

Finally, test that the DDL trigger is fired and the event is logged by creating a test table and verifying by retrieving the data from the log table:

```
create table blahBlah(ID UNIQUEIDENTIFIER, Description VARCHAR(50))

SELECT * FROM DDLLog
```

DDL triggers can also be implemented using managed code. The following code listing demonstrates an example method that responds to DDL events and e-mails an administrator the event information:

```
using System;
using System.Data;
using System.Data.Sql;
using System.Data.SqlServer;
using System.Data.SqlTypes;
using System.Web.Mail;
using System.Xml;

public class DDLTrigger
{
    public static void NotifyAdminOfDDLEvent()
    {
        SqlTriggerContext context = SqlContext.GetTriggerContext();
        XmlDocument document = new XmlDocument();
        document.LoadXml(context.EventData.Value);

        string eventType = "UNKNOWN";
        string database = "UNKNOWN";
        string commandText = context.EventData.Value;

        try
        {
            XmlNode eventTypeNode =
document.SelectSingleNode("//EVENT_INSTANCE/EventType/text()");
            XmlNode databaseNode =
document.SelectSingleNode("//EVENT_INSTANCE/DatabaseName/text()");
            XmlNode commandTextNode =
document.SelectSingleNode("//EVENT_INSTANCE/TSQLCommand/CommandText/tex
t()");

            eventType = eventTypeNode.Value;
            database = databaseNode.Value;
            commandText = commandTextNode.Value;
        }
        catch
```

```
        {
            //ingore any exceptions...
        }

        MailMessage message = new MailMessage();
        message.To = "admin@cavaliermovies.com";
        message.From = "donotreply@cavaliermovies.com";
        message.Subject = String.Format("Notification of {0} DDL Event
For {1} Database", eventType, database);
        message.Body = commandText;
        SmtpMail.Send(message);
    }
}
```

After compiling the class and loading the assembly into the database, execute the following CREATE TRIGGER command to inform the database that it should use the class we just created in response to DDL events:

```
CREATE TRIGGER DDLEmailNotificationTrigger
ON DATABASE FOR DDL_DATABASE_LEVEL_EVENTS
AS
EXTERNAL NAME
SendEmailNotificationTriggers.DDLTrigger.NotifyAdminOfDDLEvent
```

AGGREGATES

User-defined aggregate functions is a new feature in Microsoft SQL Server 2005. Aggregate functions summarize multiple values into a single value. For example, a common aggregate function is the COUNT function, which will return the number of rows returned by a query. Prior to SQL Server 2005 and its tightly integrated CLR environment, there was no way to create aggregate functions directly in the database. User-defined aggregates open a new realm of possibilities for analytical or business intelligence applications.

Implementing user-defined aggregate functions is the only programmability feature that is only possible using managed code. SQL Server 2005 does not provide the ability to implement an aggregate using Transact-SQL.

The requirements for implementing a user defined aggregate include:

- The class must be marked as Serializable.
- The class must be marked with the SqlUserDefinedAggregate attribute.
- The class must implement the IBinarySerialize interface.
- The class must provide a public Init method that returns a void and accepts no parameters.

- The class must provide a public `Accumulate` method that returns a void and accepts a parameter for a value of the applicable aggregate data type.
- The class must provide a public `Merge` method that accepts an instance of the aggregate class being implemented and returns a void.
- The class must provide a public `Terminate` method that returns a single value of the applicable aggregate data type and accepts no parameters.

Let's look at an example implementation of an aggregate that fulfills these requirements. The following example continues to use the `Weight` data type and implements a user-defined aggregate function that will summarize all of the various weight values whether stored in pounds or kilograms and return a single `Weight` value, in kilograms, that represents the average of all weights:

```
[Serializable]
[SqlUserDefinedAggregate(Format.UserDefined, IsInvariantToDuplicates =
false, IsInvariantToNulls = false, IsInvariantToOrder = true,
IsNullIfEmpty = true,MaxByteSize  = 8000)]
public class WeightAverage : IBinarySerialize
{
    public decimal TotalWeight = 0.0M;
    public int WeightCount = 0;


    public void Init()
    {
        TotalWeight = 0.0M;
        WeightCount = 0;
    }

    public void Accumulate(Weight weight)
    {
        Weight normalizedWeight = Weight.ConvertWeight(weight, "KG");
        TotalWeight += normalizedWeight.Value;
        WeightCount += 1;
    }

    public void Merge(WeightAverage average)
    {
        TotalWeight += average.TotalWeight;
        WeightCount += average.WeightCount;
    }

    public Weight Terminate()
    {
        decimal averageWeight = TotalWeight / WeightCount;
        return Weight.Parse(averageWeight.ToString() + " KG");
```

```
    }

    void IBinarySerialize.Read(BinaryReader reader)
    {
        string s = reader.ReadString();
        string[] values = s.Split('|');
        TotalWeight = Convert.ToDecimal(values[0]);
        WeightCount = Convert.ToInt32(values[1]);
    }

    void IBinarySerialize.Write(BinaryWriter writer)
    {
        writer.Write(TotalWeight.ToString() + "|" +
WeightCount.ToString());
    }
}
```

After compiling the class and loading the assembly into the database, it's necessary to inform SQL Server of the definition of the aggregate. To do this, use the CREATE AGGREGATE command, which is defined as:

```
CREATE AGGREGATE aggregate_name (@param_name data_type)
RETURNS data_type
EXTERNAL NAME assembly_name [ .class_name ]
```

aggregate_name. Specifies the name of the aggregate function you want to create.

@param_name data_type. Specifies a parameter and its data type in the user-defined aggregate.

EXTERNAL NAME assembly_name [.class_name]. Specifies the assembly and class to bind with the user-defined aggregate function.

For example, to create an aggregate function for our example class, use:

```
CREATE AGGREGATE WeightAverage (@weight Weight)
RETURNS Weight
EXTERNAL NAME WeightDataType.WeightAverage
```

Finally, to see the aggregate in action, execute:

```
SELECT WeightAverage(PackageWeight) FROM Packages
```

CONCLUSION

As we have seen in this chapter, Microsoft SQL Server 2005 provides an extremely powerful set of programmability features that will change many of the paradigms of building data-driven applications. The integration of the CLR into the database platform is an excellent feature of SQL Server 2005. However, developers may be tempted to overuse the CLR integration—either because of the "cool" factor or they may be more comfortable with the .NET languages—but this temptation should be avoided. Forcing a design to overuse CLR integration can have a severe impact on performance and scalability of your application. Proper use of the features following some of the guidelines we set forth in this book will give you the best chance at building scalable and well-performing applications.

6 ADO.NET 2.0

In this Chapter

■ New ADO.NET 2.0 Features
■ Conclusion

The original 1.0 version of ADO.NET was designed from the ground up to meet the data access requirements of loosely coupled applications. ADO.NET's disconnected data architecture is tightly integrated with XML and provides a native .NET interface to a wide variety of data sources. Microsoft had the following design goals for the first release of ADO.NET:

Support n-tier applications. ADO.NET provides excellent support for the disconnected, n-tier programming environment. Disconnected data in the form of the ADO.NET DataSet is at the core of the programming model.

Tightly integrate XML. XML support is built into ADO.NET at a low level. XML forms the basis of data contained in ADO.NET, and XML produced by ADO.NET can easily be used by other parts of the Framework.

Leverage existing ADO concepts. Since ADO was an already established and widely used data access standard, ADO.NET has a similar feel to it to allow knowledge of ADO to transfer well to the new technology.

The first release of ADO.NET met its goals well, but there is always room for improvement. ADO.NET 2.0 is a refinement of those original goals to support better performance in n-tier environments and make it easier to produce loosely coupled applications. Although ADO.NET 2.0 has a significant number of improvements, backward compatibility is preserved and the vast majority of code written using the previous version should work with the new version.

To be more easily used in distributed applications, ADO.NET is designed to separate data access from data manipulation. The DataSet is responsible for data access independent of the source of the data. Although DataSets have always offered reasonable performance, they can now be transported via binary remoting. This offers reduction in memory, CPU, and bandwidth requirements for larger DataSets. It is disabled by default, but can be turned on with the DataSet.RemotingFormat property. In addition, the indexing engine in the DataSet has been improved. Update time is close to constant rather than linear in proportion to the number of records in the DataSet.

The DataSet is composed of one or more DataTable objects along with keys and constraints that apply to the DataTables. The DataTable themselves are composed of rows and columns that contain the actual data. To improve usability of ADO.NET, some new methods have been added to the DataTable, including ReadXml and WriteXml so you can translate between DataTables and DataReaders directly. This makes a standalone data table much more useful. You might need only one table at a given time, and having to create an entire DataSet to contain that table is messy. A simple example of how you can load a DataTable directly from a DataReader is shown here:

```
SqlConnection conn = new SqlConnection(connectionStr);
conn.Open();
SqlCommand cmd = new SqlCommand("Select * from Contacts", conn);
SqlDataReader dr = cmd.ExecuteReader();
DataTable dt = new DataTable("Contacts");
dt.Load(dr);
```

Data providers are responsible for data access. The data provider components are designed for data manipulation and fast, read-only access to data. The Connection object is used to establish communication with a data source. The Command object is used to execute database commands. The DataReader encapsulates high-performance stream of data from the data source. The DataAdapter is used to bridge the provider to the DataSet and to load the dataset and marshal changes back to the data source. Figure 6.1 illustrates the fundamental ADO.NET components.

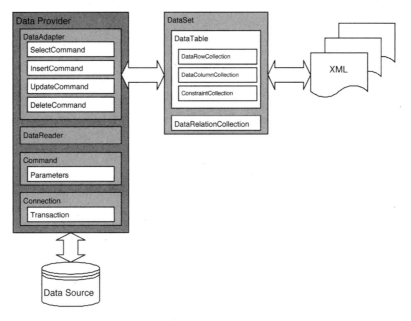

FIGURE 6.1   The main components of ADO.NET.

NEW ADO.NET 2.0 FEATURES

ADO.NET 2.0 offers many new and useful features. In this section, we describe these new features and give some examples of how they might be used.

Asynchronous Operations

One of the most pressing problems when using ADO.NET in the middle tier is asynchronous operations. In general, database operations are one of the slowest aspects of a distributed application. If database activities are channeled through a single thread, they will block and the application must wait for the operations to finish before continuing.

Assigning these long-running operations to background threads allows the application to continue to respond to other activities. Nonresponsiveness is very frustrating to users, and it is one of the tenets of the .NET Framework to provide multiple techniques to allow background threads to free the interface to continue to respond during long-running operations. Using background threads in the .NET Framework is simple: you define a delegate with the same method signature as the method you wish to call asynchronously and the CLR will generate BeginInvoke and EndInvoke methods for you. To initiate an asynchronous call, you use the generated BeginCall method using the same parameters as you would with the synchronous call with an additional parameter to specify a call. If a callback is passed to Begin-Invoke, it will be called when the target method finishes and returns. In the callback method itself, EndInvoke is called to get the return value and any in/out parameters. If there was no callback specified in BeginInvoke, then EndInvoke is used on the original thread that submitted a request.

ADO.NET 2.0 adds this same style of asynchronous operation to database tasks. The BeginExecuteNonQuery, BeginExecuteReader, and BeginExecuteXmlReader are paired with EndExecuteNonQuery, EndExecuteReader, and EndExecuteXmlReader to provide an easy way to call database tasks analogous to the way asynchronous tasks are handled throughout the .NET Framework. An example illustrating how to use polling in loop and how to wait for the result is shown here:

```
static void Main()
{
// a long running query
string commandText =
"SELECT s.Name, p.Name, SUM(o.LineTotal) as Sales " +
"FROM Sales.SalesOrderDetail o JOIN Production.Product p ON
o.ProductID = p.ProductID " +
"JOIN Production.ProductSubcategory s ON p.ProductSubcategoryID =
s.ProductSubcategoryID " +
"GROUP BY s.Name, p.Name " +
"ORDER BY Sales DESC";

using (SqlConnection connection = new
SqlConnection(GetConnectionString()))
{
connection.Open();
Console.WriteLine("Run an asynchronous command and loop while
waiting
for response");
Console.WriteLine("Press enter to continue.");
Console.WriteLine();
Console.ReadLine();
LoopAsyncCommand(commandText, connection);
Console.WriteLine("Run an asynchronous command and Wait for the
response");
Console.WriteLine("Press enter to continue.");
Console.ReadLine();
WaitAsyncCommand(commandText, connection);
Console.WriteLine("Press enter to continue.");
Console.ReadLine();
}
```

```
}

private static void LoopAsyncCommand(string commandText,
SqlConnection connection)
{
// Run the command asynchronously using the connection given.
// If the connection does not have Asynchronous Processing=true,
// this will not work and an error will be thrown.
try
{
SqlCommand command = new SqlCommand(commandText, connection);

IAsyncResult result = command.BeginExecuteReader();

// a loop that polls the IsCompleted state
// do some other (trivial) work to show
// that we are still responding on the main thread
// while waiting for the query to run
int count = 0;
do
{
count += 1;
// sleep to slow down the work a little
Thread.Sleep(200);
Console.Write(".");
} while (!result.IsCompleted);

using (SqlDataReader reader = command.EndExecuteReader(result))
{
ShowResults(reader);
}
}
catch (Exception ex)
{
Console.WriteLine("Error: {0}", ex.Message);
}
}

private static void WaitAsyncCommand(string commandText,
SqlConnection connection)
{
// Run the command asynchronously and wait for the result.
// Since we are blocking here on a single thread, it is
// like running the command synchronously.
try
{
SqlCommand command = new SqlCommand(commandText, connection);
// start the result asyncronously
```

```
IAsyncResult result = command.BeginExecuteReader();
// wait for the result (blocking)
result.AsyncWaitHandle.WaitOne();
// call EndExecuteReader to get the results
SqlDataReader reader = command.EndExecuteReader(result);
ShowResults(reader);
}
catch (Exception ex)
{
Console.WriteLine("Error: {0}", ex.Message);
}
}
```

The other way to handle asynchronous query execution is to use a callback interface. In most cases, asynchronous callbacks are the most flexible way to handle asynchronous execution since they allow other work to continue without having to explicitly check for completion of a query. An example of using an asynchronous callback appears here:

```
class CallbackAsynch
{
 private SqlConnection _conn;
 private SqlCommand _cmd;

 // a long running query
 string commandText =
 "SELECT s.Name, p.Name, SUM(o.LineTotal) as Sales " +
 "FROM Sales.SalesOrderDetail o JOIN Production.Product p ON
o.ProductID = p.ProductID " +
 "JOIN Production.ProductSubcategory s ON p.ProductSubcategoryID
= s.ProductSubcategoryID " +
 "GROUP BY s.Name, p.Name " +
 "ORDER BY Sales DESC";

 CallbackAsynch()
 {
 _conn = new SqlConnection(GetConnectionString());
 }

 ~CallbackAsynch()
 {
 _conn.Close();
 }

 public void BeginAsyncRequest()
 {
 _cmd = new SqlCommand(commandText, _conn);
```

```
  _conn.Open();
  _cmd.BeginExecuteReader(new AsyncCallback(ShowResults),new
Object());
  }

  private void ShowResults(IAsyncResult ar)
  {
  SqlDataReader reader = _cmd.EndExecuteReader(ar);
  // do something with the results here
  while (reader.Read())
  {
  for (int i = 0; i < reader.FieldCount; i++)
  Console.Write("{0} ", reader.GetValue(i));
  Console.WriteLine();
  }
  Console.WriteLine("Press enter to continue");
  }
  private string GetConnectionString()
  {
  AppSettingsReader reader = new AppSettingsReader();
  return (string)reader.GetValue("dbconnection", typeof(string));
  }

  static void Main(string[] args)
  {
  CallbackAsynch ce = new CallbackAsynch();
  ce.BeginAsyncRequest();
  // do some stuff here
  Console.WriteLine("Wait until the callback method executes.");
  Console.Read();
  }
  }
```

Multiple Active Result Sets

Related to the new asynchronous capabilities of ADO.NET 2.0, Multiple Active Result Sets (MARS) allows multiple command batches to be executed on a single connection. This is a new feature in ADO.NET 2.0 and is currently only supported in SQL Server 2005. In previous versions, only one command batch could be run at a time on a connection. Both DDL and DML operations are allowed on MARS commands, but they are executed atomically. Although the multiple commands run through MARS are not executed simultaneously, it does offer the ability to economize on expensive connection objects by multiplexing their use. To run commands simultaneously, you will need to use multiple connections, just as in the previous versions of ADO.NET. This multiplexing is not to be underestimated when you consider the expense of maintaining a connection for each of thousands of concurrent users of a busy application. Limiting the number of connections can help provide application performance and scalability.

Because MARS allows you to use one open Recordset to work with another, you can also use MARS to supplant the use of server-side cursors. As an example of how you can use one Recordset to work with another on the same connection, consider the following example, which selects a list of vendors and then selects the contacts for each:

```
static void Main(string[] args)
{
// query for list of vendors
string cmdString1 = "SELECT VendorID, Name FROM Purchasing.Vendor";
// query for contacts given a vendor id
string cmdString2 = "SELECT FirstName, LastName FROM " +
"Purchasing.VendorContact vc join Person.Contact c " +
"on vc.ContactID = c.ContactID " +
"where vc.VendorID = @VendorID";
// create a connection using the config connection string
using (SqlConnection conn = new
SqlConnection(GetConnectionString()))
{
conn.Open();
// create two commands on the same connection
SqlCommand cmd1 = new SqlCommand(cmdString1, conn);
SqlCommand cmd2 = new SqlCommand(cmdString2, conn);
cmd2.Parameters.Add("@VendorID", SqlDbType.Int);
// open a reader for the list of vendors
using (SqlDataReader dr1 = cmd1.ExecuteReader())
{
// move through the reader
while (dr1.Read())
{
Console.WriteLine(String.Format("Vendor:{0}",
dr1["Name"]));
// use the vendor id in the next query
cmd2.Parameters["@VendorID"].Value =
(int)dr1["VendorID"];
// open a reader for the contacts using the vendor id
using (SqlDataReader dr2 = cmd2.ExecuteReader())
{
// move through the reader
while (dr2.Read())
{
Console.WriteLine(String.Format("\t{0} {1}",
dr2["FirstName"], dr2["LastName"]));
}
}
```

```
    Console.WriteLine();
    }
    }
    }
    Console.WriteLine("Press enter to continue");
    Console.Read();
    }
```

Behind the scenes, MARS uses sessions to keep track of the commands that are run. Every MARS connection has logical sessions associated with it. These sessions are cached to enhance performance. The cache will contain up to 10 sessions. When the session limit is reached, a new session will be created. When a session is finished, it is returned to the cache. If the cache is full, the session is closed. MARS sessions are cleaned up when the connection is closed; there is no cleanup while the connection is open. Each session gets a copy of the SQL Server execution environment (execution context, security context, current database, format context, etc.) established by the connection.

MARS is enabled by default on connections to SQL Server 2005. To turn it off, you need to specify that it should not be used in the connection explicitly by setting the MultipleActiveResultSets property to False. If you try to run a MARS operation on a connection with the MultipleActiveResultSets property set to false, you will receive an InvalidOperationException.

Since MARS is only supported on SQL Server 2005, you might need to write code that can work both with and without it. To check for the presence of MARS, check the SqlConnection.ServerVersion value. If the major number is 9, you are connected to SQL Server 2005 and can use the MARS features (or any of the other features specific to SQL Server 2005).

User-Defined Types

As discussed in Chapter 5, "Programmability," user-defined types (UDTs) can be created with the CLR that allows objects and custom data structures to be stored in a SQL Server 2005 database. These UDTs expose data and methods as members of a .NET class or structure. UDTs are treated as first-class types in SQL Server and can be used as the data type of a column of a table, a variable in TSQL, or an argument to a stored procedure.

Mirroring the support provided in SQL Server, ADO.NET can also work with UDTs. UDTs are exposed through the SqlDataReader object as either objects or raw data. They can also be passed as parameters in SqlParameter objects. To use a UDT in a SqlParameter, the assembly must be available on the client. The SqlDbType.Udt type enumeration is used in the Add method for the parameter. The UdtTypeName property can be used to specify the fully qualified name of the UDT as it exists in the database.

To access a UDT object on a client via ADO.NET, the assembly defining the UDT must be available either through the file structure or the Global Assembly Cache (GAC). If you only want to access the raw serialized data, you do not need to have the assembly available on the client. However, if you access the raw data, you will need to create some code on the client side to interpret that stream. You can use the GetBytes, GetSqlBytes, or GetSqlBinary method to retrieve a stream of bytes from the UDT column into a buffer. Examples of how to retrieve a UDT from a SqlDataReader and how to use a UDT as a parameter in an INSERT query are shown here:

```
static void GetUDT()
{
// query to retrieve the udt
string commandText = "SELECT point from Points";
// get a connection
using (SqlConnection connection = new
SqlConnection(GetConnectionString("dbconnection")))
{
Point2D point;
connection.Open();
SqlCommand command = new SqlCommand(commandText, connection);
SqlDataReader reader = command.ExecuteReader();
while (reader.Read())
{
// check for DBNull
if (!Convert.IsDBNull(reader["point"]))
{
// first, we will convert it to a point
point = (Point2D)reader["point"];
Console.WriteLine(point.ToString());
// second, we show how to get the byte array
byte[] array = new byte[32];
reader.GetBytes(0, 0, array, 0, 32);
foreach (byte b in array)
{
Console.Write(b.ToString("X2"));
}
Console.WriteLine();
}
}
// wait for input to show the console
Console.Read();
}
}

static void InsertUDT()
{
```

```
// query that inserts a UDT
string commandText = "INSERT INTO Points (point) values (@point)";
// get a connection
using (SqlConnection connection = new
SqlConnection(GetConnectionString("dbconnection")))
{
SqlCommand command = new SqlCommand(commandText, connection);
// create a parameter for the udt
SqlParameter param = command.Parameters.Add("@point",
SqlDbType.Udt);
// assign the type name
param.UdtTypeName = "[dbo].[Point]";
// assign a new point
param.Value = new Point2D(10.2, 11.4);
// open the connection
connection.Open();
// insert the record
int rows = command.ExecuteNonQuery();
}
}
```

You can also populate a DataSet with UDT data using a DataAdapter. As a simple example:

```
string selectText = "select * from Points";
SqlConnection connection = new
SqlConnection(GetConnectionString("dbconnection")))
// create the data adapter
SqlDataAdapter da = new SqlDataAdapter(selectText, connection);

// create a dataset and populate it
DataSet ds = new DataSet();
da.Fill(ds);
```

Updating a UDT column in a DataSet can be done in one of two ways: creating custom InsertCommand, UpdateCommand, and DeleteCommand objects for a SqlData Adaptor, or use the SqlCommandBuilder to create these commands automatically. The SqlCommandBuilder treats the UDTs as a black box and cannot compare them to the original values in the rows to see if they are to be inserted or updated. To allow the SqlCommandBuilder to determine whether the UDT is to be inserted or updated, you can use a timestamp data column to label the row of data uniquely. Then, the timestamp can be used to make the comparison. An example of creating custom SqlCommand objects to update a SqlDataAdapter with a UDT is shown here:

```
static void UpdateUDTAdapter()
{
 string selectText = "select * from Points";
```

```
using (SqlConnection connection = new
SqlConnection(GetConnectionString("dbconnection")))
{

// create the data adapter
SqlDataAdapter da = new SqlDataAdapter(selectText, connection);

// create a dataset and populate it
DataSet ds = new DataSet();
da.Fill(ds);

// create the commands
//build select command
// create a select command
SqlCommand selectCmd = new SqlCommand(selectText, connection);
da.SelectCommand = selectCmd;

//build insert command
SqlCommand insertCmd = new SqlCommand
("insert into Points (Point) values(@Point)", connection);
SqlParameter param =
insertCmd.Parameters.Add("@Point", SqlDbType.Udt, 32,
"Point");
param.UdtTypeName = "[dbo].[Point]";
da.InsertCommand = insertCmd;

//build update command
SqlCommand updateCmd = new SqlCommand
("update Points set ModifiedDate=@ModifiedDate,
Point=@Point where Id=@Id",
connection);
updateCmd.Parameters.Add("@ModifiedDate", SqlDbType.DateTime,
8, "ModifiedDate");
param =
updateCmd.Parameters.Add("@Point", SqlDbType.Udt, 32,
"Point");
param.UdtTypeName = "[dbo].[Point]";
updateCmd.Parameters.Add("@Id", SqlDbType.Int, 4, "Id");
da.UpdateCommand = updateCmd;

//build delete command
SqlCommand deleteCmd = new SqlCommand
("delete from emp where Id=@Id", connection);
deleteCmd.Parameters.Add("@Id", SqlDbType.Int, 4, "Id");
da.DeleteCommand = deleteCmd;

DataTable tbl = ds.Tables[0];
// modify the data in the dataset
```

```
foreach (DataRow r in tbl.Rows)
{
r["Point"] = new Point2D(40, 40);
r["ModifiedDate"] = DateTime.Now;
}
// this will call the update command
da.Update(tbl);
}


}
```

Bulk Copy

When you need to copy large amounts of data into a database, you will usually use a bulk copy utility because it is much faster than executing individual insert statements for each row. ADO.NET 2.0 has bulk copy built in so you can use a SqlConnection to perform bulk copy operations from a DataReader or DataTable. The SqlBulkCopyOperation object can do single or multiple bulk copy operations that are part of an existing transaction or in a new transaction. Although it is a flexible tool, it is not intended to replace a full function ETL tool like SSIS, which is covered in Chapter 13, "SQL Server Integration Services." Copying data into SQL Server with SqlBulkCopyOperation is simple:

1. Connect to the source system. This is most likely to be a different database than the destination, but it can be the same.
2. Retrieve the data from the source system into a DataReader or DataTable.
3. Connect to the destination system. At this time, the only valid destination for a bulk copy operation is SQL Server 2005.
4. Create an instance of a SqlBulkCopyOperation object.
5. Set properties on SqlBulkCopyOperation for the required operation. Unless the source and destination tables have matching columns, you will need to create ColumnAssociators to map the source columns to their destinations.
6. Call WriteToServer.
7. Clean up by calling SqlBulkCopyOperation. Close or disposing the object.

Note that you can repeat steps 5 and 6 to perform multiple bulk copy operations as necessary to complete a task. This is more efficient than creating a separate instance for each individual operation. Note that if you perform several bulk copy operations using the same SqlBulkCopyOperation object, there are no restrictions on whether source or target information is equal or different in each operation. However, you must ensure that column association information is properly set each time you write to the server.

By default, bulk copy operations are done in their own transaction. You can also integrate bulk copy operations into transactions shared by other database operations and commit or roll back the entire transaction. To do this, you can pass a reference to the transaction into the `SqlBulkCopyOperation` constructor.

The following example illustrates the use of `SqlBulkCopyOperation`. Here, we are using a class called `TabTextReader` to convert a tab-delimited text file into a table that is then written to the server. In the first instance, all of the names in the `DataTable` match those in the destination table. The second instance shows how the column names can be mapped using `ColumnMappings` if there are naming discrepancies. Note that if you map one column, you have to map them all.

```
static void Main(string[] args)
{
// reads a tab-delimited text file into a DataTable with
// the same column names as the Customer table.
TabTextReader tab1 = new TabTextReader("customers1.txt");
// Read another text file with different column names.
TabTextReader tab2 = new TabTextReader("customers2.txt");
// Connect to the target server.
using (SqlConnection destConn =
new SqlConnection(GetConnectionString()))
{
destConn.Open();
using (SqlBulkCopy bcp = new SqlBulkCopy(destConn))
{
// Since all of the column names match for the first file,
// we don't have to use SqlBulkCopyColumnMapping.
bcp.DestinationTableName = "Customers";
bcp.WriteToServer(tab1.table);
// The second file has some mismatches
//and needs to be mapped.
bcp.ColumnMappings.Add("customer_id",
"CustomerID");
bcp.ColumnMappings.Add("company_name",
"CompanyName");
bcp.ColumnMappings.Add("contact_name",
"ContactName");
bcp.ColumnMappings.Add("contact_title",
"ContactTitle");
bcp.ColumnMappings.Add("address",
"Address");
bcp.ColumnMappings.Add("city",
"City");
bcp.ColumnMappings.Add("region",
"Region");
bcp.ColumnMappings.Add("postal_code",
"PostalCode");
```

```
bcp.ColumnMappings.Add("country",
"Country");
bcp.ColumnMappings.Add("phone",
"Phone");
bcp.ColumnMappings.Add("fax",
"Fax");

bcp.WriteToServer(tab2.table);
 }
}
```

Batching

Batching operations can improve application performance by reducing the number of round-trips to the database server. The `DataAdapter` in ADO.NET 2.0 has an `UpdateBatchSize` property that allows changes done through the `DataAdapter` to be done in batches. The default value of this property is 1, which means that each operation is sent to the database individually. This is the same as the behavior in ADO.NET 1.x. Setting the `UpdateBatchSize` to 0 means that all update operations will be done in a single batch. Other values of `UpdateBatchSize` send that number of commands in each batch.

The `RowUpdated` events are fired for each batch that is executed, instead of each row as in ADO.NET 1.x. If there is more than one row affected by the batch, the row details are not available in the `Row` property of the `RowUpdated`. You can access the number of rows processed in the `RowCount` property and retrieve each individual row using the `CopyToRows` method. You will get a `RowUpdating` event for each row that is processed in the batch:

```
// handler for RowUpdating event
protected static void OnRowUpdating(object sender,
SqlRowUpdatingEventArgs e)
{
 UpdatingEvent(e);
}

// handler for RowUpdated event
protected static void OnRowUpdated(object sender,
SqlRowUpdatedEventArgs e)
{
 UpdatedEvent(e);
}

static void Main(string[] args)
{
 string selectText = "select * from Person.Contact";
 using (SqlConnection connection = new
```

```
SqlConnection(GetConnectionString()))
 {
 // create a select command
 SqlCommand selectCmd = new SqlCommand(selectText, connection);
 // create the data adapter
 SqlDataAdapter da = new SqlDataAdapter(selectCmd);
 // set the batch size
 da.UpdateBatchSize = 10;
 // use the command builder to build the update statement
 SqlCommandBuilder cb = new SqlCommandBuilder(da);
 cb.QuotePrefix = "[";
 cb.QuoteSuffix = "]";
 // create a dataset and populate it
 DataSet ds = new DataSet();
 da.Fill(ds);
 DataTable tbl = ds.Tables[0];
 // modify the data in the dataset
 foreach (DataRow r in tbl.Rows)
 {
 r["ModifiedDate"] = DateTime.Now;
 }
 // add event handlers
 da.RowUpdating += new
SqlRowUpdatingEventHandler(OnRowUpdating);
 da.RowUpdated += new SqlRowUpdatedEventHandler(OnRowUpdated);
 // run the update batches
 da.Update(ds);
 // remove event handlers
 da.RowUpdating -= new
SqlRowUpdatingEventHandler(OnRowUpdating);
 da.RowUpdated -= new SqlRowUpdatedEventHandler(OnRowUpdated);
 }
}
// handle the updating event
protected static void UpdatingEvent(SqlRowUpdatingEventArgs args)
{
 Console.WriteLine(String.Format("OnRowUpdating: {0}",
args.Row["ModifiedDate"]));
}
// handle the updated event for each batch
protected static void UpdatedEvent(SqlRowUpdatedEventArgs args)
{
 Console.WriteLine(String.Format("OnRowUpdated:{0}", args.Status));
}

private static string GetConnectionString()
{
 AppSettingsReader reader = new AppSettingsReader();
```

```
    return (string)reader.GetValue("dbconnection", typeof(string));
}
```

Paging

Paging is an important way of controlling the flow of data in applications. There have been many workarounds to provide paged data; ADO.NET 1.0 and ADO.NET 2.0 have ways to page have data built in. The Command object now provides an Execute PageReader method that provides a mechanism for data paging. The Execute PageReader method takes three parameters and returns a SqlDataReader containing a page of data. The first argument defines a behavior in the form of System.Data. CommandBehavior enumeration values. The next argument indicates a row position to start at. The third argument tells how many rows to fetch. Internally, this method creates a server-side cursor against the whole set of data specified in the Command, fetches the required rows from the cursor, and then closes the cursor. As an example, consider the following code that returns a page of data from a command:

```
SqlDataReader GetPage (int idx, int size)
{
    string cmd = "SELECT * FROM Contact ORDER BY ContactID";

    SqlConnection conn = new SqlConnection
        ("server=.;database=AdventureWorks;Trusted_Connection=yes");
    conn.Open();
    SqlCommand cmd = new SqlCommand(command, conn);
    SqlDataReader dr = cmd.ExecutePageReader(
        CommanBehavior.CloseConnection, (size * idx) + 1 , size);
    return dr;
}
```

Large Data Types

As discussed in Chapter 4, "Transact-SQL for Developers," SQL Server 2005 adds a max specifier for the varchar, nvarchar, and varbinary types to allow storage of large objects, up to 2^{32} bytes in size. So, for example, you can create a column of type varchar(max) to hold large chunks of text.

In ADO.NET 1.x, you had to use the GetBytes method to retrieve and manipulate large objects. ADO.NET 2.0 supports the new data types easily with no differences between the way you work with a max value type and the smaller data types. The max types can be used as parameters in stored procedures and retrieved using a DataReader just like the smaller types. For example, you can just retrieve the data element and use the ToString() operator to convert it to a string type, as shown here:

```
while (reader.Read())
{
```

```
    string str = reader[0].ToString();
    Console.WriteLine(str);
}
```

If you want to have more control over the way the data is retrieved from a max type, there is still an option to retrieve the data manually. For varbinary(max) data, you can use GetSqlBytes or GetSqlBinary. For varchar(max) and nvarchar(max) data, you can use the GetSqlChars method to retrieve the data. Here are some examples of using these methods:

```
rdr = cmd.ExecuteReader();
while (rdr.Read())
 {
 SqlBytes bytes = rdr.GetSqlBytes(0);
 }

rdr = cmd.ExecuteReader();
while (rdr.Read())
{
 SqlChars buffer = rdr.GetSqlChars(0);
}

rdr = cmd.ExecuteReader();
while (rdr.Read())
 {
 SqlBinary binaryStream = rdr.GetSqlBinary(0);
 }

rdr = cmd.ExecuteReader();
while (rdr.Read())
{
 byte[] buffer = new byte[8000];
 long bytes = rdr.GetBytes(1, 0, buffer, 0, 8000);
}
```

Schema Discovery

Schema discovery allows applications to retrieve metadata information about database schemas from .NET managed providers. Most of the important information about a database schema such as tables, columns, and stored-procedures can be obtained. ADO.NET 2.0 offers five different types of metadata. At the option of the provider author, support for each of those types can be implemented in the data provider. The SQL Server provider has support for:

MetaDataCollections. A list of the available metadata collections.

Restrictions. The array of qualifiers for each collection that can be used to filter the schema information requested.

DataSourceInformation. Information about the database referenced by the provider.

DataTypes. Information about the data types supported by the database.

ReservedWords. Words that are reserved for that database.

As a simple example, the following code retrieves a list of the available schemas in a database from a connected database:

```
public static void GetSchemaList(string connectString)
{
// retrieve the connection string
ConnectionStringSettings s =
ConfigurationSettings.ConnectionStrings[connectString];
// create the provider factory
DbProviderFactory f =
DbProviderFactories.GetFactory(s.ProviderName);
// create the connection
using (DbConnection conn = f.CreateConnection())
{
conn.ConnectionString = s.ConnectionString;
conn.Open();
// get the available schemas
DataTable schemas = conn.GetSchema();
// write the information to the console
foreach (DataRow r in schemas.Rows)
{
foreach (DataColumn c in schemas.Columns)
{
Console.WriteLine(c.Caption + ": " + r[c].ToString());
}
Console.WriteLine();
}
}
Console.Read();
}
```

Being able to get metadata information is not new to ADO.NET 2.0; metadata access is a part of every data access API. What are different are the flexibility and the expressiveness of the API to allow access to metadata from many different providers. The information provided by metadata in ADO.NET 2.0 is useful in creating customizable database applications. If a user modifies the database schema, the application can retrieve those changes and modify the commands used with the database to match the updated schema.

Statistics

An interesting feature added to ADO.NET 2.0 is the ability to query runtime statistics on a SqlConnection. This can be quite useful when investigating performance problems, but does not replace the appropriate use of performance counters. To enable statistics for a specific instance of a connection, set the StatisticsEnabled property to True. All statistics are counted from the point when the statistics are enabled. Calling the RetrieveStatistics method returns the statistics, which are stored in a list of name-value pairs that exposes the IDictionary interface. To reset the statistics on a SqlConnection, you call the ResetStatistics method. Here is an example of looping through the statistics in the IDictionary:

```
static void Main(string[] args)
{
 string cmdString = "SELECT * FROM Person.Contact";
 using (SqlConnection conn =
 new SqlConnection(GetConnectionString()))
 {
 // enable collection of statistics
 conn.StatisticsEnabled = true;
 // open the connection
 conn.Open();
 // run a query
 SqlCommand cmd = new SqlCommand(cmdString, conn);
 // get the results and loop through them
 // to generate some activity
 SqlDataReader reader = cmd.ExecuteReader();
 while (reader.Read());
 // get the statistics and loop through them
 // to just get one, reference the key in the dictionary
 IDictionary stats = conn.RetrieveStatistics();
 foreach (DictionaryEntry entry in stats)
 {
 Console.WriteLine(String.Format("{0}={1}",
 entry.Key, entry.Value));
 }
 Console.WriteLine("Press enter to continue");
 Console.Read();
 }
}
```

There are 21 statistics available from the SqlConnection, each returning a name and a value that is an Int64 (long in C#). The available statistics are listed and briefly described in Table 6.1.

Client Failover

Database mirroring is an important way to improve the availability of crucial databases. SQL Server 2005 makes it straightforward to configure a mirror of a primary

TABLE 6.1   ADO.NET Statistics Cover Many Aspects of Data Access Performance

Name	Description
BuffersReceived	Count of Tabular Data Stream (TDS) packets received by the provider.
BuffersSent	Count of (TDS) packets (buffers) sent to database by the provider after statistics have been enabled.
BytesReceived	Count of bytes in the TDS packets received by the provider.
BytesSent	Count of bytes sent to SQL Server in TDS packets.
ConnectionTime	Amount of time the connection has been opened.
CursorFetchCount	Count of server cursors fetches.
CursorFetchTime	Amount of time it took server cursors fetches to complete.
CursorOpens	Count of cursor openings.
CursorUsed	Count of rows retrieved through cursors.
ExecutionTime	Cumulative time spent processing. This includes time waiting for replies and time executing code in the provider itself. Some short operations (e.g., GetChar) are not included in the timings.
IduCount	Count of INSERT, DELETE, and UPDATE statements executed.
IduRows	Number of rows affected by INSERT, DELETE, and UPDATE statements executed.
NetworkServerTime	Time spent waiting for replies from the server.
PreparedExecs	Count of prepared commands executed.
Prepares	Count of statements prepared.
SelectCount	Count of SELECT statements executed.
SelectRows	Count of rows selected, including all generated by SQL statements, even if they were not actually used.
ServerRoundtrips	Count of times commands sent to the server and replied to.
SumResultSets	Count of result-sets returned to the client.
Transactions	Count of user transactions started, regardless of whether they are committed or rolled back.
UnpreparedExecs	Count of unprepared statements executed.

production database that can be promoted to primary if the original primary is unable to service requests. The sequence of events when connecting to a server with a configured failover server but without a specified failover server in the SqlConnection is:

1. A SqlConnection is established to a SQL Server that has a mirror configured.
2. The server sends the name of the mirror server back to the SqlConnection object.
3. If the primary server is unable to service requests, the SqlConnection attempts to reestablish a connection to the primary server. If that does not work, the SqlConnection attempts to connect to the mirror database.

To support database mirroring in SQL Server 2005, ADO.NET allows the explicit configuration of a failover server. This can be more efficient if a connection is attempted when the primary server is in a failed state. To explicitly specify a failover server for a connection is to specify the name of the server in the connection string, as:

```
Data Source=server1;Integrated Security=SSPI;
Initial Catalog=Northwind; Asynchronous Processing=true;
Failover Partner=server2
```

Dependencies

SqlDependencies allow the tracking of changes in query results. This works by creating a callback with the server so that when the results set changes, a message is sent to the subscribing client. This is a new feature in SQL Server 2005. Notifications offer a straightforward way of using dependencies from ADO.NET 2.0. Basically, you create a SqlCommand, bind the notification to the command, and execute the command. If the data changes, an event is fired and can be used by the client. This feature is covered in depth in Chapter 7, "Notification Services."

Change Password on Connect

A nice little feature in ADO.NET 2.0 that enhances security is the ability to change the passwords of user accounts without having to log in to the database server directly. Since the SQL Server password policies can be synchronized with the password policies in a domain (see Chapter 3, "Database Security," for more details on this), passwords on databases are more likely to be changing on a regular basis, improving security. Allowing the client to change the password directly lightens the administrative burden of password management.

CONCLUSION

The improvements in ADO.NET 2.0 make it very easy to create highly scalable, disconnected applications. The important enhancements in asynchronous operations and MARS make dealing with multiple clients simultaneously much more efficient. Best of all, these features are built on the asynchronous model already provided by the .NET Framework, so the learning curve is minimal. Batching, paging, and failover are other improvements that ease the application developer's burden. Full support for new features of SQL Server 2005—UDTs, large data types, dependencies and notifications (covered in Chapter 7), and XML support (covered in Chapter 8, "XML in SQL Server 2005")—along with nice-to-have features like bulk copy, statistics, and password changing on connect make it possible to fully leverage SQL Server 2005 in your applications.

7 Notification Services

In this Chapter

- Introducing Notifications
- Notification Applications
- Management and Operations
- Conclusion

Today's information-based economy runs on having access to the right information at the right time. Everyone from stockbrokers and business people to sports fans and online shoppers derive utility from being informed of important events ranging from details about corporate mergers and acquisitions, to who won the big game, or when a package was shipped from the warehouse. We expect this information to be provided instantly, in a variety of formats, and delivered to mobile devices including PDAs, pagers, and cell phones.

Odds are if you're building a data-driven application today you have a requirement to push some sort of information out to users of that application. Your requirement may be as simple as sending a shipment notice email to a customer, or it may be a much more complicated information delivery requirement. In either case, building the software infrastructure to distribute information reliably to a wide variety of devices is, in most cases, a distraction from building the core functionality of your application. This is where Notification Services come into play.

Notification Services provide a scalable and reliable infrastructure for information delivery, giving you the ability to focus on the business problems your application solves. Notification Services were first available as a separate application installation on the SQL Server 2000 platform. With the release of SQL Server 2005, Microsoft has enhanced Notification Services and more tightly integrated it with the database platform. In this chapter, we'll look at Notification Services, including what they are, how you can use them, and how to manage them.

INTRODUCING NOTIFICATIONS

Notifications can come in a variety of formats, but generally speaking, a notification is information that is delivered to subscribers when certain events occur. An example of a notification is an email that is sent to your inbox informing you when a new movie has been released in your favorite genre. Subscribers are those who have registered (subscribed) as being interested in receiving information. The subscription defines the types of events in which the subscriber is interested. Events are occurrences of something. An event may be an elapsed timer; for instance, an event may occur daily or may be based on changes to something such as a new row added to a table or an XML file dropped into a folder. When an event occurs, Notification Services looks at what subscriptions match the event and then sends the proper notification to the subscribers of that event.

NOTIFICATION APPLICATIONS

Notification applications are constructed using a combination of XML and Transact-SQL in a declarative programming model. The combination of declarative XML configuration and Transact-SQL statements makes notification services a very flexible and robust platform for information delivery. The next few sections cover some of the key concepts and capabilities of Notification Services in preparation for building a notification application in a subsequent section.

Notification Services Architecture

For establishing a conceptual background for Notification Services, we must start with the architecture. Notification Services has a very elegant architecture with surprisingly few "moving pieces" for such a robust platform. The Notification Services architecture uses three main processing components to turn data changes into delivered notifications. The major logical processing components of Notification Services include an event provider, generator, and distributor. Earlier in this chapter, we said that Notification Services turns data changes into delivered notifications; now let's look at this process in the context of the three main logical processing components of Notification Services.

We start the process with a data change. The event provider monitors for data changes and turns them into event data. Once notification services receive new event data, the generator processes the data and matches the event data with subscriptions, subscribers, and devices. When the generator matches an event to a subscriber, it generates notification data combining the event data with the subscriber data. At this point, the distributor picks up the new notification data and formats it for delivery to the subscribed device. Figure 7.1 illustrates the major processing and data components of the Notification Services architecture.

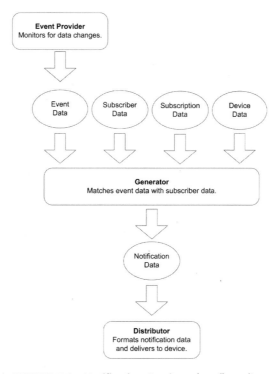

FIGURE 7.1   Notification Services data flow diagram.

Now that we have seen, at a high level, how a data change becomes a delivered notification, the next few sections further establish some key concepts for Notification Services applications.

Subscription Management

The term *subscription management* means configuring who the users are (sub-scribers), what information they want to receive (subscription), and how they want to receive that information (device).

For managing subscriptions, Microsoft provides an API in the form of a set of managed objects (and COM wrappers for the managed assemblies). The managed objects for Notification Services are included in the microsoft.sqlserver.notifica-tionservices.dll file found in the Notification Services bin folder.

Event Collection

Notification Services provides several built-in event providers for implementing your notification application, including Filesystem, SQL Server, and Analysis Services.

Filesystem Event Provider

The Filesystem Event Provider monitors a folder and fires events when files are dropped into the monitored folder. It works exclusively with XML files so events will only be fired if the file has an XML extension. The Filesystem Event Provider can be a very simple way to integrate loosely coupled systems—if a supplying application can generate an XML file, you can consume it using the Filesystem Event Provider and SQL Server's XML support.

SQL Server Event Provider

The SQL Server Event Provider runs a specified select query on an interval to find events. The event data retrieved is then provided to the notification application as events. Filtering of the event data is achieved using the WHERE clause of the select query. SQL event providers can also execute a postprocessing Transact-SQL statement after running the select query. The postprocessing statement can be a stored procedure call, or an INSERT, UPDATE, or DELETE statement. Using a postprocessing statement is a great way to mark data as "processed" so that you are not generating duplicate notifications.

Analysis Services Event Provider

The Analysis Services Event provider is similar to the SQL Server Event Provider except instead of running a SQL SELECT statement on an interval, the provider runs an MDX query on an interval. After processing the MDX query, the results of the query are mapped to the event classes defined for the notification application. Because the event classes are two-dimensional structures, the results of the MDX must also be a two-dimensional structure (e.g., a flat result set).

Custom Event Provider

The built-in event providers in SQL Server 2005 Notification Services are sufficient to meet most development requirements. For the few cases where they are not, you may implement a custom event provider to supply the functionality needed. There are two types of custom event providers, hosted and nonhosted. Custom-hosted event providers run within the Notification Services host, while nonhosted event providers run within their own process. Custom-hosted providers have the benefit of the entire Notification Services management infrastructure and can be managed similar to the other built-in providers, while nonhosted providers operate outside that infrastructure.

Custom-hosted event providers must implement the IEventProvider interface, or if the event provider can be scheduled, it must implement the IScheduledEvent-Provider interface. The interface definitions of these two types of event providers are the same. The following code listing defines the IEventProvider interface:

```
public interface IEventProvider
{
    void Initialize(
NSApplication app,
String provider,
StringDictionary args,
StopHandler stopDelegate);
    Boolean Run();
    void Terminate();
}
```

For brevity, the IScheduledEventProvider interface definition has been omitted; however, the methods defined on that interface and the parameters to the methods are the same as the IEventProvider interface.

The main difference between the different types of custom event providers is in the way they are invoked. After a continuous event provider is initialized, the Run method is invoked one time, while for a scheduled event provider, the Run method is invoked after each scheduled interval has elapsed.

The implementation of a custom event provider is left as an exercise to the reader.

Notification Formatting

In the high-level architecture overview of notification services we saw that the raw notification data is formatted in preparation for delivery. Notification Services provides an XML/XSLT formatter for controlling format of delivered notifications. Using the XML/XSLT formatter you can provide custom formatting XSLT templates that transform the raw notification XML data.

Additional notification formatting capabilities are possible by implementing a custom formatter. Custom formatters implement the `IContentFormatter` interface.

Notification Delivery

Once a notification has been formatted, it's ready for delivery to a device. The delivery of notifications is controlled by *delivery channels*. Delivery channels are defined for a Notification Services instance and carry the final formatted result from Notification Services to an external service for the specific delivery channel protocol for distribution to the device. Notification Services provides the default delivery protocols listed in Table 7.1.

TABLE 7.1   Default Delivery Protocols

Delivery Protocol	Description
SMTP	Sends email notifications.
HTTP	Sends SOAP, SMS, or other HTTP-based notifications.
File	Generates files containing the notification data.

These delivery protocols cover the most common delivery scenarios. If your requirements dictate notification delivery using a protocol other than the default protocols provided by Notification Services, you can implement the `IDeliveryProtocol` interface to supply a custom delivery protocol for notifications.

Building a Notification Application

Constructing a notification application involves a combination of XML and Transact-SQL configuration separated into two parts: instance configuration and application configuration. The instance configuration is implemented in an XML file called the instance configuration file, while the application configuration is implemented in an XML file called the application definition file. The instance configuration file specifies properties that apply to all applications defined for any instance, and what applications run on the instance. The configuration for each application is contained in a separate application definition file. In the next sections, we cover the process of building a Notification Services application that sends email notifications about new movie releases to subscribers interested in the movie from the new release genre.

Instance Configuration File

The instance configuration file is used to control the configuration notification services. The instance configuration file is an XML file that specifies the configuration metadata for the notification services instance, including name, database, and delivery channels. A minimal instance configuration file requires values for the configuration properties listed in Table 7.2.

TABLE 7.2   Elements of an Instance Configuration File

Name	Description
InstanceName	Specifies the name of the SQL Server Notification Services instance. The name must be unique for a given SQL server.
SqlServerSystem	Name of the SQL server that hosts the Notification Services database.
ApplicationName	Name of an application for the Notification Services instance. Application names must be unique for a Notification Services instance.
BaseDirectoryPath	Specifies the path containing any application-related configuration files.
ApplicationDefinitionFilePath	Specifies the path to the Application Definition File (ADF) XML file that controls the configuration of notifications for the application. The path may be specified as a relative path (relative to the BaseDirectoryPath value) or as an absolute path.
DeliveryChannelName	Logical name of the notification delivery mechanism. The delivery channel name must be unique for an instance of SQL Server notification services.
ProtocolName	Specifies the name of the protocol used by a particular delivery channel. Protocols may be any of the default protocols provided with SQL Server 2005 (SMTP, File, or HTTP) or your own custom developed protocol.

The following sample instance configuration file illustrates the structure of a minimal configuration for notification services:

```
<?xml version="1.0" encoding="utf-8"?>
<NotificationServicesInstance
xmlns:xsd="http://www.w3.org/2001/XMLSchema"
```

```
xmlns:xsi="http://www.w3.org/2001/XMLSchema-instance"
xmlns="http://www.microsoft.com/MicrosoftNotificationServices/Configura
tionFileSchema">

    <InstanceName>
CavalierMoviesNotifications
</InstanceName>

    <SqlServerSystem>
Hplaptop
</SqlServerSystem>

    <Applications>
        <Application>
        <ApplicationName>
CavalierMovies
</ApplicationName>
        <BaseDirectoryPath>
c:\cavaliermovies
</BaseDirectoryPath>
        <ApplicationDefinitionFilePath>
c:\cavaliermovies\app.xml
</ApplicationDefinitionFilePath>
        </Application>
    </Applications>

    <DeliveryChannels>
        <DeliveryChannel>
        <DeliveryChannelName>
EmailChannel
</DeliveryChannelName>
        <ProtocolName>
SMTP
</ProtocolName>
        </DeliveryChannel>
    </DeliveryChannels>

</NotificationServicesInstance>
```

Application Definition File

The application definition file is the second piece of configuration needed to build a
Notification Services application. The application definition file contains the metadata that specifies how a particular application should behave. The format of an application definition file is defined by the ApplicationDefinitionFileSchema and
typically contains six distinct configuration sections. A minimal application definition file only requires four of these configuration sections; however, the most com-

mon implementations of Notification Services applications will require the configuration sections listed here. The typical configuration sections are listed in Table 7.3.

TABLE 7.3 Elements of an Application Definition File

Name	Description
EventClasses	Defines the events for which notifications may be generated.
SubscriptionClasses	Specifies the fields needed to subscribe to a notification.
NotificationClasses	Defines the fields used as the content of a notification.
Providers	Configures the source of events.
Generator	Specifies the configuration of the engine that evaluates rules determining when notifications should be generated.
Distributor	Configures the engine that formats and delivers | notifications.

Let's see how these sections are arranged in the XML configuration file. The following sample illustrates the structure of a typical application definition file; the specific configuration within each section has been omitted and will be covered in the following sections:

```
<?xml version="1.0" encoding="utf-8" ?>
<Application xmlns:xsd="http://www.w3.org/2001/XMLSchema"
    xmlns:xsi="http://www.w3.org/2001/XMLSchema-instance"

xmlns="http://www.microsoft.com/MicrosoftNotificationServices/Applicati
onDefinitionFileSchema">
    <EventClasses>
            <!-- event class configuration -->
    </EventClasses>
    <SubscriptionClasses>
            <!-- subscription class configuration -->
    </SubscriptionClasses>
    <NotificationClasses>
            <!-- notification class configuration -->
    </NotificationClasses>
    <Providers>
                    <!-- event provider configuration -->
    </Providers>
    <Generator>
            <!-- generator configuration -->
```

```
        </Generator>
        <Distributors>
                <!-- distributor configuration -->
        </Distributors>
    </Application>
```

Event Definition

Your notification application will process events it receives and turn them into delivered notifications. As part of the application definition file's EventClasses element, you define the events your application will process and the data structure of each event. Defining an event and its fields is similar to defining a table and its columns, where the table name is the event class name, and the column names and data types are the field names and field types of the event. The following event definition was cut from the application definition file listed at the start of this section and defines the NewReleaseEvent, which contains a movie name and the movie's genre:

```
<EventClasses>
    <EventClass>
        <EventClassName>NewReleaseEvent</EventClassName>
        <Schema>
            <Field>
                <FieldName>GenreName</FieldName>
                <FieldType>varchar(50)</FieldType>
            </Field>
            <Field>
                <FieldName>MovieName</FieldName>
                <FieldType>varchar(200)</FieldType>
            </Field>
        </Schema>
    </EventClass>
</EventClasses>
```

Subscription Definition

The subscription definition section of an application definition file serves two different purposes. The first is to define the data needed to subscribe to the notifications. In our application, we are interested in subscriptions to a particular movie genre; for example, if you are interested in Sci-Fi movies, you want to subscribe to receive notifications about new releases in the Sci-Fi genre. Defining the data needed for subscription is achieved by defining a subscription class and the fields of that class. Very similar to the event classes defined in the previous section, subscription classes specify a name along with field names and data types.

The second purpose of the subscription definition section is to specify the matching rule that connects event data with subscribers interested in the data. If you recall from the architecture overview, the generator takes event data, pulls in subscription data, and then generates notifications for the matching elements. The scenario just described is configured using the event rule section of the subscription definition.

Now, let's look at the subscription definition section of our example application definition file, which specifies a subscription class requiring a genre for subscribing to the notifications and includes a matching rule that connects events to subscribers based on the genre:

```
<SubscriptionClasses>
    <SubscriptionClass>
<SubscriptionClassName>
NewReleaseSubscriptions
</SubscriptionClassName>
        <Schema>
            <Field>
                <FieldName>GenreName</FieldName>
                <FieldType>varchar(50)</FieldType>
            </Field>
        </Schema>
        <EventRules>
            <EventRule>
                <RuleName>
NewReleaseEventRule
</RuleName>                          <EventClassName>
NewReleaseEvent
</EventClassName>
                <Action>
INSERT INTO NewReleaseNotifications(SubscriberId,DeviceName,
SubscriberLocale, GenreName,MovieName)
SELECT s.SubscriberId, 'myEmail', 'en-US', e.GenreName, e.MovieName
FROM NewReleaseEvent e, NewReleaseSubscriptions s
WHERE e.GenreName = s.GenreName;
UPDATE CavalierMovies.dbo.Movie SET NewReleaseProcessed=1;
                </Action>
            </EventRule>
        </EventRules>
    </SubscriptionClass>
</SubscriptionClasses>
```

Notification Definition

The notification definition section specifies the data structure of the notification, the formatter, and parameters for transforming the notification for delivery, and the protocol used to deliver the notification. Now we will look at each of these sections.

The structure of the data for a notification is defined by the notification class and its fields and field types. Again, this is similar to defining the data structure for events and subscriptions.

The formatter and corresponding parameters are defined in the content formatter section. In our example application, we are using the XSLT formatter so we specify a base directory path that contains our XSL files and the name of the XSL file we want to use for transforming notification XML into a notification for delivery.

The protocol section specifies the delivery protocol and parameters needed for the protocol. In our application, we are using the SMTP protocol, which requires To, From, and Subject parameters. Additionally, we are submitting a BodyFormat parameter of HTML because we want our email messages formatted using HTML.

```
<NotificationClasses>
    <NotificationClass>
<NotificationClassName>
NewReleaseNotifications
</NotificationClassName>
            <Schema>
            <Fields>
            <Field>
            <FieldName>GenreName</FieldName>
            <FieldType>varchar(40)</FieldType>
            </Field>
            <Field>
            <FieldName>MovieName</FieldName>
            <FieldType>varchar(200)</FieldType>
            </Field>
            </Fields>
            </Schema>
            <ContentFormatter>
                    <ClassName>XsltFormatter</ClassName>
                    <Arguments>
                    <Argument>
                    <Name>XsltBaseDirectoryPath</Name>
                    <Value>C:\cavaliermovies</Value>
                    </Argument>
                    <Argument>
                    <Name>XsltFileName</Name>
                    <Value>NewReleaseTransform.xsl</Value>
                    </Argument>
                    <Argument>
                    <Name>DisableEscaping</Name>
                    <Value>true</Value>
                    </Argument>
                    </Arguments>
            </ContentFormatter>
```

```
            <DigestDelivery>true</DigestDelivery>
                    <Protocols>
                    <Protocol>
            <ProtocolName>SMTP</ProtocolName>
            <Fields>
    <Field>
    <FieldName>Subject</FieldName>
                            <SqlExpression>
'New Release Notification'
</SqlExpression>
    </Field>
    <Field>
    <FieldName>From</FieldName>
<SqlExpression>
'e.jason.cline@gmail.com'
</SqlExpression>
    </Field>
    <Field>
    <FieldName>To</FieldName>
    <FieldReference>
DeviceAddress
</FieldReference>
    </Field>
                            <Field>
    <FieldName>BodyFormat</FieldName>
    <SqlExpression>'html'</SqlExpression>
    </Field>
            </Fields>
                    </Protocol>
                    </Protocols>
            </NotificationClass>
        </NotificationClasses>
```

Provider Definition

Previously, we covered the event definition of an application definition file. The event definition is the data structure that is populated by a provider. The most common default providers are the SQL provider, File provider, and Analysis Services provider. Each of these providers generates events when the necessary conditions are met. The provider definition is used to define what provider(s) to use for generating events and the parameters supplied to those providers.

For the purposes of our example application, we are using the SQL provider to run a query every 60 seconds. The query looks for movies that have not yet been processed as a new release and returns the data needed to populate the EventClass structure we defined earlier.

```
        <Providers>
```

```
            <HostedProvider>
            <ProviderName>
NewReleaseSQLProvider
</ProviderName>
            <ClassName>SQLProvider</ClassName>
            <SystemName>hplaptop</SystemName>
            <Schedule>
                <Interval>P0DT00H00M60S</Interval>
            </Schedule>
            <Arguments>
                <Argument>
            <Name>EventsQuery</Name>
            <Value>
                select g.name "GenreName",
m.title "MovieName"
                from CavalierMovies.dbo.movie m
join CavalierMovies.dbo.genre g
on m.genreid = g.genreid
                            where m.newreleaseprocessed = 0
            </Value>
                </Argument>
                <Argument>
                <Name>EventClassName</Name>
                <Value>NewReleaseEvent</Value>
                </Argument>
            </Arguments>
            </HostedProvider>
        </Providers>
```

Generator Definition

The generator definition section of an application definition file specifies where the application rules will be processed.

```
<Generator>
<SystemName>hplaptop</SystemName>
</Generator>
```

Distributor Definition

The distributor definition section of an application definition file specifies where the notifications will be formatted and distributed.

```
<Distributors>
<Distributor>
        <SystemName>hplaptop</SystemName>
</Distributor>
</Distributors>
```

Deployment

To run a Notification Services application, you must deploy the XML configuration files for a Notification Services instance and application. The NSControl application that ships with Notification Services is used to deploy notification instances and applications. NSControl supports an array of commands and parameters for managing notification services and is installed in the following location:

```
<SQL Server Install Path>\90\NotificationServices\9.0.242\bin
```

All NSControl commands are submitted in a similar way. The general format of commands submitted to NSControl is:

```
NSControl <command> <command parameters>
```

We use the NSControl commands in Table 7.4 to deploy the instance configuration file and the application definition file for our notification services application.

TABLE 7.4   NSControl Commands for Deploying a Notification Services Application

Command	Description
Create	Creates a Notification Services instance and application databases defined in the input configuration file.
Enable	Enables the specified Notification Services instance or a specific component of the specified instance.
Register	Creates registry entries, performance counters, and a Windows service for the Notification Services instance.

The deployment process for our Notification Services instance and application involves a number of steps. The first step is to create the Notification Services instance and application. This step of the process is accomplished using a command similar to the following:

```
NSControl create —in InstanceConfigurationFile.xml
```

The execution of this command will create the instance defined in the InstanceConfigurationFile.xml file and the application whose configuration file (ApplicationDefinitionFile.xml) is referenced in the file.

The next step in the deployment process is to register the instance. Registration of a Notification Services instance creates configuration registry entries and installs performance counters for the Notification Services instance. The variant of the registration command we are using also generates a Windows service for the notification instance.

```
NSControl register —name CavalierMoviesNotifications —service
-serviceusername MyLocalAdminAccount —servicepassword MyPassword
```

Now that the Notification Services instance has been created, you must manually start the service:

```
net start NS$CavalierMoviesNotifications
```

Although the instance and application now exist on the system, they are not enabled by the creation process. The next step in the deployment process is to enable the instance and application. To do so, execute an NSControl command similar to:

```
NSControl enable —name CavalierMoviesNotifications —server
MySQLServerMachine
```

The enable command accepts the instance name, which is defined in the instance configuration file, and the name of the machine hosting the instance. The variation of the enable command that we used in our example enables the instance, application, and all components of the application; however, there are other variations of the enable command that provide more granular control. For more information on them, please refer to the NSControl documentation in SQL Server Books Online.

Adding Subscription Data

Before we can receive notifications, we need to set up a subscriber, device, and subscription. As mentioned earlier, Microsoft provides subscription management capabilities through an API for managing subscriptions. The API provides nice managed classes for building your own subscription management application. For a real application, you will definitely want to use the managed classes to build a robust UI for managing subscription data. However, for simplicity and the purposes of this example, we will use VBScript to invoke the API through the COM wrappers shipped with Notification Services. Note that the methods and properties used on the Notification Services subscription management objects are the same whether invoked through the COM wrapper or directly in the managed API.

```
Dim instance, app, subscription, device

'Create the objects we'll need for establishing a subscription
Set instance =
WScript.CreateObject("Microsoft.SqlServer.NotificationServices.NSInstan
ce")
Set app =
WScript.CreateObject("Microsoft.SqlServer.NotificationServices.NSApplic
ation")
```

```
Set subscriber =
WScript.CreateObject("Microsoft.SqlServer.NotificationServices.Subscrib
er")
Set subscription =
WScript.CreateObject("Microsoft.SqlServer.NotificationServices.Subscrip
tion")
Set device =
WScript.CreateObject("Microsoft.SqlServer.NotificationServices.Subscrib
erDevice")


'initialize the objects
instance.Initialize "CavalierMoviesNotifications"
app.Initialize (instance), "CavalierMovies"
subscriber.Initialize (instance)
subscription.Initialize (app), "NewReleaseSubscriptions"
device.Initialize (instance)

'create a subscriber
subscriber.SubscriberId = "test"
subscriber.Add

'create a subscription for the new subscriber
subscription.SubscriberId = "test"
subscription.SetFieldValue "GenreName", "Sci-Fi"
subscription.Add

'create a device for the subscriber
device.DeviceName = "myEmail"
device.SubscriberId = "test"
device.DeviceTypeName = "Email"
device.DeviceAddress = "e.jason.cline@gmail.com"
device.DeliveryChannelName = "EmailChannel"
device.Add
```

Generating an Event

Finally, with the notification application defined, deployed, and with a subscriber, we're now ready to add a new Sci-Fi movie to generate a new release notification. Our CavalierMovies database already has a stored procedure for adding a new movie, so we'll invoke that stored procedure with the following Transact-SQL:

```
DECLARE @movieId UNIQUEIDENTIFIER
EXEC AddMovie     'Sci-Fi',
'My Test Sci-Fi Movie',
120,
'My Test Description',
2006,
```

```
'PG-13',
@movieId OUTPUT
```

MANAGEMENT AND OPERATIONS

SQL Server 2005 Notification Services applications are managed using the NSControl application, which we have seen used for deploying applications. NSControl is a command prompt utility that supports commands for configuring and controlling Notification Services instances and applications. The NSControl application is like the Swiss army knife of managing Notification Services applications—if you can't manage it with NSControl, it probably can't be managed.

In the next few sections, we discuss some of the commonly used NSControl commands. For a detailed description of all available NSControl commands, please review the reference materials provided in SQL Server Books Online.

Administration

Thus far, we have covered the deployment of notification applications, but that is just one small part of managing the notification infrastructure in SQL Server 2005. In this section, we cover the remaining administrative tasks in Notification Services. These tasks involve management existing instance and application deployments using NSControl commands. Table 7.5 provides a brief description of the administration commands we'll be using in this section.

TABLE 7.5 NSControl Commands for Managing Notification Services Applications

Command	Description
Delete	Removes a Notification Services instance and application databases.
Disable	Stops the specified Notification Services instance or specific component of the specified instance.
Unregister	Removes registry entries, performance counters, and the Windows service for the instance.
Update	Updates the instance and applications with any changes found in the input configuration files.

Next, we'll look at how we can use these commands to perform some common administrative tasks.

Updating an Instance or Application

If your notification application is like most, it probably won't be too long after the initial deployment until you have to make your first tweak to the application. Tweaks can be good things, so don't fret. Let's say your boss gets reports from customers about how cool it is to receive notifications about newly released movies, and they want to extend it to include new releases from the new video game rental service. After updating the application definition file to generate events for new video game releases, you now must update the application that's already deployed on the server. Updating an application is a three-step process, and we'll now walk through the steps needed to update an existing application.

The first step is to disable the existing notification application. To apply an update, the notification application cannot be generating and processing events during the update, so we first issue a disable command:

```
NSControl disable —name CavalierMoviesNotifications
```

The next step is to apply the update to the Notification Services application. To do so, we'll use the update NSControl command providing the configuration file as input. The command to update the application will be similar to:

```
NSControl update —in InstanceConfigurationFile.xml
```

The update process checks the existing configuration against the configuration specified in the input file and determines what alterations are required for the instance and application. If the update reports an error, you must update the instance configuration file or the application definition file to correct the error and run the update command again.

The final step in the process is to enable the updated instance and application. To do this, we'll use the same command we executed following the instance creation:

```
NSControl enable —name CavalierMoviesNotifications —server
MySQLServerMachine
```

That's all there is to it. Your Notification Services instance and application have been updated.

Removing an Instance

It has been said that building software is like making sausage—you don't want to see what goes into it but you like what you get at the end. Through the messy process of designing and developing software you'll build test project after test project, and at some point you'll want to clean up your development system and remove all those Notification Services instances and applications you created to test your ideas. Removing applications is a multistep process, so let's walk through the removal of an instance.

The first step is to disable the instance so it stops processing events. An instance is disabled in the same manner as for updating an instance, using the command:

```
NSControl disable —name CavalierMoviesNotifications
```

Next, you must stop the generated Windows service for the notification instance before proceeding. The service names take the format NS$<instance name>. For example, the service for the CavalierMoviesNotifications instance would be NS$CavalierMoviesNotifications, and to stop the service, type the following at a command prompt:

```
net stop NS$CavalierMoviesNotifications.
```

If you did not register your application using the Windows Service option, this step can be omitted.

The third step to removing a Notification Services instance is to unregister the instance. The unregistration process removes registry entries and performance counters for the instance. Unregistration will also remove the Windows service for the instance if you are using that option. To unregister an instance, use a command similar to the following:

```
NSControl unregister —name CavalierMoviesNotifications
```

The final step is to delete the notification databases for the instance and applications. To do this, we'll use the following command:

```
NSControl delete —name CavalierMoviesNotifications —server
MySQLServerMachine
```

After issuing the command, NSControl will prompt you to confirm the deletion. Once confirmed, NSControl will proceed to remove the Notification Services infrastructure that was generated for the instance.

Monitoring

As we alluded to in our discussion of deploying Notification Services instances and applications, the Notification Services infrastructure comes complete with monitoring capabilities built in. Notification Services monitoring takes the form of performance counter objects that are generated when you register a new Notification Services instance.

The generated performance monitor objects are segmented to monitor at three different levels: component, application, and instance (Table 7.6).

TABLE 7.6   Notification Services Performance Monitoring Objects

Monitor Name	Monitor Scope	Description
Delivery Channels Object	Component	Monitors delivery channels on the local server.
Distributors Object	Component	Monitors distributors on the local server.
Event Providers Object	Component	Monitors event providers on the local server.
Generator Object	Component	Monitors the generator on the local server.
Events Object	Application	Monitors events for an application.
Notifications Object	Application	Monitors notifications for an application.
Subscriptions Object	Application	Monitors subscriptions for an application.
Vacuumer Object	Application	Monitors vacuuming for an application.
Subscribers Object	Instance	Monitors the subscribers for an instance.

CONCLUSION

In this chapter, we introduced SQL Server Notification Services, from concepts and architecture through implementation and management/monitoring. We saw that Notification Services provides a robust platform for subscription-based applications. Using Notification Services for your next subscription-based application will allow you to focus on addressing business problems rather than on building pesky infrastructure.

8 XML in SQL Server 2005

In this Chapter

- XML Basics
- Native Storage for XML
- XML Query
- SQL Server Native Web Services
- Conclusion

Extensible Markup Language (XML) is a standard developed by the World Wide Web Consortium (W3C) that specifies a standard way of structuring data in a human- and machine-readable format. The XML language is really a metalanguage; that is, a language that is used for defining other languages.

Very few technologies have had as significant an impact on software development as XML. The simplicity and flexibility provided by XML are the driving factors that have led to its use in everything from Web applications to data exchange. Some of the major advances in software development over the past few years, such as Service Oriented Architectures (SOA) and Asynchronous JavaScript And XML (AJAX), are built on XML. Innovation using XML has largely been focused on the user interface and middle tiers in software development, but the database has been largely unaffected by the advance of XML. With the release of SQL Server 2005, Microsoft is providing native XML support and storage in the database.

In this chapter, we cover the great new XML features available in SQL Server 2005. First, however, for readers who may not be familiar with XML, we'll cover the basics of XML to provide a background for its use in SQL Server 2005. Readers already familiar with basic XML structure and constructs may skip the next section where we begin the coverage of native XML support in SQL Server 2005.

XML BASICS

To describe languages, XML uses tags that are structured and grouped in a way that provides context and meaning to the data contained within the tags. This is, in concept and syntax, very similar to HTML, which uses tags to define the layout of the data contained within tags. For example, let's look at the following HTML document:

```
<html>
<head>
<title>My Simple HTML Document</title>
</head>
<body bgcolor="red">
<p>Hello World!</p>
</body>
</html>
```

You can see that the document is a set of tags and attributes that are structured with a title in the header and a single paragraph in the body of the document. The tags, for example, are <body>…</body> and <p>…</p>, while the single attribute in the document is bgcolor="red".

An XML document is very similar in syntax to the XML document we just reviewed. Both languages allow a set of tags to be grouped and structured around data to provide some context for the data. It should be noted that the similarity between these two languages is not an accident. Both HTML and XML are based on the Standard Graphics Markup Language (SGML) specification. Although similar in syntax to HTML, XML provides a couple of simple constructs that provide flexibility to application developers.

The two most significant constructs that give XML its flexibility are the ability to define custom tags and to custom define how tags should be grouped and structured. While the HTML language is limited to a specific set of tags and grouping structure, in XML you can define your own. For example, if we wanted to create an XML document that mimicked the HTML example, we could define a document tag containing title and message tags. Such an XML document might look something like:

```
<?xml version="1.0"?>
<document color="red">
<title>My Simple XML document</title>
<message>Hello World!</message>
</document>
```

Using XML you can define, structure, and group tags in any way you'd like, provided you adhere to a set of very simple rules:

All tags must have a closing tag. In our example, for every opening tag such as `<title>`, we have a corresponding closing tag such as `</title>`. Alternatively, if a tag does not contain any child tags, the following syntax is valid `<title/>`, which expresses both the start and end tags in a single tag.

All documents must have a root tag. The root tag of an XML document contains all other tags. Our example XML document uses "document" as the root tag. Notice that this tag contains all other tags in the document.

All tags must be well structured. The nesting of tags within an XML document may not overlap. For example, it would be illegal XML syntax to overlap the message and title tags we defined, such as `<title>My Simple XML Document<message></title>Hello World!</message>`.

Tags are case sensitive. Using different case tag names for opening and closing tags is invalid XML. For example, `<title>My Simple XML Document</TITLE>` is invalid XML syntax.

Attribute values must be quoted. Attributes that do not enclose their values in quotes are invalid. For example, in `<document color=red>`, `color=red` is an invalid XML attribute. Changing this to `color="red"` makes it valid XML syntax.

We have now covered the basic syntax and structure of XML. This section was intended to give those new to XML a brief introduction and serve as a background for the XML support in SQL Server 2005. In the next section, we begin covering the XML support provided by SQL Server 2005; for those interested in learning more about XML beyond the support provided by SQL Server 2005, we encourage you to read some of the numerous books available on the topic.

NATIVE STORAGE FOR XML

Although XML has been an essential technology in many aspects of modern application development, one area in which it has been largely unsupported is in the database. Storing XML in a database, such as Microsoft SQL Server 2000, typically involved storing the XML in either a textual or binary format. Storing XML as text or binary data results in a loss of the context and structure of the XML document. Without the ability to easily query and modify data within an XML stored in a text or binary format, developers often chose to represent XML data as relational structures in the database.

The ISO SQL-2003 standard addresses the storage of XML and introduces an XML data type for storing XML data directly in the database. Microsoft SQL Server 2005 implements support for this standard and additionally provides enhanced capabilities to query and operate on XML data stored in the database.

XML Data Type

With the release of SQL Server 2005, XML becomes a first-class data type. Now developers have many options for working with XML as a type for columns and variables, and input and return values for procedures and functions. Working with the XML data type is very much like working with any other data type in SQL Server. Let's take a quick look at an example of creating a table with an XML column:

```
CREATE TABLE Orders
(
    OrderId int primary key,
    OrderXML xml
)
```

After executing the preceding statement, we can add data to the table using a simple insert statement such as:

```
INSERT INTO Orders(OrderId, OrderXML)
    VALUES
    (
        1000,
        '<order>
            <item>
                <sku>12345</sku>
                <quantity>5</quantity>
                <name>Widgets</name>
                <price>10.00</price>
            </item>
            <subtotal>50.00</subtotal>
            <tax>2.50</tax>
            <total>52.50</total>
        </order>'
    )
```

Validation Checks

XML data in SQL Server 2005 has two variants called typed and untyped. Untyped XML only validates that the structure of the XML data is correct; however, no type validations or specific structure requirements are enforced. Near the end of the chapter, we cover typed XML, which supports XML structure and data type validation through *XML schemas*.

Methods on XML Data Type

For native XML storage to be useful, the system must provide robust capability to retrieve and operate on the XML data. In SQL Server 2005, much of this capability is centered around five methods on the XML data type that provide retrieving and updating XML data—`exist()`, `nodes()`, `modify()`, `query()`, and `value()`. In this section, we will be using some simple XQuery and XPath syntax that is covered later in the chapter. If you are unfamiliar with the syntax of XQuery or XPath, it may be necessary to reference the XQuery Language section of this chapter for reference. Now let's look at each of the methods and an example of its use.

The first method on the XML data type we'll cover is the `exist()` method. This method accepts an XQuery expression and is used to determine whether the item identified in the XQuery statement exists in the XML instance. If the evaluation of the XQuery statement finds the element or elements, this method will return the integer one; otherwise, it will return zero. Before we look at an example of using the `exist()` method, we need to populate the Orders table with some additional data that will be used in this example and the subsequent examples of XML data type methods. Execute the following statements to fill the table with some example data:

```
INSERT INTO Orders(OrderId, OrderXML)
    VALUES
    (
            1001,
            '<order>
                    <item>
                            <sku>234567</sku>
                            <quantity>1</quantity>
                            <name>Foo</name>
                            <price>10.00</price>
                    </item>
                    <subtotal>10.00</subtotal>
                    <tax>0.50</tax>
                    <total>10.50</total>
            </order>'
    )

INSERT INTO Orders(OrderId, OrderXML)
```

```
VALUES
(
        1002,
        '<order>
                <item>
                        <sku>567890</sku>
                        <quantity>1</quantity>
                        <name>Foo</name>
                        <price>100.00</price>
                </item>
                <item>
                        <sku>456789</sku>
                        <quantity>1</quantity>
                        <name>Bar</name>
                        <price>100.00</price>
                </item>
                <subtotal>200.00</subtotal>
                <total>200.00</total>
        </order>'
)
```

Looking at the order XML, you'll notice the last entry does not have a tax node. We'll now use the exist() method to retrieve all orders where a tax node exists:

```
SELECT OrderId
    FROM Orders
    WHERE OrderXML.exist('/order/tax') = 1
```

Executing this statement returns the two order IDs that include tax.

Now let's look at the nodes() method. The nodes() method is particularly useful for decomposing XML data into a relational data format. The method accepts an XQuery statement and returns a collection of special XML data type instances that match the evaluation criteria defined in the XQuery statement. These special XML data type instances returned by the nodes method have the same methods available as a typical XML data type instance, with the exception of the modify() method, which is not available. The following query illustrates how you can use the nodes() method to get an aggregate count of the number of unique items on each order:

```
SELECT OrderId, COUNT(*)
    FROM Orders
    CROSS APPLY OrderXML.nodes('/order/item') as T(C)
    GROUP BY OrderId
```

The modify() method on the XML data type provides the ability to alter specific values stored in the XML and to add or delete nodes within the XML document.

`Modify ()` accepts an XML data modification statement that provides extensions to the XQuery language for altering XML data. We'll cover more about the XML data modification language in a later section. For now, let's look at a simple example of using the `modify ()` method and an XML data modification statement to change all products named "Foo" to "Foo II."

```
UPDATE Orders
SET OrderXML.modify('
    replace value of(/order/item[name = "Foo"]/name/text())[1]
    with "Foo II"
    ')
SELECT Orders.OrderXML
    FROM Orders
```

To retrieve specific data from an XML column, Microsoft SQL Server provides the `query()` method. The `query()` method accepts an XQuery statement and returns the item or items resulting from the evaluation of the statement. The elegant simplicity of the query method on the XML data type illustrates how Microsoft SQL Server 2005 has made great strides in making XML a first-class data type in the database. In the following example, you can see how straightforward it is to extract an order total, stored in XML, from the database:

```
SELECT OrderId, OrderXML.query('/order/total')
    FROM Orders
```

Retrieving XML data from the database is certainly a powerful feature, but there are many times when you really need to extract scalar values from that data. A classic example of this is to create a report that shows the total revenue for a period. For this situation, the `value()` method on the XML data type comes in handy. The `value()` method works similar to the Transact-SQL CAST and CONVERT in that it will return a scalar value of the specified type. The value method accepts an XQuery statement and a valid SQL Server data type for the scalar conversion. To illustrate our example scenario, the following query extracts the order total from each order stored in XML, converts the value to the MONEY data type, and returns the summation of all order totals:

```
SELECT
SUM(OrderXML.value('(/order/total/text())[1]', 'money'))
    FROM Orders
```

We have now covered the five methods of the XML data type. Using these methods, you can operate on your XML data in ways that were unthinkable prior to SQL Server 2005. Those who have worked with XML documents stored in the filesystem and have built solutions that query and parse that data have to wonder, what about the performance of these XML queries? The engineers at Microsoft thought about this too, and along with the XML data type have provided a new index type specifically for XML data.

XML Index

Querying XML data one node at a time to determine whether it's a match can be a lot of work for a database server. Let's consider a scenario in which we have 1000 orders stored in an XML column. The loading, parsing, and querying of each of those XML documents to find, for example, all orders over $100 would involve a significant amount of processing. To reduce the overall amount of work required and eliminate the need to process each XML node individually, SQL Server provides XML indexes that are designed to speed up XML queries.

An XML index uses a tried-and-true technique that has been used to speed relational database queries for years—the B+ tree. Technically speaking, a B+ tree is a balanced search tree in which the keys are stored at the leaves of the tree. By structuring data into a balanced tree, it's possible to achieve significant improvements in the amount of processing required to locate data stored in an XML column.

SQL Server 2005 provides two kinds of XML indexes: primary and secondary. A primary XML index includes all paths and values that are part of the XML data stored in the column—the most common and applicable index for XML data. Here's an example of creating a primary index on an XML column:

```
CREATE PRIMARY XML INDEX OrderXMLIDX ON Orders(OrderXML)
```

When you create a primary XML index in SQL Server, it's actually decomposing the XML into an internal node table where each row in the table is a node in the XML document.

Secondary XML indexes come in three different flavors, and to create a secondary XML index, a primary index must first be created. The three types of secondary XML indexes are PATH, PROPERTY, and VALUE. The secondary XML indexes actually act as an index on the node table generated by the primary XML index. For example, the secondary path XML index optimizes path queries against the internal node table of the primary XML index. Creating a secondary XML index is very much like creating a primary XML index, except you must specify the primary XML index and the type of secondary index to create (e.g., PATH, PROPERTY, or VALUE). Here's an example of creating a secondary XML path index:

```
CREATE XML INDEX OrderXMLPathIDX ON Orders(OrderXML)
    USING OrderXMLIDX FOR PATH
```

When using native XML storage and queries against XML data, proper indexing is essential to ensure adequate system performance. We cover performance optimization tips in Chapter 10, "Performance Analysis and Tuning," but generally speaking, if you will be executing many queries against an XML column, you should probably create a primary XML index. If the majority of those queries are of a particular type, you should consider creating a secondary XML index.

XML QUERY

What if the SQL language had insert statements but no select, update, or delete statements? Such a scenario would seriously limit the usefulness of a database—and the same can be said for XML. Storing data in a native XML format is only useful if there's a simple way to retrieve and manipulate that data. This is one area where Microsoft surpassed the ISO SQL-2003 specification, which only requires the implementation of an XML data type, and implemented support for XML Query. XML Query (XQuery) is a language specification, currently under development by the W3C, for retrieving and modifying data contained in an XML structure.

XQuery Language

XQuery is a functional language that uses expressions to query XML data. An XQuery statement consists of a prologue and a body. In the prologue of an XQuery expression, you can define a default namespace and namespace prefix mappings that can be used in the body of the expression. The prologue portion of an XQuery expression is where you define aliases, if you will, for namespaces. The body of an XQuery expression defines the result that will be returned. The body may include an XPath expression, a FLOWR statement, or a calculation.

XPath Expressions

In its most basic form, an XPath expression defines the location of an item to retrieve from an XML document. One way to conceptualize an XPath path is as a folder path in your filesystem. For example, C:\MyFolder\MySubFolder\MySub-SubFolder specifies the path one would take to locate the MySubSubFolder. Now if we represent this folder structure in XML, it may look something like this:

```
<C>
    <MyFolder>
            <MySubFolder>
                    <MySubSubFolder />
            </MySubFolder>
    </MyFolder>
```

```
</C>
```

To retrieve the MySubSubFolder item in this structure, the XPath expression would be:

```
/C/MyFolder/MySubFolder/MySubSubFolder
```

In addition to specifying the location of data within an XML structure, XPath provides numerous functions that can be used to operate on the data. The list of available functions is too numerous for this chapter, so Table 8.1 is not comprehensive; however, you may consult the SQL Server 2005 help documentation for a full list of supported functions.

TABLE 8.1   Common XPath Functions

Function	Example
Round	SELECT OrderXML.query('round ((/order/total)[1])') FROM Orders
concat	SELECT OrderXML.query('concat ((/order/item/name)[1], " $", (/order/total)[1])') FROM Orders
Contains	SELECT OrderXML.query('contains ((/order/item/name)[1], "Foo")') FROM Orders
string-length	SELECT OrderXML.query('string-length((/order/item/name)[1])') FROM Orders
count	SELECT OrderXML.query('count(/order/item/name)') FROM Orders
sum	SELECT OrderXML.query('sum(/order/item/quantity)') FROM Orders
string	SELECT OrderXML.query('string((/order/total)[1])') FROM Orders

FLOWR Statement

Some situations require more capabilities for processing XML than can be achieved using a simple XPath expression; for example, if you need to iterate through a set of nodes, in these cases the more powerful FLOWR statement comes in handy. The FLOWR statement, which stands for FOR, LET, ORDER BY, WHERE, and RETURN, is a major part of the XQuery language. Technically, Microsoft SQL Server does not support the LET portion of the FLOWR statement. Now let's dissect each of the components of the FLOWR statement.

FOR in a FLOWR statement behaves very much like SELECT FROM in Transact SQL. The FOR portion of the statement lets you define the data the statement will be iterating over. Additionally, in the portion of the statement you may bind a variable to the iteration. Using the FOR statement along with the RETURN statement, you can replicate the basic behavior of an XPath expression. For example, let's transform the following XQuery, which uses an XPath expression into a FLOWR statement (technically, we'll just be using FR):

```
SELECT OrderXML.query('/order/item/sku')
    FROM Orders
```

The result of executing the preceding query contains the SKU XML for each item in the order. Now, let's transform that XPath statement into a FLOWR statement that returns the same results:

```
SELECT OrderXML.query('
    for $sku in (/order/item/sku)
    return $sku
    ')
    FROM Orders
```

The ORDER BY portion of a FLOWR statement works very much like the ORDER BY clause in Transact-SQL, allowing you to return results in a specific order. ORDER BY is an optional portion of a FLOWR statement, and without specifying an order, the nodes will be returned in document order. When using ORDER BY, the data will be sorted in ascending order by default, or you can specify sort direction by using the ascending or descending keywords following the element being ordered. Additionally, ORDER BY supports ordering by multiple elements, which is very similar to ordering by multiple columns in a Transact-SQL statement. The following example illustrates a FLOWR statement that returns the names of items ordered by price and SKU:

```
SELECT OrderXML.query('
    for $itm in (/order/item)
    order by $itm/price[1] descending, $itm/sku[1] ascending
    return $itm/name[1]
    ')
    FROM Orders
```

Filtering data that will be returned by a FLOWR statement is accomplished using the WHERE clause. Using the WHERE clause, you specify one or more boolean expressions that control whether the node is returned. The following example shows how to use the WHERE clause to filter the item returned to only those where the SKU is not six characters:

```
SELECT OrderXML.query('
    for $itm in (/order/item)
    where string-length($itm/sku[1]) != 6
    return $itm
    ')
    FROM Orders
```

XML Data Modification Language

The XQuery language includes some very powerful constructs for retrieving XML data. With XQuery, you can slice and dice XML data in innumerable ways; however, the language lacks any constructs for modifying XML data. In SQL Server 2005, Microsoft has extended the XQuery language to provide support for modifying XML data. These extensions are called the XML Data Modification Language (XML DML) and consist of the statements insert, delete, and replace value of.

insert

To insert one or more nodes or attributes into an XML document, use the insert XML DML command. Using the insert command, you specify the nodes to insert and where in the document to add the nodes. The insert command is defined as:

```
insert <expression>
({as first | as last} into | after | before <expression>)
```

If you recall, earlier in the chapter we illustrated an example of using the exists method on the XML data type to locate an order record that lacked a tax node. Now, let's use the insert command to add a tax node to all records that don't currently have a tax node:

```
UPDATE Orders
    SET OrderXML.modify('
insert <tax>0</tax>
after ((/order/subtotal)[1])
')
    WHERE OrderXML.exist('/order/tax') = 0
```

delete

Deleting data from an XML document is accomplished by using the delete XML DML command. The delete command is very simply defined as:

```
delete <expression>
```

To update our example data and remove the subtotal node from our XML, execute the query:

```
UPDATE Orders
SET OrderXML.modify('delete /order/subtotal')
```

replace value of

In addition to inserting and deleting nodes, the XML data modification language supports the updating of node values using the replace value of command, defined as:

```
replace value of <expression> with <expression>
```

Now, let's look at an example using the replace value of command. For this example, we will update items having an SKU of 12345 and change their SKU to 123456:

```
UPDATE Orders
SET OrderXML.modify('
replace value of ((/order/item/sku[.="12345"]/text())[1])
with "123456"
')
```

As you can see, the XML Data Modification Language extensions to XQuery round out the XML support provided in SQL Server 2005 and help make XML a first-class data type.

XML Schema Support

For those who have not worked extensively with XML, we find that there's often a perception that XML is always an untyped storage mechanism that lacks any sort of structure enforcement. The perception is that as long as the XML within a document is well formed, it is valid and XML has no way of enforcing structure or types. That is a misperception. XML documents can enforce structure and data types using XML schemas.

XML schemas provide a declarative language for specifying the structure and types that are required for an XML document to be considered valid, and are an industry standard way of enforcing structure within XML documents. Schemas are constructed using the eXtensible Schema Definition (XSD) language, a W3C standard language that is itself based on XML.

SQL Server 2005's XML data type can use schemas to support what's called typed XML variables and table columns. Typed XML data elements use user-defined schemas to validate and enforce structure and data type adherence within an XML document.

User-Defined Schemas

XML schemas play an important role in the XML support built in to SQL Server 2005 by enforcing the integrity of data stored in XML data type columns. When an XML data type column or variable is associated with an XML schema, the database will validate that all modifications to the XML adhere to the structure defined in the schema.

In this section, we look at building a user-defined schema using XSD that we can then use to create a typed XML column. Full coverage of the XSD language is beyond the scope of this book; however, there are many great references available online, and SQL Server Books Online can provide some reference information. For our coverage of XSD, we'll stick to the basics. Table 8.2 describes the most common XSD elements we will be using in our example.

TABLE 8.2 Common XSD Elements

XSD Element	Description
xsd:schema	The schema element is the root element of an XML schema, and will typically contain xsd:element names for each of the possible root nodes allowed in the XML document.

xsd:complexType	When defining an element in an XML schema, the node can contain either a simple value or other nodes. For example, `<mySimpleNode>1234</mySimpleNode>` contains a simple value, while the following contains an inner node and is considered a complex type:
	
	`<myComplexNode>`
	`    <myInnerNode1>A</myInnerNode>`
	`</myComplexNode>`
	
	Building a schema for a complex element requires the element's content to be defined within a `complexType` element.

xsd:sequence	When an element contains other elements, the inner elements of the XML structure are defined within a xsd:sequence node. The order of the elements within the xsd:sequence element are preserved and enforced during validation of XML documents against a schema.
xsd:element	The xsd:element node simply defines an XML node, which has a name and a type—either simple or complex.
xsd:attribute	The xsd:attribute node specifies that a particular element may have an attribute. Similar to xsd:elements, attributes have a name and a type.

Now, let's use these basic XSD elements to construct a schema. If you recall, we have been working with an order XML structure for most of the examples, so we will construct a schema to validate. An example of the structure follows:

```
<order>
<item>
<sku>567890</sku>
    <quantity>1</quantity>
    <name>Foo</name>
    <price>100.00</price>
</item>
<item>
    <sku>456789</sku>
    <quantity>1</quantity>
    <name>Bar</name>
    <price>100.00</price>
</item>
<subtotal>200.00</subtotal>
<tax>0.00</tax>
<total>200.00</total>
</order>
```

Describing this structure verbally, we would say an order has one or more items, with each item having a SKU, quantity, name, and price. Additionally, we would say that the order also has a subtotal, tax, and total amounts. We could further describe the specific data types of each of the elements, but we think you get the point. The process for mapping an existing XML structure into a schema is much the same as if you were to map a paper form to a database schema. If we now look at a schema representing the structure we just described, it would look something like:

```
<xsd:schema xmlns:xsd="http://www.w3.org/2001/XMLSchema">
  <xsd:element name="order" >
   <xsd:complexType>
     <xsd:sequence>
       <xsd:element name="item" maxOccurs="unbounded">
          <xsd:complexType>
          <xsd:sequence>
              <xsd:element name="sku" type="xsd:long" />
              <xsd:element name="quantity" type="xsd:int" />
              <xsd:element name="name" type="xsd:string" />
              <xsd:element name="price" type="xsd:double" />
          </xsd:sequence>
          </xsd:complexType>
     </xsd:element>
     <xsd:element name="subtotal" type="xsd:double" />
     <xsd:element name="tax" type="xsd:double" />
     <xsd:element name="total" type="xsd:double" />
```

```
        </xsd:sequence>
      </xsd:complexType>
    </xsd:element>
  </xsd:schema>
```

We now have our XML schema for the order XML structure. In the next section, recover how to load the schema into SQL Server so it is available for use with XML data types.

Schema Management

Before you can use an XML schema to validate XML structures in SQL Server 2005, the schema must be loaded into the database. SQL Server 2005 provides a CREATE XML SCHEMA COLLECTION DDL statement for loading XML schemas. The statement is defined as:

```
CREATE XML SCHEMA COLLECTION [name] AS [xml schema text]
```

To load our example XML schema into the database, we'll use the following command:

```
CREATE XML SCHEMA COLLECTION OrderSchema AS
N'<xsd:schema xmlns:xsd="http://www.w3.org/2001/XMLSchema">
  <xsd:element name="order" >
   <xsd:complexType>
    <xsd:sequence>
       <xsd:element name="item" maxOccurs="unbounded">
          <xsd:complexType>
          <xsd:sequence>
                <xsd:element name="sku" type="xsd:long" />
                <xsd:element name="quantity" type="xsd:int" />
                <xsd:element name="name" type="xsd:string" />
                <xsd:element name="price" type="xsd:double" />
          </xsd:sequence>
          </xsd:complexType>
      </xsd:element>
      <xsd:element name="subtotal" type="xsd:double" />
      <xsd:element name="tax" type="xsd:double" />
      <xsd:element name="total" type="xsd:double" />
    </xsd:sequence>
   </xsd:complexType>
  </xsd:element>
</xsd:schema>'
```

After execution of this command, the OrderSchema is available for use in variables and column definitions using the XML data type.

In addition to the CREATE XML SCHEMA COLLECTION statement, Transact-SQL also provides statements for dropping and altering XML schemas. These statements follow a pattern similar to the CREATE XML SCHEMA COLLECTION statement, and the details of using these statements can be found in the SQL Server help.

We have now defined our schema and loaded it into the database. In the next section, we cover how you can use the XML schema with table columns and XML data type variables.

Using Schemas with XML Data

XML schemas can be used in XML data type columns and variables. Binding a schema to a column or variable ensures that the XML contained in the instance will be validated against the content of the referenced schema. Binding a schema is really quite simple. To attach a schema to a variable or column, simply reference the schema collection name in the data type definition of the variable or column. For instance, if we have a variable definition similar to:

```
DECLARE @myVariable XML
SET @myVariable = N'<order>
<item>
<sku>1</sku>
    <quantity>1</quantity>
    <name>Foo</name>
    <price>100.00</price>
</item>
<subtotal>100.00</subtotal>
<tax>0.00</tax>
<total>100.00</total>
</order>'
```

Changing the declaration statement to the following will bind the XML to the OrderSchema we created in the previous section:

```
DECLARE @myVariable XML(OrderSchema)
```

The same approach can be used to bind XML columns to a specific schema. Earlier in this chapter, we created an orders table with an XML data type column for storing order XML. Now, let's update that column binding it to the OrderSchema for structure validation. To update the Order table, execute the command:

```
ALTER TABLE Orders
    ALTER COLUMN OrderXML XML(OrderSchema)
```

The OrderXML column is now bound to the OrderSchema, and all data stored in the column will be validated against its structure. To verify that the schema is enforced, we'll try to insert some invalid XML; that is, XML that would be considered valid for an untyped XML column but does not adhere to the OrderSchema. Try to execute the following statement:

```
INSERT INTO Orders(OrderId, OrderXML)
    VALUES(7654, N'<order></order>')
```

Executing the command results in an XML Validation error because the schema stipulates that an order must have one or more items along with subtotal, tax, and total nodes. If we update the XML to adhere to the schema, as in the following statement, we'll see that the new data is validated and added to the table:

```
INSERT INTO Orders(OrderId, OrderXML)
    VALUES( 7654,
N'<order>
<item>
<sku>1</sku>
                                <quantity>1</quantity>
                                <name>Foo</name>
                                <price>100.00</price>
</item>
<subtotal>100.00</subtotal>
<tax>0.00</tax>
<total>100.00</total>
</order>')
```

As you can see, XML schemas provide powerful validation capabilities to the XML data type. Whenever possible, you should consider using typed XML for the XML data stored in your database; the validation capabilities will help ensure the integrity of your XML data.

SQL SERVER NATIVE WEB SERVICES

XML Web Services have changed the way we think about interoperability. Web Services provide a simple, open, and flexible way to integrate application services using XML and the HTTP protocol. Web Services were first introduced to the mainstream Microsoft development community with the initial release of .NET. Since that time, the adoption of Web Services and architectures based on Web Services has continued to increase.

SQL Server 2000 first provided an add-on application that linked Microsoft Internet Information Server (IIS) with a SQL Server database to provide query results in an XML format over HTTP. The SQL Server 2000 add-on was called SQLXML, and since the initial release the features and functions supported by the duo of SQL

Server and IIS have increased. Although the feature set of SQLXML has expanded over the years, it has remained a relatively clunky integration of IIS and SQL Server. With the release of SQL Server 2005, the clunky integration has been dropped and SQL Server 2005 can natively host Web Services without requiring the services of IIS.

In SQL Server 2005, it's possible to expose any user-defined function or stored procedure as a Web Service hosted by the database engine. In SQL Server, these exposed Web Services are termed *endpoints*, which are created and managed using Transact-SQL.

Let's say we need to expose a Web Service to our distributors that provides the ID of a genre. The CavalierMovies database already contains a stored procedure that accepts and returns the information we're interested in, so all we need to do is expose that stored procedure as a Web Service. To do so, execute the command:

```
CREATE ENDPOINT GenreUtility
STATE = STARTED
AS HTTP
(
    SITE = '*',
    AUTHENTICATION = (INTEGRATED),
    PATH = '/sql/CavalierMovies',
    PORTS=(CLEAR),
    CLEAR_PORT = 8000
)
FOR SOAP
(
WEBMETHOD 'GetGenreId' (NAME='CavalierMovies.dbo.GetGenreId'),
    WSDL = DEFAULT
)
```

With the Web Service created, we'll now create a console application that invokes the Web Service. The simplest way to include a Web Service in a .NET application it to use the Web Reference proxy generator included in Visual Studio .NET. First, create a new Console Application named WebServiceConsumer. Next, right-click on the reference node and choose Add Web Reference. When the Web Reference dialog appears, specify the URL to endpoint we just created. The URL will adhere to the format:

```
http://<sql server machine name>/sql/CavalierMovies?wsdl
```

Figure 8.1 shows an example of the Web Reference dialog.

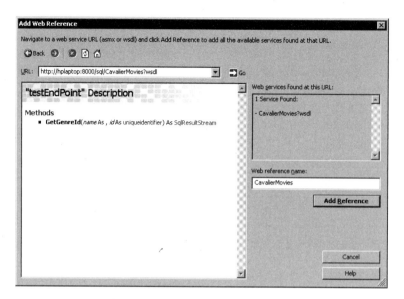

FIGURE 8.1 The Web Reference dialog.

Now, click the Add Reference button to generate the proxy for calling the Web Service. Next, update the Class1.cs with the following code:

```
using System;
using System.Net;

namespace WebServiceConsumer
{
    class TestCavalierMoviesNativeWebService
    {
        [STAThread]
        static void Main(string[] args)
        {
            if(args.Length < 1)
                return;

            String id = null;

            // create the web service proxy
CavalierMovies.GenreUtility ws
= new CavalierMovies.GenreUtility();
// we're using integrated authentication for
// the endpoint so we need to provide the
// credentials for the user that's running
// the application to the proxy so we're
// authenticated properly.  Note that if the
```

```
// user running the application does not have
// access to the database then an exception
// will be thrown.
ws.Credentials =
CredentialCache.DefaultCredentials;

                    // call the web service
ws.GetGenreId(args[0], ref id);

// print the result
                    System.Console.WriteLine
(
"The id of " + args[0] + " is " + id
);
            }
        }
}
```

Now, compile the application. After the compile completes, you can run the application by opening a command prompt and changing to the directory containing the executable for the application and type:

```
WebServiceConsumer.exe Sci-Fi
```

This command executes the application and invokes the Web Service to retrieve the ID of the Sci-Fi genre.

CONCLUSION

We have seen throughout this chapter that SQL Server 2005 has officially promoted XML to a first-class citizen of the database. In doing so, Microsoft has provided developers with a foundation for new and innovative application designs that seamlessly meld traditional relational models with hierarchical XML structures. We're very excited about the new XML capabilities in SQL Server 2005; however, we must also caution you that the new XML support is one more option in your technology arsenal for solving business problems. Just as any other technology choice, it requires proper evaluation and design to select the right tool to address a particular need. These decisions always come with tradeoffs, so choose your tool carefully.

9 Service Broker

In This Chapter

- Asynchronous Queuing
- Programming Model
- Service Broker Security
- Conclusion

In today's world of robust Web applications, it is not uncommon for application designers and developers to see requirements that stipulate an application must scale to support hundreds or thousands of users. Designing a database application that can scale to these levels is a very difficult task. With continuously improving hardware performance and its ever-decreasing price, some designers and developers approach scalability problems by investing in more powerful hardware to handle the loads. Under certain situations, such as legacy applications whose user base is increasing dramatically, throwing hardware resources at the problem can be a cost-effective way to provide increased throughput for an application. Increasing the investment in hardware, however, is not always the most effective solution. For these cases, it's necessary to design scalability into the application.

There are a variety of techniques application developers and designers use to improve both the responsiveness and the scalability of an application. The most common class of changes designers make to improve an application's responsiveness is to use asynchronous programming techniques instead of the traditional synchronous programming model. With traditional synchronous programming, an application performs one task at a time, and while the application is executing a task, it cannot respond to other requests by the user. If the tasks executed by a synchronous application run long enough, the application can appear to "hang." Asynchronous programming can dramatically improve the responsiveness of applications by allowing applications to execute long-running tasks while still responding to other requests by the user.

Asynchronous programming techniques take a variety of forms and address responsiveness issues at different architectural layers. Asynchronous programming has received a significant amount of attention over the past year with the popularity of AJAX (Asynchronous JavaScript And XML) for Web development. AJAX allows developers to build Web applications that seem to defy the conventional wisdom that Web applications can be sluggish and provide less-capable UIs than traditional Windows applications. AJAX is certainly not within the scope of this manuscript, but serves as an example of how asynchronous programming techniques can improve the perceived performance of an application. What AJAX did for the front end of a Web application, a queuing architecture can do for the back end of an application. Asynchronous queuing can maximize scalability while improving the perceived performance of an application.

The tools to build applications using asynchronous queuing have been around for a while. The most notable tool on the Microsoft platform for implementing queuing is probably Microsoft Message Queue (MSMQ). MSMQ was a standalone queuing service that provided no direct integration with the database, which was okay for some applications that did not have a backend database. Applications that use queuing but lack a backend database are a minority of the applications that use the architecture. A significant portion of applications that use an asynchronous queuing architecture will have a corresponding backend database. Without integration into the database, things like transaction management require complicated and slow solutions such as distributed transactions (two-phase commits) to ensure data integrity. With a majority of queuing applications backed by a database and the problems that arise when messaging and databases are not integrated it just makes sense to move messaging services into the database platform—which is what SQL Server Service Broker is all about.

Microsoft SQL Server 2005 Service Broker provides built-in support for the asynchronous queuing architecture. In the remainder of this chapter, we cover asynchronous queuing and the built-in support provided by SQL Server 2005 Service Broker.

ASYNCHRONOUS QUEUING

Asynchronous queuing is an architecture that enables applications to send requests to other services and continue execution without waiting for the results of the request. The classic example of a messaging-based architecture is email. You compose an email message for your local government official and send it. The message is routed through the Internet and eventually ends up in the inbox of the official to whom you are writing. Once the official has time to read your message, he or she writes a reply and the process starts again.

In this example, after writing the message and clicking Send, you were able to continue with other tasks while the message was processed and routed to the appropriate server and inbox. This loosely coupled architecture abstracts the specifics of the receiver's server and inbox from the sender, allowing the communication to occur. Another significant benefit of the asynchronous queued architecture is that you did not have to wait at your computer to receive the response from your government official. While it may seem a bit absurd to wait at your computer for response to a message you sent, that's exactly what happens with synchronous programming—every task must complete before you can move on to the next. This concept is better demonstrated by the graphical timeline in Figure 9.1.

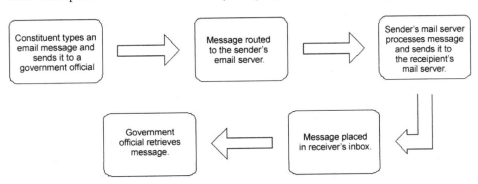

FIGURE 9.1 Graphical timeline illustrating an asynchronous queued architecture and a synchronous architecture.

Asynchronous queuing is a very powerful design option for building scalable applications. The next few sections cover some of the key points of an asynchronous queued system and how SQL Server 2005 addresses those points.

Message Ordering and Coordination

Asynchronous message-based infrastructures typically process messages in the order in which they were received. For example, if message A was sent to a queue and message B was later sent to the same queue, but due to routing delays, the queue received message B before message A, then the traditional messaging infrastructure would process message B first and then message A. For some applications, this ordering difference can pose a major problem and lead designers to seek alternative architectures for problems where message ordering is important. Microsoft SQL Server 2005's built-in Service Broker solves this ordering problem and will guarantee that messages are processed in the order in which they were sent to the queue—not the order in which they were received in the queue. Therefore, using the previous example, with Service Broker, the system would process message A and then message B, because that was the order in which the messages were sent to the queue—even though message B was received before message A.

In addition to message ordering, another common problem in asynchronous message-based applications is the identification of duplicate messages. Most applications want to process messages once and only once and in the order the messages were sent. Traditional messaging infrastructures leave the identification and processing of duplicate messages up to the application. Service Broker supports duplicate message identification and guarantees that your application will process messages once and in the proper order.

Transactions

Messaging services that live outside the database platform, such as MSMQ, must use special semantics and protocols to ensure data integrity. These semantics and protocols are generally called two-phase commits. The two-phase commit was introduced in the 1980s and provides a way to handle transactions across distributed systems. A two-phase commit, also called a distributed transaction, allows multiple distributed database operations to be performed and simultaneously commit all transactions or simultaneously roll back all of the transactions if any transaction fails.

Distributed transactions are notoriously slow, and can typically be an order of magnitude slower than the same transaction managed entirely by the database engine. Slowing transaction processing will increase the time database tables are "locked" and can ultimately bring performance to a crawl. When designing high-throughput applications, distributed transactions should be avoided wherever possible. When messaging services are provided outside the database engine, however, distributed transactions are the only viable option you have for ensuring data integrity.

Moving messaging services into the database engine can in most cases eliminate the need for distributed transactions. With messaging services provided by the database, the engine can manage all its transactions internally, just as it would for a stored procedure updating data, without needing the services of an external transaction coordinator. Transactions are managed using the same familiar BEGIN TRANSACTION and

COMMIT TRANSACTION semantics. The performance improvements gained by switching from distributed transactions can be quite dramatic.

Multithreading and Multireader Queues

There are generally two ways to scale queue processing: add queues or add readers. The first approach we'll discuss is to scale queue processing with multiple queues. Every time you add a queue, you add a corresponding reader for that queue. In real life, you'll find this sort of approach at the checkout of your local mega discount store.

Adding queues can work pretty well in both a messaging system and in real life, as long as each "job" requires about the same amount of time to complete. When the jobs require variable amounts of time to complete, some queues can back up while others may be empty. Imagine this situation at your mega discount store checkout. We've all been there. You enter the express checkout line with only one person in front of you and the cashier has to call for a price check on one of the items that person is buying. You're only purchasing a single item, but by the time the cashier gets a price check, someone with a whole cart full of items can be checked out and headed out the door. The same thing can happen in a messaging system when a short-running task is blocked by a long-running task, even when other queues may be empty.

Another approach to improve queue processing throughput is to have a single queue and add multiple readers to pull messages from the queue. This approach helps to balance the overall workload across multiple readers. With a multiple reader approach, you would never have a situation as described in the multiple queue approach where the one queue is backed up while another sits idle. In a single queue, multiple reader architecture, as long as there is work to be processed you will not have idle readers. In real life, you'll typically see this sort of queuing approach in customer service departments where there is a single queue with a winding velvet rope herding you to a counter with multiple agents. Once an agent becomes available, the next person is pulled from the queue.

It can be difficult to implement multiple queue readers on multiple threads while ensuring that a message is only processed one time. In most applications, it is imperative that messages not be processed multiple times. Think about the situation where you have built your own home-grown messaging infrastructure for processing incoming orders. To maximize the throughput of your system, you implement multiple queue readers so the system can process multiple messages simultaneously. Imagine the consequences to your company if your messaging infrastructure did not synchronize the resources properly and sent the same order for 10,000 widgets multiple times to the factory floor—you just might be looking for a new job.

Support for multiple queue readers and the assurance that message will be processed one and only one time comes out of the box with SQL Server 2005

Service Broker. To take it one step further, Service Broker also provides the capability to dynamically grow or shrink the number of queue readers based on the rate of incoming messages. The dynamic management of queue readers is called activation.

Message Fragmentation

Another feature of Service Broker that is designed to improve the overall throughput of the messaging system is called message fragmentation. When large messages are sent to a queue, they may be divided into smaller fragments and sent to the queue, which then reassembles the small fragments.

Breaking large messages into smaller pieces helps the overall throughput of the system by allowing small messages to be processed at the same time as fragments of larger messages are being processed. Fragmenting large messages is particularly beneficial if you are sending large messages between SQL Server systems across a relatively slow network.

Another benefit of fragmenting large messages is the retransmission of a message if it failed to reach the queue. In the event a message fragment fails to reach the queue and must be retransmitted, Service Broker will only retransmit the individual message fragment, not the entire message.

Load Distribution

SQL Server Service Broker is flexible enough to scale up, using more processing power on the same machine, or scale out, distributing the message processing across multiple SQL Server machines. We discussed the scale-up capability earlier in this chapter. The scale-up support is called activation, and if you recall it involves dynamically bringing queue readers online to match the rate of incoming messages. SQL Server can also scale out to distribute loads across multiple machines.

Service Broker routing and message forwarding allows you to scale your messaging-based application across multiple machines. Message forwarding allows a Service Broker instance to accept a message and forward it to another Service Broker instance. Because the routing of the message to another instance is handled totally by Service Broker, your application can be completely oblivious to whether the load is a single instance or if there are 10 instances sharing the load.

Now that we have covered some general messaging concepts, issues with messaging, and briefly touched on how Service Broker addresses the issues, we will now look into the Service Broker programming model.

PROGRAMMING MODEL

The programming model for Service Broker involves just a handful of types used for creating applications: Message Type, Contract, Service, and Queue. These types are all interrelated and required for building a Service Broker application. We cover each of the types later in this section, but first, let's walk through these types and their relationships so we can start with a conceptual understanding of the various pieces of the Service Broker programming model. The following is a 50,000-foot view of the programming model:

- A *Service* reads messages from a *Queue*.
- The Service operates under one or more *Contracts*.
- Each Contract specifies one or more *Message Types* allowed under the Contract.
- Optionally, a Message Type may stipulate a particular XML *Schema* to which messages must adhere.

Figure 9.2 illustrates the high-level Service Broker programming model.

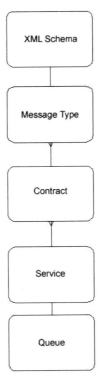

FIGURE 9.2 Service Broker programming model.

All of the types found in the Service Broker programming model are created, managed, and operated on using Transact-SQL. Programming Service Broker applications does not require you to learn an extensive set of specialized messaging APIs. The few Transact-SQL extensions for Service Broker can be picked up easily, which is a significant benefit over some other messaging platforms that require developers to learn extensive APIs just to send and process messages.

In the remainder of this section, we take a closer look at the pieces that make up the Service Broker programming model. As part of this coverage, we will be constructing a sample Service Broker application.

Message Types

To have a meaningful conversation with someone, you both need to understand the language the other is speaking. The same can be said for Service Broker conversations; for a conversation to occur, the information being sent and the response that is returned must be known. This information is specified using message types, which specify the type of data that will be exchanged between sender and receiver.

Message Types typically specify that the data exchanged (e.g., messages) follow an XML format. The unspoken rule is that messages should contain XML data; however, this is not required. In fact, messages can contain almost any kind of data. To be more precise, messages can contain any kind of data that can be converted and stored as varbinary(max), which is the data type used to hold the messages in a queue.

Now that we have learned a little more about message types, let's look at how one would create a message type. As mentioned previously, each of the types in the Service Broker programming model can be managed using Transact-SQL. To create a Message Type, use the following Transact-SQL syntax:

```
CREATE MESSAGE TYPE <name>
[VALIDATION = {NONE | EMPTY | WELL_FORMED_XML |
    VALID_XML WITH SCHEMA COLLECTION <schema name>]
```

The syntax for creating messages is relatively straightforward. The only required input for creating a Message Type is the name of the type. The optional VAL-IDATION portion of the statement is where you specify how Service Broker should check messages for adherence to a particular format. It's a good idea to use XML for your messages and to specify a schema for validation. To do this, use the VALID_XML WITH SCHEMAL COLLECTION option. Using XML and schemas helps your Service Broker application more easily process messages by ensuring message data adheres to a specific structure, making it easier for you to parse, query, and process the message content. The other options for validation include NONE, which can be used if you want to pass anything other than XML; for example, passing a date as the content of a message. The EMPTY validation option will check that the message has no content, and can be useful if you just want to receive notification or acknowledgment in a message but no data. The remaining option is WELL_FORMED_XML, which will verify that the message content contains structurally valid XML data but does not enforce a particular format or other restrictions on the arrangement or content of the XML data.

Let's look at an example of creating a message type. Following our recommendation, we will create a message type that uses an XML schema for validation, so we first create the schema by executing:

```
CREATE XML SCHEMA COLLECTION MovieRatingSchema AS
N'<xsd:schema xmlns:xsd="http://www.w3.org/2001/XMLSchema">
  <xsd:element name="movieRating" >
   <xsd:complexType>
    <xsd:sequence>
        <xsd:element name="customerId" type="xsd:string" />
         <xsd:element name="movieName" type="xsd:string" />
        <xsd:element name="stars" type="xsd:int" />
    </xsd:sequence>
   </xsd:complexType>
  </xsd:element>
</xsd:schema>'
```

As you may have guessed from the schema, our Message Type and the entire sample application is for processing customer movie ratings. We're sure you have seen the star ratings on various Web sites that contain music or movies, where you click on a rating and through the magic of AJAX an update occurs behind the scenes to store your rating. We will be constructing a scalable backend service for processing these types of events. Now, let's create the message type for our Movie Rating Service Broker application:

```
CREATE MESSAGE TYPE [//CavalierMovies.com/MovieRating]
VALIDATION = VALID_XML WITH SCHEMA COLLECTION MovieRatingSchema
```

For our Message Type, we specify a name and the XML schema we created earlier for validation. Notice the format of the Message Type name, which follows the generally accepted naming convention for Service Broker types:

```
//<company domain>/<unique path and name>
```

With our new Message Type we just created, we can now create contracts that stipulate usage of the Message Type.

Contracts

When doing business with another company or person, it's a good idea to have a contract to protect the interests of everyone involved. Contracts can be very specific, but typically provide a framework that outlines the expectations of the interaction.

Contracts, in the context of SQL Server Service Broker, are no different. Service Broker contracts define what message types can be sent and what direction they will be sent. You can think of a contract as providing a framework that describes the rules of a Service Broker conversation. Let's look at how to create a Service Broker contract:

```
CREATE CONTRACT <name>
    (
{<message_type_name> SENT BY {INITIATOR | TARGET | ANY} }
[ ,...n]
)
```

All contracts require a name and one or more Message Type specifications. The Message Type specification portion of the statement requires defining who will be sending the messages. Specifying INTIATOR means the contract will allow the initiating service to send messages of the specified type. The TARGET option means the receiving service can send messages of the specified type, and the ANY option means that either the initiating service or the receiving service can send messages of the specified type. The ANY option is provided because a message type can be included in a contract definition only one time. That means it would be invalid to say TYPEA SENT BY INITIATOR, TYPEA SENT BY TARGET. Instead, you must create the contract using TYPEA SENT BY ANY.

The sample application we are building is a "fire and forget" Service Broker application. We are only interested in sending messages from the initiating service to the target service. To specify the contract for our sample application, execute:

```
CREATE CONTRACT
[//CavalierMovies.com/SpecifyMovieRating]
(
    [//CavalierMovies.com/MovieRating] SENT BY INITIATOR
)
```

Notice the naming convention the contract follows is the same pattern we used for the Message Type and we have specified the Message Type name we created earlier. Next, we will look at queues. Although queues do not directly use a contract, services use contracts, so the ordering may seem a little counterintuitive. However, because of the creation dependencies, in order to create a service, we have to first have a queue.

Queues

Queues make up the core of the Service Broker messaging platform. In a nutshell, queues store messages; therefore, the receivers are able to process them as they please. The sender of a message does not have to wait on the receiver to process the message because it is persisted in the query awaiting retrieval and processing. Since the sender doesn't have to wait for the message to be processed, applications can achieve dramatic improvements in throughput and scalability of some operations.

The job of a queue is to store incoming messages until a reader becomes available to process them. Queue readers are known as service programs and are responsible for reading messages from a queue and then processing the messages. Figure 9.3 illustrates the flow of messages through a queue to be processed by a service program.

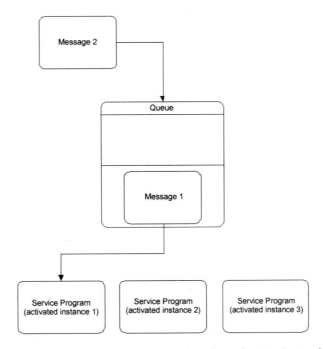

FIGURE 9.3   Flow of message data through a Service Broker queue.

You may recall our brief discussion earlier in the chapter about activation and how Service Broker can scale up on a singe machine. Activation involves a balancing of throughput handled by a queue and service programs. The activation process works by automatically creating instances of service programs to process messages from a queue when all existing service programs are busy processing messages. The activation option is specified when a queue is created and provides parameters to control what service program should be called, and the maximum number of service programs to have running at any given time.

The term *service program* sounds quite exotic and specific to Service Broker; however, in reality, a service program is nothing more than a stored procedure. Service programs do all the heavy lifting in a Service Broker application, including reading and processing all messages in the queue.

Now, let's review the syntax for creating a queue. The following DDL syntax creates Service Broker queues:

```
CREATE QUEUE <name>
[WITH
    ACTIVATION
    (
        PROCEDURE_NAME = <proc name>,
        MAX_QUEUE_READERS = <num of queue readers>,
        EXECUTE AS {SELF | '<user name>' | OWNER}
    )]
```

The CREATE QUEUE command has several additional optional components we have omitted for brevity. The SQL Server online help lists the full syntax if you are interested.

CREATE QUEUE requires only a name to be specified; however, the ACTIVATION segment of the command is something you will want to specify the majority of the time. If the ACTIVATION portion of the command is not specified, you will have to manually invoke a service program to read from and process messages from the queue. A scenario in which you would not specify the ACTIVATION parameters would be if you want to process messages in a batch instead of as they are sent to the queue. ACTIVATION parameters include the name of the stored procedure to invoke, the maximum number of readers that should be running at any given time, and since the activation happens automatically, you must specify who the procedure should be run as. Let's see how this syntax works with an example.

We are interested in processing messages as they are sent to the queue, so we definitely want to use the ACTIVATION option. To do so, we have to first create the stored procedure that will be activated before we can create the queue.

This procedure processes movie rating messages by reading the first message from the queue, extracting some data (customer, movie, and rating) from the message XML, adding the review to the database, and finally ending the conversation and committing the transaction. To create the service program stored procedure, execute:

```
CREATE PROCEDURE MovieRatingProcedure
AS
    BEGIN TRANSACTION;
    DECLARE @message XML,
        @messageTypeName NVARCHAR(128),
        @response XML,
        @conversationGroup UNIQUEIDENTIFIER,
```

```
        @conversationHandle UNIQUEIDENTIFIER,
        @customerId UNIQUEIDENTIFIER,
        @movieName VARCHAR(200),
        @stars INT,
        @reviewId UNIQUEIDENTIFIER;

SET @message = NULL;
SET @messageTypeName = NULL;
SET @conversationGroup = NULL;
SET @conversationHandle = NULL;
SET @customerId = NULL;
SET @movieName = NULL;
SET @stars = NULL;

WAITFOR
(
    RECEIVE TOP(1)
    @conversationHandle = conversation_handle,
    @messageTypeName = message_type_name,
    @message = CAST(message_body AS XML)
    FROM [//CavalierMovies.com/MovieRatingQueue]
), TIMEOUT 5000;

IF @conversationHandle IS NOT NULL
BEGIN
IF @messageTypeName
    <> '//CavalierMovies.com/MovieRating'
    BEGIN
        END CONVERSATION @conversationHandle;
        COMMIT TRANSACTION;
        RETURN;
    END;

    SET @customerId = @message.value
        (
        '(/movieRating/customerId/text())[1]',
        'uniqueidentifier'
        );

    SET @movieName = @message.value
        (
        '(/movieRating/movieName/text())[1]',
        'varchar(200)'
        );
```

```
            SET @stars = @message.value
                (
                '(/movieRating/stars/text())[1]',
                'int'
                );

            EXEC CavalierMovies.dbo.AddReview@customerId,
                @movieName,
                @stars,
                NULL,
                @reviewId OUTPUT;

            END CONVERSATION @conversationHandle;
        END
    COMMIT TRANSACTION;
```

With the service program ready, we can now create the queues for our example application. To do so, we specify the service program, limit the number of queue readers to 10, and have the procedure run as the owner. Execute the following command to create the queue:

```
CREATE QUEUE [//CavalierMovies.com/MovieRatingQueue] WITH
    ACTIVATION
    (
        PROCEDURE_NAME = MovieRatingProcedure,
        MAX_QUEUE_READERS = 10,
        EXECUTE AS OWNER
    )
```

With a queue created, we have almost generated all the messaging infrastructure we'll need for our application. The one remaining piece is the service, and we will cover that next.

Services

Services act as a logical grouping of queues and contracts. Services are the endpoints in a Service Broker application and are the logical source and destination of conversations. The syntax to create a service is straightforward. The following Transact-SQL syntax is used for creating services:

```
CREATE SERVICE <name>
    ON QUEUE <queue name>
    [(<contract name> [,...n])]
```

The Transact-SQL for creating a service requires a name and a queue. Optionally, you may specify one or more contracts for messages sent to the queue.

Let's switch back to our example application. Since we now have a contract and queue for our example application, we can go ahead and create the service. Execute the following command to generate the service:

```
CREATE SERVICE [//CavalierMovies.com/MovieRatingService]
    ON QUEUE [//CavalierMovies.com/MovieRatingQueue]
([//CavalierMovies.com/SpecifyMovieRating])
```

All of the infrastructure pieces of our Service Broker application are in place. We have created a message type, a contract, queue, service process, and now a service. These pieces provide all the plumbing for our application. Next, we'll look at how we can actually send messages through this plumbing by using a dialog conversation.

Dialog Conversations

Services communicate via a dialog conversation. The dialog is established by specifying the sending and receiving services along with the contract under which the dialog will operate. Dialogs can be created where the sending and receiving services are the same—we actually have this situation in our example application. Whether a dialog is created for two distinct services or a service is having a conversation with itself, dialogs will ensure that messages are ordered; that is, they are delivered in the order in which they are sent. This is called exactly once in order (EOIO) delivery. The ordering of messages in a dialog is persisted and will survive restarts and crashes.

Dialog conversations are uniquely identified by a conversation handle. The conversation handle is important, because after a dialog is established, this handle is used to send messages between the services in the dialog.

Sending a message is a two-step process. First, you must establish a dialog between two services, and then send the message. Establishing a dialog and sending a message is accomplished using two new Transact-SQL commands: BEGIN DIALOG and SEND ON CONVERSATION, respectively. First, let's look at BEGIN DIALOG. The following Transact-SQL is used to establish a dialog between two services:

```
BEGIN DIALOG @dialogHandle
    FROM SERVICE <initiator service name>
    TO SERVICE '<string representing name of target service>'
    [ ON CONTRACT <contract name> ]
```

The begin dialog statement defined here includes the most widely used options for establishing a dialog. For the full list of parameters and options, please see the SQL Server online help.

Now, let's cover the meaning of each of these parameters. The first parameter is the dialog handle variable. The dialog handle variable must be declared prior to passing in to the BEGIN DIALOG statement and should be declared as a UNIQUEIDENTI-FIER. When the dialog is created, the dialogHandle variable will be populated with the GUID representing the dialog conversation. The FROM SERVICE segment of the command names the initiating service, and the TO SERVICE portion of the command specifies a string containing the name of the target service. Optionally, the dialog can specify a contract that dictates the types of messages that may be exchanged as part of the conversation.

The SEND ON CONVERSATION command is the second step in submitting a message for processing. The Transact-SQL for SEND ON CONVERSATION is specified as:

```
SEND
    ON CONVERSATION conversation_handle
    [ MESSAGE TYPE message_type_name ]
    [ ( message_body_expression ) ]
```

The first parameter to this command is the conversation or dialog handle that was created during the call to the BEGIN DIALOG command. The remaining options allow you to specify the message type and the message content.

Now that we have covered the syntax of sending messages to Service Broker, let's continue our example and build a stored procedure we can call to submit our messages. Using a stored procedure to establish a dialog, build, and then send a message is a great way to expose your Service Broker application to a wide array of users—everything from other stored procedures to .NET Web applications can easily execute stored procedures and provide your application to the masses. Our example procedure is called FireAndForgetMovieReview. We call it "fire and forget" because it sends the message to the service but doesn't have to wait for the message to be processed, returning immediately after the message is sent to the queue. The following code listing illustrates a stored procedure that invokes our Service Broker application:

```
CREATE PROCEDURE FireAndForgetMovieReview
    (
        @customerId UNIQUEIDENTIFIER,
        @movieName VARCHAR(200),
        @stars INT

AS
    DECLARE @dialogHandle UNIQUEIDENTIFIER,
        @movieRating XML(MovieRatingSchema) ;

    SET @movieRating =
```

```
                    '<movieRating>' +
                        '<customerId>' +
                            CAST(@customerId AS VARCHAR(36)) +
                        '</customerId>' +
                        '<movieName>' +
                            @movieName +
                        '</movieName>' +
                        '<stars>' +
                            str(@stars) +
                    '</stars>' +
'</movieRating>';

        BEGIN DIALOG @dialogHandle
            FROM SERVICE
                [//CavalierMovies.com/MovieRatingSenderService]
            TO SERVICE
                '//CavalierMovies.com/MovieRatingReceiverService'
            ON CONTRACT
                [//CavalierMovies.com/SpecifyMovieRating]
            WITH ENCRYPTION = OFF;

        SEND ON CONVERSATION @dialogHandle
            MESSAGE TYPE [//CavalierMovies.com/MovieRating]
            (@movieRating) ;
```

Now, to test the stored procedure and our Service Broker application, query to retrieve a customer ID and a movie name using the following two queries:

```
SELECT * FROM CUSTOMER

SELECT * FROM MOVIE
```

Once you have a valid customer ID and a valid movie name, you may call the stored procedure passing in an integer value of one to five for the rating. An example of a call to the stored procedure is:

```
EXEC FireAndForgetMovieReview
'E6C11522-84FC-48EC-8DBC-61486BF4464A',
'Star Wars',
5
```

After executing the procedure, you can check the MovieRatings table to verify the entry was created.

Routes

We have mentioned that services are loosely coupled and independent of their physical location. When you call a service, you are calling a logical representation of the service that may exist on another physical system. Additionally, if you write your application to call a particular service but that service is later moved to another machine, you don't have to update your code because you are referencing the service as a logical rather than physical component.

Of course, at some point, the rubber meets the road and a logical reference has to be resolved to a physical location. The physical attributes of a service are maintained using ROUTES. Service Broker routes are determined using a routing table. This follows a pattern similar to the resolution of a domain name (e.g., microsoft.com) to an IP address.

The process works like this:

1. A dialog is started using the logical name of the service.
2. When a message is sent, the Service Broker does a lookup in the routing table.
3. If an entry is found, the properties specified in the routing table will be used to locate the service. If an entry is not found in the routing table, the system will use the local database.

Anytime you want to access a service on a remote machine—for example, to scale out across multiple machines and share the processing load—you must create an entry for the routing table. Routes are created using the Transact-SQL command:

```
CREATE ROUTE <route name>
    WITH
        SERVICE_NAME = '<service name>',
        ADDRESS = '<address>'
```

To use the most common parameters for creating a route, you would specify a route name, the name of the service that will be using the route, and an address to the service. Service Broker route addresses adhere to the format:

```
TCP://address:port
```

The address may be a DNS name, NetBIOS name, or an IP address. The default listening port number for Service Broker is 4022.

SERVICE BROKER SECURITY

Security is an important aspect of every application. Service Broker provides flexible and high-performance options for securing your messaging applications. It can secure both the content of conversations, termed *dialog security*, and what servers may connect to Service Broker, called *transport security*. In the remainder of this section, we cover both security options.

Dialog Security

Individual conversations are secured using dialog security, which allows your application to encrypt messages sent outside of the current service instance. Local messages are not encrypted. Dialog security has two variations: full security and anonymous security. Both variations encrypt all messages exchanged over the network between two service instances. The major difference between the two variations is the user or role under which operations are performed in the receiving database.

Full security protects Service Broker from sending messages to or receiving messages from untrusted databases. When a dialog uses full security, both the sending and receiving databases must be trusted. Trust between two databases is established by the installation of certificates that identify each instance. When configuring the trust of a remote system, it's necessary to define a service binding that specifies the local user account that will be used to execute operations required by the receipt of remote messages.

Anonymous security requires that the service sending a message must trust the receiver of the message; however, the receiver of the message does not have to trust the sender of the message. As with full security, all messages sent over the network are fully encrypted. Because the receiver of the message cannot identify the sender, all operations performed by the receiver are executed under the public role.

Transport Security

Transport security allows administrators to control what systems on a network may connect to Service Broker and provides encryption between the instances. Using transport security, Service Broker can authenticate its identity using either Windows- or certificate-based authentication. Using Windows-based authentication, the systems must be on the same domain; the same restriction does not exist for certificate-based authentication. With certificate-based authentication, a certificate is created using both a public and private key in the master instance, and a corresponding certificate is created in the remote instance using just the public key.

CONCLUSION

As we saw throughout this chapter, Service Broker provides a fairly simple and elegant model for building asynchronous messaged-based applications. We also saw how Service Broker addresses many of the problems of classic messaging applications, such as clunky two-phase commits for transactions and message ordering across multiple transactions. The bottom line is that Service Broker is in every way an enterprise class messaging system and provides another weapon in a developer's arsenal for building highly scalable data-driven applications on SQL Server 2005.

10 Performance Analysis and Tuning

In this Chapter

- A Journey, not a Destination
- Performance Factors
- Tools
- Conclusion

erformance is paramount in application development. Even if you have implemented what you would consider the next killer app, it's a simple fact of software development that if the performance is horrible, people won't use the application. In the corporate world, sometimes you don't have any other choice but to continue using a poor performing application—a situation even worse than users not using the application at all. If you have ever had the misfortune of supporting a corporate application with significant performance problems, you understand what we're talking about. In the eyes of a captive user base, a poor performing application that users must continue to use on a daily basis can do absolutely nothing right. The users see the slow performing application and almost immediately the focus switches to what's wrong with the application—poor performance. The bottom line is that users expect software to respond promptly.

Slow performing applications and databases are not built intentionally. A developer doesn't start a project and think, "How can I slow this application down?" It just doesn't work that way. Generally speaking, developers have the best of intentions when it comes to performance. For a variety of reasons, some of which are under the control of the developer and some are not, these good intentions do not automatically translate into good performance. This is especially true for database applications where the environment is ever changing with more and more data being added every day.

In this chapter, we survey the performance tuning landscape available in SQL Server 2005. First, we cover the various factors that impact the performance of your database applications, followed by the tools provided with SQL Server 2005 to help you both monitor and improve performance. Then, we finish with coverage of some of the significant features in SQL Server 2005 that will help you implement high-performance database applications.

A JOURNEY, NOT A DESTINATION

Database applications can be a difficult class of application to optimize. With a desktop application, the amount of processing required for the application doesn't typically change over time. If you open Notepad and type a paragraph, the performance of the application will be about the same today as it would be in six months. Database applications don't have the benefits of a static execution environment because they operate in an environment where the data they are working with continues to change on a daily basis. The set of operating data for most production databases continues to grow over time. In this environment, even if your application performs well when first put into production, that doesn't mean it will perform well after the first month of operation.

Performance tuning as a single task is one misperception that application developers often have concerning database application tuning. If an application developer optimizes an algorithm in a pure desktop application—for example, Notepad—the performance of the algorithm isn't likely to change over time, so for a pure desktop application, performance improvements are generally a one-time task. With database application development, performance tuning and optimization is an ongoing process. Database performance tuning is not a destination; rather, it is a process of understanding the factors that influence performance, measuring performance, making alterations, and measuring the results of the alterations. Figure 10.1 illustrates the continuous improvement cycle.

This continuous cycle of improvement should continue as long as your application is being used.

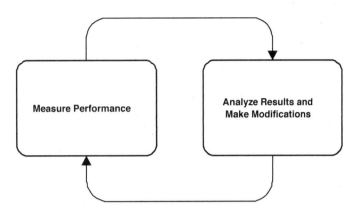

FIGURE 10.1   Continuous performance improvement cycle.

With database performance it's about making tradeoffs to provide the best overall system response and throughput. It is important to make the distinction that performance (response time) is not the same as scalability (throughput). *Performance* is the response time for a single user, while *scalability* refers to the throughput or load an application can handle. Design and implementation decisions that select the best performing option do not mean the choice is the most scalable, and of course the opposite is also true—the most scalable choice may not be the best performing option. It's all about tradeoffs. You will want to start with your typical application load and then optimize the performance while adhering to your scalability requirements.

PERFORMANCE FACTORS

The performance of database applications is not typically dependent on any individual factor. More often, database application performance is dependent on many different variable combinations.

Hardware

Database server hardware can have a significant impact on the performance of your database application. The hardware used to run your database application must be properly sized to match the requirements and demands of the database application. Because hardware can have such a significant impact on the overall performance of your database application, it is one of the main areas to monitor when analyzing a potential performance issue. When sizing hardware for a database application or monitoring hardware for performance analysis, you need to take into account the following hardware systems:

- Storage system
- Network system
- Memory
- Processor

Now let's look at each of these systems to see how changes may impact overall performance of your database application. First, let's review one of the most important aspects of database hardware—storage.

Storage System

In a database system, the performance of the storage system (e.g., the disk(s)) is one of the most common bottlenecks on a database server. Database systems, in addition to abundant disk space to support ever-growing database sizes, need a fast enough disk system to support the I/O requirements of a database application. Database servers require a high amount of disk I/O because it's generally not possible to cache today's large databases in-memory. For instance, if your application's database is 10 GB but your server has 1 GB of physical memory, the server is only going to be able to cache a small portion of your database in the system's physical memory.

Since it's not possible to fit an entire database such as this into memory, when you run a "large" query the database is going to have to move information from the physical disk into memory for processing—a process called swapping. Some swapping is unavoidable with today's large databases (and a 10 GB database is small by today's standards), but excessive swapping is a performance killer. Any excessive disk I/O is bad because the disk system has physical limitations on its performance. Think about it. With physical memory you have electronic signals moving across "wires," but with a disk you have a motor spinning magnetic platters with a reader head that must be physically moved from one location to another to read data, the simple physics of which limit the performance one can achieve with disk I/O. There are some disk configurations that can help overcome the physical limitations of an individual disk. These configurations are called redundant arrays of independent disks (RAID). Multiple disks with a RAID configuration can reduce the delays of waiting on a platter to spin to a particular location and a reader head to move to a location to read data. Even with the improvement provided by RAID, there are real physical limitations on the performance of disks.

To optimize the performance of your application, you must "right-size" both the capacity and performance of the disk system for your server. We use the term *right-size* because in addition to optimizing performance, there is also an economic aspect to decisions to purchase or upgrade hardware. For instance, you could implement a sophisticated RAID storage system to support a workgroup database with three users, but in reality, this may not be economically feasible.

Network System

Network resources available for a database server need to closely match the amount of data pulled "across the wire" by your application. Today it's not uncommon to see gigabit or faster networking infrastructure within an office. However, if you have a distributed system or field offices accessing your database application across a slow wide area network (WAN), then the network can decrease the performance of your application. As with all other hardware components, you must measure the network resources consumed by your application and adjust your application or the networking infrastructure accordingly.

Memory

SQL Server loves memory. Physical memory is expensive, though, when compared to the cost of disk space, especially when you jump into the realm of enterprise applications where you need 8, 16, or even 32 gigabytes of physical memory for your database system. Consequently, the decision about the amount of memory needed for you application definitely has an economic component. Generally speaking, though, you want to get as much data into physical memory as possible. Physical memory is orders of magnitude faster than disk I/O, so when you run a query you want to see the data pulled from memory and not disk.

Processor

Processors also play a role in the performance of a database server. Both number and speed of the processors contribute to the responsiveness of the database server. Processors are one of the performance factors that should be monitored over a period of time to determine if your system has adequate processing power. As a general rule, if you are seeing processor utilization stay at 80% or higher for an extended period of time (not just spikes to 80% or higher), then either your system does not have enough processing power or there is a problem with how your database application is using the database server. Poorly written queries can tax the processors, making them do excessive work to return the results you requested. Again, measure your application performance and see if your system needs more processing horsepower or your queries need tweaking.

We have now briefly covered the major hardware systems that contribute to the performance of your database application. Every database and application and every deployment environment is unique, so we encourage you to follow the continuous improvement cycle and measure the performance of your application under its typical load. In the next sections, we cover some of the other factors that contribute to database system performance.

SQL Server Configuration

Historically, SQL Server has positioned itself as a system that runs smoothly out of the box, and SQL Server 2005 is no different. SQL Server 2005's default configuration parameters are set to allow SQL Server to dynamically manage most parameters related to performance. For most databases, these settings are fine; however, for very large databases or databases supporting a large number of users, some parameters may impact your system performance.

The parameters are accessed from within the SQL Server Management Studio by right-clicking on a server node and choosing Properties. The Properties dialog when it is first loaded lists the general operating system and SQL Server configuration values. The settings listed on the general page of the Properties dialog are not changeable from this dialog, so they are meant for informative purposes only. Figure 10.2 illustrates the general server Properties dialog.

FIGURE 10.2 The Properties dialog.

Now, we'll switch to the Memory page of the Properties dialog. The Memory page, as illustrated in Figure 10.3, gives you the ability to control the memory allocated to SQL Server.

The first option listed on the Memory page of the Properties dialog is the usage of AWE. AWE stands for address windowing extensions and can be used for massive enterprise-scale database systems that need to address up to 64 GB of physical memory. You will need to enable AWE for SQL Server instances that need to address over 4 GB of memory.

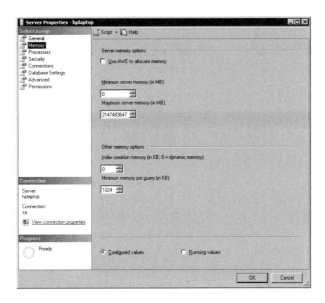

FIGURE 10.3   The Memory page.

Next on the Memory page of the Properties dialog are the Minimum and Maximum server memory configuration settings. The values listed for these settings are specified in MB. SQL Server uses these values to control the amount of memory allocated to the server.

The Minimum server memory setting is very useful if your database server is competing with other processes (including the operating system) for available memory. Specifying a value for the available memory will guarantee that SQL Server keeps at least the specified amount of memory at all times. If your database server is also a Web server, this setting can help ensure that the memory requests made by the Web server don't cause SQL Server to release too much of its allocated memory. Remember, one of the main keys to database performance is to reduce I/O, so you want to keep as much data in physical memory as is feasible. For dedicated database servers, this is the one setting you want to look at and specify the minimum amount of memory you think your database application will require.

The Maximum server memory setting is set by default to essentially have no maximum. In most cases, this is fine, especially when the server is a dedicated database server. SQL Server is going to allocate and deallocate memory between the minimum and maximum you have specified, so unless you have a special situation, don't be concerned that the value is so large. One special situation in which you may want to consider putting an upper bound on the memory allocation is if your system is used for more than a dedicated database server. For instance, if your server also runs a Web application and you find that the database is chewing up all the available memory causing the performance of your Web application to suffer when it makes requests for memory, you may want to consider lowering the maximum amount of memory that can be allocated to SQL Server. Of course, for that scenario you may also want to consider separating the Web application and the database server to different systems, or adding memory so it is not so scarce.

The remaining two settings on the Memory page of the Properties dialog are the Index creation and Minimum query memory. Both of these settings are specified in KB. The Index creation memory setting controls the amount of memory allocated to index creation sorts. Using a value of zero allows SQL Server to manage the amount of memory devoted to index creation sorts. Keep in mind that specifying a large value here will only take resources away from other operations on your SQL Server.

The last setting is the Minimum amount of memory to allocate for each query. This setting, too, works best with its default value of 1024 KB, and there are very few cases where it would be advisable to increase this value. One case where you would consider an increase to the minimum memory setting would be if you have a dedicated database server with plenty of memory available and you run a relatively low volume of large queries. Increasing the setting for that scenario may provide some performance benefit, but typically, the default value for this setting is fine and should not be changed.

The next set of performance options available for SQL Server are processor-related settings. To see the options, choose the Processor page in the Properties dialog (Figure 10.4).

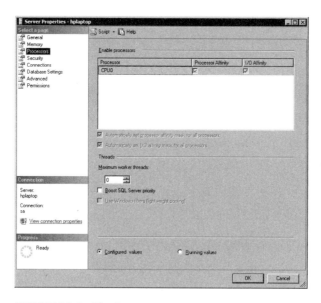

FIGURE 10.4 The Processor page.

The first settings on the Processor page of the Properties dialog control the processor and I/O affinity. The settings provide control over what processors are used to execute specific work. For example, with these settings you could specify what processors in a system are used for processing disk I/O, and which processors run specific threads. By default, SQL Server will manage the processor work assignments, and for all but the most extreme cases this is fine. We recommend leaving these settings at their default values, which allow SQL Server to manage the system processing.

The next setting on the Processor page of the Properties dialog is the Maximum worker thread setting. Worker threads are the threads SQL Server uses to process user queries. SQL Server will create worker threads for each connection to SQL Server up to the maximum number of worker threads specified by this setting. The default value of this setting is zero, which allows SQL Server to dynamically manage the number of threads used by the system. When SQL Server manages the threads, the maximum number is governed by the number of processors and whether you have a 32- or 64-bit system. Table 10.1 shows the maximum number of worker threads the default setting in SQL Server will allow.

TABLE 10.1 Maximum Number of Worker Threads for a Specific Number of Processors and System Architecture

Processors	32-Bit Architecture	64-Bit Architecture
1	256	512
2	256	512
4	256	512
8	288	576
16	352	704
32	480	960

For most situations, the default worker thread setting is fine, and changing the number of worker threads is not generally recommended.

The next option on the Processor page is the Boost SQL Server priority option. Anytime you see a setting that says, "Boost...," you immediately have grand visions that this must be the ultimate performance setting providing everything you ever dreamed of. Now, back to reality, and let's see what this setting does before we start singing its praises.

To understand the Boost SQL Server priority option, you must first understand a little about Windows process scheduling. Every process in Windows is assigned a priority to determine how requests for processing made by the process should be scheduled. Processes with a higher priority will be given processor time ahead of those processes that have a lower priority. It's like triage at the emergency room, where those who need the most help get it and those who need less immediate help must wait until resources become available. Therefore, choosing this option will increase the priority of the SQL Server process, which makes the operating system yield processing time to SQL Server over other processes.

If your server is shared with other applications, such as a Web server, then choosing this option can adversely affect the other applications. If, however, you have a dedicated database server where SQL Server is the only application running on the system, you can enable this option, but typically, you won't notice a perceivable difference. Increasing the processor time given to SQL Server only means that you may be starving the operating system from the time it needs to effectively run the server, so you may notice no difference with this setting enabled.

The last setting on the Processor page is "use Windows fibers." This setting is only available on Windows 2003 Server. On Windows 2003 Server, threads can have smaller units called fibers, which are lightweight processing units. These smaller units are much more efficient at context switching than threads in multiprocessor systems. Using this setting can show some performance improvement, but only on systems where processing is the bottleneck.

In this section, we covered some of the SQL Server configuration options that contribute to the performance of your system. Although we saw some options that could provide marginal improvements under certain situations, there were no silver bullets, and in general allowing SQL Server to manage its own performance is the best idea.

Quantity of Data

The amount of data you have in your database and returned by your queries is going to be a significant factor in the overall performance of your system. SQL Server is very good at handling large databases, but that's not to say that there is no penalty for size. Much of the penalty incurred by having large databases comes in the form of I/O cost. If your database does not fit 100% into memory, then at some point SQL Server is going to go to the disk to retrieve data—and disk I/O is slow.

What can you do to decrease the size of your databases? In some cases, not much. If you need 10 gazillion rows for your application, then you need 10 gazillion rows, and that can't change. In other cases, you can employ "archiving" schemes where you move old data into a data warehouse or another system, keeping your production database limited to only the data you need to work. This will eliminate the historical data that no longer matters to your application but keep the data available for analysis and trending.

Another area where you can negatively impact performance is returning too much data as part of your query results. If you don't specify any conditions on your query, SQL Server is going to do a full table scan and process all the rows in your table. Specifying conditions, especially on indexed or key columns, allows SQL Server to quickly retrieve data without the expense of processing every single row. It's important that columns involved in your conditions be indexed. SQL Server uses its indexes just like you use the index of a book. Thumbing through page after page looking for a particular topic would take an inordinate amount of time; however, using the index you can quickly find the page a topic is listed on and quickly locate it. Using conditions on your queries sounds like a simple thing to do—and it is. However, there are a significant number of applications out there that for one reason or another don't have properly conditioned queries, and their performance suffers because of it.

Database and Query Design

The design of your database and the queries you run against it is the number-one cause of poor performance. However, on a positive note, this is where the real performance gains can be achieved. Sure, you have to have the right hardware and you can't run an extremely high-performance system with bonehead SQL Server configuration or 10 gazillion terabytes of data, but the "Wow" performance gains are usually found in the design of the database and your application queries.

The first thing you need to consider about the design of your database is how it will be used. Does it need to process business transactions (order entry, etc.), or is the purpose of the system to aggregate and analyze data? For online transaction processing (OLTP) databases, you will want to have a highly normalized model for data integrity and high-performance inserts and updates. If your system is really about the analysis of data, an online analytical processing (OLAP) system or data warehouse, you want to aggregate the data in the data model so retrieval of data is optimized. If this question is not answered properly, you will end up with less than optimal system performance.

Part of a proper database design is including the appropriate indexes in your data model. We mentioned indexes earlier and how they are helpers for how SQL Server retrieves data. Indexes can have a negative impact on performance, too. If you have an OLTP system that is heavily indexed, the inserts and updates will be slower because the database must update the index when the data changes. Designing the right indexes for a system can be difficult, but SQL Server 2005 provides a tool to help you determine the indexes that will improve your application's performance—we cover that later in the chapter.

Poorly designed queries will definitely impact the performance of you application. If your query retrieves unnecessary data or too many rows, that's unnecessary processing and retrieval time for the database server. Another area where developers can get into trouble is with too many table joins. This situation can occur when you don't answer the OLTP versus OLAP question correctly. A highly normalized model that must be reaggregated to analyze the results means that your queries will involve many, many table joins. Table joins can impact performance and make it more difficult for SQL Server's query optimization engine to construct an efficient execution plan for the query.

We have now seen some of the factors that contribute to the performance or lack of performance for your database application. In the next section, we look at the tools that can help you identify which factors are impacting your performance.

TOOLS

The first part of the continuous performance improvement process is to measure the performance of your application. If you start making changes to "optimize" your application without measuring, you could be making some (potentially expensive) changes that provide little or no benefit to the resulting performance. For measuring the performance of database application built on SQL Server 2005, we use a variety of tools that are provided with SQL Server 2005 and the Windows operating system to help us do our jobs better and more efficiently.

System Monitor (PerfMon)

The Microsoft System Monitor, also called PerfMon, is the standard tool for monitoring and logging performance-related information on Windows systems. You can access the System Monitor on a Windows system by running PerfMon from the Windows run dialog. Figure 10.5 shows the System Monitor (PerfMon) application.

PerfMon provides a set of performance objects, including Processor, Memory, Network Interface, Physical Disk, and a whole series of SQL Server performance objects. Every performance object has a set of counters; for example, some of the counters available for the Memory performance object include "Available Mbytes," "Pages/sec," and "% Committed Bytes In Use." As you can see, some performance counters will provide absolute measurements such as "Available Mbytes," while others provide rates or percentages such as "Pages/sec" and "% Committed Bytes In Use," respectively.

PerfMon can be used to interactively monitor a system's performance and log counter data to a file to analyze later. This is a great feature, especially for testing environments where you will analyze the performance of your application. This is not a chapter specifically about the PerfMon tool, so we won't go into the details about

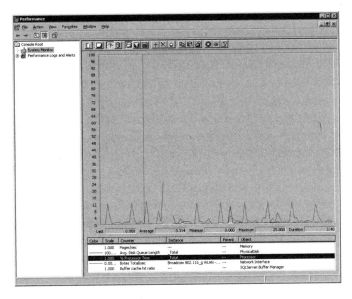

FIGURE 10.5   PerfMon.

how to configure PerfMon. However, the help included with the application provides a great step-by-step guide on how to configure the tool for logging.

When monitoring your database system, there are many, many counters you may want to consider. If you try to monitor too many counters, you can quickly be overwhelmed by the data, so we find it best to monitor a few important counters to isolate what aspect of your database system is the bottleneck. Once you have identified the area of the bottleneck, if you need more information, you can add additional counters specific to that factor. Table 10.2 lists the minimal set of counters for analyzing the hardware of your SQL Server 2005 database.

TABLE 10.2   Performance Counters for Monitoring SQL Server

Object	Counter	Description
Processor	% Processor	Monitors the percentage of the processor being used. Sustained values over 80% indicate the processor is being overutilized.
Memory	Pages/sec	Monitors the number of pages of memory that must be swapped to/from the physical disk. A high value for this counter indicates that the system is unable to keep all the data it needs in physical memory. →

Object	Counter	Description
Network Interface	Bytes/sec	Monitors the activity on the network. You can determine how much of the network resources are being used by taking this number in bytes, multiplying it by 8 bits, and then dividing it by the available megabits on your network (e.g., 10, 100 megabits), which will give you a percentage of the network being used. If that calculation results in a value over 80%, you have a network bottleneck.
PhysicalDisk	Avg. Disk Queue Length	Monitors the disk requests waiting to be executed. The disk queue should not average a value higher than two. Values higher than two may indicate the disk is being over utilized. If the value is over two but you're still not certain the bottleneck is the disk, you can add the % Disk Time to verify that the % Disk Time is high while experiencing the performance problem.
SQL Server: Buffer Manager	Buffer cache hit ratio	Monitors how well SQL Server's cache is working. This value should be as close to 100 as possible. A value close to 100 means that SQL Server is finding most of the requested data in physical memory. A low value means that SQL Server has to go to disk to get the data it needs. This can indicate that the SQL Server minimum memory needs to be increased or that the amount of physical memory does not match the load being experienced by the server.

Using these performance objects will help you isolate what general area of your system is the likely source of your performance problem. You may find it necessary to drill into the bottleneck area with additional counters and monitoring. The System Monitor application help provides explanations for all the available counters and is a good reference for the meaning of the counters.

Dynamic Management Views

SQL Server 2005 provides detailed internal performance information through its dynamic management views. The dynamic management views provide an astounding amount of very detailed performance information about the internal operations of SQL Server. Dynamic management views and table valued functions are part of the system views provided in SQL Server 2005. The views are divided into the following broad categories:

- CLR
- Mirroring
- Database
- I/O
- Query Notifications
- Execution
- Full-Text Search
- Index
- Replication
- Operating System
- Transaction

Within each of these categories are views and table valued functions that provide data germane to the particular category. Because of the sheer number of views available and the amount of information provided by each, we will not be providing details on all the available management views. SQL Server's online help provides an excellent reference on the available dynamic management views.

Now, let's look at some of the interesting views provided in the execution category. Within the execution category, you will find the views in Table 10.3 useful for isolating "bad queries" on your system.

TABLE 10.3   Dynamic Management Views

View/Table Valued Function Name	Description
sys.dm_exec_connections	Provides information about the current database connections. Using this view, you can find problems with applications that open connections but neglect to close them.
sys.dm_exec_sessions	Provides information about user sessions; for example, you can find the login information for a particular connection. →

View/Table Valued Function Name	Description
sys.dm_exec_sql_text	A table valued function that accepts a SQL handle (which can be retrieved from the sys.dm_exec_requests view) and returns the SQL text that is being executed by a particular request.
sys.dm_exec_requests	Provides information about the execution requests. Using this view you can retrieve the SQL and Plan handles to get the specific details about a request's SQL and corresponding execution plan. Additionally, this view provides the execution time and other counter information about the request.
sys.dm_exec_query_stats	Provides detailed performance information about each execution of a particular query.
sys.dm_exec_query_plan	A table valued function that accepts a plan handle and returns the execution plan XML. You can analyze the execution plan to determine how the database will process the query, which can help you implement the proper indexes to optimize your performance.

You can query these views and table valued functions just like a normal table or view. Let's look now at an example of how to use these views. In today's business environment where IT shops are consolidating systems to reduce operating costs, it's pretty common for an application to share a database server with several other applications. If you are receiving trouble reports that your application is performing poorly, it would be very nice to look into the core of the database and see if the slow performance is due to your queries. With dynamic management views you can do just that. The following query illustrates how you can join dynamic management views to capture what users are executing queries, the text and execution plan of the query, and how long the query takes to execute:

```
SELECT sess.login_name as "User",
conn.client_net_address as "Location",
(
SELECT sqltext.text
FROM sys.dm_exec_sql_text(req.sql_handle) sqltext
) AS "SQL",
(
```

```
SELECT planxml.query_plan
FROM sys.dm_exec_query_plan(req.plan_handle) planxml
) AS "Plan",
stats.max_elapsed_time "Elapsed Time"
    FROM sys.dm_exec_sessions sess
            JOIN sys.dm_exec_connections conn
ON sess.session_id = conn.session_id
            JOIN sys.dm_exec_requests req
ON sess.session_id = req.session_id
            JOIN sys.dm_exec_query_stats stats
ON req.sql_handle = stats.sql_handle
ORDER BY stats.max_elapsed_time DESC
```

This is powerful stuff for performance issue isolation and tuning. Dynamic management views open the internal operations of the SQL Server database engine like never before.

SQL Server Profiler

The SQL Server Profiler tool gives you the ability to capture and log information about SQL Server events over a specific period of time. For those of you who have worked with the Profiler on SQL Server 2000, you will find the core functionality remains, but the SQL Server 2005 version provides some very useful enhancements. For those not familiar with the SQL Server Profiler, we provide a brief overview.

The SQL Server Profiler records queries and events that are executing on the instance being monitored. The information captured can be saved to a file, called a trace file, or alternatively stored in a database table. Capturing events using the SQL Server Profiler is simple. After launching the application, choose the "New Trace" option. You will then be prompted for login information to the server you want to monitor. With the login information specified, the Trace Properties dialog will appear. The Trace Properties dialog helps guide you through the process of defining what you want to capture and where you want to place the captured information. Figure 10.6 illustrates the general Properties tab of the Trace Properties dialog.

The General tab gives you options to name the trace you are performing and to specify how the trace data will be stored. You may also choose not to automatically persist the trace information if you just want to view the events interactively. Most of the time, however, you will want to persist the trace information to a file so you can analyze, archive, and easily share trace results over time. In addition to the storage location, the General tab provides a set of trace templates from which to choose. Choosing a trace template will automatically have the trace capture a specific set of events. The events captured by a particular template are displayed on the Events Selection tab of the Properties dialog, illustrated in Figure 10.7.

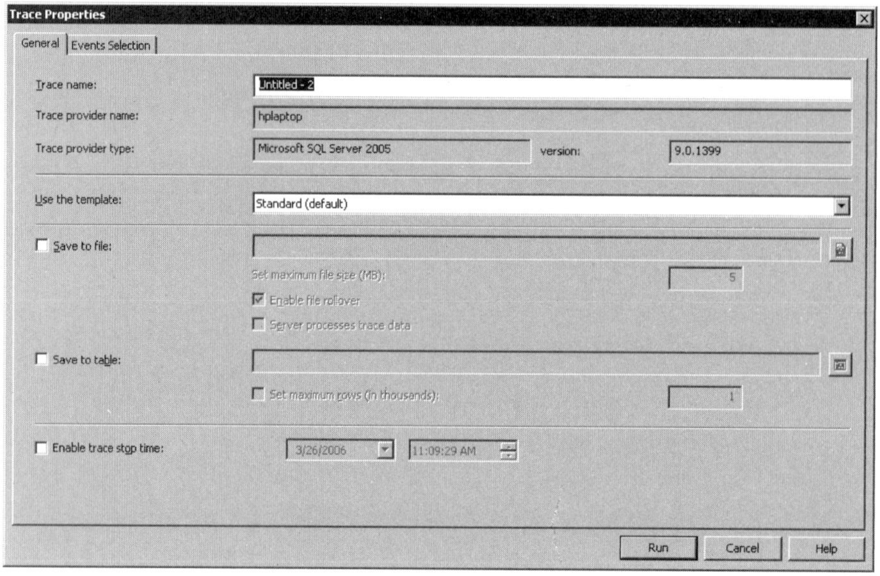

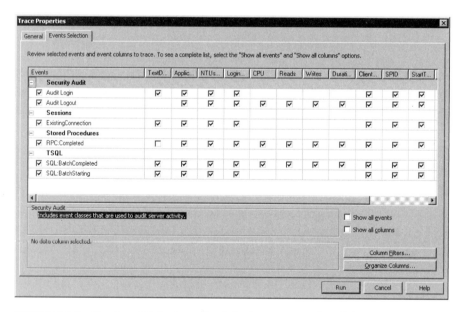

FIGURE 10.6   The Properties tab of the Trace Properties dialog.

FIGURE 10.7   The Event Selection tab of the Trace Properties dialog.

On the Event Selection tab, you can see the events selected for the trace template you have chosen. This is where you can customize your trace and change what events will be captured. After finalizing the events selected for your trace, you can start your trace by clicking Run. At this point, you can begin exercising the functionality of your application you want to profile. As your application executes queries and interacts with the database server, you will see events logged in the Trace window. The data captured by the profiler can be very useful for understanding exactly how an application is interacting with the database. For IT shops supporting third-party database applications, this can help you understand how the application is interacting with the database.

In addition to some usability improvements in the SQL Profiler user interface, especially in the area of event selection, the SQL Profiler now provides some very useful integration with PerfMon. The profiler's integration with PerfMon gives developers the ability to view counter log data alongside profiler event data so you can analyze the events in the specific context of the stress on the machine at the point in time where the event occurred. Now let's look briefly at how you can use this integration to analyze your events and counter logs.

The profiler and PerfMon integration is only for analyzing saved traces and counter logs. It does not support interactively coordinating events with counter data. For the SQL Server profiler, that means you must choose to save your trace to a file or a database table. We typically choose a file just because we find it easier to work with, and share trace files. For PerfMon, that means you have to create counter logs. Earlier in this chapter we showed you how to interactively view performance monitor data; to integrate the counters with the profiler we have to take a slightly different approach to log the counter data. After launching PerfMon, expand the Performance Logs and Alerts node. Next, right-click on the Counter Logs node and choose New Log Settings as illustrated in Figure 10.8.

At this point, we provide a name for the log, and a dialog will appear to configure the data captured in the log. Now, we will select the same counters we chose earlier in this chapter when performing interactive monitoring. In addition to adding the counters, we also specify a sample interval of 1 second to give us granular performance information. Figure 10.9 illustrates the counter log definition.

With the counters added, we click OK to save the counter log. Unlike the interactive monitoring where you can see the counter information visually, with counter logs nothing is happening visually but the system is logging the counter data to the file(s) we specified.

Now that the counters are capturing information, we can start our SQL Profiler trace. Define a trace that captures events to a file and run the trace. It's important that both the trace and the counter logs capture information at the same time. It's not necessary to have them start at exactly the same instant, but you want to start the counter logs, and within a minute or so at the most, start the SQL profiler trace.

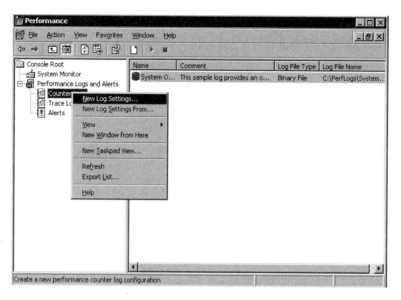

FIGURE 10.8 Defining new performance log settings.

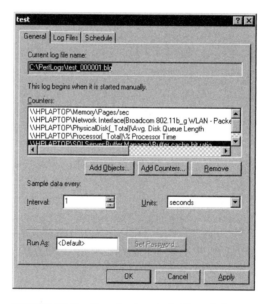

FIGURE 10.9 Counter log definition dialog.

To capture some interesting data, exercise the pieces of your application you're interested in monitoring. For our test, we simply ran a couple of Transact-SQL queries just to generate several events and some counter data. When you have finished executing the part of your application being profiled, stop the SQL Profiler trace by clicking the Stop button, and then stop the counter logs by right-clicking the log and choosing Stop.

Now we can analyze the data that was just captured. First, inside the SQL Profiler, choose File → Open → Open Trace File and select the file you specified when creating your trace. With the saved trace file open in the SQL Profiler, choose File → Import Performance Data and locate the file you specified when defining the counter log. After choosing the log data, the Trace window will be updated to display the counter information graphically and in a tabular format as illustrated in Figure 10.10.

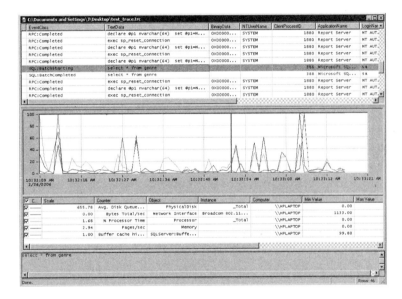

FIGURE 10.10 Trace window containing performance data.

You can see the counter values for a specific event by selecting the event. The counter values at the point in time of the selected event are indicated by the thick vertical line on the counter graph.

Database Tuning Advisor

Thus far, we have covered the factors that contribute to the performance of your database and some of the tools we can use for capturing and analyzing performance-related information. Now we'll look at a tool that can provide specific suggestions for improving the performance of your database application—the Database Tuning Advisor (DTA).

The DTA uses a workload you provide that is representative of what your database application will do in a production environment. The workload can be a saved SQL Server Profiler trace file, which makes it simple to capture a realistic workload for your application. Figure 10.11 illustrates the Database Tuning Advisor configured to run a saved SQL Server Profiler trace file.

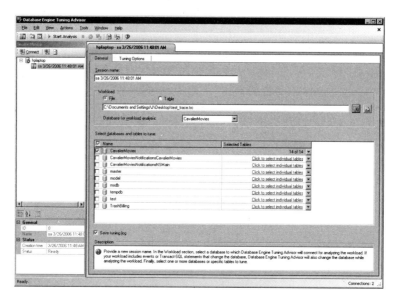

FIGURE 10.11 Database Engine Tuning Advisor window.

DTA then executes that workload and will make recommendations concerning indexes, partitions, and other physical database changes that will improve the performance of your application. Along with each recommendation, the tool also provides an estimation of the performance improvement you could see as a result of making the modification.

The DTA is primarily concerned with physical changes to the database for improving performance and does not include logical data model or design recommendations, so it generally falls with the realm of the database administrator. However, if you find yourself wearing the hats of both a database application developer and a database administrator, this tool can help you look like a pro.

CONCLUSION

In this chapter, we covered the primary factors that contribute to the performance of your application, tools for analyzing and capturing performance data, and tools for using that data to recommend alterations. The performance tuning and analysis features in SQL Server 2005 far exceed the capabilities of its predecessors and provide robust analysis features to help you build the best performing applications possible on the SQL Server platform.

11 Business Intelligence

In this Chapter

- Challenges
- Providing Value
- Delivering Value
- SQL Server 2005 Business Intelligence Features
- Conclusion

In a business world that places so much emphasis on being connected, all too often key business applications are anything but connected. A company might have supply chain applications that are only in operation in one division, CRM systems that only touch a single customer channel, and multiple ERP systems as the result of mergers and acquisitions. It is difficult to get a picture of how the business as a whole is doing from all these separate systems. Business intelligence pulls all of the disparate data together to form a unified view of the enterprise that can generate insight into the vitality of business processes.

Better information presented in a way that encourages analysis coupled with the ability to act on the recommendations adds up to bottom-line results. According to consulting firm McKinsey and Company, if an average S&P 1500 company can increase prices 1 percent while holding sales volume steady, they will experience an 8-percent improvement in operating profit. Given that kind of leverage, it isn't surprising that IDC has found that business analytics applications have an average five-year return of 431 percent, with 63 percent of projects achieving payback within a two-year period. Broad results for business intelligence projects should be viewed skeptically due to differences in the solutions, technologies, and organizations in which they are applied. However, these impressive results are a good indicator of generally solid returns on business intelligence investments.

This chapter begins with a discussion of a general framework for business intelligence solutions, and then describes the features in SQL Server 2005 that support the design, construction, and ongoing operation of these solutions. The subsequent chapters cover the specifics of business intelligence solutions with SQL Server 2005, such as ETL, reporting, OLAP, and data mining in greater detail.

CHALLENGES

In concept, business intelligence is readily accepted. Who can argue against working smarter? However, many business intelligence solutions fall far short of their potential. The source of the largest benefits attributable to a BI (business intelligence) project is operational improvements because of better information flow and decision making. However, measuring these "better decisions" is very difficult. The business case for business intelligence needs to build on specific areas of improvement. The true measure for success of BI in an organization should be how effectively they facilitate "closing the loop" and integrate fact-based decision making into improved operational practice and results. However, many solutions fail to deliver the value that was envisioned when first embarking on the project. Weaknesses in business intelligence solutions can come from many sources. Some of the most common problem areas are:

- Functional orientation
- No single version of the truth
- Low usage levels
- Poor data quality
- Static solutions
- Costly operations
- Lack of business context

Functional Orientation

Business intelligence is not a new phenomenon, but for the most part of its two decades of existence, BI has been focused on functional areas within organizations, most often finance and marketing. As a result, most BI applications are targeted at specific functional problems, which leads to fragmentations of the truth, incomplete solutions, and an overpopulation of tools. For example, a solution focused on vendor performance might succeed in reducing costs, but result in declining manufacturing yields and profitability if the vendor performance metrics were not interlinked with manufacturing metrics.

Initially, BI tools were sold on a departmental basis and favored creating solutions that were local in scope. Data warehousing was conceived of at the enterprise level and focused exclusively on collecting and rationalizing data across the entire enterprise. As the departmental solutions were swept into enterprise-wide efforts, the complexity and capabilities of the solutions were dramatically expanded. Today, enterprise BI environments include many different tools:

- Extract, transform, and load tools
- Relational data warehouse
- Multidimensional database
- Reporting tools
- Data mining
- Metadata repository
- Database design tools
- Database management tools
- Data quality tools
- Web portals

As a direct result of the functional orientation of the applications, many organizations have a large number of business intelligence tools. In many cases, different departments use different tools that are not always compatible. This leads to increased costs due to multiple licensing and support agreements, and high integration costs.

No Single Version of the Truth

Different applications and departments calculate metrics using different algorithms and data, leading to a confusing array of reports and difficulty in distinguishing which version is the "true" story. The post-Enron environment of increased skepticism and mistrust of corporate practices has placed a premium on risk management. Forces that threaten an organization's viability create a demand for information and practices that allow managers and directors to know the true state of the business and react before things get out of hand. Without accurate and timely information, executives are flying blind, unable to see the real issues that confront the business. The numbers generated by a BI application might be from different sources and provoke disagreement over the veracity and meaning of findings.

Usage Levels Are Low

There is a natural usage pattern to business intelligence solutions. Typically, they will come out of the gate strongly because of initial training and promotion efforts. The true test comes after a few quarters of existence. Successful systems may see some reduction in usage at this point or at least a leveling off of growth as initial excitement fades, some limits to the solution are hit, and people who don't benefit from the solution drop out of the user pool. Unsuccessful solutions will see a drop-off after the initial pop and never recover momentum. Systems that are not used are not going to achieve their ROI targets. In many organizations, the furthest along the path of business intelligence they get is having business analysts or information technology people create reports that are consumed by business users and executives. The business users never get their hands dirty analyzing data and executive dashboards go unused. An examination of those companies that have had success in implementing enterprise applications reveals that what most of them have in common is a framework for integrating, analyzing, sharing, and reacting to the information in their applications. What sets industry leaders apart from their peers is not the size and scope of their information systems, but how those systems are used in an integrated fashion to drive business strategy. The key to their success is using data to drive better decision-making. Common causes for low usage include:

- Lack of training
- Poor usability
- Difficulty integrating solution with other operations
- Value of the intelligence is low
- Poor data quality

The best way to understand why people are not using the solution is to ask them. Surveys, interviews, and discussions with interested groups to identify the issues are often very enlightening. In many cases, users will not be aware of features that already exist in the solution, so additional training will help them use the solution. Usability expertise can be applied to problems where users are simply unable to work with the application. Sometimes, performance can be a major usability issue, necessitating some throughput improvements. If the value of the intelligence is low or users cannot use what they have learned in other systems, they will not go to the trouble of using the solution. In these cases, exploring a closer integration with the transactional systems is a good idea. Poor data quality is a big challenge.

Poor Data Quality

Data quality is one of the biggest risks in a business intelligence project. Failing to address issues of data quality early and often will lead to data quality issues down the road when it will be very expensive to fix. Sometimes, you will find that the data quality is too poor to achieve the business requirements. In these cases, you want to identify the issues early before you spend a lot of time and money implementing a solution that cannot work. You will need to go back to the sponsors of the project and deliver a concrete list of the issues and proposed solutions before proceeding. As the project evolves, data quality issues will be identified. For example, two systems might have customer address records. Which one is correct? You need to have the data owners identified and be ready to work with them to hammer out data integrity and consistency problems. If users cannot trust the results provided by the solution or the data is out of date, they will not use it. Common data quality issues are:

- Incomplete or inaccurate data
- Too much data latency
- Errors in BI solution calculations or assumptions

These problems can be solved with data quality initiatives. Make sure that data owners have been established and that executive sponsorship allows you to work with them on data integrity problems. Make sure the ETL processes are correct and that the sources are the best possible. Data latency issues can be solved by shortening the time between data refresh or using advanced caching techniques. Review the calculations in the solution to make sure they are correct and test them with real production data. Often, flaws will be revealed in systems that have only been tested with test data systems.

Solution Is Too Static

Business changes, and so should your business intelligence solution. Solving yesterday's problems does not do much good. The solution will become perceived as part of the problem. Some tendencies of static solutions include:

- Lack of ownership
- Inflexible design
- No plan for evolution

To solve these problems, make sure first and foremost that you have a clear business owner of the solution and strong sponsorship. If you have management backing for making changes to the system, review the design for tightly coupled areas that preclude expansion and changes with an eye toward possible refactoring or redesign. This will help separate the various components of the solution so they can be upgraded as things change.

It is important to have a plan for incorporating new data sources or business imperatives. A good plan starts with solid documentation of the system as it currently exists. Even if the original development team is in-house, they will not be able to remember the details of what they did six months or a year ago. In addition to opening up to changes by a development team, build in power user flexibility so power users can make some modifications. This kind of self-service can go a long way in winning over business users as allies.

Costly Operations

Sometimes a BI application will be successful in terms of usage and impact on the business, but will still be a business failure because of high operational costs, which can be caused by:

- Lack of automation
- Inflexible design
- Poor documentation and training for operations

Review the operations and design to reveal problem areas and automate anything that can be automated. Establish metrics for operational cost and responsiveness and monitor them over time to be able to spot problem areas before they become acute. Properly document the system for operations and train the team on operating procedure. If warranted, redesign pieces of the solution to facilitate lower operational costs.

Lack of Business Context

In many cases, business intelligence is not used effectively because it is tangential to the actual work done by the organization. Unless the business intelligence solution is aligned with strategy and integrated into the systems that run the company, it will have difficulty providing value. Although business intelligence solutions might provide a better flow of information to decision makers, the decision-making process is still done on an ad hoc basis. This is a particular problem with business intelligence programs that are spearheaded by an information technology group. There is a large volume of data collected, but there is no way for business users to find their way around in it.

PROVIDING VALUE

To leverage business intelligence solutions, organizations must use the tools to find value in their growing mountains of data. Good business intelligence solutions share some common characteristics:

- Operate on business processes
- Drive analysis to decision makers
- Encourage usage
- Have meaningful ownership
- Support change
- Reduce workloads

Operate on Business Processes

Departmental analysis only goes so far and tends to focus on finding locally optimal solutions. Business intelligence solutions that focus on a business process, rather than on strictly departmental concerns, are more likely real solutions to business problems. For example, a business intelligence system that is focused on the entire customer acquisition process could be used to analyze how well the organization does at every step of marketing, sales, delivery, and after-sales support. One that is just focused on analyzing delivery performance might neglect the other parts of the value chain and recommend "fixes" that reduce overall value. For example, profitable customers might really like expedited shipping although this might not make sense at the departmental level.

Drive Analysis to Decision Makers

Too many business intelligence solutions are divorced from what decision makers do on a daily basis. These half-solutions require them to go through many steps of extracting data from a data warehouse into Excel and then producing their own reports to make decisions with on a daily basis. Instead, solutions should be built with a firm understanding of the information and decisions that need to made on a daily basis, and allow decision makers to reduce the steps required for a decision and reduce work, not increase it. This doesn't mean that ad hoc analysis is precluded from the solution, but the focus should be on where the rubber meets the road. This also requires that you apply context to the numbers. Instead of just presenting numbers, allow experts to provide annotation to make them more meaningful.

Encourage Usage

The first and most obvious indicator of a valuable business intelligence solution is whether people actually use it. If the solution is being used, it must provide benefits to the users that exceed the costs in time and effort of using it. If it is not being used, then the value provided by the solution is suspect.

The simplest measure of usage can be obtained by monitoring the database and network to see how much traffic the solution gets overall. It is useful to be able to break down the usage patterns of the application to pinpoint which areas get the most use and which are relatively neglected, so you can understand which areas are important to the user population. In addition, interest is a good indicator of usage. A steady stream of issue reports and enhancement requests indicate that people are interested in the well-being of the solution and want it to work better. Of course, too many issues might indicate that the solution is not meeting user expectations, but if they are still using it, you will have a chance to make changes to the solution and improve the overall satisfaction.

Meaningful Ownership

Long term, there is probably nothing more important to the success of a BI solution than ownership. There needs to be ownership established both over the solution itself and over the source data systems. If nobody owns the solution long term, no one will be willing to make the ongoing investments in time and resources to make the solution a success. The existence of a dedicated support team for the solution is an excellent indicator that the management team takes ownership of the solution seriously. This team will be responsible for working with business users to make sure the application continues to meet their needs, and working with the owners of the source systems to ensure relevant, consistent, and high-quality data.

Support Change

The design of a business intelligence solution should support the current business goals and allow for changing goals and future growth. There are a large number of options for designing a BI solution. In some cases, a simple relational database that stages production data for reporting might be adequate. In others, a full-blown data warehouse will need to be constructed that integrates every major system in place in the company and provides advanced data mining and data visualization tools. In between, there are many solution designs that will result in an application that will support the business need at minimum cost.

A well-designed business intelligence solution should allow for appropriate response times and simple maintenance. The different pieces of the application should be distinct and loosely coupled so changes in one area will not break applications in another. Careful attention should be paid to automating repetitious activities so ongoing operational costs can be minimized.

Also important is extensive logging and error reporting. If something goes wrong during routine operations, the appropriate people need to know as soon as possible so they can take action to restore operations. In almost all cases, the business intelligence solution should not pull data directly out of the transactional data store. Instead, a staging area should be used to minimize the impact on the transactional applications and provide an opportunity to merge disparate data sources. Strong change management practices should be followed to ensure that changes to the system are planned and can be rolled back if necessary.

Metrics to measure the effectiveness of a particular design can be generated by looking at the ongoing costs of maintaining and modifying the solution. If it is very expensive to make common and expected changes, the design may be inadequate.

Reduce Workloads

A business intelligence solution should reduce workloads. You want people to do more with less, not spend time fishing for data. Ideally, the BI solution should have a user interface that is approachable for the novice, but also provides enough depth for the expert user. Power users will want access to sophisticated analytic and data mining tools that support deep investigations of the data. Casual users will want to be able to get to meaningful information quickly and easily.

User education is a big component of ongoing solution efficiency. Documentation should be prepared that covers the operation and usage of the solution. Comprehensive documentation should cover the standard stuff of normal day-to-day operations, routine maintenance, and disaster recovery. In addition, it should cover user definitions of metadata and instructions for modifying and evolving the solution. Appropriate training should be given to the users and sustainers of the system so they can use and support the system efficiently.

DELIVERING VALUE

To provide value, a business intelligence solution should be focused on the business, not the technology. The tools that deliver the information are secondary, but also important to establishing and maintaining a valuable application. To enhance the value of a business intelligence solution, try to:

- Link solutions to strategies
- Consolidate infrastructure and data
- Establish relevancy

- Prepare the data
- Provide appropriate analysis tools
- Share the results
- Enable action

Linkage of Solutions to Strategies

In too many cases, organizations take a "build it and they will come" approach to creating business intelligence solutions. Instead, the focus should be on allowing the business to guide the decisions about what data should be gathered and how it should be analyzed. The solution must be aligned with corporate strategies. Of course, this means you must understand those strategies and how business intelligence relates to them. If the corporate strategy is to be the low-cost provider of a good or service, BI solutions should be focused on the cost aspects of the business and allow decision makers to drive costs out. Ideally, you should pick three or so goals for your business intelligence efforts to give them a focus that is aligned with your corporate strategies and give multiple sources of benefit. For example, if your business strategy is to be a low-cost provider, your solution might focus on supply chain analysis, forecasts of raw materials costs, and manufacturing optimization.

If you don't understand the relevant problems, you run the risk of developing a business intelligence solution that is poorly conceived and, rather than becoming an integral part of the operation of the business, becomes a solution in search of a problem. You need to understand that the technologies do not create a business solution in and of themselves. The business intelligence project must address a specific and meaningful business requirement and must be adaptable to change as business requirements change. In many cases, a smaller project that addresses low-hanging fruit will reduce the time to benefit and provide a more immediate return on investment. From that beachhead of success, you can extend the platform into other operational areas in the order of importance to the business.

Consolidate Infrastructure and Data

Disconnected BI solutions are expensive. Multiple software purchases, maintenance fees, and additional labor and hardware costs to host and integrate all of the different tools can add up to a considerable chunk of change. In addition, a multiplicity of tools contributes to the problem of having multiple versions of the truth. Making sure that all the tools have been synchronized with the same metadata and metrics definitions is a headache. You should try to eliminate as many point solutions as possible and migrate toward a more encompassing business intelligence infrastructure. Ideally, this will have a single technology foundation. In addition to the software and hardware infrastructure, you need to pay attention to the data infrastructure and make sure data owners have control over the definition of key terms like *customer*, *order*, and *supplier*, and the data sources and algorithms that are used to calculate metrics.

Once you have a sufficient understanding of the business problem, you will need to create a plan for collecting the data. Business intelligence requires data. To provide worthwhile business intelligence, your solution must have accurate and timely data. Corporate data can reside almost anywhere. Most companies have a wide variety of applications that have evolved to meet business needs over time. Important data can reside in legacy mainframe systems, custom applications, and Excel spreadsheets on laptops. Divisions that were acquired and even sometimes those that have always been with the company but separated by geography or product line often have different financial and operational applications from the rest of the company. In many cases, these systems will have different meanings for common terms like *customer*. In one system, a customer is simply any entry in the customer table. In another, a customer must have outstanding orders. Resolving definition issues between systems and departments can be a very time-consuming and potentially politicized situation. It is very important to have full buy-in from top executives before embarking on such a project. There will be situations where you will need their influence to break impasses.

Data quality is a critical success factor for any business intelligence solution. Poor quality data undermines trust in the solution. No matter how good the analytic applications are or how usable the interfaces are, poor data will undermine trust in the system. If the decision makers don't trust the underlying data, they won't use the system. It is very difficult to get ROI out of a system that is not used.

In many cases, data quality turns out to be worse than anyone anticipates before the scrutiny of a business intelligence project. In the best cases, the transaction systems that have been collecting the data have proper constraints and business rules and there has been some managerial attention paid to making sure the data is correct. In these cases, the biggest problem might be data that is out of date due to external changes. A common example of that would be a customer moving without informing the company. In other cases, the data might be close to unusable and there will be a considerable effort to change the systems that are collecting the data and make sure those responsible for data collection are properly trained.

In addition to the mundane complexities of data integration and quality, you may encounter legal barriers. In many instances, it is illegal or unethical to share customer transaction information across multiple systems. For example, hospitals will have financial analysis that needs to be separated from medical analysis. There is simply no need for a financial analyst to know which patient had which treatment. In these cases, the data might still be usable for analytical purposes if it is sufficiently blinded to make the customer anonymous. Privacy is also a big and growing concern. The European Union has much stricter privacy and information sharing laws than those of the United States. Any program that intends to share customer information between European and U.S. divisions of a corporation requires special scrutiny.

One of the most difficult things about a BI initiative is gathering the *metadata*, the data that describes your data. For example, the definition of a customer identifier as a nine-digit number generated sequentially based on the date the customer was entered in the system would be a form of metadata. Without accurate metadata that is agreed upon by all the relevant parties, decision makers won't be able to discern the specific meaning of a given analysis correctly. Are sales gross or net? Does cost of goods sold include allocated overhead or not? Understandably, metadata is notoriously hard to define and track down. Attaining and keeping a consistent definition of enterprise metadata requires the full support and cooperation of your organization's subject matter experts and executives.

Establish Relevancy

Make sure the business intelligence solutions provide information that leads to action. This means creating automated BI solutions that scan for changes in conditions and alert decision makers to problems or opportunities. Your business is impacted by external events, so your decisions need to take that into account. To provide proper basis for decision making, you need to ensure that your business intelligence solutions also incorporate external data sources. Most importantly, your BI solutions need to be used to refine the business processes themselves. When a problem or opportunity in a process is discovered, information from the business intelligence solution can be used to redesign the process.

Provide Appropriate Analysis Tools

After finding, collecting, and cleansing the data, you need to provide tools for analyzing the data. Most users will be primarily consumers of intelligence. A minority of users will produce most of the content consumed by the others. Although some data analysis tasks might be reserved for specialists, the tools to analyze the data should be placed as broadly as possible through the organization to get the most benefit. It is a good idea to provide a tool that business users are already familiar with, like Excel, or at least one that requires a minimum of training and familiarization. That way, the people who really know the business are able to access business intelligence and make better decisions. These are the people who can do the most with the information and you should cater to their needs.

This is in contrast to the older, more centralized style of decision support systems, which were targeted at directing information up the chain to the executive suite so that good decisions could be handed back down the chain. In fact, executives delegated access to a subordinate who presented them with the results of the analysis. In today's world of flattened hierarchies and empowered employees, the information and tools to analyze it need to be spread throughout the organization.

Share the Results

In addition to providing pervasive access to the data and the means to analyze it, you need to provide the means to publish and share the results of analysis. The value of business intelligence is subject to strong network effects: it is more valuable the more people in the organization know about it. In addition, creating conduits for sharing and discussing analysis makes the organization more capable of reacting to change. The more people see the writing on the wall, the more likely they are to read it and take, or at least accept, the appropriate actions.

Enable Action

The reason to build a business intelligence solution is to improve decision-making capabilities. This means the information needs to be easy to analyze, and must be presented in a format that is easily actionable. Actionable means that the information can facilitate change in the organization. Ideally, the same systems that give you the information for a decision allow you to act on it with very little latency between decision making and action.

SQL SERVER 2005 BUSINESS INTELLIGENCE FEATURES

As we have discussed, business intelligence solutions are built on many different supporting technologies. Essential technologies for business intelligence include tools for data extraction and transformation, data warehousing, reporting, data mining, data visualization, and multidimensional databases. In addition to managing the data, there are tools that manage the metadata that describes the data used in the solution. Ideally, these technologies will be able to support real-time, actionable information and can be integrated so decisions can be acted upon without delay. Let's move from a general discussion of business intelligence solutions to how SQL Server 2005 fits into the picture.

SQL Server 2005 is a comprehensive business intelligence platform that provides tools for almost every aspect of a business intelligence solution. Table 11.1 links the generic components of a business intelligence solution to the components available in SQL Server 2005.

TABLE 11.1   Business Intelligence Components that Are Available in SQL Server 2005

Business Intelligence Component	SQL Server 2005 Component
Extract, transform, and load	SQL Server 2005 Intragration Services (SSIS)
Relational data warehouse	SQL Server relational database
Multidimensional database	SQL Server 2005 Analysis Services
Reporting	SQL Server 2005 Reporting Services
Data mining	SQL Server 2005 Analysis Services
Metadata repository	Unified Data Model (UDM)
Database design tools	Business Intelligence Development Studio
Database management tools	Management Studio
Data quality tools	N/A
Web portals	SharePoint Portal Server

Extract, Transform, and Load

Extract, transform, and load (ETL) functions are provided by SQL Server 2005 Intration Services (SSIS), which has been significantly upgraded from previous versions and now has enough breadth and depth to create enterprise-scale ETL applications. These include improved functionality in the areas of:

Package development. The Business Intelligence Development Studio supports designing, developing, and debugging SSIS packages. These packages are now stored as XML in the filesystem or the database and can be kept under source control. The Business Intelligence Development Studio is hosted in Visual Studio, allowing access to all of the tools available in that environment. For debugging, the development environment allows the setting of breakpoints, and attaching a data viewer to see the data at each stage of the process. Deployment of packages has been enhanced to make it simple to bundle together all of the related elements for a test or production system.

Control flow. Control flow has been separated from data flow to make the logic in a SSIS package more easily understood. The control flow itself can support many different kinds of precedence and looping constructs. There are many different predefined tasks available for common work, including send mail, bulk insert, execute SQL, reading data from the filesystem or FTP, and working with Analysis Services. Customized tasks can be created using VB.NET scripting or with the SSIS object model.

Data flow. Multiple sources, transformations, and destinations are supported in the data flow pipeline. Data from multiple sources can be merged together using Join, Lookup, or Union operators without creating temporary tables. The data stream can be split into multiple streams using conditional split and multicast transforms. Many different kinds of row-based data transforms are available to map data from source to destination, including basic data conversions, character mapping, derived column transforms, and more sophisticated multirow aggregation and sorting transforms. In addition, there is support for complex logic to create fuzzy matching, time dimension generation, and pivoting of data in a straightforward manner.

Relational Data Warehouse

The SQL Server 2005 database engine has several specific features that allow for the creation of optimized relational data warehouses, including:

Partitions. Partitioned tables and indexes have their data divided into groups of rows that can be separated on different disks or servers. Partitioning can improve query performance and manageability by breaking the data up. Partitioning also enables fast data loading and simplified maintenance for very large tables.

Transact-SQL improvements. Transact-SQL improvements, including new data types and analytic functions that provide important functionality for data warehousing. Recursive queries are also available to create more flexible self-joins.

Snapshot isolation. Concurrency is often an issue when providing business intelligence solutions. Because BI is often based on read-only applications that run multiple queries against transactional databases with constantly changing data, something more than standard concurrency control is necessary. Snapshot isolation allows these queries to run with a minimum impact to the running transactional application while providing transactionally consistent data to the queries.

Indexed views. Views are extremely useful for developing business intelligence solutions. Indexed views provide a performance boost to views in three ways: by allowing aggregations to be computed ahead of time and retrieved during query execution, by prejoining tables, and by caching combinations of joins or aggregations. The Database Tuning Advisor can suggest when indexed views are appropriate.

Database mirroring. Creating a read-only database mirror of a transactional database is an excellent way of offloading reporting and data warehouse extraction loads from a transactional system.

Multidimensional Database

The OLAP portion of Analysis Services 2005 provides multidimensional database functionality in SQL Server 2005. Analysis Services 2005 blurs the line between relational and multidimensional databases. The Unified Dimensional Model combines the query performance and analytical richness of OLAP with the flexibility and zero latency data of the relational model. SQL Server 2005 has the following features for multidimensional databases:

Proactive caching. Data latency is a big problem for most OLAP databases since they are typically at the end of the ETL chain. Proactive caching allows cubes to automatically refresh when transactions occur on the source database, minimizing the data latency. Proactive caching has many tunable parameters that allow you to configure the right combination of latency and frequent data loading for your transactional systems.

Key performance indicators. SQL Server 2005 provides a framework for defining values, goals, and trends for key performance indicators.

MDX scripts. Multidimensional Expressions (MDX) is a powerful language that you can use to specify multidimensional queries. For SQL Server 2005, MDX has been expanded to allow for scripts that create server-defined objects such as cubes, calculated members, and cell calculations. These scripts follow a procedural model where the scripts are applied in order and can be debugged to evaluate the state at every line of script.

Tools and wizards. There are many tools and wizards defined for some of the most common and troublesome tasks in designing and building multidimensional databases, including semi-additive measures, time dimensions, financial aggregation, and currency conversions.

Data source views. Data sources contain the information used to connect to source data. Data source views define a subset of relevant tables in a source database. The metadata in a data source view can be augmented with information like relationships, friendly names, and calculated columns. These views can be shared between projects and are very useful when you have a large number of data sources and source columns that you wish to reuse across different applications.

Native Web services. XML for Analysis (XMLA) is now a native protocol for communicating with Analysis Server. This makes zero and light footprint client applications much easier to build and deploy.

Reporting

Reporting is one of the cornerstones of solid business intelligence. Reporting Services is a complete platform for creating, managing, and delivering static and interactive reports. Report Server's modular design and flexible application programming interfaces (APIs) allow enterprises to tightly integrate reporting with their business intelligence solutions. Some of the features that make Reporting Services a solid solution include:

Authoring tools. Reporting Services features the Report Designer, which is hosted in Visual Studio to create reports that are stored in an XML-based report definition language (RDL). The open nature of the report format means that it is possible to have reports generated in an automated way.

Data sources. In addition to supporting data hosted in Microsoft SQL Server and Analysis Services, Report Services can access data stored in a database that can be accessed through an OLE DB or ODBC driver.

Report presentation. Reporting Services offers a number of different basic formats for reports, including freeform, table, matrix, and charting. In addition, there is full support for parameterized filtering of report contents and sorting and grouping. If static reports are not enough, Reporting Services offers dynamic drill through and linked reports. The presentation of a report is a separate process from querying the data, so that the same report may be rendered in different formats.

Report management. There is a role-based security model that protects both reports and data sources. Reports can be scheduled for execution and delivery or obtained on demand. Users can subscribe to reports to receive updates on a regular basis or when important data is updated. Reporting Services also maintains a stored snapshot or the report dataset at the time the report was run for auditing purposes and to help establish trends.

Report delivery. Reports can be delivered in a wide variety of formats, including HTML, PDF, Excel, XML, and CSV. The reports can be posted to a portal, emailed, or accessed via Web or shared folders.

Data Mining

Data exploration, pattern discovery, and prediction are integral to successful business intelligence. The data mining technologies to support these are fully integrated into SQL Server 2005. The goals for the data mining features in SQL Server 2005 were to provide a complete, easy-to-use, integrated set of features that extend the market for data mining applications. Although building a successful data mining model requires a strong understanding of the data and the business drivers behind the data, SQL Server makes this process as easy as possible. SQL Server supports the most popular data mining algorithms, including:

Decision trees. This classification algorithm is often a good starting point for data exploration. It is also good for predicting both discreet and continuous variables. In effect, the algorithm tries to find a combination of input states that predict specific outputs.

Naïve Bayes. This algorithm calculates probabilities for each state of the input attribute given each state of the results. Although it only works on continuous variables, it is also very quick to compute.

Clustering. Clustering groups records that have similar characteristics. It is often an excellent way to better understand the relationships in the data and to create simple predictions.

Association. This algorithm is mostly used for market basket analysis and finds correlations in sets of data.

Sequence clustering. This algorithm combines clustering with an analysis of the sequence of events in a dataset. It is particularly useful in the analysis of click stream information from Web sites.

Time series. Time series analysis is used to create predictions of continuous variables over time. The specific algorithm used by SQL Server 2005 reduces the statistical knowledge necessary to create accurate time series models from datasets.

Neural networks. This is an artificial intelligence technique that explores all the relationships in the data for data exploration, classification, and prediction. Although neural networks are very flexible, they are also very slow to train and consume a large amount of computing power.

Metadata Repository

The Unified Data Model (UDM) provides excellent support for creating metadata that provides a single view of a variety of physical data sources. The benefits of UDM include:

Friendly names. The raw contents of data sources such as ERP systems are often very difficult to understand. UDM allows the creation of friendly names for important data elements.

Spans heterogeneous data sources. Interesting information is often distributed across multiple data sources that can be difficult to reconcile and connect.

UDM allows these to be presented in a uniform way to client tools such as Excel.

Aggregated information. Most transactional data stores hold very detailed data, while most business users are concerned with the big picture. UDM provides aggregated views of relevant data.

Business rules. Raw data sources must be interpreted without the benefit of the business rules that accompany them. UDM captures business rules in the model to support richer analysis.

SQL Server 2005 does not have a specialized metadata repository application. Instead, Analysis Services metadata information is stored as XML files that are managed by Analysis Services. These files can be stored under version control.

Database Design Tools

The Business Intelligence Development Studio is used to build and maintain BI applications. You can use the BI Development Studio to define a cube or mining model. Functions of the BI Development Studio include:

1. Defining all details of Analysis Services objects (cubes, dimensions, mining models, security roles...), and testing/debugging those definitions (including browsing the data).
2. Defining all details of other components of the application, including Reporting Services reports and SSIS packages.
3. Based on the Visual Studio Development environment, creating a cube or mining model will be a parallel task to creating any kind of project in Visual Studio. Extensive customization of the development environment is possible.

Database Management Tools

The Management Studio is used to manage database servers and Analysis Services, Reporting Services, and SSIS servers. This supports the management of a deployed application, and the functions that can be carried out include:

- Management tasks, such as backup/restore, and processing.
- Defining those details of Analysis Services objects that are deemed relevant to management activities; for example, adding a new partition, or adding a user to a security role. There are no design tools provided to define or change other details; for example, adding a new dimension to a cube is not considered a management activity.

- Browsing data, and issuing MDX and DMX queries.
- Scripting objects and tasks, and issuing XMLA queries (to create objects, delete objects, process, etc.).
- Changing a server property (e.g., the log file location).

Data Quality Tools

Microsoft does not provide any specific tools for data quality with SQL Server 2005. However, the programmability through both CLR integration and TSQL inherent in the platform provides enough flexibility to implement advanced rules in the data store to enhance the quality of transactional data that comes into the database. In addition, the flexibility of the SSIS to validate the content, quality, and structure of the data coming in from disparate systems provides an excellent basis for a data quality program.

Portals

Although SQL Server 2005 doesn't include a Web portal, Microsoft SharePoint Services fulfills this role. Note that to use SharePoint with SQL Server 2005, you will need to apply the SharePoint Service Pack 2 (SP2). More details on this service pack can be found at *http://office.microsoft.com/en-us/assistance/HA100806971033.aspx*. Covering SharePoint in any depth would require a book all its own, so we will leave you with a short list of useful SharePoint resources if you wish to learn more.

The SharePoint Products and Technologies on MSDN section offers links to development details and examples (*http://msdn.microsoft.com/library/default. asp?url=/library/en-us/odc_2003_ta/html/sharepoint.asp*).

The SharePoint Portal Server Home page offers high-level descriptions of what SharePoint is and how it can be used (*http://office.microsoft.com/en-us/ FX010909721033.aspx*).

- The Microsoft SharePoint Community has a large list of discussion threads, articles, and tips for working with SharePoint (*http://msd2d.com/default_section. aspx?section=sharepoint*).

CONCLUSION

This chapter discussed a framework for business intelligence solutions and linked it to the features available in SQL Server 2005. First, we outlined the challenges inherent in creating business intelligence. Then, we moved on to describe how business intelligence can create value out of the overwhelming quantity of information available in today's business environment. We offered some advice on how to best align the business intelligence solution with both the business and the underlying technology. Finally, we described the features of SQL Server 2005 that apply to each aspect of building a successful business intelligence solution. Next, we will move on to describe each of these pieces in detail.

12 ▪ Data Warehouse

In this Chapter

- ▪ Top-Down versus Bottom-Up
- ▪ Data Warehouse versus Transactional Systems
- ▪ Dimensional Modeling
- ▪ Sizing of a Data Warehouse
- ▪ Data Preparation and Cleansing
- ▪ Loading Data
- ▪ Conclusion

A *data warehouse* is a foundation for business intelligence. The purpose of a data warehouse is to be a repository for consolidated and organized data that can be used for analysis. This data can come from a large variety of sources, including online transaction processing (OLTP) databases, legacy systems, spreadsheets, and external sources. Data warehouses range from very, very large with many terabytes of data to smallish collections of a few megabytes.

A *data mart* is conceptually similar to a data warehouse. However, instead of being based on data across the entire enterprise, a data mart is a subset of corporate data that is targeted for a specific business department or set of users. This subset can be extracted directly from enterprise system data or from a larger data warehouse. The term *data warehouse* is often used broadly in practice to encompass both of these meanings. Bill Inmon in *Definition of a Data Warehouse* (Inmon Associates, *www.inmoncif.com/library/articles/dwdef.asp*, August 25, 2003) defines a data warehouse as a collection of data used to support decision making that is:

- Subject-oriented
- Integrated
- Time-variant
- Nonvolatile

Subject-oriented means that the data warehouse is organized around particular subjects instead of ongoing operations. For example, a data warehouse might have a section organized for the analysis of sales by date, product, and region. Contrast this to a database designed to support ongoing operations that would have this same information stored in a set of transactional tables supporting point of sale and inventory applications. In general, the format of this data will be optimized for the transactional applications that use it, but much less so for analysis outside of those applications.

Integrated means that the data warehouse contains data gathered from a variety of sources, and then merged into a coherent view. Primarily, this means that data is collected from all of the transactional systems in the enterprise that have relevance to the subject. Even if a company has distinct sales systems across different divisions, in order to get a holistic view of company sales, all that data needs to be brought together in the data warehouse. In addition to data collected inside the enterprise, sometimes data from outside the enterprise is included in the warehouse to improve the quality and analytical value of the data. Continuing with our sales example, the sales data might be augmented with external market research or demographic data to assist in analyzing and understanding sales patterns.

Time-variant means the data is related to a particular time period. To be useful in business analysis, data needs to be placed in a temporal context. For example, our sales data will have a date attached to it either directly taken from the transactional systems or as it is inserted into the data warehouse.

Nonvolatile refers to the static nature of the data after it is copied into the data warehouse. Unless a data error is found, the data isn't modified in the data warehouse. Instead, the data is maintained in the transactional systems, and then copied to the data warehouse in a process called extraction, transformation, and loading (ETL). In SQL Server 2005, the ETL process is facilitated by SQL Server Integration Services (SSIS), which we discuss further in Chapter 13, "SQL Server Integration Services."

An important conceptual note is that sometimes the terms *OLAP* and *data warehouse* are used interchangeably. However, these are two very distinct things. A data warehouse, as we described previously, is typically a relational database and contains potentially huge volumes of data. OLAP, in contrast, is a specific technology that enhances multidimensional analysis of the data, such as the OLAP services provided by SQL Server Analysis Services. It is possible to have a data warehouse without OLAP and do multidimensional analysis using only SQL queries. It is also possible to have an OLAP database without the presence of a data warehouse. In that case, the data might be pulled directly from the transactional systems to create the cubes used for multidimensional analysis. What data warehouses and OLAP have in common is that they are both designed to make reporting of business data more efficient.

TOP-DOWN VERSUS BOTTOM-UP

As with almost any topic of some complexity, the proper way to design and build a data warehouse is a subject of some controversy. In general, data warehousing has a historical divide into two camps: top-down and bottom-up.

Top-down

The unified data warehouse advocates who believe that the proper way to construct a data warehouse is to create one centralized repository for the entire enterprise. Bill Inmon, the man who coined the phrase "data warehouse," is the leader of this group with his vision of a "Corporate Information Factory" that places the data warehouse at the center of all business intelligence activities (for more information, see W. H. Inmon, Claudia Inhoff, and Ryan Sousa—2000). This data warehouse, typically designed as a normalized enterprise data model, provides a single version of the truth and is very robust against changes in the business. From this central repository, dimensional data marts are created for specific analytical tasks. Typically, a top-down approach offers excellent consistency across the various data marts because they are all designed together.

However, this consistency comes at the cost of a much larger and longer project. Monolithic, top-down data warehousing projects can take many years to complete and can be inflexible to departmental needs and concerns. Such a project can take years and cost many millions of dollars. The return on investment for such undertakings is distant and uncertain and can be difficult to justify in business terms despite the elegant data engineering.

Bottom-up

Contrasting with top-down is the bottom-up method that is championed by Ralph Kimball, another luminary in the data warehousing field (for more information, see "The Data Warehouse Toolkit: The Complete Guide to Dimensional Modeling," Ralph Kimball and Margy Ross—2002, p. 16). In the bottom-up approach, a comprehensive data warehouse is built up over time through a series of data marts that are focused on specific areas and coordinated through data warehouse bus architecture. Defining a standard bus for the overall data-warehousing environment means that different data marts can be plugged together. The bus analogy stems from the usage of the term in personal computer hardware, where the inception of the ISA and subsequent PCI bus standards made it much easier to assemble pieces made at different times by different manufacturers in one personal computer.

Starting with a relatively limited and focused scope provides a way to kick-start a business intelligence platform. Since each data mart is a relatively small project, it can begin to deliver value more quickly than a larger data warehouse project. Once the data marts have begun to prove their worth to the enterprise, it is much easier to justify an ongoing investment in developing additional marts. Each additional application or process focus that is added will benefit the value of the whole through the network effect—each additional element adds perspective and insight to the other elements. This more evolutionary approach has the advantage of producing more immediate results at the long-term risk of not achieving successful integration between the data marts.

However, the fragmentation engendered by the bottom-up approach, if not managed properly, can lead back to the bad old days of stovepipe reporting systems and information confusion. Less structured and comprehensive business intelligence efforts are great for achieving immediate results. However, eventually, the incongruities between departmentally focused efforts will stifle the flow of information across the entire enterprise and reduce the competitive advantage gained from business intelligence.

Hybrid Approach

More recently, a hybrid model has evolved. The top-down approach has accepted that it is necessary to deliver value more quickly, and the bottom-up approach recognizes that a failure to adequately plan for future integration can be a costly mistake. Everyone wants to achieve the same result: a flexible data repository that adapts to business changes and provides a single version of the truth. Finding a middle ground between these two approaches is essential. To make sure these focused applications don't become silos, careful attention needs to be paid to making sure that the strategic goal of providing information for the entire enterprise is not compromised.

To do this, you need to pay careful attention to developing enterprise-wide metadata. Be sure to establish and maintain a core list of common elements. Make sure to design a solid and extensible staging area for collection, cleaning, and distribution of your enterprise data. In addition to simply providing the means for business intelligence, make sure to measure utilization and results to establish return on investment. To help build and maintain momentum, publicize successes that are made possible by improved business intelligence.

DATA WAREHOUSE VERSUS TRANSACTIONAL SYSTEMS

A data warehouse is much different from a transactional system. Most of this difference derives from the different purposes of the two systems. Transactional systems focus on updating and adding single records, with the key element being fast and efficient processing of transactions. Data warehouses provide access to many records, with a key element being very quick access to information for reporting and analysis. Since form generally follows function, the differences in design are not surprising. Many people coming to data warehouse design from transactional system design make the classic mistakes of ignoring these distinctions. Or, they make the even worse mistake of using a transaction system directly as a data warehouse.

Dimensional modeling is the most effective way to design a data warehouse. It is the process of creating a logical model that is optimized for query and analysis performance. In many cases, a data schema produced by a dimensional model of a system is much simpler than the schemas of the transactional databases supporting the same system. Although many people believe that dimensional modeling is a recent development, it has been around for quite some time. The first known references to what we now understand as dimensional modeling are from a joint General Mills and Dartmouth University research project in the 1960s (see Wayne Eckerson, "Data Quality and the Bottom Line," *The Data Warehousing Institute*, 2002, p. 5).

One reason for this relative simplicity is that data warehouses don't need to support transactions. Transactions greatly complicate the design of a database because of the critical properties that must be met to support transactions. The four properties that are generally agreed upon to be necessary to support transactions are:

- Atomicity
- Consistency
- Isolation
- Durability

Taken together, these properties are commonly referred to by their acronym: ACID. Systems professionals often say, referring to these properties, that their transactional systems have "passed the ACID test." It is no simple matter to design a system to properly support ACID transactions, and the resulting databases are less than optimal for generating reports of meaningful business phenomena.

Atomicity

Atomicity means that a transaction either completes in its entirety or not at all. There is no possibility that only a part of a transaction is completed. If only part of a transaction can be completed, the whole transaction is undone. The canonical example of the importance of atomicity is the example of a doing a transfer in a banking system. In such a system, the first account is debited and the second one is credited. If a customer attempts to transfer money from one account to another, there would be big problems if the transaction were left in a half-completed state. Either the customer would have the first account debited without the corresponding credit to the second account, which would make the customer unhappy, or the second account would be credited without the corresponding debit, which would make the bank unhappy.

Consistency

Transactions must preserve the internal consistency and integrity of the database. If the database satisfies all of its integrity constraints before the transaction, it must also satisfy those conditions after the transaction. Although many kinds of integrity constraints are possible for a database depending on the type of application it supports, some constraints such as uniqueness of primary keys and referential integrity are consistently applied across all applications.

Isolation

A transaction must act as if it is running entirely on its own, even though there might be thousands of other transactions occurring nearly simultaneously. Basically, this means that the system behaves as if all of the transactions are conducted in a series. In most cases, the isolation of transactions is supported by database locks. Managing table locking is a very important and complex part of the job of a transactional database system.

Durability

Durable means that the results of the transaction will not be lost in a system failure. Since many transactions in a database are done between an enterprise and its customers, this is an important property. You would not want to charge customers twice for the same transaction or not at all. This typically requires that the transactions be recorded to a disk immediately after they are completed in the form of a log that can be restored in the event of a system failure.

Performance Impact

In most cases, transactional databases are in a highly normalized form that requires multiple joins to get to elements that are meaningful to business users. Although these joins make transactions more efficient by reducing the size of the tables that need to be locked for a given transaction, the presence of joins makes typical business intelligence activities like creating reports and analyses more difficult and complex. Instead of dealing with tables that represent business entities, a strong knowledge of SQL is required to piece together business facts from a series of normalized tables.

In addition to the complexity of extracting business facts from normalized tables, reporting directly off transactional databases imposes a large performance penalty. Running complex queries on a live transactional system to support reporting and analysis can have a devastating effect on transaction throughput of the system. The biggest performance problems arise from database locking. As discussed previously, the purpose of database locking is to prevent a record from being accessed simultaneously by two different database tasks. A long-running query might prevent transactional tasks from being processed and cause system bottlenecks, or a transaction might stop queries from being processed. Either way, the contention caused by additional queries will result in suboptimal response time for transactions.

Indexing is another area where the priorities of transactional processing and data warehousing collide. Since indexes add time to insertions and deletions (as much as 20 percent), databases designed primarily for transactional processing tend to have minimal indexes—potentially only on primary and foreign keys. Data warehouses, on the other hand, can benefit from many more indexes to facilitate retrieval of data. The drawback of slowed insertions and deletions does not impact data warehousing very much.

Different Uptime Requirements

In addition, due to their different usage in the enterprise, data warehouses and transactional systems often have different uptime requirements and backup and restore strategies. Transactional systems often have elaborate support for on-the-fly backup of the transactions (the D in ACID). Organizations spend great amounts of money ensuring that their transaction logs are backed up, often keeping mirrored systems that can resume operations almost immediately in the event of a failure.

On the other hand, data warehouses, since they operate with static historical data, can simply be backed up on a regular schedule. There is little chance that sales data from three years ago are going to be updated in the normal course of business. This means that full backups on a data warehouse don't need to happen very often. Instead, it makes much more sense to use incremental backups when data is updated and rely on periodic full backups. This might mean that recovery from a complete failure of the data warehouse would require a year's worth of incremental backups to be restored. Imposing unnecessary reliability requirements on data warehousing applications can result in increased cost that doesn't add value.

Operational Data Store

Transactional systems and data warehouses have dramatically different requirements, designs, and implementations. The *operational data store* represents a middle ground between these two extremes. An operational data store is typically a set of tables that support near real-time reporting on operations. A typical example of this is in a call center where customer data is stored in an easily retrievable denormalized format to expedite the process of servicing customer inquiries. Although this isn't a full data warehouse, it does facilitate some analysis and remove the burden of supporting queries from a transactional system. Figure 12.1 shows how an operational data store might fit in with a call center application.

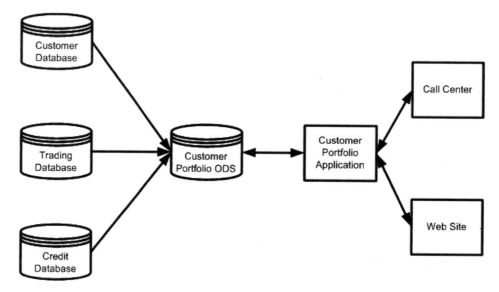

FIGURE 12.1 Operational data store.

The operational data store (ODS) is sort of halfway between a transactional system and a data warehouse. In general, they are designed to directly support operations and not ad hoc analysis. However, they are often an excellent source of data for a data warehouse since they are typically a first level extract of data from a transactional system and contain information that is directly related to the business. Although an ODS does not have all of the characteristics of a data warehouse, it can be very useful as a starting point for building one.

DIMENSIONAL MODELING

Now that we've highlighted the difference between transactional systems and data warehouses to place them in context with each other, we will explore dimensional modeling in more depth. As noted previously, dimensional modeling is the process of creating a logical model that is optimized for query and analysis performance and ease of use. Dimensional models are the foundation for a well-constructed data warehouse. They have proven to be very robust over time and, because they are organized around elements that are important to the business, they provide decision makers with an understandable and flexible platform for ad hoc queries and analyses. This simplicity and understandability is one of the best features of the dimensional model.

Star Schema

A distinguishing feature of a dimensional model is a set of business facts surrounded by multiple dimensions that describe those facts. In most cases, a data warehouse is organized in a *star schema* with central *fact tables* surrounded by *dimension tables*. A fact table is the primary table in a dimensional model, and is where the numeric data that is the focus of analysis is stored. Facts are the measurements of interest to the business. It is best to define facts at the most granular level possible. A good fact might be revenue taken at the invoice level. A dimension table is an axis of analysis on the fact table. It is possible to slice and dice the data along any combination of the dimensions included in the schema.

A dimensional schema is a *star schema* if all dimension tables can be joined directly to the fact table. A star schema with a central sales fact table and dimension tables for time, product, and store is shown in Figure 12.2.

In Figure 12.2, note that the central fact table has multiple foreign keys that join the facts directly to the primary keys of the dimension table. The facts themselves are specific, numeric columns in the fact table. It would be possible to lump everything together into one table by collapsing all of the dimensions into one flat table, but this would be a very broad table that is more inflexible in the face of change. Quite often, it becomes necessary to add dimensions after the fact table has already been constructed, and the single table approach would make this much more difficult. The dimensions are usually thought of as independent facets of a transaction, and are rarely strongly statistically independent, but are instead logically independent. For example, customer and store would often be statistically correlated because shoppers would tend to shop at the same stores. However, they are logically independent in that an analyst might be interested in partitioning by customers or stores or both.

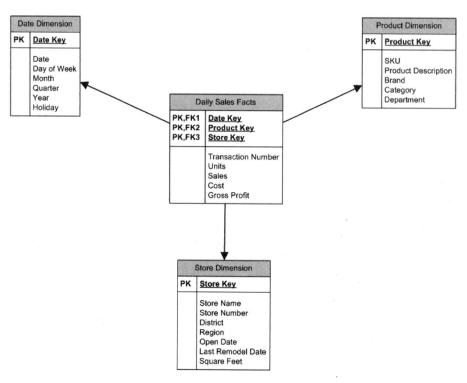

FIGURE 12.2   A simple star schema for retail sales.

Sometimes, a transaction in the fact table will have one or more missing dimensional elements. For example, if you have a promotions dimension, some products may be sold without an associated promotion. In this case, instead of setting the promotions foreign key in the fact table to null, it is preferable to add a "No Promotion" record in the dimension table and set the foreign key to point to that record. This makes the representation of no value consistent with the rest of the data and makes querying and analysis easier.

Slowly Changing Dimensions

Some dimensions have a tendency to evolve over time, a phenomenon called *slowly changing dimensions*. Slowly changing dimensions present a problem because the axes of analysis can change over time. A common change is a reorganization of the sales structure. For example, if the sales regions are changed, then salespeople may be reassigned across those different regions. Therefore, an analysis of the "new" Eastern region might not include sales from the same salespeople as the "old" Eastern region.

The word *slowly* refers to the speed of change compared to the fact table. Fact tables typically change with every update to the data warehouse, while dimensional changes occur on a periodic basis. Although the changes, like a sales force reorganization, may occur all at once in what feels like a rapid manner, the structure of the sales force dimension still changes more slowly than the data in a sales fact table.

Ralph Kimball, in *The Data Warehouse Toolkit: The Complete Guide to Dimensional Modeling*, proposes three different strategies for handling changing dimensions. He categorizes the solutions into three types, which he calls Type One, Type Two, and Type Three.

The strategy for Type One is to simply replace the data in the dimension table with the new data. Replacing the data is very appropriate if the old data was erroneous or it is unlikely that the changes will materially affect important analyses. However, simply replacing the data makes it impossible to do an apples-to-apples comparison of old data versus new data. Therefore, following the sales example, it would be impossible to analyze sales in the old sales structure since it would no longer be present in the database.

The second strategy, Type Two, adds the new data into the dimension table, while preserving the old data. In this case, we would add a new row to the sales table for the new Eastern region and record new sales data against it. This preserves the old structure and allows analysis of old versus new structure. This strategy can lead to a lot of data in dimension tables, since the old records are kept in the table. Since dimensional tables are orders of magnitude smaller than fact tables, this is not usually a huge problem.

Type Three preserves a version of the history by adding it to the dimension record. For example, to preserve the category changes for a product, you would have a field for the old category and the date it was changed. This strategy has the advantage of preserving the old data for analysis across one change, but can't support multiple changes in the data. In addition, queries to analyze data across old and new values can be complex. In general, Type Three dimensions are rarely worth the extra complexity and rarely seen in actual application.

Each strategy for handling slowly changing dimensions has its place. For correcting erroneous entries or information that does not need to be tracked over time, the simplicity of the Type One solution has the most appeal. For changes that are separable over time, a Type Two solution is the most sensible. Finally, for changes where being able to find the previous values and analyze with them, a Type Three solution is appropriate.

SQL Server 2005 has support for slowly changing dimensions. There is a slowly changing dimension wizard that can create a solution for maintaining a Type One or Two dimension. We cover management of slowly changing dimensions in SQL Server 2005 in Chapter 15, "OLAP."

Shared Dimensions

It is a typical analysis requirement to provide consistent dimensions across different subjects. For example, it is useful to be able to query on sales and purchase orders over the same time and product dimensions. Since sales and purchase orders are different business processes and have different facts, they will be stored in different fact tables, but will share the time and product dimensions. Careful modeling of your architecture will result in the sharing of as many dimensions as possible. Sharing dimensions over multiple fact tables is sometimes called a *fact constellation*. In a very complex organization composed of multiple fairly independent business units, it might not be possible to cover the entire organization with a large set of shared dimensions. Some might not share any other dimensions except time, which can usually be consistently mapped between different subjects.

Sometimes, dimensional designers are tempted to create *snowflake schemas*. A *snowflake schema* is like a star schema, except one or more dimension tables are not joined directly to the fact table. Instead, they must be joined through other dimension tables. A schema that has been snowflaked along the product dimension is shown in Figure 12.3.

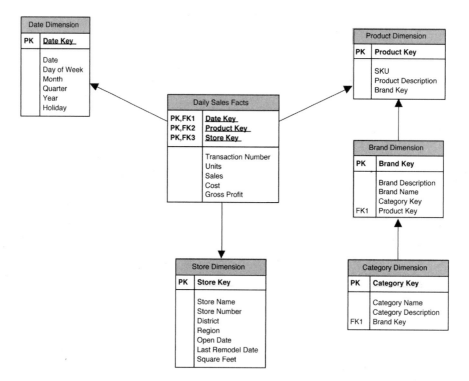

FIGURE 12.3   A snowflaked product dimension.

Although snowflaking appeals to the relational database designer because it is a normalization of the database, we should resist the urge to snowflake a dimensional schema if at all possible. In the context of a data warehouse, the additional complexity in querying and understanding the schema is not worth the nominal space savings and simplified updates provided by a more normalized schema. If you have a subject matter expert look at a pure star schema, he or she will almost always be able to identify with the process that is captured in the design. The same is not true for a heavily snowflaked design. Database experts have no problem understanding multiple levels of foreign keys, but the abstract concept of keys tends to confuse most business decision makers.

Compared to the sizes of the fact tables, the size of the dimension tables is inconsequential. If we have a 100,000-row product dimension table and we save 28 bytes per row by replacing a 30-byte category description with a 2-byte code, we will save about 2.67 MB worth of disk space. That isn't a bad thing, but it pales in comparison to the 10 GB of data we might have in our fact table. It is a matter of relative importance, and spending time and effort to address something of minor importance is just not sensible. The only time it would make sense is if you had a truly massive dimension table that was in the area of 10 percent of the size of the fact table.

As a rule of thumb, a data warehouse for an organization will contain somewhere between 10 and 25 fact tables describing the business operations. Smaller and simpler organizations may have fewer fact tables. Five to 15 dimensions will describe each of these fact tables. Too few dimensions will inevitably limit the queries that are possible. If you only have a few dimensions, you need to think more about different ways decision makers are going to want to slice and dice the data. If you have too many dimensions, there is a good chance that at least some of the dimensions are not independent or useful.

SIZING OF A DATA WAREHOUSE

It is valuable to have an estimate of the size of a data warehouse to be able to plan for storage, backup, and networking requirements—not just the size it is right now, but an estimate of the future size. Where possible, it is a good idea to do both bottom-up and top-down estimates. To approximate the size of a data warehouse made up of fact and dimension tables from the bottom up, you just need to estimate the size of the fact tables. Dimension tables are typically fairly small in comparison to the fact tables and can be ignored for purposes of sizing the data warehouse.

To estimate the size of a fact table, multiply the size of a row in bytes by the number or rows in the fact table. For column types that have a variable length, you can use a sample of existing data to generate an average value. This simple estimate ignores complexities of index sizes, storage efficiencies of different data types and page sizes, but it does give a good ballpark estimate of the amount of data you will have in a data warehouse. An estimate of the number of rows in a fact table is created by multiplying the number of transactions per day during typical operations and multiplying that by the number of days in operation over a given time period. To get the result in kilobytes, divide by 1024, and again by 1024 to get the size in megabytes. For example, let's say we generate an average of 10,000 line items of point of sale data every day. For the design we put together previously for the central fact table, an average line of point of sale data is 316 bytes in length, so every day, we are generating 3,160,000 bytes of data, or a little over 3 MB of data. If we operate 365 days a year, that amounts to approximately 1095 MB per year, or a bit over 1 GB of data.

A different way of calculating the size of a data warehouse that is related directly to sales information is to start with the top-line financial number for a given unit of time and divide by the average sale. As an example, let's say we have top-line revenue of $50 million per year with an average point of sale line item of $15. That means we generate approximately 3,333,333 line items of data per year. Multiplying by the same length we used before, 316 bytes, we arrive at a total of 1,053,333,333 bytes, which is close enough to our bottom-up estimate that we can feel pretty comfortable that we are talking about storing about 1 GB of new data per year.

Extraction, Transformation, and Loading

Source data from transactional systems is brought together in data warehouses through the process of extraction, transformation, and loading (ETL). ETL tools are responsible for the cleaning and translation of raw data from its native format in transactional systems and loading it into data warehouses. Basically, they convert the raw inputs from the transactional systems into something that can be analyzed in a data warehouse. An overview of the ETL process is presented in Figure 12.4.

As corporate information systems have become more complex, so has ETL. In many cases, ETL tools need to support many different systems and applications, spanning from large-scale ERP and CRM systems, to electronic commerce applications, to homegrown operational applications. In addition, ETL tools need to support getting data from external sources. External sources can add a lot of analytical value to a data warehouse by providing information on industry benchmarks and standard performance that can be used in comparing performance against industry norms or augmenting the analysis that is possible with internal data only. An example of useful external data is financial information from credit scoring bureaus like Dun and Bradstreet. Incorporating this data into a customer table would enable analysis of the data by customer revenue, credit rating, and the like.

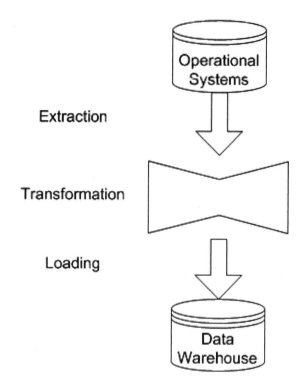

FIGURE 12.4 The ETL process.

As we have discussed, SQL Server 2005 includes a very capable ETL tool in the form of SQL Server Integration Services (SSIS). SSIS provides a one-stop shop for almost all of the requirements of a sophisticated ETL solution. We discuss the specifics of SSIS in more depth in Chapter 13.The first step to ETL is identifying the sources and the data they provide. If there are multiple sources for the same data, you will need to evaluate each of the sources on the basis of:

Correctness. Some systems have more accurate data than others do.

Completeness. Some sources contain an entire fact or dimension table, while others might just contain a subset. It is easier to work with systems that contain all of the data.

Timeliness. A source that is updated continually is better than one that is updated only periodically.

Origination. A source that is the point of origination for the data is better than one that receives a copy of the data.

Complexity. A source with a simple schema will have simpler conversion code than one with a very complex schema, all other things being equal.

After identifying the internal and external data sources, you will need to map the source data to the data warehouse. This mapping is part of the role of metadata.

Metadata

A complete set of ETL tools should manage the integration of heterogeneous environments, and the creation and management of metadata. Metadata is data about data. It describes the data that exists in the data warehouse so decision makers can use the data effectively. The usual analogy used to describe metadata is that it is like the card catalog in a library. The cards describe the books in terms of their author, content, and location in the stacks. Without the card catalog (or its modern computerized equivalent), finding a book in a library would be hopeless. How would you know which books addressed a certain subject? If you could find out which books were relevant, how would you locate them in the library? Searching for the proper book would be a tedious process of trial and error.

In terms of business intelligence, metadata has nothing to do with books, but it does provide the same benefits as a card catalog. Instead, the metadata describes the data kept in the data warehouse and in transactional systems. The information captured about the data is everything from technical details like size and data type to the definition in terms of the business. The metadata helps people understand which information to use for which purposes and where to find it. For example, what does net profit on a line of point of sale data mean? Is it just the cost of goods subtracted from the selling price, or is some element of allocated costing used in the calculation? Without metadata, the only way to know would be to recalculate it yourself and compare the results, or dig through source code to see how it was calculated. Neither of these methods is very efficient or appealing.

Metadata has been around for a very long time in the form of database schemas and data-flow diagrams, but the emergence of widespread business intelligence has made metadata a much more visible and important factor. Metadata used to be predominantly technical metadata that provides developers and technical staff information on where the data comes from and how it is to be maintained, essential to the ongoing operation of the data warehouse. Examples of technical metadata include:

- Logical data models
- Physical data models
- Transactional systems feeding data warehouse
- Identification and mapping of source system fields

- Transformations performed on source data
- Security information
- Program names and descriptions
- Versioning information
- Extraction schedules and logs

Business metadata, on the other hand, provides business users with a roadmap for accessing data in the data warehouse. Solid business metadata allows the decision makers using the information to use it better by reducing the search times for specific data and increasing the trust level in the data. Examples of business metadata include:

- Subject areas
- Table names with business definitions
- Field names with business definitions
- Description of field mappings and transformations from source system
- Confidentiality and security rules
- Data owner
- Data refresh dates and schedules

Metadata is very difficult to gather, organize, and maintain. The gathering of metadata is a very time-intensive task and, to be done right, requires interviewing business users to find out how the data is calculated and used. Information systems departments being what they are, there is always a search for a silver bullet that will protect us from having to talk to actual business users, but there is no substitute for directly interviewing subject matter experts when it comes to creating metadata.

Even after the metadata is gathered and codified, it tends to change at the speed of the business. New business models and systems change the calculation and use of the metadata continuously. A common pitfall is to come out of the gate at the beginning of a data-warehousing project and create an excellent initial repository of metadata that becomes outdated as soon as the excitement of the new project wanes. Outdated metadata is often irrelevant, or even worse, misleading.

SQL Server 2005 has good support for collecting, managing, and storing metadata in the form of data source views. A data source view is a named, saved subset of a relational schema. The data source views are shared between SSIS and Analysis Services so the same definitions can be used in data integration and analysis. A data source view consists of:

Identifier. The identifier consists of a name, a text description, and a unique identifier (GUID).

Definition. The definition specifies the schema that is of interest in the data source, including tables, views, unique keys, and foreign key relationships.

Attributes. Many different attributes are available to improve the usability of the view, including friendly names, named queries, calculated columns, logical primary keys, and relationships.

SSIS can use data source views directly to define sources and destinations for data flows, and as a source for reference tables for lookup transformations. Data source views provide many benefits to your ETL process, including:

Reuse. A data source view can be defined once and then used by multiple data adapters and transformations in SSIS.

Refresh. A data source view can be refreshed to reflect changes in its underlying data sources. You can review changes before choosing whether to implement the data source changes in the data source view.

Caching. A data source view caches the metadata from the data sources on which it is built. This means you can use data source views even if you are not connected to the data sources.

You can build multiple data source views on a data source and tailor each data source view to the needs of a SSIS task, data adapter, or transformation. For example, by using a data source that references your Sales database, you can build one data source view that includes only order information, and a second data source view that includes only customer information.

DATA PREPARATION AND CLEANSING

Data cleansing is an important factor in a successful data warehouse. Data cleansing checks data for errors like duplication, incorrect spelling, and abbreviations. As data volumes have grown, so have the volume of errors in data. Business intelligence, like most systems, follows the "garbage in, garbage out" principle. Even the best software solution can be made irrelevant by presenting bad data. As soon as decision makers lose faith in the accuracy of a business intelligence system, the system becomes worthless. It is difficult to recover a reputation for accuracy once it is lost. Unfortunately, it is very easy to introduce poor quality data into a data warehouse.

If you are doing a solid job of creating your source data in a transactional system with 97 percent accuracy on each field with a customer record consisting of 10 elements (first name, last name, first address, second address, city, state, zip code, phone number, fax number, and email address), you will have 300 errors per 1000 customer records. And that is not the worst of it. Despite your best efforts, data is a perishable good and will spoil over time. For example, about 2 percent of customer records become obsolete in a month because people move, change marital status and die (see Wayne Eckerson, "Data Quality and the Bottom Line," *The Data Warehousing Institute*, 2002, p. 5). The same dynamic applies to inventory and point of sale information as vendors add new products and discontinue old ones.

In addition to the dynamic nature of data, business rules and systems change over time, resulting in even more inconsistencies in data. Some of these may be inconsequential, but others can cause real problems. The Data Warehousing Institute has estimated that poor quality customer data alone costs $611 billion a year in excess postage, printing, and staff overhead (see Wayne Eckerson, "Data Quality and the Bottom Line," *The Data Warehousing Institute*, 2002, p. 10). In addition to those direct costs, the costs of misaligned promotions and lost customer loyalty could be even greater.

Before data can be added to a data warehouse from a transactional system, it must be prepared and cleansed. One of the easiest ways to facilitate this operation is to create a data preparation area that is a separate database from the data warehouse. This holding area is where you can start to transform the data from transactional data to warehouse data.

Some common transformations necessary to move data from transactional systems into a data warehouse include:

Date mapping. Date fields need to be mapped into date dimension tables.

Field lengths. Different transactional systems might have different field lengths for common fields. The data warehouse needs to use a common length.

Data types. The same field can be stored as different types in different databases. The data warehouse needs to use one data type.

Encodings. Transactional systems might map values to different codes; for example, using T and F or 1 and 0 for true and false.

Units of measure. Transactional systems might deal in different units. A warehouse application might deal in cases, while a point of sales system might work with individual units.

Duplicates. Transactional systems might have duplicates of the same data that need to be reconciled.

Capitalization. Transactional systems might use different standards of capitalization.

Missing data. Systems might use different conventions for missing data.

These are by no means the only errors that might be encountered when moving data from transactional systems to a data warehouse. In fact, data transformation for a data warehouse is one of the most challenging tasks in a data-warehousing project, sometimes taking more than half of warehouse development efforts.

Transformation can involve some manual steps to reconcile inconsistent or ambiguous entries. These should be avoided if at all possible since they tend to be an avenue for errors and can be a great expense in the ongoing operations of the data warehouse. A significant number of manual interactions are a good indicator that the source data might be too rough for use in the data warehouse without changes to the source system.

If the data is in poor condition, it might be easier to make changes to the source systems than to try to fix all the problems in the ETL process. However, attempting to fix transactional systems might be a potent distraction to the primary purpose of a data-warehousing effort and should be done only as a last resort. It is usually easier to attack the problem by using ETL tools. However, sometimes the problems are intractable and must be remedied at the level of the transaction system. Since this will halt progress on the data-warehousing project until the problems are resolved, this is definitely a risk to keep in mind when planning a data-warehousing project.

Although SQL Server 2005 does not have a specific data-cleansing tool, it does have features that support cleaning data as it passes through the ETL process. One of the more interesting tools available in SSIS is the availability of Fuzzy Lookup and Fuzzy Grouping. Fuzzy Lookup enables you to match input records with clean, standardized records in a reference table. The matching process is resistant to data errors that are present in the input. Fuzzy Lookup finds the closest match and tells you how confident you can be in the quality of the match. For example, customer information added during a new sales transaction may not exactly match any record in the existing Customers table because of typographical or other errors in the input data. Fuzzy Lookup returns the best matching record from the Customers reference table, even if no exact match exists, and provides measures to indicate the match quality.

Fuzzy Grouping allows you to group records in a table so each group corresponds to the same real-world thing. The clustering is resilient to commonly observed errors in real data, because records in each group may be close, but not identical. For example, Fuzzy Grouping is useful for grouping together all records in a Customers table that describe a single real customer for the purposes of removing duplicates.

LOADING DATA

After you have decided on your data sources and created your transformation and cleaning processes, you are ready to load the data into the data mart. It makes the most sense to load the dimensional data first and then load the fact table that references the dimensional data through foreign keys. You have to make sure to preserve database integrity when loading a data mart, so if you are using a bulk loading facility like SQL Server's bcp, make sure it is configured to enforce referential integrity on inserting data. As data is loaded, the indexes will need to be recalculated. If you are loading more than 10 to 15 percent of the rows, it makes sense to drop the indexes to facilitate quick inserts and then rebuild the indexes after the data has been loaded. It usually makes sense to load data marts one at a time during off hours so you impact the performance of transactional systems as little as possible.

There are some options to decide when to update data warehouse data. It can be difficult to detect what has changed since the last update. Some techniques for detecting changes and updating a data warehouse include:

Snapshot. Compare source data with a prior copy.

Trigger. Use a trigger to update the data warehouse as transactions occur.

Transaction. Use the transaction log as the basis for updates to the data warehouse.

Full. Create a complete new copy of the source data.

An interesting new feature useful for data warehousing introduced in SQL Server 2005 is the database snapshot. A database snapshot is a read-only, static view of a source database—a sort of copy of a database representing its state at a particular time. This can be used to capture the contents of a database at a specific moment in time to provide a read-only mirror of a database for reporting purposes or as a source for populating a data warehouse.

To create a database snapshot, use the CREATE DATABASE T-SQL statement with all of the usual modifiers (the unique name of the snapshot, name of the database file, etc.), with the AS SNAPSHOT OF clause followed by the database name. For example, to create a snapshot of the pubs database, you could execute the following SQL statement:

```
CREATE DATABASE [pubs_snap] ON
(NAME = pubs,
FILENAME = 'C:\Program Files\Microsoft SQL
Server\MSSQL\data\pubs_snap.ss')
AS SNAPSHOT OF pubs;
GO
```

Any snapshots you create show up in the Database Snapshots folder of SQL Server Management Studio. Once you have created a snapshot, you can use the content. In addition, you can revert the original database to the copy. This capability makes snapshots handy as a quick backup before doing risky changes to a database.

CONCLUSION

Data warehousing is a fundamental building block of business intelligence and is very well supported by features in SQL Server 2005. There are two basic schools of thought on constructing a data warehouse: top-down, which emphasizes data integrity across the entire organization, and bottom-up, which emphasizes achieving useful results quickly. A hybrid between these two approaches is an excellent way to proceed with a data-warehousing project. Dimensional modeling is the best way to design a database for analysis because of its simplicity and fidelity to the business model. Extraction, transformation, and loading are some of the principle challenges to any data warehouse. SQL Server 2005 provides excellent facilities for supporting ETL, as we discuss in the next chapter.

13 SQL Server Integration Services

The information we use every day has increased manyfold over the past 20 years. This increase of information requirements has led to a proliferation of applications storing information throughout almost every organization. A direct implication of this growth in the number of applications is that key corporate data resides in many different systems. Getting to a single view of the business has become quite difficult. The fractured views of customers, suppliers, and business processes offered by enterprise applications are often insufficient for fact-based decision making. Data is stored in various systems, in a variety of different formats and databases scattered throughout the organization. To improve the information available to make decisions, you need to be able to consolidate data.

There are a number of options available for data consolidation. At the lowest level, you can write your own custom applications to move data between data sources. Some of the features we discussed in Chapter 6, "ADO.NET 2.0," provide

283

a solid basis for building custom data migration applications. Custom coding has the advantage of being very flexible, since you can create any kind of custom logic required to map data from one system to another. However, this flexibility comes at a high price in terms of initial development and maintenance costs. Systems change over time, and it is very expensive to run custom development projects to keep up with the changes in your source and destination systems. Although custom ETL code used to be a common choice, today there are much better options available.

Instead of building your own data consolidation layer from scratch, it is usually better to use an integration toolset that provides much of the plumbing. These tools take much of the pain out of creating and maintaining this vital layer in your data warehouse. Many different vendors provide comprehensive tools for building ETL applications. However, many of these tools are very expensive and difficult to use. In earlier versions of SQL Server, Microsoft provided a simple ETL tool bundled with SQL Server called Data Transformation Services (DTS). Although DTS had its strengths, it also faced many limitations that limited its usefulness. With the release of SQL Server 2005, Microsoft has redone DTS to turn it into a much more robust tool called SQL Server Integration Services (SSIS).

SSIS is an enterprise data transformation and integration solution useful for extracting and transforming data from disparate sources and consolidating it to single or multiple destinations. SSIS offers connectivity to many different kinds of data sources, a set of tools and services to build data transformation solutions that meet your business needs and help manage the process on an ongoing basis. The comprehensive graphical tools allow you to build a complete solution without writing a single line of code in many cases. However, if the complexity of your requirements exceeds the capabilities offered by the graphical tools, you can access the objects and application programming interfaces (APIs) to craft a customized solution. Common tasks that can be done using SSIS include:

- Consolidate data from different sources
- Extract data into data warehouses and data marts
- Data cleansing and standardization
- Perform initial data loads into new systems
- Automate data management jobs

In this chapter, we discuss the basic organization of SSIS and introduce some of the tools used to construct SSIS solutions in SQL Server 2005 so you can get started on creating solutions for your own organization. If you are completely new to the integration tools in SQL Server, you will see that SSIS offers a complete ETL package. If you have used DTS in the previous versions of SQL Server, you will see that SQL Server 2005 offers many new capabilities and greatly enhances the previous version.

SSIS PACKAGES

The fundamental building block of an SSIS solution is the SSIS package. An SSIS package is an executable collection of connections, tasks, transformations, and workflows that defines a series of steps that are executed when the package is run. The package is the root level object from which all of the other objects are attached. All the other SSIS objects—tasks, containers, and precedence constraints—are stored in collections in the package. Tasks and containers can be grouped and run repeatedly as the package executes. When a package is run, it coordinates all of the other flows that occur in the package. In a typical SSIS package, the execution of a package will connect to a data source, copy the source data, do some transformations, and then send notifications about the status of the execution.

A package consists of a control flow and usually one or more data flows. A control flow defines the tasks and containers that execute when the package runs. These tasks and containers can be organized with precedence constraints to execute sequentially or can occur in parallel. Control flow provides a workflow structure to a package by providing conditions and precedence for the tasks defined.

A data flow is the source and destination adapters that link to the data sources, the transformations that convert the data from source to destination, and the data paths that link the adapters to the transformations. Data flow configures the data sources, transformations, destinations, and paths to connect the various components in a data flow graph. This graph will usually include at least one source and one destination and will often feature a transformation between them. Paths define the connections between the elements of a graph in sequence. The path editor shows the metadata and allows you to define data viewers on the path to observe the data as it goes through the path. This can be extremely useful for debugging because you can isolate where problems are occurring in a complex data flow. A data flow can also incorporate error handling for row-level errors. If an error occurs, the rows causing the problem can be routed to a different destination to help in troubleshooting and preserving the functionality of the rest of the process. You can include many unrelated graphs in a data flow.

In addition to the structural features in a package, SSIS has features that enhance the maintainability and operations of packages, including:

Restarting. Checkpoints can be set in a package to configure where the package will resume if it is interrupted in the middle of a run. This can be a large time-saver if a long-running process is halted toward the end of execution by avoiding repetition of slow tasks such as downloading large XML files or loading large amounts of data. The lowest level of a package that can be check pointed is the task container.

Security. Digital signatures can be applied to a package. This establishes a mechanism so only trusted packages are executed. In addition, packages can be encrypted with a password or a user key.

Transactions. Transactions allow a package, or containers and tasks within a package, to be configured to succeed or fail as a whole. This helps preserve data integrity. Transactions can be used in packages to enforce consistency by making sure all the database actions either succeed or are rolled back. This allows you to bundle several different tasks together and maintain data integrity. These transactions can be distributed across different data sources and destinations to bind them all into a single transaction.

Configurations. Configurations allow you to preset variable values in a configuration file that can be deployed with a package. When the package is run, it will use the values in the configuration file. You can create a variable configuration in the SSIS Configuration Wizard in the SSIS Designer.

CONTAINERS

The SSIS architecture is based on nested containers, with the package being the topmost container. Each container can include other containers, and is run in the order specified by the precedence constraints configured in the package. If a package is stopped while a transacted container is running, the transaction stops, and work that has been done in the container is rolled back. When the package is run, the container is rerun as well. A container is finished when all of its child containers have finished. Each container returns success or failure when it is finished. If the container fails, the SSIS engine compares the total count of failures to the `MaximumErrorCount` property defined in the package. If `MaximumErrorCount` is exceeded, the package execution fails. Containers can influence the results of their parents by `FailParentOnFailure` and `FailPackageOnFailure`, causing the immediate parent and the containing package to fail on the failure of the container, respectively.

Containers provide structure for SSIS packages. Containers can include other containers and tasks. Containers offer many options for iterative control flows and grouping of tasks into significant elements of work. You can use containers to repeat a task for each item in a collection or until a specified expression is true. Tasks and containers can be grouped into units that succeed or fail as a group. There are four types of containers in packages:

ForEach Loop container. Provides an iterative, for each element enumerator.

For Loop container. Provides an iterative container that is stopped when an expression evaluates to true. If you are a SQL Server 2000 DTS user, you will see that this is a dramatic improvement and will avoid the hacks that were necessary to perform looping in the older version of DTS.

Sequence container. Groups tasks and other containers into subsets of the overall control flow.

TaskHost container. Contains a single task.

In addition to the collections that are in all containers, packages have three additional collection types: connections, log providers, and configurations.

- Connections are used in SSIS for connecting to data sources such as text files and databases.
- Log providers provide a mechanism that the package and its containers use to record activities.
- Configurations are collections of values that are used for the properties in the package when it is run.

Every container has the properties listed in Table 13.1.

TABLE 13.1 Container Properties Define Descriptive Information and Run-time Aspects for Containers

Property	Description
DelayValidation	A value that specifies whether container validation is delayed until the package runs. The default value for this property is False.
Description	A description of container functionality.
Disable	A value that specifies whether the container is disabled. The default value of this property is False.
DisableEventHandlers	A value that specifies whether the container event handlers run. The default value of this property is False.
FailPackageOnFailure	A value that specifies whether the package fails when an error occurs in the container. The default value of this property is False.
FailParentOnError	A value that specifies whether the parent container fails when an error occurs in a container. The default value of this property is False.
ForcedExecutionValue	If ForceExecutionValue is set to True, a value that specifies the execution value that the container returns. The default value of this property is 0.

Property	Description
ForcedExecutionValueType	The data type of `ForcedExecutionValue`. This property is available only in SSIS Designer.
ForceExecutionResult	The forced execution result of the container. The default value of this property is `None`, which indicates that the container does not force its execution outcome. The values are `None`, `Success`, `Failure`, and `Completion`.
ForceExecutionValue	A value that specifies whether the execution value of the container is forced. The default value of this property is `False`.
ID	The container GUID, which is assigned when the container is created. This property is read-only.
IsDefaultLocale	A value that specifies whether the container uses the default locale. This property is read-only and set to `False`.
IsolationLevel	The isolation level of the container transaction. The values are `Unspecified`, `Chaos`, `ReadUncommitted`, `ReadCommitted`, `RepeatableRead`, `Serializable`, and `Snapshot`.
LocaleId	A Microsoft Win32® locale. The default value of this property is the locale of the parent container.
LoggingMode	A value that specifies the logging behavior of the container. The valid options are `Disabled`, `Enabled`, and `UseParentSetting`.
LoggingOptions	The internal name for SSIS logging options. This property is read-only.
MaximumErrorCount	The maximum number of errors that can occur before a container stops running. The default value of this property is 1.
Name	The container name.
TransactionOption	The transactional participation of the container. The options are `NotSupported`, `Supported`, and `Required`. The default value of this property is `Supported`.

Every container has the collections listed in Table 13.2.

TABLE 13.2   Collection Properties Define Event Handlers, Variables and Precedence for Container Collections

Collection	Description
EventHandlers	The container-level event handlers. The collection can include an event handler for each event the container raises.
Executables	The container-level tasks and containers in the container. The collection can include the tasks and containers that SSIS provides and custom tasks and containers.
PrecedenceConstraints	The precedence constraints that link container-level containers and tasks into an ordered workflow.
Variables	The system variables that SSIS provides for containers, and the container-level custom variables the container uses.

WORKFLOW

Workflow defines the sequence of events in a package. Precedence constraints allow tasks to be conditional on the success (or lack thereof) of another task. You can use constraints to establish parallel branches of execution. If no constraints are defined, the step is run immediately when the package runs.

The workflow consists of tasks arranged with precedence and constraints. This workflow is process-oriented with a distinct beginning and end. The idea is that you process objects as they pass through with each step. Each step is a task and has a completion result of success or failure. Therefore, the fundamental component of an SSIS workflow is a task, which is a discrete set of functionality, executed as a single step. A task defines work performed as part of the data movement or data transformation process, or as an external job to be executed. Using containers, tasks can be grouped together and run in a loop or as a single unit of work.

Tasks can be enabled or disabled depending on logic defined in the workflow.

SSIS has a number of tasks that are built in and can be readily accessed through the SSIS Designer or through custom code. Tasks are configured by setting properties. Each task has custom properties that are unique to that type of task and common properties that are present in all types of tasks. These properties can be accessed by using the SSIS Designer custom dialog boxes, the Properties window in the Business Intelligence Development Studio, or programmatically. A package can contain multiple tasks of the same type that are configured in different ways. These tasks can be configured to address a large number of common situations. For example:

Importing and exporting data. SSIS can use any OLE DB data source to import or export data. These data sources or destinations can include text files.

Data transformation. Mapping of columns between source and destination.

Copying database objects. Transfer indexes, views, logins, stored procedures, triggers, rules, and user-defined types between databases.

Sending messages. Programmatically send email or message queue messages depending on execution state.

Custom tasks. These are written in .NET.

Precedence constraints specify conditions that organize executables into a defined workflow. They can be placed between any type of task and the For Loop, ForEach Loop, and Sequence containers. Packages cannot be linked directly together using precedence constraints, but you can use an Execute Package task to establish an indirect precedence condition between two packages. Event handlers can also use constraints to link their executables into a workflow.

Precedence constraints are created in SSIS Designer by connecting two executables. The precedence constraint is evaluated after the first executable is run to determine whether the second executable is run. This constraint is added to the `PrecedenceConstraints` collection in the container. Precedence constraints can be created in packages, event handlers, For Loop, Foreach Loop, and Sequence containers. The Package Explorer in SSIS Designer can be used to edit the precedence constraints in a container.

All tasks have properties that control the operations performed by the task. Some properties are read-only and can be set only at design time; other properties can be set either at design time or updated while the task is running. Table 13.3 lists the properties that are common to all tasks.

TABLE 13.3 Task Properties Define Descriptive Information About the Task and Control Run-time Aspects.

Property	Description
DelayValidation	Specifies whether task validation is delayed until run-time. The default is `False`.
Description	A description of the task. The default is the task name.
Disable	Specifies whether the task is disabled. The default is `False`. $\rightarrow$

Property	Description
DisableEventHandlers	Specifies whether the task's event handlers are disabled. The default is False.
ExecutionProcess	Specifies how the task is executed: InProcess, OutOfProcess, and Remote. The default is InProcess.
ExecValueVariable	Specifies the name of a custom variable for the execution value of the task. It can be either none or the name of a custom variable. The default is <none>, indicating that the task does not store its execution result.
FailPackageOnFailure	Specifies whether the task fails on error. The default is False.
FailParentOnFailure	Specifies whether the package fails when an error occurs in a task component. The default is False.
ForceReturnValue	Specifies the outcome of task execution. Valid values are None, Success, Failure, and Completion. The default is None.
ID	A GUID assigned to an instance of a task when the task is added to a package. Read-only.
IsDefaultLocale	Specifies whether the task uses the default locale. Read-only.
IsolationLevel	Specifies the isolation level of the transaction. Valid values are Chaos, ReadCommitted, ReadUncommitted, RepeatableRead, Serializable, and Unspecified. The default is Serializable.
LocaleId	Specifies the task locale. Any valid Windows locale can be used in a task. The default is the locale of the parent container.
LoggingMode	The logging mode of the task. Valid values are UseParentSetting, Enabled, and Disabled. The default is UseParentSetting.
MaximumErrorCount	Specifies the maximum number of errors that can occur before a package stops running. The default is 1.
Name	The unique name of the task instance. The default value of this property is the task name.
TransactionOption	The transaction attribute of the task. Valid values are NotSupported, Supported, and Required. The default is Supported.
Version	The version of the task. Read-only.

The core type of task performed by most workflows is the data flow task, which moves data from source to destination, as described in more detail here. Other tasks can be grouped into the following categories:

- Data preparation tasks
- Workflow tasks
- SQL Server tasks
- Scripting tasks
- Analysis Server tasks
- Database Maintenance tasks

Data preparation tasks do things like loading and moving files. The specific data preparation tasks are:

Filesystem. Performs operations on files and directories stored in the filesystem.

FTP. Performs operations on FTP servers to download data.

Web Services. Performs operations on Web Services to download data.

XML. Performs operations on XML files to validate, merge, and compare the data.

Workflow tasks are used to create workflow operations, including executing other tasks and sending messages. Briefly, the workflow tasks are:

Execute Package. Runs an SSIS package in the context of the current workflow.

Execute DTS 2000 Package. Runs SQL Server 2000 DTS packages in the context of the current workflow. This is used to provide backward compatibility with tasks written in the previous version of SQL Server.

Execute Process. Runs an application or batch file in the context of the workflow.

Message Queue. Posts or receives messages from a Message Queue.

Send Mail. Sends email messages.

WMI Data Reader. Retrieves data from Windows Management Instrumentation (WMI).

WMI Event Watcher. Waits for events raised by WMI.

SQL Server tasks perform specialized activities on a SQL server database. These include:

Bulk Insert. Directly copies data from text files into SQL Server tables. This is the fastest way to load data into SQL Server.

Execute SQL. Runs single or multiple SQL commands in a database.

Scripting tasks are used to run custom code to perform functions that aren't provided in SSIS. There are two types of scripting tasks available:

ActiveX Script. Runs scripts created in ActiveX Scripting languages such as VBScript or JScript. This capability is similar to that offered in SQL Server 2000 DTS scripting.

Script. Runs scripts created in Visual Basic .NET. In general, new scripts should be created as Script tasks because it offers better integration with SSIS Designer and has enhanced debugging support.

Analysis Services tasks are used to manipulate data in Analysis Services. There are three kinds of Analysis Services tasks:

Analysis Services Processing. Used to process cubes or databases in Analysis Services.

Analysis Services Execute DDL. Can create, modify, delete, and process analytic objects in Analysis Services.

Data Mining Query. Runs predictions on data mining models built in Analysis Services.

Database Maintenance Tasks can be used in an SSIS job to perform maintenance activities. Note that these tasks are intended to be used primarily from the SQL Server Agent and are not included in the Toolbox when you are building a Control Flow in SSIS, but they can be used if needed. The available tasks include:

Back Up Database. Performs SQL Server backups.

Check Database Integrity. Checks the allocation and integrity of a SQL Server database.

Defragment Index. Reorganizes the indexes in a table or view for better efficiency.

History Cleanup. Deletes historical backup and restore information.

Execute SQL Server Agent Job. Used to run any SQL Server Agent jobs, which are used mostly for administrative tasks that are performed on a repeated basis.

Notify Operator. Sends a notification to an operator via the SQL Server Agent.

Reindex. Rebuilds indexes for tables and views.

Shrink Databases. Shrinks a database and associated log files.

Update Statistics. Updates key information for a table or view.

EVENT HANDLERS

Event handlers can be included in a package to respond to events that are raised by a task or container. These event handlers are constructed in a manner similar to packages and have a control flow and optional data flows. Event handlers are stored as a collection in the package, and can be used to respond to events raised by containers and tasks. Event handlers can do a variety of tasks, including sending email or running error handling routines. They can be constructed for packages, the ForEach Loop container, the For Loop container, the Sequence container, and individual tasks.

Events are raised in executables in response to something happening. You can create custom handlers to work with these events when they happen. An event handler is a special container that is run in response to an event. Information about the event is passed into the container. If an event has no event handler defined, the event is raised in the container next up in the container hierarchy. This is repeated until we run out of containers, in which case the event is handled by the default event handler.

Creating an event handler is comparable to creating a package in that event handlers have sequenced tasks and containers in control flow and may include data flows. SSIS Designer has an Event Handlers design surface for creating custom event handlers.

DATA FLOW

Data flow in SSIS is a data-oriented structure that is oriented around producing and consuming rows of data. A data flow defines data sources, transformations, destinations, and error handling. Rows are fed in as inputs to one end of the data flow, are transformed, and then emerge as outputs into a data provider. If errors occur in the data flow, they can be handled with defined error handlers.

The data flow is a graph of components, with each component having zero or more inputs and zero or more outputs with paths connecting the outputs to the inputs. Inputs and outputs can be left unconnected. The data flow is treated as a task in the workflow.

Performance is very important in the data flow. To achieve high performance, the data flow is performed in as concurrent a manner as possible. Copying is minimized and data is spooled to take advantage of lag times between components.

Components in a data flow include data source adapters, data destination adapters, and transformations. SSIS is compatible with many different kinds of data providers as both sources and destinations. OLE DB and ODBC providers are supported, as well as a large variety of file-based providers including text and XML, and nonrelational providers including Microsoft Exchange Server and Active Directory.

Paths define the route between the components and include the metadata about the data that is moved on the path. These paths form a graph of the routing of the data from source to destination and can include one or more sources, transforms, and destinations.

Transformations change data as it proceeds through the graph. A singleton transform changes each row as it is processed. This includes Derived column transforms, character mappings, data conversion, and lookup. Other transforms are based on the whole set of data and wait for the entire batch before transforming any data. These include the sort and aggregate transforms. Others are set oriented, but do not wait for the entire batch to process the data; for example, Pivot and UnPivot and MergeJoin. Other transformations have multiple inputs and outputs, such as UnionAll, Multicast, and Conditional Split.

Data flow and workflow work together to provide ETL services. Workflow provides the execution environment and controls the overall execution of the work. Data flow is just a task that is plugged in to this workflow to copy and manipulate the data. A schematic of the data flow is presented in Figure 13.1.

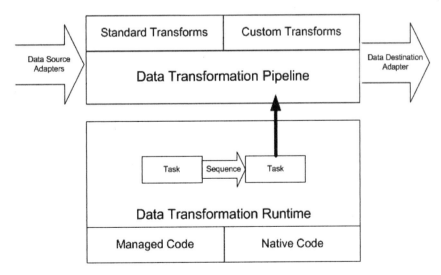

FIGURE 13.1 The data flow in SSIS maps data from the data source, through transformation and to the data destination.

VARIABLES

Variables can be used in SSIS to communicate between objects in packages and between parent containers and their children. A variable is created in the Variables collection at the scope of a container and is available to all of its child containers. You can create variables with package scope, For Loop scope, ForEach Loop scope, Sequence scope, or task scope. You can also organize variables by NameSpace. By default, SSIS creates custom variables in the User namespace, but you can create your own namespaces to help organize variables in large and complex SSIS packages. In addition to custom variables, SSIS has a set of system variables defined for each container.

EXPRESSIONS

Expressions are used in SSIS to define conditions for case statements, update data values, and assign values to variables. In addition, you can use expressions to define Conditional Split and Derived Column transformations, and Precedence constraints and For Loops. The expression builder in the SSIS Designer shows a list of available data columns, variables, functions, and operators that you can use in an expression.

LOGGING

SSIS has sophisticated and flexible logging capabilities. Logging can be enabled for the package overall or for individual tasks and containers in the package. The level of logging can be customized by selecting the events that should be logged and the information that should be logged for each. Many different logging providers are supported, including Text file, SQL Profiler, SQL Server, Windows Event Log, or XML file. Defining logging options for packages can be done in SSIS Designer using the Configure SSIS Logs, or programmatically. In addition, you can define common logging configurations and save them as templates to be applied to other packages in the SSIS Designer.

Packages can be created in a variety of ways. The easiest is with the SSIS Import/Export Wizard. The SSIS Designer has a graphical interface that allows the construction of a package from its component parts. Lastly, you can directly use the SSIS object model for creating a package. We discuss creation of SSIS packages in the remainder of the chapter.

SQL SERVER IMPORT/EXPORT WIZARD

The easiest way to create an SSIS job is to use the Import/Export wizard. This tool leads you through a step-by-step builder that creates a job that will perform simple data migration tasks. By default, the Import and Export wizard has minimal transformation capabilities. The only column-level transformation that can be done is to set the name and data types. You can edit the packages created by the Import/Export wizard in the SSIS Designer and use them as starting points for more complex data migrations.

Creating an SSIS package using the Import/Export wizard is easy. There are a few options to start the wizard. One of the easiest is to right-click on any database in the SQL Server Management Studio, select Tasks, and then select Import or Export. You will see the Welcome screen displaying some general information about the wizard as shown in Figure 13.2.

FIGURE 13.2   The Welcome screen displays some general information about the Import and Export Wizard.

Selecting Next takes you to Choose a Data Source where you pick a data source from the listed providers shown in Figure 13.3. Data sources supported in the wizard are:

- SQL Server
- Flat files
- Access
- Excel
- Other OLE DB providers

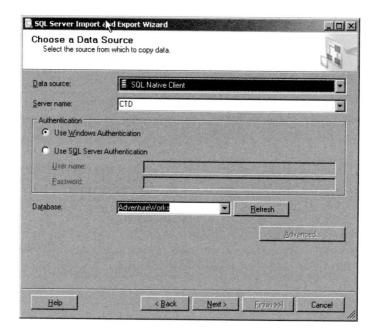

FIGURE 13.3 The Choose a Data Source screen lets you pick a data source for the wizard.

When you start the wizard by right-clicking on a database in the SQL Server Management Studio, the SQL Native Client will be chosen with the current server and database selected.

The next step in the wizard is Choose a Destination. The providers supported as destinations are the same as the source providers. In the example shown in Figure 13.4, we have chosen a Flat File Destination and picked a file on the local disk drive called customers.txt.

After choosing the destination, we select the data to be copied in the Specify Table Copy or Query dialog shown in Figure 13.5. In this dialog, you can select whether you want to copy an entire table or view of data from your source, or create a query to customize the data that will be copied. We chose to copy an entire table.

After choosing to copy a table or a query, you specify what should be copied. Since we chose to copy a table in the previous dialog and chose a flat file destination,

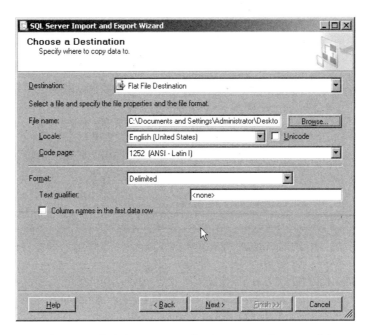

FIGURE 13.4 The Choose a Destination screen lets you pick a destination for the wizard.

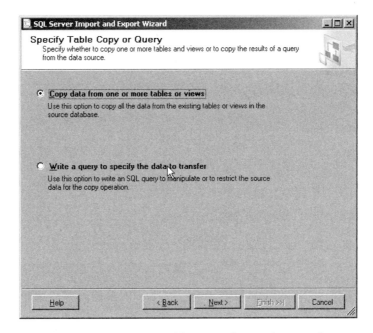

FIGURE 13.5 The Specify Table Copy of Query lets you choose whether to copy an entire table or limit the source using a query.

we get the Configure Flat File Destination dialog shown in Figure 13.6. Here we set the source table to be copied to be [Adventure Works].[Sales].[Customer] and configure the delimiters for the destination file.

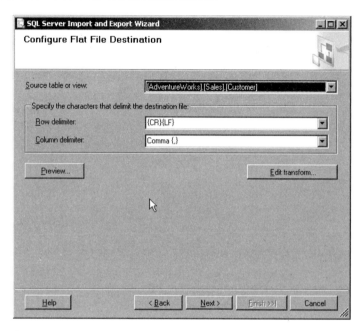

FIGURE 13.6 The Configure Flat File Destination screen lets you define the format for the flat file.

If we select the Edit Transform button, we can change the transformations used in the page to a limited extent. The only changes we can make to the transformation in the wizard are to the name, the data type, and the data type properties of columns in new destination tables. You can, for example, set the length of string columns and the precision and scale of numeric columns. You can also specify the nullability of the destination columns and whether they should be ignored during the transformation. If the data is copied to an existing table, you cannot change the data type or nullability properties of the destination columns, but you can ignore columns so they are not copied.

Since we have defined all the information required to run the SSIS package, we go to the Save or Schedule Package dialog shown in Figure 13.7. Here we have the option of running the package immediately, scheduling it for later execution, and saving the package. We can save the package either to SQL Server or to the filesystem as a DTSX file.

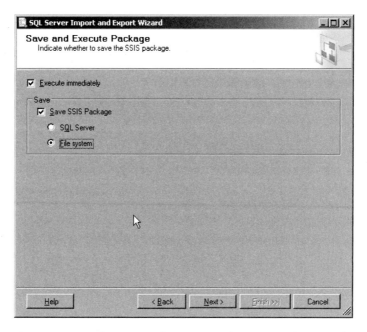

FIGURE 13.7 The Save and Execute Package screen lets you choose whether to save the package for later execution.

Since we chose to save the package, we have to choose the level of protection for the package. The options are:

- Do not save sensitive data
- Encrypt sensitive data with user key
- Encrypt sensitive data with password
- Encrypt all data with user key
- Encrypt all data with password

Sensitive information includes any password or connection string information that could be used to compromise the server. By encrypting all data with a user key, only the same user who encrypted the package can load it. Encrypting sensitive data with a user key means that sensitive information (e.g., passwords) is blank when the package is opened by another user. Password encryption is similar except that any user who knows the password can access the encrypted information.

Next, we get the Save SSIS Package dialog shown in Figure 13.8. Here, we choose the name for the saved package and where it should be saved.

After we have filled out the name and destination, we select the Next button to go to the Complete the Wizard screen, shown in Figure 13.9, where we are shown

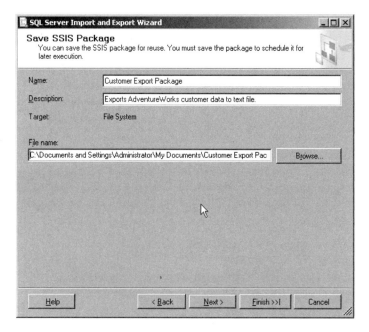

FIGURE 13.8 The Save SSIS Package screen lets you define the name, description and file for the saved SSIS package.

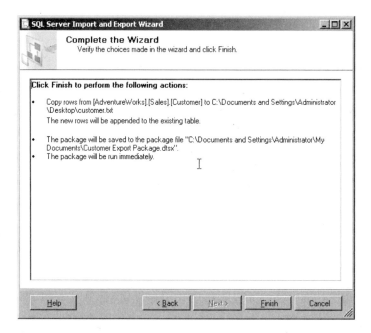

FIGURE 13.9 The Complete the Wizard Screen verifies the selections made in the wizard.

the choices we have made in the wizard. If we see something we don't like here, we can go back through the wizard and change the selections.

After we select the Finish button, we see the execution dialog, which will update the progress of the package as it runs and report the final status back to us as shown in Figure 13.10. Since our package was executed successfully, we see the steps that were run and how many rows were moved to our destination file.

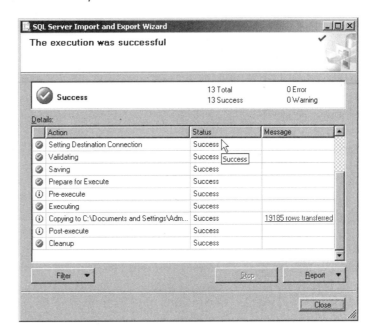

FIGURE 13.10 This screen shows the results of the package execution.

DESIGNER

The SSIS Designer is part of the Business Intelligence Development Studio and has a graphical, Visual Studio-like interface for creating SSIS packages. Each project in SSIS Designer has a collection of packages, data source views, and additional files that are associated with the project. Using SSIS Designer, you can construct packages that implement complex data transformations and workflows. It includes separate windows for constructing all of the elements of an SSIS package, including control flow, data flow, and event handlers. A number of wizards and specialized editors can be used in the SSIS Designer to add functionality to your package. The Package Editor has a Properties pane, which displays the properties of the selected package, and a toolbox where you can drag and drop components into your solution.

In addition, SSIS Designer has integrated debugging that can employ breakpoints and watches.

Like Visual Studio, the SSIS Designer includes a Package Explorer, which allows you to edit all of the elements in the hierarchy of a package. This hierarchy has the package container at the top, with all of the connections, containers, tasks, event handlers, log providers, precedence constraints, and variables displayed below it. The containers and tasks include event handlers, precedence constraints, and variables. The For Loop, ForEach Loop, and Sequence containers can have other containers and tasks. Data flow containers have the Data Flow task and the components used in the data flow.

Control flow in an SSIS package is built using the Control Flow window in the SSIS Designer. In that window, we see a design surface for creating the control flow, and the Control Flow Items tab in the SSIS Designer toolbox will be active, showing the available tasks and containers that can be added to the workflow. Items can be placed in workflow order by using their connectors to establish precedence constraints between the connected items. You can implement repeating flows, group tasks, define customer variables, and add annotations to your control flows.

In conjunction with the control flow, you can also design a data flow in the SSIS Designer. In the Data Flow window in the SSIS Designer, we see a design surface for the graph of that data flow where we can drag Data Flow Items from the toolbox. Each data flow is associated with a Data Flow task. A package can define multiple Data Flow tasks, with each having a different definition.

Event handlers are constructed using the Event Handlers design surface in SSIS Designer. Event handlers can include control flow, data flows, and variables, and are constructed in a way similar to packages.

The easiest way to learn the SSIS Designer is to use it. We will walk through the creation of a simple SSIS package that will import an XML file into the Cavalier Movies database. To implement this package, you will:

- Use the Business Intelligence Development Studio to create a new project.
- Create a new data source.
- Define a data flow.
- Define a control flow.
- Execute the package.

The first thing we need to do is launch the SSIS design environment. To do so, select Start | All Programs | Microsoft SQL Server 2005 | Business Intelligence Development Studio from the Windows task bar. After the Business Intelligence Development Studio has started, select File | New | Project. In the Project Types pane of the New Project dialog box, select the Business Intelligence Projects folder. In the Templates pane, click the Integration Services Project icon. In the Name text box, replace the default name with Import Movies. In the Location text box, select a location to save the project. These actions will create a new SSIS project called Import Movies in a new solution and an empty package named "Package," as shown in Figure 13.11.

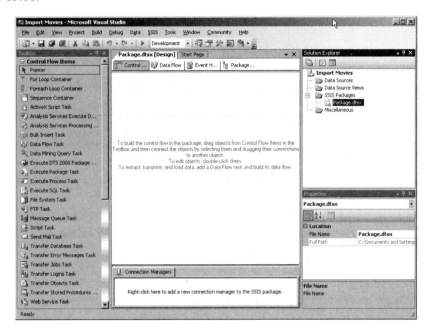

FIGURE 13.11   This screen shows an empty SSIS package in the Business Intelligence Developer Studio.

After we have created the package, we will create a new data source. The Data Source wizard will create a data source that can be reused across multiple projects. To do this, select the Solution Explorer, expand the Import Movies solution, right-click the Data Sources folder, and select New Data Source from the context menu. In the Data Source Wizard dialog box, click Next on the Welcome to the Data Source Wizard page. On the "Select how to define the connection page," click the New button. In the Connection Manager dialog box, in the "Select or enter a server name" drop-down list, type "localhost" or your server name. Under "Enter information to log on to the server," select the Use Windows NT Integrated security. In the "Select the database on the server" drop-down, select the CavalierMovies database, as shown in Figure 13.12, and then click OK. Back in the Data Source Wizard dialog, click Next. In the Completing the Wizard page, review the Connection string properties and then click Finish.

FIGURE 13.12 The Connection Manager is used to configure the connection used in the data source.

Now, we need to create a connection to the data source. Toward the bottom of the screen you will see a Connections tab. Right-click the empty connections pane and click New OLE DB Connection. In the Select Data Connection dialog box, highlight the localhost.CavalierMovies connection and click OK. This will add a new connection that points to the CavalierMovies data source and can be used with different package tasks.

Make sure the Control Flow tab is selected at the top of the design surface and show the toolbox by selecting the View | ToolBox menu item. If you like, you can click the Pin icon at the top of the Toolbox window to keep the window from minimizing. In the Control Flow Items list of the Toolbox, right-click the Control Flow Items and click Sort Items Alphabetically (Figure 13.13). You can navigate through the list using the arrows to move up and down. Select the Data Flow Task item from the Toolbox and drag and drop it on to the Control Flow Editor. Double-click the Data Flow Task you have just added.

Now, the Data Flow tab should be selected and you will notice that the Data Flow Items are visible in the Toolbox and the Data Flow Editor is open. In the Toolbox, in the Data Flow Items list, drag and drop an XML Source Adapter to the Data Flow Editor, as shown in Figure 13.14. In the Data Flow Editor, double-click the XML Source. In the XML Source Editor dialog box, select the Browse button next

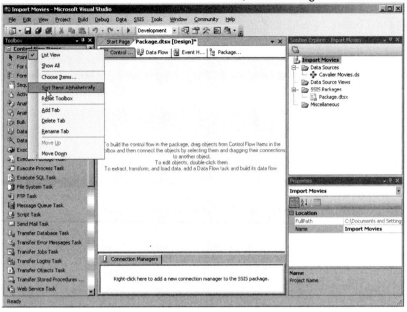

FIGURE 13.13   Sorting the items in the Toolbox alphabetically can make them easier to find.

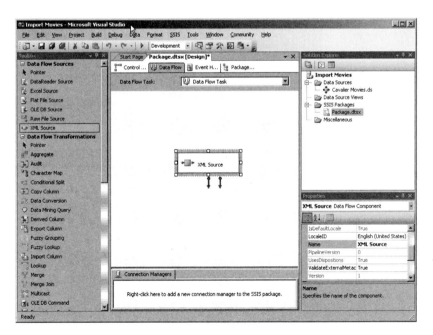

FIGURE 13.14   After you drop the XML Source on the Data Flow Editor, it will be ready to configure.

to the XML Location text box. In the Open dialog, navigate to the movies.xml file and click OK. Next, click the Generate XSD button. Generating an XML Schema or XSD is not strictly necessary, but it will speed execution of the job since if there is no schema, the structure of the XML will have to be inferred every time the job is run. In the Save As dialog, navigate to the folder containing the movies.xml file and click Save. Back in the XML Source editor dialog box, click on the Columns entry in the select box on the left-hand side. Make sure Movie is selected in the Output Name drop-down list and select Title, Description, Length, and Year checkboxes in the Available External Columns panel, as shown in Figure 13.15. Select the OK button to close the XML Source Editor dialog.

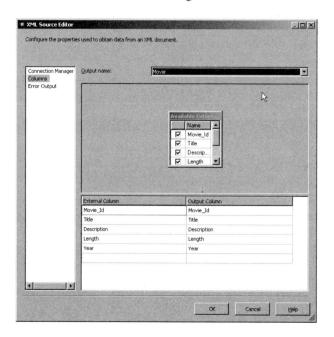

FIGURE 13.15 The XML Source Editor is used to select the data to be used from the XML document.

Next, drag and drop a Data Conversion item from the Toolbox onto the Data Flow Editor as shown in Figure 13.16. The Data Conversion item will map the data types from the source to match the data types in the destination. Connect the XML Source Adapter to the Data Conversion by clicking on the XML Source Adapter and selecting the green line extending from the bottom of the item and dragging it to the Data Conversion. The Input Output Selection dialog will appear. Select Movie from the Output drop-down list, as shown in Figure 13.17, and click OK to close the dialog. Double-click on the Data Conversion item. In the Data Conversion Editor dialog box, make sure the following Available Input Columns are checked:

- Title
- Description
- Length
- Year

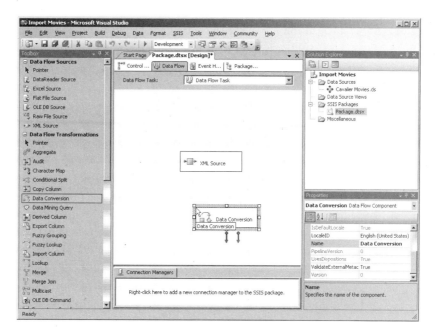

FIGURE 13.16 After dropping the Data Conversion Transformation on the Data Flow Editor, it is ready to configure.

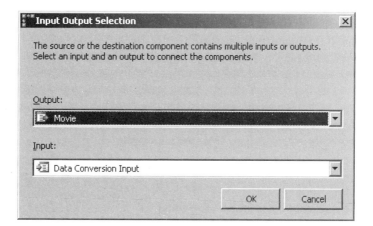

FIGURE 13.17 The Input Output Selection lets you select the inputs and outputs for the connection.

In the grid at the bottom of the Data Conversion Editor dialog, change the data type of the items to those in Table 13.4.

TABLE 13.4   The Input Columns Are Mapped to an Output Alias and Data Type

Input Column	Output Alias	Data Type	Length
Title	Copy of Title	string[DT_STR]	200
Description	Copy of Description	text stream[DT_STR]	
Length	Copy of Length	four-byte signed integer [DT_I4]	
Year	Copy of Year	four-byte signed integer [DT_I4]	

Now, drag and drop a SQL Server Destination item from the Toolbox onto the Data Flow Editor. Connect the Data Conversion to the SQL Server Destination by clicking on the Data Conversion item, selecting the green line extending from the bottom of the item, and dragging it to the SQL Server Destination object. Double-click the SQL Server Destination item. In the SQL Server Destination Editor dialog, select Connection Manager from the list on the left-hand side of the dialog. Select the New… button next to the OLE DB Connection drop-down list and select lo-calhost.CavalierMovies. Next, select [dbo].[Movie] from the "Use a table or view" drop-down list. Click the Preview button to see the contents of the table. Click Close on the Preview Query Results dialog to return to the SQL Server Destination Editor dialog.

After we have set the connection, select the Mappings item in the list on the left-hand side of the SQL Server Destination Editor dialog. The mappings are shown in a graphical format toward the top of the dialog and in a grid at the bottom, as shown in Figure 13.18. You can map the columns either by drag and drop from the Available Input Columns to the Available Destination Columns in the graphical display, or by selecting the appropriate element from the drop-down lists in the grid. Map the columns as shown in Table 13.5.

TABLE 13.5   The Input Columns Are Mapped to Destination Columns

Input Column	Destination Column
Copy of Title	Title
Copy of Length	Length
Copy of Description	Description
Copy of Year	YearReleased

After you have mapped the columns, click OK to close the SQL Server Destination Editor dialog.

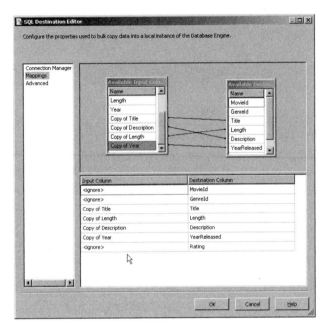

FIGURE 13.18 The SQL Destination Editor displays the mappings of Input Columns to Destination Columns.

Now we are ready to save and execute the package. Select the File | Save All menu item. Select the Data Flow tab at the top of the designer. In the Solution Explorer, right-click the Package.dtsx package and select Execute Package to run the package. As an alternative, you can select the Debug | Start menu item. While the package executes, you will see the colors of the boxes change indicating the following:

- **Gray**: Waiting to execute
- **Yellow**: Currently executing
- **Green**: Successfully finished
- **Red**: Failure

Each box will indicate at the top how many records have been processed (Figure 13.19). After the package has finished execution, select Debug | Stop Debugging to return to edit mode.

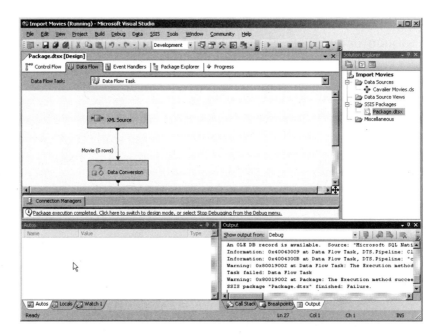

FIGURE 13.19   After running the package, the Data Flow Editor will display the number of rows that were processed.

To verify that the package has run, we will query the contents of the Movie table. From the Windows task bar, select Start | All Programs | Microsoft SQL Server 2005 | SQL Server Management Studio. If asked to authenticate, accept the default values and click OK. Select the New Query button in the upper-left of the toolbar, and then select New SQL Server Query from the drop-down menu. If asked to authenticate, accept the default values and click OK. In the Query window, type the following query:

```
USE CavalierMovies
SELECT * FROM Movie
SELECT COUNT(*) FROM Movie
```

Press F5 to run the query and verify that the data from the XML file has been loaded into the database. You should have the movies listed in Table 13.6 added to the database.

Note that the GenreId will be set to 00000000-0000-0000-0000-000000000000 because the movies have not been classified in a specific genre, and the MovieId will be a random globally unique identifier.

TABLE 13.6   These Movie Titles Should Appear in the Database After the Import Has Been Run

Title	Length	Description	Year Released
Dr. Strangelove	123	Apocalyptic dark comedy.	1960
I'm Gonna Git You Sucka	88	Spoof of blaxploitation movies from the 1970s.	1988
Caddyshack	109	Comedy about a golf course.	1979
The Matrix	136	Computer hacker discovers nature of reality.	1993
2001: A Space Odyssey	134	Something strange found on the moon.	1968

CONCLUSION

SSIS is an excellent tool for creating data migration solutions. It is organized around the concept of containers, with the top-level container being the package. The containers hold all of the workflows and data flows defined for the job. The flexibility of nested containers allows for easier construction and reuse of solutions. Tasks are predefined for most of the common tasks involved in data migration. Some of its many management features include support for many different types of logging, transactions to make sure jobs succeed or fail as a whole, checkpoints to resume operations that are halted, and configurations to allow for simple package deployment. In addition, the SSIS Import/Export wizard and SSIS Designer make it possible to create complex solutions without writing code.

14 SQL Server Reporting Services

In this Chapter

- Reporting
- Report Design
- Reporting Services Architecture
- Conclusion

In Chapter 11, "Business Intelligence," we briefly described the features of SQL Server 2005 Reporting Services (SSRS). In this chapter, we discuss the fundamental elements of corporate reporting and report design and then go on to describe how SSRS can be used to provide an effective reporting solution for corporate data.

REPORTING

SQL is an excellent language for accessing and analyzing corporate data. However, the tools we have used for querying data are not suitable for broad distribution to a wide population of nontechnical users. In addition to merely querying data, a successful business intelligence solution shares the results of any analysis that has been performed in a way that is easy for the target audience to access and comprehend. The value of business intelligence is subject to strong network effects: it is more valuable the more people in the organization know about it. How do we share the information we have gathered? The most common answer is "reports."

Although sometimes still associated with the ugly, static "green-bar" reports that were printed from mainframe applications and delivered by a person walking around the office with a cart full of accordion paper, reporting has evolved considerably in the last 20 years. When the laser printer became commonplace, reports migrated from the mainframe to the PC. As email achieved widespread adoption, it became the most common distribution media for reports. This evolution has continued, and reports currently come in all kinds of formats—Web pages, PDF, PDA screens, and voice mail. Sometimes, it can be difficult to determine exactly what we mean by reporting since the line between reports and the applications that generate the data has blurred.

Despite all the change, one thing has remained constant: reporting is all about providing timely, useful information to the people who need it. Good reports deliver information in a format that consumers can easily interpret and understand in time to allow them to act on the information they have received. Although formats and technologies have changed, reporting is arguably the most important output of any information system.

With new legislative mandates and increasing pressure from the world at large for enhanced corporate accountability, it is vital that important information be communicated clearly and unambiguously to those responsible for making decisions. It is no longer good enough for managers to say, "I didn't know." High degrees of corporate accountability have been legislated by Congress in the form of the Sarbanes-Oxley Act of 2002, which requires publicly traded companies to report material changes in financial condition or operations on a rapid and current basis, among other strict reporting requirements. Even privately held and foreign corporations are subject to more rigorous regulation and oversight because of these far-reaching measures because they have dealings with companies subject to Sarbanes-Oxley and must provide relevant reporting to their business partners. In addition, litigation is a constant threat for companies. The potential problems and costs of adverse legal consequences are increased when management doesn't have a good handle on the activities that are occurring in the corporation.

Communicating complex information is difficult. People are easily overwhelmed with reports that are confusingly labeled or arranged and often fail to understand the meaning of the information they have been given. It is vital to be able to provide well-designed reports that are highly usable and understandable. This means more than just a series of tables and columns of figures; it means meaningful graphics and appropriate summaries and definitions of terms. It also means being able to drill through the information on a report to view the granular information that went into creating the report.

In addition to the challenge of providing understandable information, business strategies and tactics are constantly changing. Reporting requirements change as often as the business does. The increased competitive climate and rapid pace of change present in most businesses require that new views of corporate activity be created on a regular basis. It is important that a business intelligence solution be able to respond quickly to these changes and not require a large custom development effort to respond to routine changes in information requirements.

In this chapter, we show how SSRS provides flexible reporting capabilities that support good decision-making. Our focus is on traditional reporting techniques involving both printed and screen output. We will not cover reports that are delivered via PDA or other technologies in detail. Many of the same general principles apply, and adapting the approaches shown in this chapter to include alternate display devices should be reasonably straightforward.

REPORT DESIGN

Before creating a report, there are some important issues to consider. As with most projects, the place to start is with the requirements. Much like creating requirements for a software project, figuring out the basic requirements that go into a report is essential for it to meet the user's needs. From there, the report is designed, implemented, and tested. The basic steps for creating a report are:

1. Understand the report's intentions.
2. Understand the users and uses of the report.
3. Collect the data sources for the report.
4. Create a layout for the report.
5. Determine distribution for the report.

To create a successful report, the first thing you need is to understand the high-level intention of the report, which is crucial to creating a report that meets the needs of the users. As in software development, shortcomings in understanding the requirements are often fatal to the success of the product. It is an excellent idea to formulate a short description of the use and intent of the report to establish a starting point and create further requirements for the report. For example, the intention of the report might be to create a top-level revenue report for the whole corporation broken down by division and product line, or to create a view of slow-moving inventory broken down by region and SKU. Whatever the specific purpose of the report, writing a brief one- or two-sentence descriptor will help to make sure that the intention of the report is clear in the minds of both the developers of the report and the consumers.

In addition to understanding the purpose of the report, you need to understand who is going to be using the report and the context in which they will be using it. In many cases, this will be a large and diverse group of people, each with different areas of concern. For example, a top-level revenue report for the entire company might be used by almost everyone in the company from the Chief Executive Officer (CEO) on down and by analysts and investors outside the company. Regardless of the number and type of users, it is important to consider what they are going to consider important in the report. The CEO would use the report to evaluate the revenue generating performance of the divisions and might want to coordinate the numbers with other reports showing the costs associated with each division and the bottom-line contribution for each. A divisional general manager might be concerned with the same things, but on a divisional basis. A divisional sales manager might be concerned with the detailed breakdown of revenue generated by salesperson and product line. A salesperson or product manager would be chiefly concerned with the performance of his or her particular domain.

Understanding who is using the report and how they will be using it can help refine the purpose. If the uses of the report and the purpose don't line up, it might be a good idea to investigate whether the report is indeed appropriate for the intended use and can be modified to suit, or whether another report is needed. As long as the numbers gathered from the data warehouse provide a single version of the truth, creating different reports for different uses is not a problem—unless different reports give different answers.

As part of deciding who will be using the report, you will define the security model that needs to be implemented to provide the proper level of access control. It is important to keep control over the access list for a report so the information contained is not distributed to those who shouldn't have it. It is always easier to start with a small list of authorized users and expand access as needed, rather than attempt to put the genie back into the bottle after the information has been distributed broadly.

Based on understanding the intention and use of the report, we next determine the data that should be contained in the report. In many cases, it might require considerable effort to track down a reliable source for the data. In any event, you will need data that will allow the intention of the report to be fulfilled. Sometimes, at this point, you will discover that the report cannot be created without considerable investment in time and resources to collect the data. This is where the effort to collect the metadata for your data warehouse really pays off.

As we discussed in Chapter 11, the metadata in a data warehouse describes the data much like a card catalog describes the books in a library. Being able to determine whether the appropriate data exists in the data warehouse and find it easily considerably shortens the time and effort required to create a report. If the metadata is not kept up to date, finding the data scattered throughout the organization becomes a tedious process of trial and error.

In addition to providing the data fields that will be present in the report, you will need to consider the organization of the report. In what order should the data be sorted? What should the data be filtered by? At what level should the data be summarized? How much ad hoc analysis should be allowed? In some cases, the answers to these questions will be obvious; in others, it might be quite difficult to determine. Again, answering these questions becomes much easier with accurate metadata that describes the grain and source for the data.

While defining the data fields for the report, you want to begin to create the report layout. One of the first things to consider when creating a report layout is the title of the report. It should be indicative of its purpose to those who will be reading the report. In the best cases, the title can be easily derived from the purpose statement that was written when the process of creating the report was started. For example, the top-level revenue report described previously might be titled "Corporate Revenue Report." In other cases, creating a title can be very difficult, but it is a vital step in maximizing the value of the report. In most cases, you want to avoid cryptic naming for a report—titles like "R101A" are not very useful. Cryptic titles inhibit sharing the information in the report because people who might benefit from the contents of a report will have no idea from the title what it is about and might never discover it unless someone who is "in the know" points them to the report.

Another important element in the layout is how to highlight exceptional data. Most people tend to manage by exception, and the rules for defining what an exception is and how it is to be indicated on the report are important. Many possible conditions can be used to determine which elements are exceptions. Using a formula different from the one expected by the users of the report can lead to fairly serious consequences if conditions that should be addressed are not because they are not flagged as exceptional. Alternatively, the opposite can happen, and a report can flag too many elements as exceptional even though they are not beyond the normal range of expected operations. In this case, the report can "cry wolf" and cause real exceptions to be ignored when they do occur. Where possible, the formula used to define the exceptions should be shown on the screen or page along with the data. This way, the viewer of a report understands how the exceptions were generated and can take that into account as the information is digested.

It is difficult to overestimate the significance of the formatting and presentation of data in a report. In his seminal book, *Visual Explanations*, Edward Tufte, a noted expert on information design, presents some very compelling examples of both good and bad information presentation impacting important decisions. In the tragic case of the space shuttle Challenger accident in 1986, an engineering report that showed the relationship between cold temperatures and failed o-rings was shown to management before the fateful decision to launch on a very cold January day. This report failed to sway their decision because it was very difficult to disentangle the true meaning of the data that was displayed. Poorly designed charts and graphs made discerning the true story behind the data difficult. In this case, it is possible that a better-designed report would have averted a disaster (Edward R. Tufte, *Visual Explanations*, Graphics Press, CT, 1997, pp. 38–53).

Although most business reports don't have the same criticality as the Challenger example, it is still important to pay careful attention to the layout of a report and the impact it has on the understanding of the data conveyed by the report. An excellent report will enable the reader to comprehend the situation described quickly and unambiguously.

Layout considerations for a report to be delivered online are different from those delivered on paper. The greater interactivity allowed by online reports is counterbalanced by the lower resolution that is generally available on computer monitors versus the printed page. Understanding who will be using the report and how they will be using it can be very useful in optimizing a report for either printed output or viewing on a screen. In addition to the standard print and computer screen outputs, modern reports are sometimes viewed on PDAs or other devices without full-screen capabilities. Designing reports for these devices can be difficult, but basically the less screen resolution and real estate you have to work with, the more carefully designed the report needs to be to make sure the information is understandable.

Strongly consider creating a prototype to show to the report consumers after gathering some initial requirements. It is often much easier to critique and improve upon something that is more concrete than a list of fields. An iterative process is the best way to generate refined and useful reports. A good first step is to create a mockup in a word processor or spreadsheet that can be used to elicit feedback from the users of the report. Any tool you are comfortable and efficient with can be used for a mockup—a word processor, spreadsheet, or even pencil and paper.

A mockup is easy to do and is extremely useful in reducing miscommunication between the stakeholders and the report designer. It is frustrating to go to great lengths to secure a particular piece of information for a report just to find out that it really isn't useful to the intended users and could just as easily be omitted. Conversely, sometimes the crucial data is readily accessible but isn't included in the report because it is simply overlooked. In any case, the point is that consumers of a report will be much more likely to notice discrepancies in a mockup that is closer to the real thing than a list of fields to be included in the report. In addition, prototyping will help identify what information might be required in the future. This will help to future-proof the report as much as possible by allowing you to anticipate user requirements. You can use this input in your next iteration of your data warehouse to be sure the required information is captured and ready to build reports that more fully meet user needs.

One caveat about prototypes is to avoid spending too much time on them; you could easily spend as much time creating an elaborate prototype as creating the actual report. Concentrate on providing a prototype that is good enough for users to understand and give feedback on. The key to the successful use of prototypes is iteration and feedback, and overly elaborate efforts just get in the way.

After we have gone to the trouble to understand the requirements for the report and produce a design, we need a tool to create the report and manage distribution. The next sections describe an excellent technology to do just that: SQL Server Reporting Services.

REPORTING SERVICES ARCHITECTURE

SSRS is a service-based reporting platform designed to provide enterprise-class reporting on a variety of data sources, publish reports in a variety of file formats, and manage and secure report access. At the core of SSRS is the Report Server, a Windows service that provides report management, processing and delivery services, and a Web service that provides interfaces used to access reports. The Report Manager is a Web-based management tool for Internet Explorer 6 used for administering the Report Server. The Report Builder is an end user tool that provides ad hoc reporting capabilities on reporting models. The Report Designer is integrated into Microsoft Visual Studio and provides a full-featured report design tool. The Model Designer is used to build models for consumption by the report builder. The Reporting Service Configuration tool is used to configure the report server and manage virtual directories, service account, encryption keys, email delivery, and reporting database configuration. Many of these same functions are available through a command-line interface to provide more flexible management. Figure 14.1 shows how all of these pieces fit together in the overall architecture of SSRS.

Web Services

SSRS is designed to be extensible and flexible. The Report Server Web Service exposes all of its functions and can be called directly from a custom application to customize the management and execution of reports. The Management Web Service is defined in the Web Services Description Language (WSDL) found at *http://<server_name/reportserver/ReportService2005.asmx?wsdl*. The Execution Web Service is defined in the WSDL at *http://<server_name/reportserver/ReportExecution 2005.asmx?wsdl*. A WSDL file describes the operations, parameters, and return

values for a SOAP service. Either of these Web services can be consumed by any development environment that supports SOAP by referencing the WSDL file.

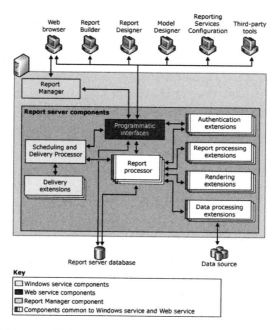

FIGURE 14.1 SSRS has multiple components.

URL Access

All of the reports, resources, folders, and data sources published in SSRS are accessible via a URL. This is an easy way to integrate custom reporting into a portal or business application by simply embedding a link to a report URL. The format for the URL:

```
<protocol>://<server>/<root>?[/<path>][&<[prefix:]paramname=value>[&<[p
refix:]paramname=value>]…]
```

Protocol is the type of request for the report (e.g., HTTP or HTPPS). *Server* is the name of the report server (e.g., reportsrv or reportsrv.myco.com). *Root* is the virtual root for the report server (e.g., reportserver). *Path* is the full path description for the report to be displayed (e.g., FinanceReports/BalanceSheet). The parameters are described by a name value pair with an optional prefix (e.g., rc or rs). If no prefix is specified, the parameters are passed to the report. The prefix rc is used to supply device rendering information; rs is used to pass parameters to the report server; dsu and dsp are used to specify username and password, respectively, to access a data source.

Some examples show just how simple it is to access an SSRS through a URL. The following URL accesses the Balance Sheet report and renders it as an Excel file:

```
http://reportsrv/reportserver?/FinanceReports/BalanceSheet&rs:Format=
Excel
```

This URL shows an item navigation page, illustrated in Figure 14.2, for the FinanceReports folder:

```
http://reportsrv/reportserver?/FinanceReports&rs:Command=ListChildren
```

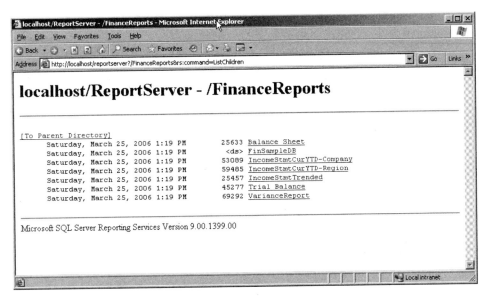

FIGURE 14.2 The report server displays a very simple report listing.

.NET API

A .NET API is available to create custom extensions for data processing, delivery, security, and report rendering. Extensions are grouped into four broad categories:

- Data Processing
- Delivery
- Rendering
- Security

Data processing extensions allow the creation of custom data sources that can be consumed by reports in SSRS. Out of the box, SSRS includes data processing extensions for SQL Server 2005, OLE DB, Oracle, and ODBC. You can create your own extensions for a custom business application using the same interfaces as the standard data processing extensions to support comparable functionality.

Delivery extensions enable the delivery of published reports by a specific mechanism. SSRS includes delivery extensions for email and file shares. You can create delivery extensions that support other delivery mechanisms, such as FTP, and enroll them in subscriptions just like the out-of-the-box extensions.

Rendering extensions transform report layout and data into a specific format. The included extensions are for XML, CSV, Image, PDF, Excel, and HTML. As with the other extension types, to create your own rendering extension, you implement the required interfaces and it will work as the Microsoft delivered extensions. Custom rendering extensions are regarded as the most difficult type of extension to create because of the number of report elements and properties that must be supported, so carefully consider your options before implementing your own rendering extension.

Security extensions allow flexibility for securing reports in SSRS by allowing custom definitions of users and groups for authentication and authorization. SSRS uses Windows-based authentication by default, which might not be appropriate for use on the Internet or in an organization that uses an alternative user management system. Since security is critical in reporting, think carefully about writing your own security extension. The capabilities provided by the Windows authorization system are suitable for the vast majority of SSRS implementations.

In addition to excellent descriptions of creating extensions in the online help, there are examples of data processing, delivery, and security extensions available for SSRS. These samples are located in C:\Program Files\Microsoft SQL Server\90\Samples\Reporting Services\Extension Samples and are an excellent starting point for your own extensions.

Report Definition Language

SSRS reports are defined in Report Definition Language (RDL), an XML schema used to define the layout and data sources for a report. Custom .NET assemblies and code can be defined in a report to customize report items, styles, and formatting. These assemblies are deployed in the application folders of the Report Designer and the report server and referenced in the RDL for a report. In addition, VB.NET code can be written to provide custom methods directly in the report without having to reference an external assembly.

In addition, it is possible to programmatically generate RDL in a custom report builder. This could be done in many different ways using any tool that can output XML. The online help for SSRS has a tutorial "Generating RDL Using the .NET Framework" if you are interested in creating your own custom RDL generator.

CONCLUSION

SSRS is an enterprise-class reporting engine that can provide access and analysis for corporate data. It is an excellent tool for providing timely, useful information to the people who need it. SSRS is based on flexible Web services and offers a great deal of extensibility for custom solutions.

15 OLAP

Multidimensional analysis is a key component for effective business intelligence. The ability to slice-and-dice data by relevant characteristics enables much better understanding of business data. There are many different types of multidimensional analysis in common usage today. For example, executives use multidimensional analysis to observe and understand the key performance measures for their businesses, and financial analysts use multidimensional analysis to examine the health of fiscal inflows and outflow. However, the most commonly used example of multidimensional analysis is in sales and marketing to analyze product lines and customer buying behaviors and patterns.

In this chapter, we will start with an overview of SQL Server Analysis Services 2005 (SSAS 2005). We will then describe some basic principals of OLAP and give an overview of the Unified Dimension Model. After that, we will describe the architecture of SSAS 2005 and close with an example. Please understand that this chapter is just a small sampling of the features and functions in SSAS. There are many other aspects of SSAS that cannot be covered in a single chapter that are described in the SQL Server Books Online.

INTRODUCTION TO ANALYSIS SERVICES

As we described in Chapter 11, "Business Intelligence," Analysis Services is the core of business intelligence in SQL Server 2005. SSAS provides two basic services: multidimensional databases and data mining. The focus in this chapter is on the multidimensional database functionality. The data mining functionality is covered in Chapter 16, "Introduction to Data Mining in SSAS 2005."

In general, there are two main classes of database applications. OnLine Transaction Processing (OLTP) applications are designed for fast, scalable processing of business process data. However, they are not well suited for reporting and querying because these applications rely on highly normalized tables.

On the other hand, OnLine Analytical Processing (OLAP) applications are designed for fast querying of business process data. OLAP applications rely on denormalized tables with meaningful metadata that allows data to be sliced and diced along different analytical dimensions.

Although OLAP applications can be built on relational databases, such as SQL Server 2005, there are advantages to using a special-purpose multidimensional database. These advantages are well described by a term coined by Nigel Pendse: *Fast Analysis of Shared Multidimensional Information,* or *(FASMI)* (Pendse, Nigel, 2005, "What is OLAP?" Retrieved from *www.olapreport.com/fasmi.htm* on 3/29/2006).

Fast. The system is designed to return results within five seconds.

Analysis. The system supports the creation of customized statistical and business analyses by end users.

Shared. The system is designed for multiple users.

Multidimensional. The data must be viewable from different perspectives.

Information. The application contains all of the relevant information to be able to analyze a business process.

Leveraging the FASMI attributes of SSAS requires some understanding of how the data is stored and accessed.

OLAP BASICS

Analysis Services stores data in multidimensional cubes. A cube organizes a set of data, called *measures*, into *dimensions* to form a logical model that can be queried. Measures are the numerical data or facts that users analyze. Quantity Sold is a typical example of a measure.

Dimensions are the categories of analysis for the cube. These categories are derived by classifications that make sense to the business. A sales cube might have a product dimension, a location dimension, and a time dimension as shown in Figure 15.1.

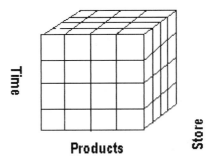

FIGURE 15.1   Cubes are organized into dimensions.

Each of the dimensions is organized into *hierarchies*. The members of a hierarchy are organized into *levels*, which are used for navigation and aggregation in the cube. The hierarchies are characterized by *attributes*. These attributes correspond to the columns in the table used to construct the hierarchies. For example, you might have a Location dimension that is broken into levels by Country, Region, and City attributes.

Each of the members of the lowest level, City in this case, is a *leaf*. The leaf level also represents the *granularity* of the cube with respect to that dimension. So, therefore, in this case, we have data down to the City level in location. Each of the members of the other levels, Region and Country, are *nonleaf*. The nonleaf members have a higher granularity than the leaf members. A dimension can also include an *All* member at the top level.

Measures exist at every intersection between dimensions and are thought of as a special measures dimension. Every cube must contain at least one measure. Measures can be additive in that they are meaningful when summed across dimensions, or nonadditive if they can't be meaningfully summed across dimensions. Unit sales are almost always an additive measure, while inventories might be a nonadditive measure because they cannot be meaningfully summed over time (what is the meaning of the inventory at the end of January plus the inventory at the end of February?).

In addition to measures that are taken directly from transaction data, calculated measures can be defined that combine the data with different mathematical and logical operations. For example, a profit measure could be created by subtracting a cost measure from a sales measure. Defining a calculated member in a cube only stores the definition of the calculation, not the results. Although you don't impact the size of the cube significantly, the performance impact can be considerable if the calculation is complex or very data intensive.

If you pick a specific product, location, and time, the intersection of the three dimensions would give the measure associated with them. This is called a *slice*. Slicing a cube defines a member or group of members that are evaluated across other dimensions. In effect, you are looking at a subset of the cube. Slicing is not limited to selecting one element from each dimension; you can also take slices by specifying a subset of the dimensions and then summing over the others. For example, to retrieve the total sales for a particular product over all times and locations, you would end up with a plane that is perpendicular to the x-axis as shown in Figure 15.2.

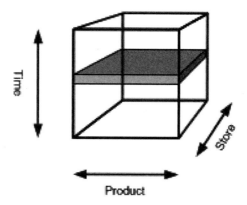

FIGURE 15.2   Slicing is used to look at a subset of a cube.

An alternate, more technical, term for a slice is *tuple*, which is defined as an ordered collection of one member from one or more dimensions. The tuple identifies specific sections of a cube where these dimensions intersect. In other words, each specified dimension in a tuple narrows down the records that are members of the tuple. All other things being equal, the fewer dimensions specified, the more records in the tuple. A tuple that is described by one member from each dimension of a cube specifies a cell. Figure 15.3 illustrates a specific cell that is identified by an intersection of all three dimensions.

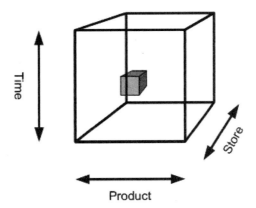

FIGURE 15.3 The more dimensions specified in a slice, the fewer records that are selected.

Although slicing is easy to conceptualize with a small number of dimensions, it is important to remember that cubes can contain an effectively unlimited number of dimensions in SSAS 2005. High dimensional orders can become a challenge to work with, but it is important to have the flexibility to model all of the relevant dimensions that are useful for analysis. Most of the time, data is viewed from the perspective of only a few dimensions at a time for a given application. Since people live in a four-dimensional world (the three physical dimensions of space and the dimension of time), most people have a great difficulty understanding and manipulating more than a handful of dimensions. However, from the perspective of having a single version of the truth, it is important that a cube can be used for many different types of analyses involving different dimensions.

THE UNIFIED DIMENSIONAL MODEL

Data access presents many challenges in the typical business intelligence scenario. In most cases, business intelligence solutions include data from varied data sources. These include data warehouses with summarized historical data, operational data stores with granular transaction data, and flat files with simple structure and limited metadata. All of these sources use distinct access methods, and each requires considerable technical skills to use it effectively—creating proper joins between disparate data sources is typically beyond the skill of business users. To create meaningful results, they need to get support from their IT departments or external consultants, resulting in considerable expense and delay in some cases.

Even with professional help, these disparate data sources require considerable effort to consolidate and it is difficult to do well. Simply locating the proper data and understanding its meaning in business terms can be quite difficult. In many cases, different applications are used to access each of the different data sources. This can result in multiple versions of the truth emerging as different business users produce a variety of Excel spreadsheets in an ad hoc manner. A very simple traditional business intelligence scenario is illustrated in Figure 15.4.

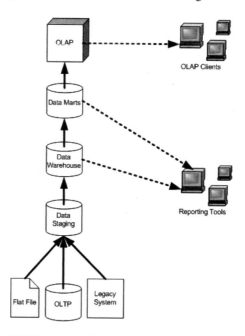

FIGURE 15.4 The typical business intelligence scenario involves different tools to browse different data sources.

Instead of the chaos of the typical business intelligence scenario, the Unified Dimensional Model (UDM) provides a more cohesive approach to business intelligence. UDM allows more efficient access, understanding, and analysis of business intelligence information. UDM models your data warehouse, data marts, third-party data, and nonrelational data sources such as Web services and flat files dimensionally as a set of cubes. In addition, UDM provides aggregated data, incorporates business rules, and includes key performance indicators (KPIs).

Although building a complete UDM requires considerable effort, much of the information required needed to use corporate data will be defined during the design and creation of the UDM, paying off over the long run. After creating a UDM, the data source views and cubes have been defined and made available for querying. The XML-based data access provided by UDM allows consistent access to a wide variety of data sources with the information presented in business-relevant terms that eliminate the need to understand the technical structure of the transactional systems.

The entire data model is more easily understood by business users because of UDM's provision of consistent semantic metadata. The business entities are represented by attributes, representing business-relevant terms such as *Customer* and *Supplier*, which are then grouped into dimensions that represent joins between different underlying tables. The business-relevant key figures for numeric measurements are stored in measures. UDM metadata can define the units for these measures as well as important formatting information. For example, if a financial indicator is below zero, it should be presented in red. These measures can be aggregated on the dimensions defined in UDM. Since business users require different levels of detail for different types of analysis, UDM allows retrieval of different levels of summarization from granular records to aggregate data using the same interface.

The basic structure used in UDM to provide the friendly names and calculations is the *data source view*. A data source view is a defined subset of data from each relevant data source. Not only does the data source view enable the collection of logically related data, but it also enables a sophisticated caching mechanism called *proactive caching*. Proactive caching allows the administrator to set the level of latency according to the needs of the application. If query performance over a large and relatively static data set is the most important aspect of the application, the data can be stored in precalculated MOLAP cubes. On the other hand, if the freshness of the data is the most important aspect, the query can be done directly on the source database as a ROLAP query. There are also settings in between these extremes to enable the tradeoff between latency and query performance.

ANALYSIS SERVICES ARCHITECTURE

This section gives a brief overview of how the major pieces of SSAS 2005 fit together in a solution. The diagram shown in Figure 15.5 is helpful in understanding how all of the pieces fit together. On the left side of the diagram, we have all of the different clients that can be used to access SSAS. Thin clients can access the server through XML for Analysis (XMLA), Win32 clients have access through the OLE DB for OLAP standard, and .NET clients use the ADOMD.NET connector. The major elements of the SSAS architecture are described next in the sections below.

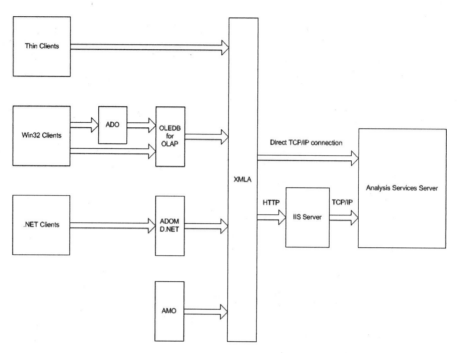

FIGURE 15.5   The SSAS architecture enables access to the Analysis Services Server by many different kinds of client.

Analysis Services Server

The Analysis Services Server in SSAS 2005 is a Windows service called MSMD-SRV.EXE. The service provides the core storage and calculation services and is accessed by clients directly through TCP/IP or indirectly through Internet Information Server (IIS).

OLE DB for OLAP

OLE DB for OLAP is published by Microsoft and establishes an API standard for multidimensional data access that is broadly used for OLAP on the Windows platform. OLE DB for OLAP consists of a set of objects and interfaces that extends the relational database access provided by OLE DB to include multidimensional data. The use of OLE DB as the core of OLE DB for OLAP allows the reuse of the interfaces that provide common data handling and manipulation and minimizes the number of multidimensional specific objects and interfaces that have to be added to the architecture. The language used to access data through OLE DB for OLAP is MDX. The architecture of OLE DB for OLAP and the relationship to OLE DB are shown in Figure 15.6.

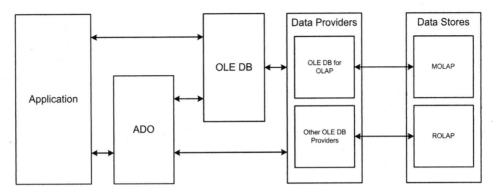

FIGURE 15.6 OLE DB for OLAP architecture.

ADMOD.NET

ADOMD.NET is a .NET object model used for building applications that access an XMLA data provider, such as SSAS. ADOMD.NET has facilities for retrieving data and metadata and can be used to modify data structures. A very simple example showing how ADOMD.NET is used in code is shown below:

```
string ReturnCommandUsingCellSet()
{
//Create a new string builder to store the results
System.Text.StringBuilder result = new System.Text.StringBuilder();

//Connect to the local server
using (AdomdConnection conn = new AdomdConnection("Data
Source=localhost;"))
{
conn.Open();

//Create a command, using this connection
AdomdCommand cmd = conn.CreateCommand();
cmd.CommandText = @"
WITH MEMBER [Measures].[FreightCostPerOrder] AS
[Measures].[Reseller Freight Cost]/[Measures].[Reseller Order
Quantity],
FORMAT_STRING = 'Currency'
SELECT
[Geography].[Geography].[Country].&[United States].Children ON ROWS,
[Date].[Calendar].[Calendar Year] ON COLUMNS
FROM [Adventure Works]
WHERE [Measures].[FreightCostPerOrder]";

//Execute the query, returning a cellset
```

```
CellSet cs = cmd.ExecuteCellSet();

//Output the column captions from the first axis
//Note that this procedure assumes a single member exists per column.
result.Append("\t");
TupleCollection tuplesOnColumns = cs.Axes[0].Set.Tuples;
foreach (Tuple column in tuplesOnColumns)
{
result.Append(column.Members[0].Caption + "\t");
}
result.AppendLine();

//Output the row captions from the second axis and cell data
//Note that this procedure assumes a two-dimensional cellset
TupleCollection tuplesOnRows = cs.Axes[1].Set.Tuples;
for (int row = 0; row < tuplesOnRows.Count; row++)
{
result.Append(tuplesOnRows[row].Members[0].Caption + "\t");
for (int col = 0; col < tuplesOnColumns.Count; col++)
{
result.Append(cs.Cells[col, row].FormattedValue + "\t");
}
result.AppendLine();
}
conn.Close();

return result.ToString();
} // using connection
}
```

AMO

Analysis Management Objects (AMO) is a set of .NET objects that allow you to implement management features in a .NET application. AMO provides access to all of the SSAS object hierarchy, including servers, databases, data source views, cubes, dimensions, mining models, and roles. Although it wouldn't typically be used in an end user application, AMO is a good way to automate administrative tasks.

XML for Analysis

In SSAS 2000, PTS is the primary channel through which data is extracted from the server. PTS followed a thick client-server architecture and required that the client component be installed anywhere the data was accessed. The primary role of PTS was to provide client-side caching of the data being queried via MDX and, in some cases, was a boost to performance. However, PTS was difficult to deploy and manage and was especially troublesome in server-side applications.

PTS has been removed from SSAS 2005. Communications between client and server are handled via an XML specification called XML for Analysis (XMLA). XMLA is a standard specification that uses the Simple Object Access Protocol (SOAP) as a delivery mechanism for messages. XMLA was developed primarily by three leading companies in the business intelligence arena (Microsoft, Hyperion-Hyperion, and SAS) and has broad adoption. SSAS 2005 uses the 1.1 version of the specification, which is freely available at *http://www.xmla.org*.

XMLAs power derives directly from its simplicity. There are only two key methods that are used to interact with an XMLA server: Discover and Execute.

The Discover method is, as it sounds, the mechanism used to find the description, or metadata, for OLAP systems. For example, a Discover call is used to get a list of cubes that are defined in an SSAS 2005 instance. A subsequent call might be used to get more detailed metadata about one of those cubes (e.g., the dimensions, members, etc.). Commonly, Discover is called to obtain information useful for the other method defined in XMLA: Execute.

Execute is used to take action on an OLAP system. The Execute command can be used for both DDL and DML tasks. Most DDL tasks in SSAS 2005 are described using Analysis Services Scripting Language (ASSL). ASSL is defined by an XML schema that defines the DDL commands that can be issued to SSAS 2005. The DDL grammar defines the objects that can be created in SSAS 2005. If you want to see the DDL used by SSAS, right-click on an object in BI Studio Solution Explorer and choose View code. It is possible to use MDX for DDL tasks, but, in general, the DDL support provided by ASSL is more flexible than the equivalent in MDX.

DML tasks in OLAP take the form of MDX queries that are issued to the database. The results of an MDX query are returned in the form of an MDDataSet that is communicated back to the client via XMLA.

MDX

The key technology for querying multidimensional data in Analysis Services is MDX, MDX is a full-featured query language that is designed specifically to work with multidimensional data. MDX is a very powerful language that can do many, many things. In general, the format of a simple MDX query is the following:

```
SELECT {[axis specification]} ON COLUMNS,
{[axis specification]} ON ROWS
FROM [cube name]
WHERE ([slicer specification])
```

There are many similarities between SQL and MDX. They both allow you to create and process a query that returns results. Many of the same things that can be done in MDX can also be done with SQL (albeit with considerable cost in complexity and performance). However, MDX and SQL have different contexts, and the syntax, although sharing the same words, has different semantics.

As you would expect, MDX provides a set of standard operators that are similar to those provided by SQL. These include the most commonly used arithmetic, comparison, and logical operators such as addition (+), subtraction (-), (−), multiplication (*), division (/), equals (=), greater-than (>), less-than (<), less-than-or-equal-to (<=), greater-than-or-equal-to (>=), NOT, AND, OR, and XOR.

MDX also supplies a large selection of built-in functions. These functions can be categorized into Logical functions, Numeric functions, String functions, Set functions, Tuple functions, Member functions, and Utility functions. These functions are readily usable from within an MDX statement without any special considerations. An exhaustive list of the MDX built-in functions and operators can be found in the SSAS Books Online. If Excel is installed on the server, Excel functions are also available. In addition to the built-in and Excel functions, user-defined functions can be created for specialized requirements.

MDX SCRIPTS

An MDX script is a collection of commands that defines the calculations for a cube. We can think of an MDX script as being executed like a program, in the order they are specified. Each command creates a new pass so the commands are always consistent with the results of the script. The presentation of the calculations in the form of a script makes it much easier to understand how the cube is created and simplifies maintenance of complex calculations.

Every cube must have a script. When a cube is initially created, a simple default script is created that defines a calculation pass for the entire cube. After the cube is created, you can modify the scripts. A script can contain the following MDX statements:

- Calculate
- Freeze
- Scope
- Create Member
- Create Set
- Conditional statements
- Assignment expressions

When first populated, the cube contains the fact data only with no calculations. This is called pass 0 and is the initial state of a cube. MDX scripts execute to create the calculations added to the raw data in pass 0. Every assignment, freeze, and calculate statement in a script creates a new pass. Although we think of the script as executing, it really represents the state of the cube so calculated members always exist even if they are created in a later pass. If no script is explicitly defined, the cube uses the default implicit script with a single `Calculate` command. If an empty script is defined, nothing is calculated.

A calculated cell is defined in a script as

```
<subcube definition> = <expression>;
```

For example,

```
(Sales, Budget) = 10;
Sales = Sales * 1.1;
```

Recursive assignments are handled by using the value from the prior pass on the right-hand side of the assignment to avoid infinite recursion. So,

```
Sales = Sales * 1.1;
```

is equivalent to

```
Sales = CalculationPassValue(Sales, -1, RELATIVE) * 1.1;
```

An example of the effects of the steps that are followed in the default MDX Script on a cube is helpful in understanding how they work. Initially, the cube is empty.

	[All]	VA	Richmond	Roanoke	NC	Raleigh	Wilmington
[All]							
Q1							
Jan							
Feb							
Mar							
Q2							
Apr							
May							
Jun							
Q3							
Jul							
Aug							
Sep							
Q4							
Oct							
Nov							
Dec							

In pass 0, the fact table is loaded:

	[All]	VA	Richmond	Roanoke	NC	Raleigh	Wilmington
[All]							
Q1							
Jan		15	10			20	11
Feb		17	9			22	8
Mar		20	14			21	7
Q2							
Apr		18	12			21	15
May		15	15			25	13
Jun		16	13			24	15
Q3							
Jul		23	17			25	17
Aug		25	20			27	20
Sep		20	19			27	21
Q4							
Oct		18	13			19	14
Nov		16	11			20	15
Dec		15	9			21	17

After CALCULATE, each cell is either a value loaded from the fact table or the results of an aggregation:

	[All]	VA	Richmond	Roanoke	NC	Raleigh	Wilmington
[All]	825	380	218	162	445	272	173
Q1	174	85	52	33	89	63	26
Jan	56	25	15	10	31	20	11
Feb	56	26	17	9	30	22	8
Mar	62	34	20	14	28	21	7
Q2	348	170	104	66	178	126	52
Apr	66	30	18	12	36	21	15
May	68	30	15	15	38	25	13
Jun	68	29	16	13	39	24	15
Q3	261	124	68	56	137	79	58
Jul	82	40	23	17	42	25	17
Aug	92	45	25	20	47	27	20
Sep	87	39	20	19	48	27	21
Q4	188	82	49	33	106	60	46
Oct	64	31	18	13	33	19	14
Nov	62	27	16	11	35	20	15
Dec	62	24	15	9	38	21	17

A `scope` definition limits statements to a specified subcube. Once defined, MDX evaluates MDX expressions and statements in that subcube. If not defined, the default `scope` is for the entire cube. A `scope` is defined as:

```
Scope(<subcube definition>);
    <statement>

...
End Scope;
```

`Scope` statements can be nested, and each nested `scope` statement inherits its parent's scope unless it is explicitly rescoped. Since `scope` statements are not iterative, this is used to separate a cube for further calculation. For example:

```
Scope(Customers.State.VA);
    Scope(Customers.City.Roanoke)
            <scope is Roanoke, VA>
    End Scope;
  <scope is VA>
  End Scope;
End Scope;
```

The keyword represents the current subcube in an MDX script. This is often used to set the value of cells within the current subcube, usually with the `Scope` statement to set the current subcube. To show how this works, consider the cube that we defined previously in CALCULATE above. SCOPE(VA) applies to the shaded region of the cube.

	[All]	VA	Richmond	Roanoke	NC	Raleigh	Wilmington
[All]	825	380	218	162	445	272	173
Q1	174	85	52	33	89	63	26
Jan	56	25	15	10	31	20	11
Feb	56	26	17	9	30	22	8
Mar	62	34	20	14	28	21	7
Q2	348	170	104	66	178	126	52
Apr	66	30	18	12	36	21	15
May	68	30	15	15	38	25	13
Jun	68	29	16	13	39	24	15
Q3	261	124	68	56	137	79	58
Jul	82	40	23	17	42	25	17
Aug	92	45	25	20	47	27	20
Sep	87	39	20	19	48	27	21
Q4	188	82	49	33	106	60	46
Oct	64	31	18	13	33	19	14
Nov	62	27	16	11	35	20	15
Dec	62	24	15	9	38	21	17

The effect of using this operator in a scope is as follows:

```
SCOPE(VA)
    This = 100
END SCOPE
```

	[All]	VA	Richmond	Roanoke	NC	Raleigh	Wilmington
[All]	825	100	218	162	445	272	173
Q1	174	100	52	33	89	63	26
Jan	56	100	15	10	31	20	11
Feb	56	100	17	9	30	22	8
Mar	62	100	20	14	28	21	7
Q2	348	100	104	66	178	126	52
Apr	66	100	18	12	36	21	15
May	68	100	15	15	38	25	13
Jun	68	100	16	13	39	24	15
Q3	261	100	68	56	137	79	58
Jul	82	100	23	17	42	25	17
Aug	92	100	25	20	47	27	20
Sep	87	100	20	19	48	27	21
Q4	188	100	49	33	106	60	46
Oct	64	100	18	13	33	19	14
Nov	62	100	16	11	35	20	15
Dec	62	100	15	9	38	21	17

The effect of using a refined scope is as follows:

```
SCOPE(VA)
    Q4 = 100
END SCOPE
```

	[All]	VA	Richmond	Roanoke	NC	Raleigh	Wilmington
[All]	825	380	218	162	445	272	173
Q1	174	85	52	33	89	63	26
Jan	56	25	15	10	31	20	11
Feb	56	26	17	9	30	22	8
Mar	62	34	20	14	28	21	7
Q2	348	170	104	66	178	126	52
Apr	66	30	18	12	36	21	15
May	68	30	15	15	38	25	13
Jun	68	29	16	13	39	24	15

	[All]	VA	Richmond	Roanoke	NC	Raleigh	Wilmington
Q3	261	124	68	56	137	79	58
Jul	82	40	23	17	42	25	17 →
Aug	92	45	25	20	47	27	20
Sep	87	39	20	19	48	27	21
Q4	188	100	49	33	106	60	46
Oct	64	31	18	13	33	19	14
Nov	62	27	16	11	35	20	15
Dec	62	24	15	9	38	21	17

The Freeze statement is used to fix cell values during the script so that they are not assigned values transitively. For example,

```
A = 2;
A = B;
B = 3;
```

After this script, A and B equal 3. Using Freeze:

```
B = 2;
A = B;
Freeze(A);
B = 3;
```

After this script, A = 2 and B = 3. Freeze(<scope>) during pass p is the equivalent of CalculationPassValue(<scope>, p, ABSOLUTE).

The calculate statement creates the aggregates for a cube according to the formulas defined. Cell calculations for nonleaf cells are defined by the structure of the cube. Most of the time, this is aggregation to up the dimensions. However, a dimension can have custom member and level calculations. Before Calculate is run, all of the nonleaf cells have a null value.

The Root() command returns the intersection at the All members for each attribute. Calling Root(<dimension>) returns the intersection from the All member of each attribute in the dimension. Calling Root(<tuple>) returns the intersection from each attribute in the tuple.

EXAMPLE

In this example, we will create a simple cube from the Cavalier Movies DW database to show some of the features in SSAS. The first step is to start the Business Intelligence Studio (BITS). After you are in BITS, choose File…New…Project from the menu. Make sure Business Intelligence Projects is chosen in the Project types

Types list and select Analysis Services Project from the Templates pane. Type "Ch15 Analysis Services Project" into the Name text box, leave the "Create directory for solution" checkbox checked, and select OK as shown in Figure 15.7.

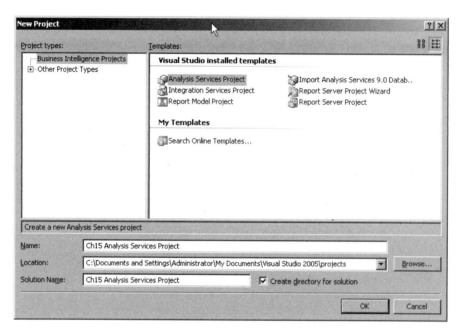

FIGURE 15.7 The New Project dialog lets you set the name and location for the project.

This will create the new Analysis Services project. Go to the Solution Explorer and choose the Data Sources folder. Right-click on the folder and choose New Data Source from the context menu. This will show the Data Source Wizard window. Select Next to skip over the welcome page.

On the next page, make sure the "Create a data source based on an existing or new selection" radio button is selected, and choose the New... button to open up the Connection Manager. In the server name combo box, type in "localhost" or your server name and select CavalierMoviesDW from the database name combo box as shown in Figure 15.8.

Choose OK to return to the Connection Definition page of the Data Source Wizard. Make sure the data source you just created is selected, and click the Next button to go to the Impersonation Information page. Choose the default radio button as shown in the Figure 15.9 and select Next to bring up the final page of the wizard. Put "Cavalier Movies DW" in the data source name text box on the last page of the wizard and click the Finish button to create the data source.

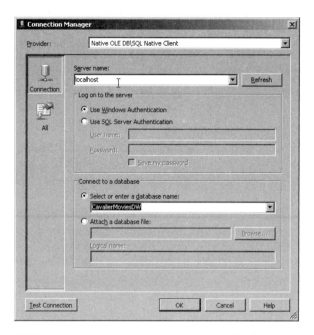

FIGURE 15.8 The Connection Manager dialog sets the connection for the data source.

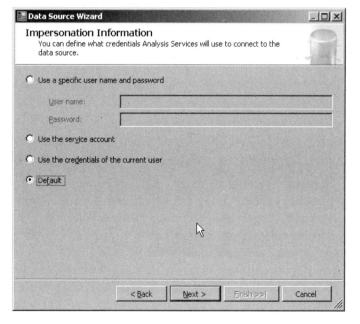

FIGURE 15.9 The Impersonation Information sets the credentials used to connect to the data source.

After creating the data source, we will create the data source view for the cubes. In the Solution Explorer, select the Data Source Views folder, right-click on it, and select New Data Source View from the context menu. This will open the Data Source View Wizard. Choose the Next button to skip over the Welcome page and show the Select a Data Source page. Select the Cavalier Movies DW data source we created earlier and click the Next button. On the Select Tables and Views page, move all of the available objects into the included objects list. The final list should look like Figure 15.10. Choose Next to go to the last page in the wizard.

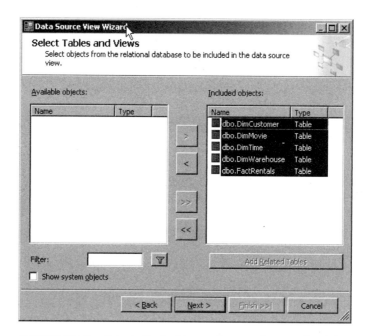

FIGURE 15.10 Select all of tables and move them to the right side of the screen.

On the Completing the Wizard page, set the Name text box to "Cavalier Movies DW View" and click the Finish button to create the data source view and close the wizard. The data source view will appear in the interface as shown in Figure 15.11.

After creating the data source, we are ready to create the cube. To create the cube, right-click on the Cubes folder in the Solution explorer and select New Cube... from the context menu. This will open the Cube Wizard. Select Next to skip the welcome page. On the Select Build Method page, make sure the "Build the cube using a data source" radio button is selected, the Auto Build checkbox is checked, and Create attributes and hierarchies is chosen in the drop-down list as shown in Figure 15.12. and click Next.

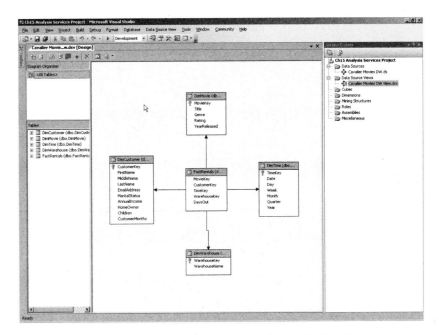

FIGURE 15.11 The data source view is shown in the design view.

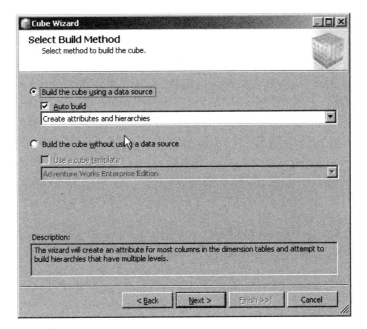

FIGURE 15.12 Select "Create attributes and hierarchies" on the Select Build Method screen.

On the Select the Data Source View page, select the "Cavalier Movies DW View" data source view created earlier from the available data source views list and choose Next. The wizard will scan the data source view and find fact tables and dimensions. Select the Next button from the Detecting Fact and Dimension Tables page to show the Identify Fact Tables and Dimension Tables page. Uncheck the check box in the Fact column in the DimTime row, select DimTime in the time dimension table drop-down list as shown in Figure 15.13, and select the Next button.

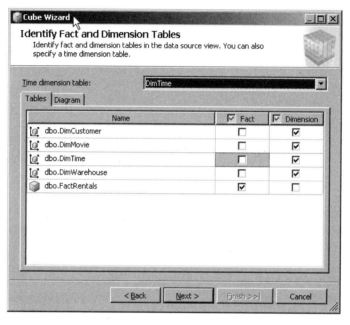

FIGURE 15.13 The fact and dimension tables are identified by the checkboxes.

On the Select Time Periods page, select the table columns and assign them to the properties according to Table 15.1 below. When you are done, the screen should look like Figure 15.14. To move on, select the Next button.

On the Select Measures page, leave the defaults selected as shown in Figure 15.15 and choose the Next button to detect the hierarchies. The Detecting Hierarchies page will show the progress of finding the hierarchies in the data. After it is done, choose the Next button to go to the Review New Dimensions page. Here you can explore the dimensions, hierarchies, and attributes that the wizard will create. When you are done, select the Next button to move to the last page of the Wizard.

TABLE 15.1   The Time Properties Are Mapped to the Time Tables Columns.

Time Property Name	Time Table Columns
Year	Year
Quarter	Quarter
Month	Month
Date	Date
Week	Week
Day of Month	Day

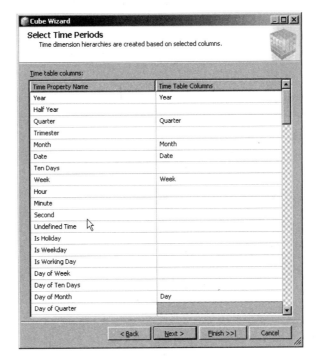

FIGURE 15.14   The completed time mappings are shown here.

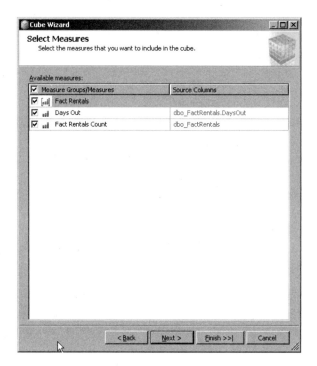

FIGURE 15.15   The default measures are preselected on the Select Measures screen.

On the last page of the wizard, set the Cube Name to Cavalier Movies Rentals Cube and select Finish to build the cube. This will show the Cube Structure tab in the Cube Designer, shown in Figure 15.16. The Cube Structure tab can be used to edit the structure of the cube by editing the measures, dimensions, attributes, and hierarchies that are used in the cube.

The next tab is the Dimension Usage tab shown in Figure 15.17. On this tab, you maintain the relationships between dimensions and measure groups.

The Calculations tab shows the MDX script used to populate the cube, illustrated in Figure 15.18. In this example, we see the default CALCULATE script. If you choose to modify the MDX script to produce custom calculations in the cube, you can do so here.

In this simple example, we will skip over the KPI, Actions, Partitions, Perspectives, and Translations tabs. The KPI tab is used to define Key Performance Indicators on the cube, the Actions tab is used to define actions for the cube, the Partitions tab is used to define cube partitions, and the Perspectives tab is used to manage the cube perspectives. Each of these is well described in the Books Online.

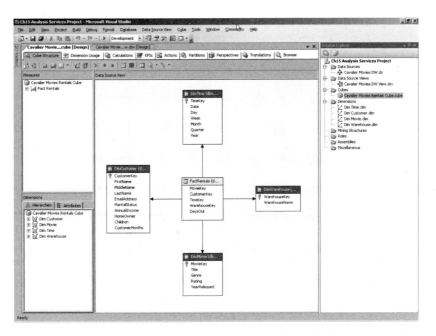

FIGURE 15.16 The Cube Structure tab can be used to edit the structure of the cube.

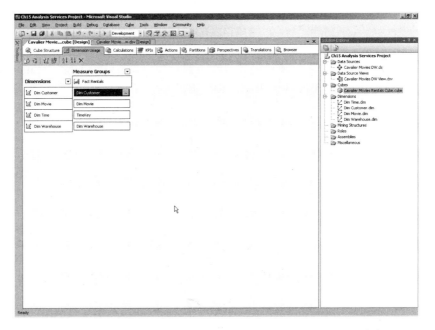

FIGURE 15.17 The dimensions and measure groups are related on the Dimension Usage tab.

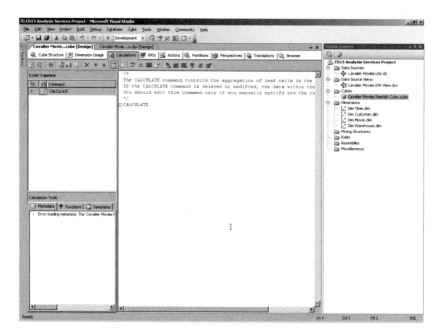

FIGURE 15.18 The Calculations tab shows the default MDX script.

The Browser tab is used to browse the cube data. Before we go to the Browser tab, choose Build…Deploy Ch15 Analysis Services Project from the menu. This will show open the Deployment Progress window to show the progress of deploying the project to the SSAS server and processing the cube so the data is available to browse. After the deployment is completed, close the Deployment Progress window.

Let's take a look at some of the data. First, drag the measures group into the "Drop Totals or Detail Fields Here" area. Next, click on the + symbol to the right of the DimMovie dimension to open up the list of attributes, and drag the Genre attribute into the "Drop Column Fields Here" section. Next, open the DimTime dimension and drag the Year-Quarter-Month-Day hierarchy on to the "Drop Row Fields Here" section. The results should look like Figure 15.19. You can continue to experiment with the different combinations of items in the Browser tab to get a feel for the data in the cube.

In our example, we have created a simple cube from a database schema, processed it, and browsed some data. Although we have just touched the surface, you can see how easy it is to do these tasks in SSAS.

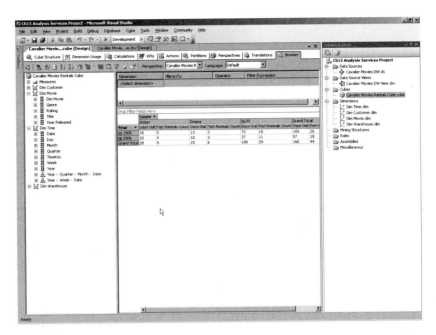

FIGURE 15.19 The data contained in the cube is shown in the Browser tab.

CONCLUSION

SSAS offers comprehensive multidimensional analysis capabilities on the SQL Server platform. Allowing business users to slice and dice data along the dimensions that are most relevant to their information needs is very powerful. In addition, SSAS extends the typical multidimensional database through the UDM, which bridges the gap between relational and multidimensional reporting, allowing seamless access to a single version of the truth.

16

Introduction to Data Mining in SSAS 2005

In this Chapter

- Data Mining Fundamentals
- Conclusion
- References

I n Chapter 15, "OLAP," we introduced the core services in SSAS 2005 and discussed OLAP. The second service, data mining, is discussed in this chapter. We present the fundamentals of data mining, the services for data mining provided in SSAS 2005, and how to construct data mining models.

DATA MINING FUNDAMENTALS

Data mining is a relatively new technology that has only become widespread in the past 15 years or so with dramatic reductions in the price of computing power. As the cost of data storage has plummeted (from $11,540 per GB in 1988 to considerably less than $1 in 2006), the volume of data has grown dramatically. A study in 2003 found that at that time, over 800 MB of data were produced for each of the 6.3

billion people on earth and that the volume was growing by 30 percent per year (P. Lyman and H. R. Varian, 2003, "How Much Information 2003?" Retrieved from *www.sims.berkeley.edu:8000/research/projects/how-much-info-2003/index.htm* on 3/11/2006). Despite this growth in data, most of our tools used to process it have not kept pace. We are drowning in data. Data mining allows us to extract information from large sets of data with the goal of putting some of those massive quantities of data to use. Data mining has its roots in academic work in databases, statistics, and artificial intelligence. The academic name for data mining, knowledge discovery in databases (KDD), is descriptive. In essence, that is what data mining is about.

Data mining has three main uses: data exploration, pattern discovery, and prediction. For example, an enterprise may have a huge database of customer transactions that contains valuable information about the behavior of customers and the patterns of product purchases. Data mining tools can discover these patterns and create predictive models. For example, a common data mining analysis is *market basket analysis* where large volumes of retail transactions are searched to find items that are commonly purchased together, such as diapers and beer. Data mining won't help explain why this correlation exists. However, even without knowing why, this previously unknown information gleaned from a large data set can be leveraged for commercial advantage.

Microsoft first included data mining capabilities with SSAS 2000. Although this initial product had a limited feature set, it did represent one of the first shipments of data mining technology in a broadly available, nonspecialist software package. SSAS 2000 Data Mining only supported two algorithms (decision trees and clustering) and had fairly primitive tools for building and tuning models. SSAS 2005 takes the pioneering efforts started in SSAS 2000 to the next level and makes data mining truly useful for a broad audience.

Data Mining and OLAP

OLAP and data mining are complementary technologies. OLAP is based on the directed slicing and dicing of data organized dimensionally. This is a very powerful technique for cutting through the clutter of large quantities of information to answer specific questions about business metrics; for example, how much of a certain product was sold in a certain timeframe to a specific category of customers.

However, OLAP is not as useful for discovering patterns that aren't known to exist. For example, a specific category of customers might be likely to purchase a certain product during a specific time of year. It is theoretically possible to discover such information by manual exploration in OLAP, but the amount of work required makes it impractical. Data mining can discover this hidden relationship in the data.

Data Mining and Statistical Analysis

Although they share some commonalities, data mining should not be confused with traditional statistical analysis. Data mining starts with a general goal you wish to learn more about. This is in contrast to statistical analysis where you form a formal hypothesis and conduct various statistical tests to determine whether the hypothesis can be rejected. In fact, the term *data mining* can have a pejorative meaning in the statistics field where it meant looking through piles of data for interesting results without any theoretical guidance.

However, traditional statistical analysis and data mining can be complementary. Data mining using techniques like association and clustering is an excellent way to identify areas in the data where it might be useful to conduct a more formal statistical analysis. For example, data mining might help you discover a grouping of customers who share a characteristic, say boat ownership, and tend to spend more than other customers. You can then follow that initial analysis up with a statistical analysis of the data to confirm that, indeed, the boat owners spend more money. If your business involves boats, this analysis would be trivial to the point of absurdity. However, if you business is not related to boating, then identifying the characteristic, understanding the causes, and changing your promotion and sales strategies (maybe offering your product for sale in marinas) might help you target this audience more effectively.

Data Mining Goals

Data mining can be done with a number of objectives in mind, the most common of which are association, classification, clustering, regression, and forecasting. All of these objectives are covered by algorithms available in SSAS 2005.

Association is about summarizing data and discovering relationships between subsets of the data. Although associations can be used for prediction, they are usually used to understand data relationships more fully. The most common application of this is *market basket analysis*, described earlier, where related item sets are discovered. Other kinds of association analysis are:

- Collaborative filtering
- Product recommendation
- Product proximity

Classification enables the prediction of one or more fields of categorical data by evaluating the historical information to establish the relationships between the variables in the training data set and use those to make predictions. Classification problems are encountered quite often. A brief list of common classification problems includes:

- Credit scoring
- Spam filtering
- Voice and handwriting recognition
- Consumer profiling

Clustering involves finding groups in the data that consist of similar subsets of records. Instead of predicting a field in the model, clustering finds groupings of data. Often, this segmentation into subgroups is a step toward other objectives. For example, it would be useful to create clusters of market baskets, those that contain baby items or those that contain alcohol, before applying market basket analysis. However, clustering can also yield results that are useful in themselves. For example, a cluster of all addresses in a geographic area with high income and education might be targeted for mailing of an opera fundraiser. Other common examples of clustering are:

- Spatial data analysis
- Text categorization
- Targeted marketing

Regression is similar in many ways to classification, except that the predicted values are continuous rather than discrete. So, instead of simply classifying customers into buckets of good and bad risk, a regression analysis could be used to predict customer default likelihood. Forecasting uses regression to project a time series into the future. For example, if product sales can be correlated with other time series data such as interest rates and commodity prices, sales can be forecast by using estimates of those prices in the future. Common examples of regression and forecasting include:

- Sales prediction
- Economic prediction
- Lifecycle prediction

Algorithms

SSAS 2005 provides seven of the most common algorithms that are applied to common data mining problems:

Association. Association is a very scalable and simple algorithm used primarily for association analysis and prediction.

Clustering. The clustering algorithm is used for segmentation and profiling. It uses standard clustering techniques (K-means and EM) with some special enhancements to support high-cardinality attributes and automatic feature selection.

Decision tree. Decision tree is a very accurate algorithm for classification, regression, and association. SSAS 2005 uses both standard techniques and patent-pending technologies in this algorithm.

Naïve Bayes. Based on Bayesian theory with the naïve assumption, meaning no distribution is assumed for the data. Naïve Bayes is a very fast algorithm and can be used for quickly exploring large data sets.

Neural network. Neural network is the most broadly applicable algorithm and can be used for classification, segmentation, and association. The SSAS 2005 neural network algorithm uses a conjugate gradient method with optional hidden layers and automatic feature selection.

Sequence clustering. This is a segmentation analysis based on sequences following a Markov model. It is much like the clustering algorithm, but accepts a nested table with a time key sequence.

Time series. Used for analyzing and predicting time-series data, this is a decision-tree-based regression analysis. It can handle data that has periodic patterns (e.g., retail sales increase every December) and is integrated with OLAP forecasting.

In some cases, multiple algorithms might be applied to a specific objective, and judgment will need to be used to select the optimal algorithm for the task at hand. Table 16.1 lists the different data mining problems, on the horizontal axis, and the algorithms that apply to those problems, on the vertical axis.

TABLE 16.1   The Algorithms Apply to Various Data Mining Problems

	Association	Classification	Clustering	Regression	Forecasting
Association	X				
Clustering		X	X	X	
Decision Trees	X	X		X	
Naïve Bayes		X			
Neural Network		X	X		
Sequence Clustering		X	X	X	
Time Series					X
Custom	?	?	?	?	?

If none of the algorithms provided in the box is suitable, custom algorithms can be created to suit the task at hand. These custom algorithms can directly use all of the existing SSAS 2005 platform features and can be created to work just like the built-in algorithms. MSDN has an excellent article outlining the requirements for building plug-in algorithms for SSAS 2005 at *http://msdn.microsoft.com/library/default.asp?url=/library/en-us/dnsql90/html/ssdmpia.asp.*

SSAS 2005 Data Mining Architecture

The foundation for data mining in SSAS 2005 is OLE DB for Data Mining (OLE DB for DM). It is an extension to the OLE DB standard designed to provide access to data mining functionality in a standardized API. The overall goal of OLE DB for DM is to make data mining applications much easier to create and deploy.

Prior to the introduction of OLE DB for DM in 1999, data mining was not well suited for deployment in many corporate environments. Although there were many excellent data-mining applications on the market, they were mostly geared toward specialist researchers and incompatible with popular business applications. The highly specialized knowledge of statistics and pattern recognition required to create the mining models using these tools are not very widespread in typical corporate information technology departments. More importantly, most of the tools assumed that the data to be mined would be stored in memory or in large flat files extracted specifically for data mining.

While this specialized data storage is a reasonable assumption for a specialist data miner, it is not as good for a corporate database environment. Creating a series of export and transformation scripts and potentially large export files in effect creates a parallel data management system, separate from the rest of the business intelligence infrastructure. The additional overhead of maintaining the data sources for data mining and keeping them in synch with the rest of the data warehouse adds considerably to the cost and complexity of data mining applications.

In addition to the difficulties of maintaining data consistency, there was not much attention paid to how the trained models could be deployed in an organization to improve existing processes. In a sense, the state of data-mining software was similar to that of database software before the emergence of SQL as a standard for data management. Before SQL became the standard, each database had its own query language and required specialist knowledge to use it effectively. Now, although the various flavors of SQL vary from vendor to vendor, the basic ANSI standard language elements are portable from database to database.

To improve on these shortcomings with traditional data-mining tools and make it easier for nonspecialists to create and use data-mining models, OLE DB for DM is based on a concept corporate developers understand well: the relational database. Since OLE DB is the de facto standard for data access, it made sense to create the data-mining API based on that standard.

One of the central concepts of OLE DB is support for SQL to create database structures and to query them. Supporting data-mining models in a database-like environment means that the same concept should apply: SQL can be used to support the creation and use of data-mining models. To make this translation from data mining to SQL work, OLE DB for DM treats important elements of data mining like tables and defines a language called Data Mining Extensions (DMX) to manipulate them. DMX is an extension to SQL that adds mining specific syntax for both DDL and DML.

Data Management

Since data mining is very data intensive, it is important to understand how data is used in data mining. In data-mining terms, a *case* is an entity or observation we want to learn about. For example, we might want to know about product purchasing behavior for a customer fitting a certain demographic profile. Complex cases that have a hierarchical structure used to train the model or make predictions in SSAS are treated as a table. This contrasts with traditional data-mining tools where the tables need to be manually flattened.

Creating a flattened view involves duplicating a large portion of the data. For example, the schema depicted in Figure 16.1 has a very common hierarchical organization. In this schema, the customer is related to both products purchased and publications subscribed to. To read this schema, we say, "A customer has purchased zero or more products" and "A customer subscribes to zero or more publications."

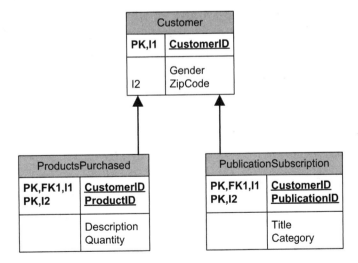

FIGURE 16.1 Customer data is often linked to multiple types of transactions.

The terminology describing the relationships implies a hierarchy. If we want to analyze the data with one case per customer, we will need to flatten this hierarchy.

Consider the single customer record shown in Figure 16.2. This particular customer has purchased five products and subscribes to three magazines.

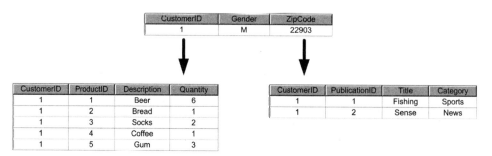

FIGURE 16.2 A single customer record can be associated with multiple purchases.

To replicate this hierarchical data organization in a flattened rowset used for data mining, we have to query against the three tables and retrieve each individual record. This means there will be 10 records returned in our flattened data set for data mining:

Customer ID	Gender	ZipCode	Product ID	Description	Quantity	Publication ID	Title	Category
1	M	22903	1	Beer	6	1	Fishing	Sports
1	M	22903	1	Beer	6	2	Sense	News
1	M	22903	2	Bread	1	1	Fishing	Sports
1	M	22903	2	Bread	1	2	Sense	News
1	M	22903	3	Socks	2	1	Fishing	Sports
1	M	22903	3	Socks	2	2	Sense	News
1	M	22903	4	Coffee	1	1	Fishing	Sports
1	M	22903	4	Coffee	1	2	Sense	News
1	M	22903	5	Gum	3	1	Fishing	Sports
1	M	22903	5	Gum	3	2	Sense	News

However, instead of relying on flattened records, a feature of SSAS called *data shaping* allows you to work directly with hierarchical data. This means that the cases can be created in a compact format from a relational database without going through the intervening step of creating a flattened table. In this case we would get a record set that looked like Figure 16.2, with each customer row having a set of product and publication records related directly to it. Once we have a set of cases in a hierarchical record set, we can use it directly in a mining model.

Mining Models

The definition of a mining model in DMX is parallel to the definition of a table in SQL, although a mining model is more complex than a table. To define a table in SQL, you specify the name of the table, the fields it contains and their data types, and keys and constraints. Similarly, in SSAS, to define a data model you specify the name of the mining model, the algorithm and parameters used to build the model, and the fields, data types, and relationships of the cases. Table 16.2 compares DMX mining models to SQL tables.

TABLE 16.2   DMX Mining Models and SQL Tables Have Similar Constructs

	Mining Model	Table
Schema	Attributes	Columns
Contents	Rows	Cases
Data Definition Operations	Create, Alter, Drop	Create, Alter, Drop
Data Manipulation Operations	Train, Predict, Browse	Insert, Delete, Select

The basic syntax for defining a mining model looks like:

```
CREATE MINING MODEL «mining_model»
(
    «column_definition_list»
) USING «dmm_algorithm»
```

where `mining_model` specifies the name of the mining model (enclosed in square brackets if there is a space in the name), `column_definition_list` defines the columns that are to be used in the model, and `dmm_algorithm` specifies the mining algorithm to be used to create the model (e.g., `Microsoft_Decision_Trees`). A concrete example of creating a mining model from a relational data source looks like:

```
CREATE MINING MODEL [Gender Prediction]
(
[Customer ID] LONG KEY,
[Gender] TEXT DISCRETE PREDICT,
[Zip Code] TEXT DISCRETE,
[Products] TABLE (
```

```
[Product ID] LONG KEY,
[Description] TEXT DISCRETE ))
USING Microsoft_Decision_Trees
```

In addition to creating a relational mining model, you can create a mining model based on an OLAP cube. To do so, use:

```
CREATE OLAP MINING MODEL «mining_model» FROM «cube»
(
 «olap_def»
)
USING «dmm_algorithm»
```

where, as previously, `mining_model` specifies the name of the mining model (enclosed in square brackets if there is a space in the name), `olap_def` defines the values that are used in the model by dimension and level, and `dmm_algorithm` specifies the mining algorithm to be used to create the model. For example:

```
CREATE OLAP MINING MODEL [MyOlapModel] FROM [Sales]
(
CASE
DIMENSION [Customers]
LEVEL [Name]
PROPERTY [Marital Status],

PROPERTY [Education],

PROPERTY [Gender] PREDICT

)

USING Microsoft_Decision_Trees
```

`CREATE MINING MODEL` uses different content types to specify the meaning of the columns to the mining model. The content type allows the mining model to use the column properly. The content type is independent from the data type of the column. There are six different column content types:

- Key
- Attribute
- Relation
- Table
- Qualifier
- Prediction

Key columns are used to uniquely identify a case. The key column in a mining model is analogous to the key in a relational database table. You must have a key column defined for each mining model. In the previous example, we are using [Customer ID] as our key column.

Attribute columns are the most common columns in mining models, and contain the attributes of the case to be used in constructing the model. In addition to the specification of the column name, attribute columns include domain information about the range and type of possible values for the attribute. In the previous example, Gender and Zip Code are attribute columns with Discrete domains. There are six possible domain types: CONTINUOUS, CYCLICAL, DISCRETE, DISCRETIZED, ORDERED, and SEQUENCE_TIME.

CONTINUOUS values are ordered and have a defined way of measuring distance and magnitude. A continuous variable can be characterized further by a description of the statistical distribution that it follows, either normal or uniform. A normal distribution is distributed in a bell curve, with the most common of values occurring in the middle of the range. A uniform distribution has values that are equally likely to occur anywhere in the range.

CYCLICAL values define an ordered cyclical set. As an example, consider the numbered months of the year with the values 1 for January, 2 for February, and so on.

DISCRETE values are categorical, with each distinct value representing something separate from every other. They do not imply any kind of order or distance. An example of discrete data is gender or zip code.

DISCRETIZED have continuous data values, but are transformed into ordered data for the analysis. This is to help data-mining algorithms that cannot handle continuous data.

ORDERED values define an ordered set that can be ranked. As an example, a skill level can be an ordered set of low, medium, and high.

SEQUENCE_TIME values are a time measurement range. This can be a number that indicates any kind of time interval.

In addition to the basic attributes, some provider-specific attributes can be used to help the data-mining algorithm build better models using the attributes, including MODEL_EXISTENCE_ONLY, NOT NULL, IGNORE NULL, and NULL INFORMATIVE.

MODEL_EXISTENCE_ONLY tells the algorithm that the value of the column is less important than the fact that it is present.

NOT NULL tells the algorithm that there should never be a null value in this column and it is an error if a null is present.

IGNORE NULL tells the algorithm to ignore any null values.

NULL INFORMATIVE means that the null information implies a missing state that is meaningful to the mining model.

Qualifier columns can be used to provide information about other attribute columns. OLE DB for DM supports the following qualifier columns: PROBABILITY, VARIANCE, STDEV, SUPPORT, PROBABILITY_VARIANCE, PROBABLILITY_STDEV, and ORDER.

PROBABILITY gives the probability of the associated value.

VARIANCE is the variance of the associated value.

STDEV is the standard deviation of the associated value.

SUPPORT is the weight of the associated value.

PROBABILITY_VARIANCE is the variance of the probability of the associated value.

PROBABLILITY_STDEV is the standard deviation of the probability of the associated value.

ORDER is the ordering of the associated value.

RELATION columns are used to further classify an attribute by establishing a relationship between a column and another column. This allows a simple mapping from a relational database to a data-mining model.

TABLE columns contain a nested table. As discussed previously, this nested table is built by using Data Shaping and contains other columns. For each case, the value of a Table column is the entire contents of the associated nested table. In our previous example, each customer has all of his or her products included in the case.

PREDICTION columns are used as the output of a mining model. Predictions carry a simple estimate, and can also contain more information about the predicted value, such as the confidence level or standard deviation. Extracting all of the information out of a prediction is done with transformation functions that can return either scalar data about the predicted value such as the probability, or nested tables that contain data such as histograms and the like.

After creating a model, it needs to be trained with cases. To train a model in DMX, we use the INSERT statement. Instead of adding records to a table as INSERT does in SQL, INSERT on a data-mining model adds the inserted cases to the body of cases used to train the model. The basic syntax for inserting cases into a model looks like this:

```
INSERT INTO «mining_model»
(
    «column_ list»
) «data»
```

As an example, consider the following INSERT statement:

```
INSERT INTO [Gender Prediction]
(
[Customer ID],
[Gender],
[Zip Code],
/* Define the nested table */
[Products] (
[Product ID],
[Description])
)
SHAPE
{
OPENROWSET('SQLOLEDB', 'INITIAL CATALOG=FoodMart 2000;',
'SELECT [Customer ID], [Gender], [Zip Code]
FROM Sales
ORDER BY [Customer ID]'
}
APPEND
(
(OPENROWSET('SQLOLEDB', 'INITIAL CATALOG=FoodMart 2000;',
'SELECT [Customer ID], [Gender], [Zip Code]
FROM Sales
ORDER BY [Customer ID]')
)RELATE [Customer ID] To [Customer ID]
AS [Products]
}
```

There are few things to note in this INSERT statement. First, to get to the training data, you use the OPENROWSET statement. This allows you to open any OLE DB data source and run a query. The syntax for OPENROWSET is:

```
OPENROWSET('<<Provider>>',
'<<Connection String>>',
'<<Query>>')
```

where Provider specifies any OLE DB data provider, Connection String specifies the connection string to be used to open the data source, and Query specifies the data that should be returned from the data source.

The second point of interest is the use of the SHAPE command to return the nested records for the case. The first OPENROWSET retrieves the parent rows followed by the APPEND statement that creates the nested table relationship and another OPEN-ROWSET statement to retrieve the child rows. It is important to order the records in the parent and child rows to make sure that all of the records in the nested table can be properly joined and returned. In this case, we have ordered both the parent and child rows using the Customer ID field.

For prediction queries, we use the PREDICTION JOIN .. ON clause to link the source data to the mining model. If the names of the source data and the mining model are identical, the NATURAL statement can be used to match up the data. If not, the column mappings can be specified in the ON clause (Figure 16.3).

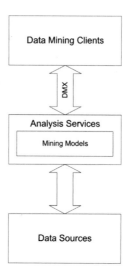

FIGURE 16.3 Data sources provide the data to mining models, which are displayed in clients.

After defining and training our data mining model, we can use it for creating predictions. Making predictions in DXM uses the SELECT statement. Generically, the SELECT statement for prediction looks like this:

```
SELECT [FLATTENED] <Fields> FROM <mining model>
PREDICTION JOIN <source data query> ON <join condition>
[WHERE <WHERE-expression>]

As an example of a prediction query, consider:
SELECT t.[Customer ID], [Age Prediction].[Age]
FROM [Age Prediction]
PREDICTION JOIN
(
  SHAPE
  {
  SELECT [Customer ID], [Gender], FROM Customers ORDER BY [Customer ID]
}
APPEND
  (
```

```
  {SELECT [CustID], [Product Name], [Quantity] FROM Sales ORDER BY
[CustID]}
RELATE [Customer ID] To [CustID]
  )
  AS [Product Purchases]
) as t
ON [Age Prediction] .Gender = t.Gender
  and
  [Age Prediction].[Product Purchases].[Product Name] =
  t.[Product Purchases].[Product Name] and
  [Age Prediction] .[Product Purchases].[Quantity] =
  t.[Product Purchases].[Quantity]
```

Training and prediction queries are very similar. They both use the same structures to insert the cases that are used in the model, the differences being that the cases for prediction don't include the variable to be predicted. The source query returns the cases to be used for prediction, and the join describes the way in which the cases are to be used in the prediction model.

In addition to creating predictions, you can also browse the data-mining model using the SELECT statement in DMX. Browsing the content of the model is important in understanding the structure of the data that was used to create it and might suggest additional ways of analyzing the data.

The simplest way to browse a mining mode is simply to return the contents of the model in a query:

```
SELECT * FROM MyOlapModel.CONTENT
```

This query will return all of the content of the mining model in the MINING_MODEL_CONTENT schema. We discuss this schema later in the context of the XMLA. In addition to simply selecting all of the elements in the model, you can create queries that look at distinct parts of the mining model. For example:

```
SELECT Age
FROM HairColorPredictDMM.Content
WHERE Gender = 'Male' and HairColor = 'Black'
```

will return the content of the mining model only for elements in the model specified by the query.

In addition to simply browsing the model by DMX, data-mining clients provide the front-end for querying the mining models and displaying predictions. This can range from the Microsoft-provided data viewers available in BI Studio to customized business applications. In addition to simply viewing the results in a client, the predictions from a mining model can be used as a dimension in a cube or as input to SSIS. One of the more common ways to view the outputs of a data-mining model is in Reporting Services.

It is also possible to query the content of a mining model to find specific cases that match some criteria to better understand the model. For example, the following query will return all of the node rules that have a probability greater than 50 percent:

```
SELECT NODE_RULE
FROM <dmm>.CONTENT
WHERE NODE_PROBABILITY > 0.5
```

In addition to the basic features of DMX already discussed, the language is extensible. The easiest method is to use any of the already available VBA or Excel functions to provide basic string, mathematical, and statistical capabilities. Custom-defined prediction functions can also be built through the plug-in API. Also available are user-defined functions written in .NET stored in the database.

Data-Mining Structures

In SSAS 2005, the data mining models are stored in a *data-mining structure*. A data-mining structure is a schema that can be used with multiple mining models to find the one most suited to the task at hand. The data loaded into the structure when it is processed is shared by all of the models defined in the structure. For example, you might have a structure that represents a marketing campaign that then contains a clustering, decision tree, and neural network model that all share the same data for training and prediction.

There are some limitations to the reusability of the data in the structure. Not all algorithms support all data types. For example, the Naïve Bayes algorithm only supports discrete data. Any continuous columns in the mining structure need to be discretized before they can be used in a Naïve Bayes mining model. This can be done using the Data Mining Designer to select the bucket count and method used for translating a continuous variable into discrete buckets.

As records are added, changed, or deleted from the source data, the mining models need to be retrained to maintain predictive accuracy. This training can be done when the containing structure is processed to refresh the data for all mining models or independently for each mining model, which can save time when there are many models and a large quantity of data. A structure needs to be processed when the structure definition is modified by adding or removing columns or when there is new data. However, a structure will not need to be processed if the only change is to the mining models contained in the structure. When a structure is processed, the data is compressed and stored in dimensions and measures that optimize the performance of the models.

There are three options for processing the models and structures in SSAS. ProcessFull processes the structure and all of the models in one pass. ProcessStructure generates the metadata, loads the structure with data, and stores it on the server. ProcessDefault is used to process the mining models once the data is stored in the structure. You can schedule these processes, run them as part of a SSIS job, or do them by hand in the SQL Server Business Intelligence Studio.

A Data-Mining Process

Successful data mining involves much more than just knowing which buttons to push in SSAS. Stepping back from the specifics of SSAS for a moment, let's discuss a framework for managing data-mining projects. Like most projects, data-mining projects benefit from following a methodology to make sure all the relevant tasks are covered in the right order. A vendor-agnostic methodology for data mining is Cross Industry Standard Process for Data Mining (CRISP-DM). CRISP-DM provides a useful structure for a data-mining project. Like most projects' plans, it starts with requirements definition, and continues with design and construction of the solution, verifying the solution and deploying to users. The CRISP-DM model has six steps, illustrated in Figure 16.4 and briefly explained here. More details on the CRISP-DM model are available on the Web site listed in References at the end of the chapter.

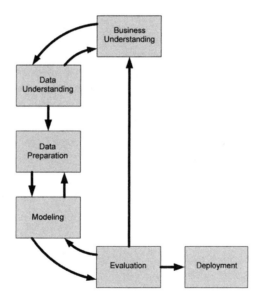

FIGURE 16.4   The CRISP-DM model has six steps.

Step 1: Business Understanding

An essential first step for any project is gathering the objectives, and a data-mining project is no different. The initial phase in the CRISP-DM model is about understanding the business objectives and translating these into data-mining terms and requirements. The result of this step should be a set of requirements and a project plan used to guide the rest of the project.

You need to make sure you understand what you hope to gain from data mining. The most appropriate questions for data mining are about the patterns of behavior in a business process. Data mining is about improving a business process, not reporting on a current process. It can help you learn about the process, but the results are typically fed directly back into the process, not consumed directly by decision makers. If business users are complaining about the timeliness and accuracy of reports that are being delivered to them, data mining will do no good. Don't treat data mining as a "one size fits all" solution— it is just one data analysis tool.

Step 2: Data Understanding

After understanding the business objectives, understanding the data in that context becomes possible. This step includes the initial data collection, familiarization with the scope and substance of the data, identification of problems and weaknesses in the data, and to begin initial data exploration and hypothesis formation.

Sometimes, it is useful to combine internal company data with data gathered from outside sources. Since data mining performs better when cases have a large number of input fields, adding relevant external data can be a good way to enhance your mining results. For example, if you have stored data by zip code, you can get demographic information about that zip code to provide more insight.

Other important considerations for your data might revolve around making sure it is legal for you to construct mining models with that data and use the results of the analysis. If your organization rents a mailing list, for example, it may go beyond your licensed use of the data to do anything with it beyond sending a mailing. There may be other legal constraints around mining with different types of data that vary from jurisdiction to jurisdiction. The European Union has much tighter privacy rules than the United States, so some types of customer analysis that is perfectly legal in the United States might run you afoul of the authorities in the European Union. In addition, creating a mining model that causes discrimination against protected classes in any country could cause legal trouble down the road. In short, be careful about using data that might be illegal or unethical, and if in doubt, seek legal council before doing something that could cause great long-term damage to your company and career.

In many cases, the initial exploration of the data will result in further understanding of the data-mining requirements developed in the first step and refinement of those objectives with the newfound information. The result of this step is a raw data set, ready for further processing.

Step 3: Data Preparation

In this step, we construct the final data set used for modeling using the raw data set gathered in the previous step. Although each of these techniques may require different kinds of data (discreet versus continuous, aggregated versus granular), the basic requirement they have in common is that they need consistent, clean data. As with any analysis involving data, the "garbage-in, garbage-out" principle is very strong with data mining. If the data we feed into the analysis is somehow misleading or biased, the results will be, at best, irrelevant, and at worst, harmful. To make sure we have the best possible data, it is strongly advisable to use either data directly from the data warehouse, or has already been cleaned and verified through our ETL process. In this step, we will transform and clean the data for input into the data mining tools.

Step 4: Modeling

Finally, we get to the creation of the data-mining models. This involves selecting the proper algorithm for application to the business problem and data set at hand, and then training the models to calculate the optimal parameters. This is sometimes as much of an art as a science, and you many have to try different mining models to achieve satisfactory results. Often, because different data-mining algorithms have different data requirements, we will have to return to step 3 to do further data preparation.

Step 5: Evaluation

After creating and training a model, we evaluate it against the defined business objectives. Sometimes, it will be necessary to revisit the requirements because the model or the data does not match the given business requirements. This might involve an expansion of requirements if the data yields results that weren't anticipated at the beginning of the project, or a reduction if there isn't anything valuable to be found. At the end of this step, we have a model that is ready to be deployed.

Step 6: Deployment

In some cases, the only goal for a data-mining project is to understand a data set better. In this case, deployment may only consist of creating and disseminating a report to the interested parties. In other cases, the model will be deployed and used in a business process in an automated fashion. For example, a credit scoring model might be integrated in an application used to process credit applications. Regardless of what is done with the model at completion, the only way to get value out of the model is to get it where it can be useful to decision makers.

Example

In our example, we will follow the CRISP-DM model outlined earlier and apply it to a data-mining problem in SSAS 2005.

Step 1: Business Understanding

For this example, we will keep the business objective simple. You company is promoting a new product and wants to introduce it to existing customers. The business objective is to produce a list for a direct marketing campaign that will maximize the response to the campaign at minimum cost. This list will be taken from the existing customer list and should be more effective than simply randomly selecting a list of customers from the existing list.

Step 2: Data Understanding

ON THE CD

To support the business objective, data is available for a similar campaign that was conducted in the past. This data is in the Ch16_data.xls spreadsheet on the CD-ROM, which contains internal data and some demographic data gathered externally about the customers. This data comes from a much larger list of customers who were solicited about the product and has been randomly sampled to pick 2000 records for training the data models, shown in the train tab in the Ch16_data.xls spreadsheet. Another 150 records were similarly selected to provide some data for evaluating the model and are shown in the Predict tab of the spreadsheet. The fields in the data set are described in Table 16.3.

TABLE 16.3 This Table Lists the Fields in the Sample Data Set with Their Types and Meanings

Field	Type	Meaning
Response	Boolean	1 if customer responded to previous campaign, 0 if not
Gender	Character	Customer gender: M for male, F for female
TotalSpend	Int	Total lifetime spending by customer
Trans	Int	Total number of transactions by customer
Products	Int	Number of distinct products purchased by customer
MnthCust	Int	Number of months as a customer
FHeadHsld	Float	% households headed by female in customer demographic region $\rightarrow$

Field	Type	Meaning
LoneParHsld	Float	% households headed by lone parent in customer demographic region
MarHsld	Float	% households headed by married couple in customer demographic region
ChildHsld	Float	% households with children in customer demographic region
EngHsld	Float	% English-speaking households in customer demographic region
MultlinHsld	Float	% multilingual households in customer demographic region
RelHsld	Float	% households with relatives in customer demographic region
PerRoom	Float	Number of people per room in customer demographic region
AvgInc	Int	Average income in customer demographic region
MedInc	Int	Median income in customer demographic region

Step 3: Data Preparation

In this step, we will import the spreadsheet of customer data into a database and make it ready to use in our modeling.

First, we will need to create a database to store the data. Start the SQL Server Management Studio. Connect to your SQL Server database on localhost, and right-click on the Databases folder. Select New Database… from the context menu to open the New Database dialog. Type "Ch16" into the Database name field and then click the OK button to create the database.

Right-click on Ch16 database Tasks…Import to show the SQL Server Import and Export wizard welcome page. Select the Next button. On the next page, choose a Data Source, pick Microsoft Excel, and set the file path to point to the Ch16_data.xls file. Leave the version set at Microsoft Excel 97–2005 and make sure the "First row has column names" checkbox is checked, as shown in Figure 16.5. Select Next.

Choose a destination. Leave SQL Native Client selected and put your server name or localhost in the Server name drop-down list as shown in Figure 16.6. Select Next.

In the Specify Table Copy or Query page, choose the "Copy data from one or more tables or views" radio button and then select Next.

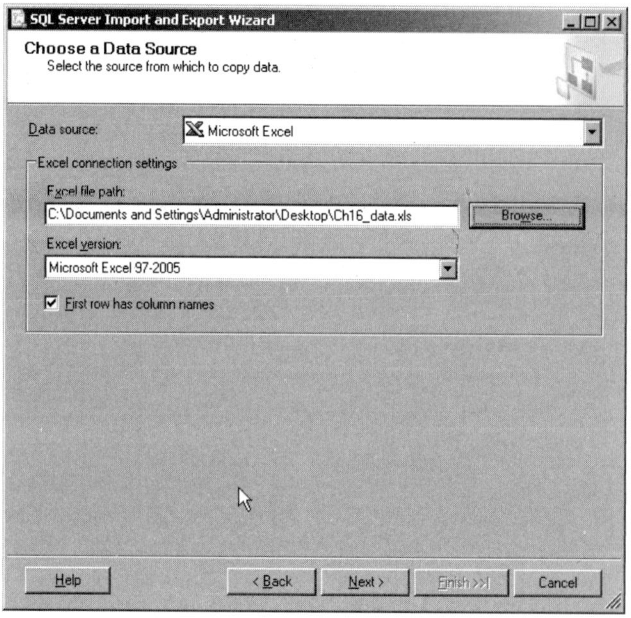

FIGURE 16.5 Select Microsoft Excel as the data source.

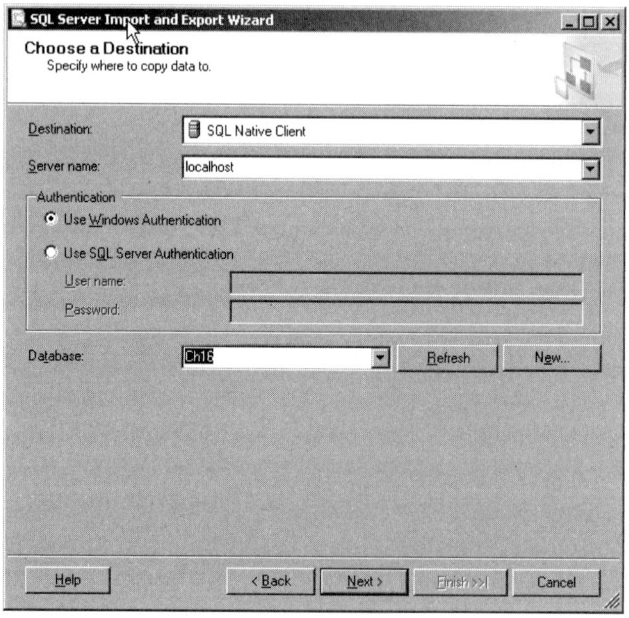

FIGURE 16.6 Select your server as the destination.

Select Source Tables and Views and choose the "predict$"' and "train$" source tables as shown in Figure 16.7.

Choose the Edit… button next to "predict$" in the source column. Change the column mappings to match those in Figure 16.8. Chose the Edit… button next to

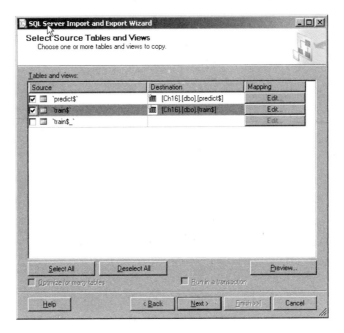

FIGURE 16.7   Select "predict$" and "train$" as source tables.

"train$" and reapply the same mappings. After you have mapped both tables, select Next.

On the Save and Execute Package page, select the "Execute immediately" checkbox. If you want to save the package for later execution, click the Save SSIS Package checkbox and choose where you want to save it. Select Next to run the package. After the package runs, you will see a success page as shown in Figure 16.9. Select Close to finish the Import wizard. At this point, you are ready to create a model.

Step 4: Modeling

Now that we have imported the data, we are ready to create the mining models. Since generating the list is a classification type of problem, we will start with the Decision Trees algorithm. To get an understanding of how to compare different mining models, we will also create a model based on the Naïve Bayes algorithm.

Start the SQL Server Business Intelligence Development Studio (BIDS) from the Windows Start menu. After BIDS has started, select File…New…Project… from the

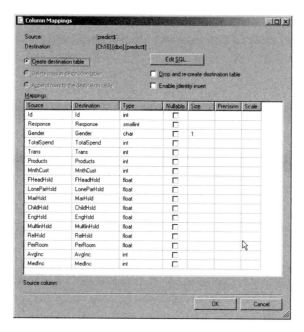

FIGURE 16.8 Set the column mappings to match those shown here.

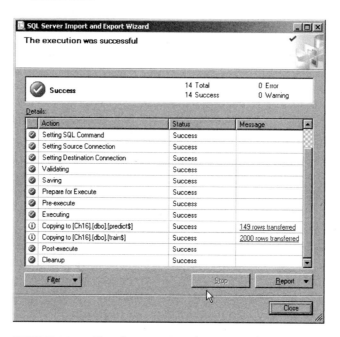

FIGURE 16.9 After the Import package runs, the number of rows transferred is reported.

menu to show the New Project Dialog. Select Business Intelligence Projects from the type list on the left pane, and Analysis Services Project from the template list. Name the project Ch16 Data Mining Project and save it in an appropriate folder.

To get the data into the mining models, we need to create data source views in the project. Right-click on the Data Source Views folder in the Solution Explorer to open the Data Source View wizard. Select Next on the Welcome page. On the Select a Data Source page, choose the New Data Source... button to open the Data Source wizard dialog. Select Next on the Welcome page. On the Select How to Define the Connection page, choose the New... button to open the Connection Manager dialog. Populate the Server name combo box with "localhost" or your server name. In the "Connect to a database section," Select Ch16 from the Select, or enter a database name combo box and select the OK button, as shown in Figure 16.10.

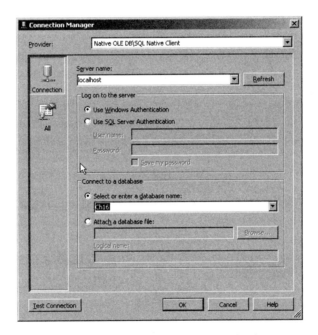

FIGURE 16.10 Populate the server and database names on the Connection Manager screen.

Back in the Data Source wizard, select Next. On the Impersonation Information page, select the default radio button to go to the Completing the Wizard page. On this page, enter "Ch16 Data Source" into the Data source name text box and choose OK to go back to the Data Source View wizard.

In the Select a Data Source page, choose "Ch16 Data Source" from the list of relational data sources, and click the Next button. In the Name Matching screen, unselect the "Create logical relationships by matching columns" checkbox and choose

Next. In the Select Tables and Views page, choose both of the available tables and move them into the included objects as shown in Figure 16.11. Choose Next. On the Completing the Wizard page, enter "Ch16 Data Source View" into the name text box and select Finish.

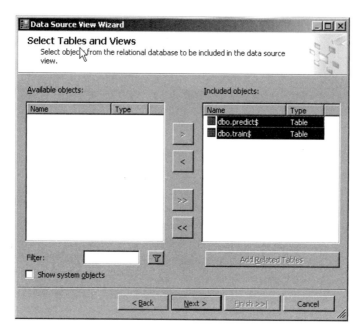

FIGURE 16.11 Choose both of the available tables to be included objects.

To create a mining structure, right-click on the Mining Structures folder in the Solution Explorer and select New Mining Structure... from the context menu to show the Data Mining wizard dialog. Click Next to skip the Welcome page. On the Select the Definition Method page, choose the "From existing relational database or data warehouse" radio button and select Next. On the Select the Data Mining Technique page, select "Microsoft Decision Trees" from the drop-down list and select Next. On the Select Data Source View page, select the "Ch16 Data Source View" from the available source views and choose the Next button. On the Specify Table Types page, select the case checkbox next to the train$ table as shown in Figure 16.12. Select the Next button.

On the Specify the Training Data page, select the columns for training as shown in Figure 16.13 and select Next.

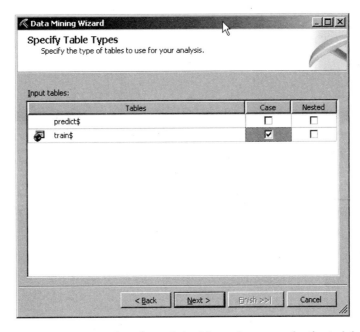

FIGURE 16.12   Select the train$ table as the source for the training cases.

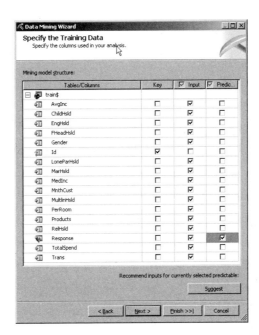

FIGURE 16.13   Select the columns used for training the mining model.

On the Specify Columns' Content and Data Type page, select the Detect button to update the content types to reflect their structure (Discrete or Continuous) and select Next. On the Completing the Wizard page, enter "Ch16 Mining Structure" at the structure name and "Decision Tree" as the model name as shown in Figure 16.14 and select Finish to complete the Data Mining wizard.

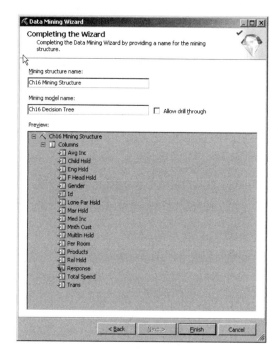

FIGURE 16.14 Name the mining structure and model to complete the wizard.

After the wizard is complete, the Data Mining Designer opens in the Mining Structure view where you can view and edit the mining structure as shown in Figure 16.15.

Because the Naïve Bayes algorithm only works with discrete values, let's create some discretized columns corresponding to the continuous variables. To do so, right-click on the Columns node under the Ch16 Mining Structure and select Add a column… from the context menu to show the Select a Column dialog. In the Select a Column dialog, choose Products from the Source column tree and click OK as shown in Figure 16.16.

A warning appears, saying that a column already exists and asks if you wish to continue; select Yes. A new column called Products 1 is added to the Columns node. Right-click on the Products 1 node and select Properties from the context

FIGURE 16.15   The Data Mining Designer appears after the wizard is completed.

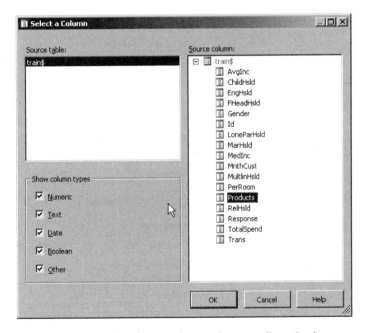

FIGURE 16.16   Select the Products column to discretize it.

menu to show the Properties window, shown in Figure 16.17. In the Properties window, change the name of the column to Products Discrete. If you are prompted to use the same name to all related columns as well, select No. Change the content to Discretized, put a 5 in the DiscretizationBucketCount, and leave the Discretization-Method as Automatic. After you have made the new column for Products Discrete, follow the same process to create a discretized copy of Total Spend called Total Spend Discrete.

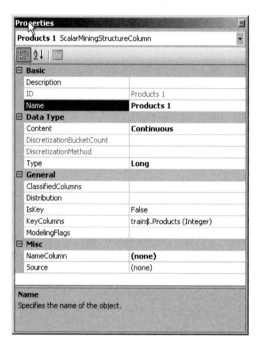

FIGURE 16.17 The properties display for the Products column.

Switch to the Mining Models view and select Mining Model…Insert new model to show the New Mining Model dialog. Set the name in this dialog to Naïve Bayes and select the Microsoft Naïve Bayes algorithm. You will get a warning that the Naïve Bayes model will ignore all of the continuous columns. Select Yes to continue. The new model will appear in the Mining Models view. Select the Products Discrete row under the Naïve Bayes model column and change the value to Input. Also, change the Total Spend Discrete value to Input as shown in Figure 16.18.

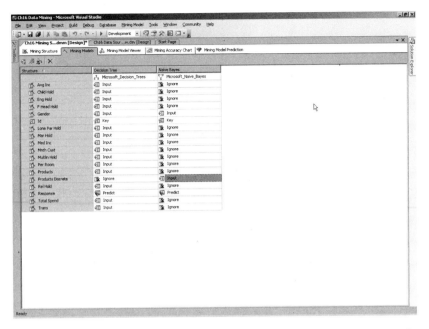

FIGURE 16.18   The Mining Model view shows the columns selected for each model.

To build and deploy the mining model, select Build...Deploy Ch16 Data Mining from the menu. This will build, process, and deploy the model to the server. After it is done, you will see a message in the Deployment Progress window indicating that the deployment was successful. After building and deploying, you can switch to the Mining Model Viewer tab to see the results of training the model.

Step 5: Evaluation

On the Mining Model Viewer tab, you can explore the patterns discovered by the data-mining model. Each of the algorithms included with SSAS 2005 includes a model viewer so you can see the results of the model.

The Decision Trees Viewer is displayed when you pick the Decision Tree model in the Mining Model drop-down list and is shown in Figure 16.19. Let's examine this viewer more closely. Each predicted column has its own decision tree. Since we just have one predicted column, there is only one tree available in the Tree drop-down list called Response.

When the Background drop-down is set to All Cases, we can see which factors are important in determining a response to a product offer. In the model shown, the most important factor is gender. If you hover the mouse over one of the nodes in the tree, you will see the number of cases in that node and the breakdown of response values (0 or 1).

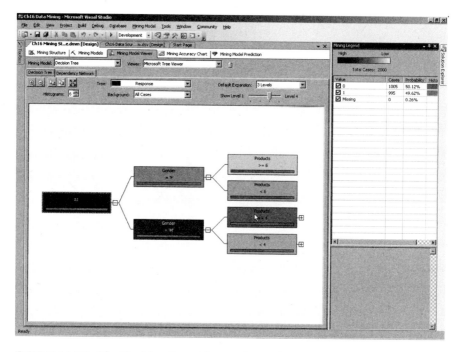

FIGURE 16.19 The Decision Trees Viewer shows the structure of the mining model.

Clicking on the node shows the count, probability, and a histogram of each response value as shown in Figure 16.20. The background colors indicate the relative importance of each node, with nodes that have higher importance displayed in a darker color. Therefore, you can tell at a glance what the most important indicators are.

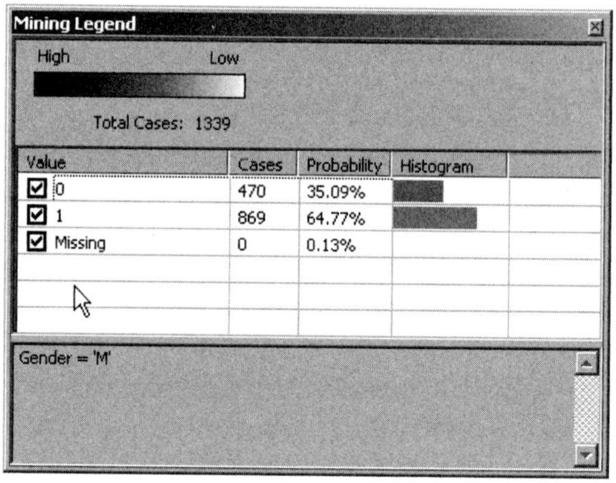

FIGURE 16.20 The histogram shows the breakdown of each response value.

Another view of the Decision Tree is provided by the Dependency View as shown in Figure 16.21. Navigate to the Dependency View by selecting the Dependency Network tab. This view shows all of the dependencies in the model. In this case, there are three dependencies shown. To just show the strongest dependencies, move the slider on the left of the diagram down. This slider has as many scales as there are nodes in the model, so picking the lowest value will only show the link from Gender. Moving the slider up adds Products and so on. This view isn't very useful with the small number of nodes identified in this analysis, but it is if you have many nodes.

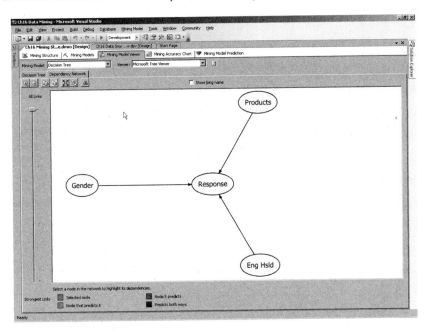

FIGURE 16.21   The Dependency View shows the node dependencies in the model.

Now, let's examine the results of the Naïve Bayes model. Select Naïve Bayes from the Mining Model drop-down list. The first view shown is the Dependency Viewer, which looks and acts like the Dependency Viewer for the Decision Tree. The Attribute Profiles view shows an overall breakdown of the attributes in the model, as shown in Figure 16.22. The columns in the histogram give a visual breakdown of the values in each attribute. If you hover over the one of the histograms, the exact values are displayed. To find the strongest correlations for a predictable value (in this case, we have only one: response), look at the relative distribution between the Population (All) column and the predicted value of interest (0 or 1 in this case).

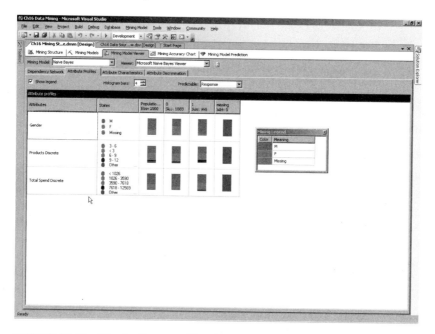

FIGURE 16.22   The Attribute Profiles shows a histogram for each attribute.

A more descriptive view of a particular classification can be found by switching to the Attribute Characteristics tab shown in Figure 16.23. This tab shows a chart containing the ranked probabilities for a chosen attribute value by each characteristic. In this case, we can see that the strongest correlation for a positive Response is with the Gender value M (87.337%).

Lastly, we have the Attribute Discrimination tab that shows the attribute values together. From this, you can make comparisons about the different values in the attributes. In our example, you can see that Gender value F strongly favors Response value 0, while Gender M strongly favors Response 1. Similar breakdowns are shown for all the attribute values.

The Mining Accuracy Chart view can be used to assess the accuracy of the predictions made by each of the models. Select the Mining Accuracy Chart tab to display the view. Click the Select Case Table... button on the Select Input Table(s) window to show the Select Table dialog. Pick the "predict$" table from the Ch16 Data Source View and select OK. This will add the columns from the predict$ table and map them to the mining model. Since the predict$ table has the same structure as the mining model, you don't have to do any manual mapping. Select 1 from the Predict Value drop-down to test the model for positive responses. The screen should look like Figure 16.24.

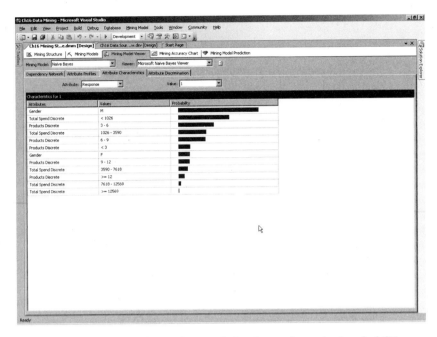

FIGURE 16.23   The Attribute Characteristics shows the ranked probabilities for each attribute.

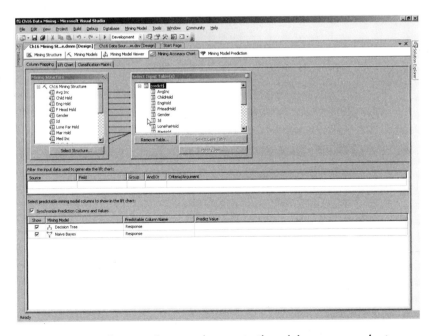

FIGURE 16.24   The mappings used to create the mining accuracy chart.

Click on the Lift Chart tab in the Mining Accuracy Chart view to see the lift chart comparing the two models. Lift is a measure of how much better the data-mining model is over random guessing for predictions over a given result set. The chart, shown in Figure 16.25, takes some interpretation. The lift chart has four lines and plots the percentage of the target population on the vertical axis, and the percentage of the total population on the horizontal axis. In general, the faster a line goes up, the better the predictive power of the model. The top line is the ideal model that has perfect prediction of the Response. This line hits the top of the chart just after the middle of the overall population. The bottom line is the percentage correct that is generated by randomly guessing. This doesn't hit the top of the chart until the upper right-hand corner. The two middle lines represent the accuracy of the mining models we have created. Overall, the Decision Tree model outperforms the Naïve Bayes model in this case.

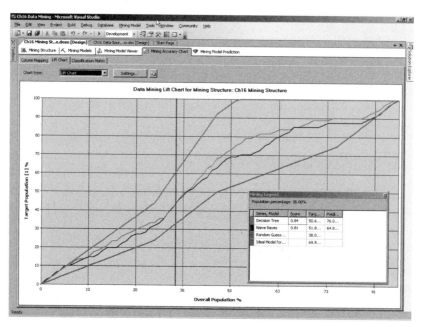

FIGURE 16.25 A lift chart is a good way to compare the effectiveness of different models.

The Profit chart allows you to create what-if scenarios to predict the profit of a targeted campaign using the models and is shown in Figure 16.26. We can enter values for the population, cost and revenues anticipated in the market, and see how the models perform in dollar terms. Select the Settings… button at the top of the chart display to open the Profit Chart Settings dialog. Enter the following values:

Population 10000
Fixed cost 50000
Individual cost 50
Revenue per individual 100

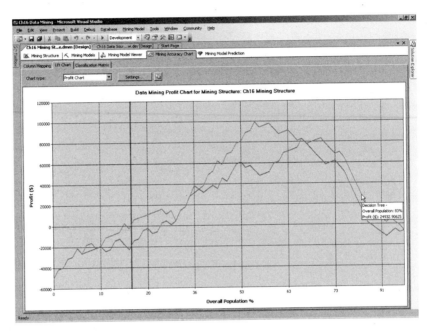

FIGURE 16.26 The Profit chart allows what-if analysis on the profitability of a mining model.

The last tab on the Mining Accuracy Chart view is the Classification Matrix, which shows the predicted values for a model on the rows and the actual values on the columns. This is useful for getting a numerical check on the accuracy of the model.

Finally, we can do a prediction using the model. Since we've identified that the Decision Trees model is more accurate than the Naïve Bayes model, we will use that to do our predictions. The tool to do this is the DMX query designer, which is very similar to the SQL query designer. First, open the Mining Model Prediction view and make sure Decision Tree is chosen as the mining model. Next, select the "predict$" case table as we did previously with the lift chart. After choosing the case table, you can create a DMX query that runs predictions against that data. First, add the columns for the predicted dataset. Drag the Id field from the predict$ table into the Source column. Next, add the prediction function by selecting Prediction Function from the drop-down on the source column on the next empty row. In the field column of that same row, select the first Predict function in the list (there are two) from the drop-down. Next, drag the Response element from the Decision Tree mining model into the Criteria/Argument column. Lastly, to check the results, drag the Response element from the predict$ table into the Source column of the next empty row. Your query should look like Figure 16.27. To see the results of this prediction query, select Mining Model...Result from the menu. To see the DMX code, select Mining Model...Query from the menu. You can edit the DMX query here as well, but be advised that changes you make on this page will be overwritten if you switch back to the query designer.

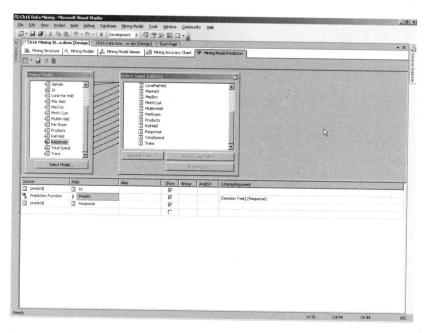

FIGURE 16.27 The DMX Query Builder allows the construction of prediction and other DMX queries.

In addition to doing prediction queries based on an input table, you can run singleton prediction queries directly against the model. A simple way to do this is to use the DMX query screen. Switch to the query view, replace the code you see there with the following DMX query, and then open the query result view:

```
SELECT
 [Decision Tree].[Response]
From
 [Decision Tree]
NATURAL PREDICTION JOIN
(SELECT 'M' AS [Gender]) AS t
```

The model predicted Response from the supplied input (Gender = 'M') is returned. This type of functionality can be used from any application and is an excellent way to leverage a data-mining model in a business application through ADOMD.NET.

CONCLUSION

Data mining is a powerful tool for making the most of the data collected by your organization. SSAS 2005 offers a flexible tool that allows you to create and manage mining models effectively in your organization. This chapter provided a brief overview and introduction to data mining in SSAS so you can begin to apply it successfully to your own projects.

REFERENCES

OLE DB for Data Mining Specification (OLEDB DM) *www.microsoft.com/ downloads/details.aspx?FamilyID=01005f92-dba1-4fa4-8ba0- af6a19d30217&DisplayLang=en*

Cross Industry Standard Process for Data Mining (CRISP-DM) *www.crisp-dm.org/*

About the CD-ROM

The CD-ROM included with *SQL Server 2005 for Developers* includes all of files necessary to complete the tutorials in the book. It also includes the images from the book in full color, and demos for you to use while working through the tutorials and exercises.

CD FOLDERS:

- IMAGES: All of the images from within the book in full color. These files are set up by chapter.
- TUTORIALS: All of the files necessary to complete the tutorials in the book including, Transact-SQL scripts, C# code files, XML files and Excel spreadsheets. These files are all in common formats that can be read by standard text editors, SQL Server Management Studio, or Visual Studio .NET, and they are set up in chapter folders.

SYSTEM REQUIREMENTS:

- Windows 2000/XP
- Pentium Processor+
- CD/Hard drive
- 128 MB RAM
- 20 MB free disk space

In addition, you will need Microsoft SQL Server 2005. There are differences between each of the SQL Server 2005 versions available. To take full advantage of all chapters in the book, we recommend SQL Server 2005 Developer Edition or Enterprise Edition. For a full listing of all of the versions and the differences between them, see *http://www.microsoft.com/sql/prodinfo/features/compare-features.mspx.*

INSTALLATION:

To use this CD, you just need to make sure that your system matches at least the minimum system requirements. You should contact the developer directly if you have any problems running the tutorial materials.

Index

Symbols
@param_name data_type, 125
@parameter_name, 114

A
access control lists (ACLs), 31–33
access to data, in ADO.NET 2.0, 147
accountability, 31–32
Accumulate methods, 124
ACID (atomicity, consistency, isolation, and durability), 265–266
ACLs (access control lists), 31–33
actions, enabling, 251
activating queues, 200, 205–206
Active Directory security model, 38
ActiveX Script, 293
adding subscription data, 166–167
ADMOD.NET, 335–336
ADO, 128
ADO.NET 2.0, 127–149
  asynchronous operations in, 129–133
  batching with, 141–143
  bulk copy utility of, 139–141
  change password on connect, 148–149
  client failover configuration in, 148
  conclusions, 149
  dependencies from, 148
  large data types and, 143–144
  Multiple Active Result Sets in, 133–135
  overview of, 127–129
  paging with, 143
  schema discovery, 144–146
  statistics in, 146–147
  user-defined types and, 135–139
affected users, defined, 37
AFTER INSERT triggers, 119–120
AFTER triggers, 119
aggregate_name, defined, 125
aggregate functions
  programmability and, 123–126
  in Transact-SQL, 66–67
  in Unified Data Model, 257
AJAX (asynchronous JavaScript and XML), 196
algorithms
  association, 256
  clustering, 256
  data mining, 256, 358–360
  Decision Trees, 256
  Naïve Bayes, 256
  neural networks, 256
  sequence clustering, 256
  time series, 256

ALTER ANY permissions, 43
ALTER permissions, 43
AMO (Analysis Management Objects), 336
Analysis Management Objects (AMO), 336
analysis of database security, 34–37
Analysis Services and OLAP, 333–343
  ADMOD.NET and, 335–336
  AMO and, 336
  Analysis Services Server, 334
  architecture of, see architecture, of Analysis Services and OLAP
  generally, 328
  and MDX, generally, 337–338
  MDX scripts and, 338–343
  OLE DB and, 334–335
  XML for Analysis and, 337
Analysis Services Event Provider, 154
Analysis Services Server, 334
analysis tools, in business intelligence, 250–251
anonymous security, in Service Broker, 213
APIs (application programming interfaces), 166, 284
ApplicationDefinitionFilePath, 157
application definition files, 158–164
ApplicationName, 157
application programming interfaces (APIs), 166, 284
applications, in Notification Services, 152–168
  Analysis Services Event Provider, 154
  architecture and, 152–156
  building, generally, 156
  Custom Event Provider, 155
  delivery of, 156
  event collection in, 154
  File System Event Provider, 154
  formatting of, 155–156
  SQL Server Event Provider, 154
  subscription management, 154
  updating, 169
architecture
  of Analysis Services, see architecture, of Analysis Services
  asynchronous queueing and, 197
  in Notification Services, 152–156
  of OLAP, see architecture, of Analysis services and OLAP
  of SQL Server Reporting Services, see architecture, of Reporting Services
architecture, of Analysis Services, 360–370

data management and, 361–363
data mining and, 360–361
generally, 333–334
mining models and, 363–370
OLAP and, see architecture, of Analysis Services and OLAP
structures in, 370–371
architecture, of Analysis Services and OLAP, 333–343
  ADMOD.NET and, 335–336
  AMO and, 336
  Analysis Services Server and, 334
  and MDX, generally, 337–338
  MDX scripts and, 338–343
  OLE DB and, 334–335
  XML for Analysis and, 337
architecture, of Reporting Services, 321–324
  .NET API in, 323–324
  URL access, 322–323
  Web services and, 321–322
arithmetic operators, in Transact-SQL, 68
assemblies, 100–103
assembly_name, 108–109
association, as data mining objective, 357
association algorithms, 256, 358–359
asynchronous JavaScript and XML (AJAX), 196
asynchronous operations, in ADO.NET 2.0, 129–133
asynchronous queueing, in Service Broker, 197–201
  generally, 197–198
  load distribution and, 200–201
  message fragmentation in, 200
  multithreading and multireader queues, 199–200
  programming model for, generally, 201–202
  transactions in, 198–199
atomicity, consistency, isolation, and durability (ACID), 265–266
atomicity, of data warehouses, 265–266
attributes
  assigning to entities, 25
  columns for, in mining models, 365
  in database design, 10
  of hierarchies, 329–330
  Serializable, in Transact-SQL, 104–108
  SqlFunction and, 116–118
  SqlUserDefinedAggregate and, 124
  SqlUserDefinedType and, 104–108
Attributes function, in Data Source View, 278

397